Activists in Transition

Activists in Transition

Progressive Politics
in Democratic Indonesia

Edited by Thushara Dibley and Michele Ford

SOUTHEAST ASIA PROGRAM PUBLICATIONS
an imprint of
Cornell University Press
Ithaca and London

First published 2019 by Cornell University Press

Library of Congress Cataloging-in-Publication Data
Names: Dibley, Thushara, editor. | Ford, Michele, editor. | Sastramidjaja,
   Yatun L. M. Student movements and Indonesia's democratic transition.
Title: Activists in transition : progressive politics in democratic
   Indonesia / edited by Thushara Dibley and Michele Ford.
Description: Ithaca : Southeast Asia Program Publications, an imprint of Cornell
   University Press, 2019. | Includes bibliographical references and index.
Identifiers: LCCN 2019016193 (print) | LCCN 2019018069 (ebook) |
   ISBN 9781501742491 (pdf) | ISBN 9781501748301 (epub/mobi) |
   ISBN 9781501742477 | ISBN 9781501742477 (cloth) |
   ISBN 9781501742484 (pbk.)
Subjects: LCSH: Democratization—Indonesia. | Indonesia—Politics and
   government—1998– | Social movements—Indonesia. | Protest movements—
   Indonesia. | Political activists—Indonesia.
Classification: LCC DS644.5 (ebook) | LCC DS644.5 .A287 2019 (print) |
   DDC 322.409598—dc23
LC record available at https://lccn.loc.gov/2019016193

Contents

ACKNOWLEDGMENTS

This volume would not have been possible without the support of the University of Sydney's Faculty of Arts and Social Sciences, which funded the workshop at which the initial drafts of the chapters were presented. It would also not have been possible without logistical support from our team at the Sydney Southeast Asia Centre (SSEAC). Michele's participation in this project was supported by an Australian Research Council Future Fellowship (FT120100778).

Putting a volume like this together is a challenging task. Beside the general question of selection, the community of scholars working on social movements in Indonesia is quite small—and, as a result, some obvious topics for inclusion (most notably, the environment movement) have fallen out because of the lack of author availability. In addition, we have challenged many of our contributors to broaden their focus in order to capture the changes over time in the different social movements featured in the book.

We would like to thank all our authors not only for committing to the project, but for their patience in working and reworking their chapters to ensure a high level of comparability in focus and time frame across the volume. We would also like to acknowledge the efforts of our discussants—Edward Aspinall, Vedi Hadiz, Elizabeth Hill, Jeff Neilson, and Sonja van Wichelen—who provided valuable input at the workshop. A special thanks to Edward Aspinall, who also commented on later drafts of a number of chapters. Finally, we are grateful to the other members of the multidisciplinary social sciences group of Indonesia specialists at the University of Sydney, whose stimulating discussions inspired us to put this volume together.

ABBREVIATIONS AND TERMS

adat	customary law or practice
AGRA	Aliansi Gerakan Reforma Agraria (Alliance of Agrarian Reform Movement)
Ahok	Basuki Tjahaja Purnama (politician)
AKAK	Advokasi untuk Komisi Anti-Korupsi (Advocacy for a Corruption Eradication Commission)
AMAN	Aliansi Masyarakat Adat Nusantara (Alliance of Indigenous People of the Archipelago)
APC	Asian Peasant Coalition
API	Aliansi Petani Indonesia (Indonesian Peasant Alliance)
ARC	Agrarian Resource Center
asas kekeluargaan	family principle
ASV	Aliansi Satu Visi (One Vision Alliance)
becak	pedicab
BIN	Badan Intelijen Negara (National Intelligence Agency)
blusukan	impromptu visits
BPD	Badan Perwakilan Desa (Village Representative Council)
BTI	Barisan Tani Indonesia (Indonesian Peasants' Front)
buaya	crocodile
BUBT	Badan Usaha Buruh Tani (Peasant-run Collective Enterprise)
cacat	crippled
CBM	Christian Blind Mission
CEDA	Canadian International Development Agency
CEDAW	Convention on the Elimination of All Forms of Discrimination against Women
cicak	gecko

CLD-KHI	Counter-Legal Draft–Kompilasi Hukum Islam (Counter-Legal Draft on the Islamic Law Compilation)
CPRD	Conventions on the Rights of Persons with Disabilities
dakwah	proselytization
DFID	Department for International Development (United Kingdom)
Dinas Sosial DIY	Yogyakarta Social Affairs Office
DNIKS	Dewan Nasional Indonesia untuk Kesejahteraan Sosial (Indonesian National Council for Social Welfare)
DPR	Dewan Perwakilan Rakyat (People's Representative Council)
Dria Manunggal	Institute of Research, Empowerment and Development for People with Different Abilities
eLSAD	Lembaga Studi Agama dan Demokrasi (Institute for the Study of Religion and Democracy)
FAKTA	Jakarta Citizens Forum (Forum Warga Jakarta)
FAMI	Front Aksi Mahasiswa Indonesia (Indonesian Student Action Front)
FAMRED	Front Aksi Mahasiswa untuk Reformasi dan Demokrasi (Student Action Front for Reform and Democracy)
FBR	Forum Betawi Rempug (Betawi Brotherhood Forum)
FITRA	Forum Indonesia untuk Transparansi Anggaran (Indonesian Forum for Budget Transparency)
FNPBI	Front Nasional Perjuangan Buruh Indonesia (National Front for Indonesian Workers' Struggle)
Forkot	Forum Kota (City Forum)
Forsol Buruh	Forum Solidaritas untuk Buruh (Solidarity Forum for Workers)
FPI	Front Pembela Islam (Defenders of Islam Front)
FSPI	Federasi Serikat Petani Indonesia (Federation of Indonesian Peasant Unions)
FSPMI	Federasi Serikat Pekerja Metal Indonesia (Federation of Indonesian Metalworkers Unions)
GAPB	Gerakan Anti Politisi Busuk (Movement against Rotten Politicians)

GBI	Gerakan Buruh Indonesia (Indonesian Labor Movement)
GeRAK	Gerakan Anti-Korupsi (Movement against Corruption)
Gerindra	Partai Gerakan Indonesia Raya (Great Indonesian Movement Party)
Gerkatin	Gerakan untuk Kesejahteraan Tuna Rungu Indonesia (Indonesian Movement for the Welfare of the Deaf)
GGW	Garut Governance Watch
GSBI	Gabungan Serikat Buruh Independen (Association of Independent Labor Unions)
Hanura	Partai Hati Nurani Rakyat (People's Conscience Party)
HGU	Hak Guna Usaha (Commercial Lease Rights)
HKTI	Himpunan Kerukunan Tani Indonesia (Indonesian Farmers' Harmony Association)
HMI	Himpunan Mahasiswa Indonesia (Islamic Tertiary Students' Association)
HPMJT	Himpunan Petani Mandiri Jawa Tengah (Central Java Independent Peasant Association)
HWDI	Himpunan Wanita Penyandang Disabilitas Indonesia (Indonesian Association of Women with Disabilities)
HWPCI	Himpunan Wanita Penyandang Cacat Indonesia (Indonesian Union for Crippled Women)
IAIN	Institut Agama Islam Negeri (State Islamic Institute)
ICMI	Ikatan Cendekiawan Muslim Indonesia (Indonesian Islam Intellectuals' Association)
ICW	Indonesian Corruption Watch
ILGA	International Lesbian, Gay, Bisexual, Trans and Intersex Association
ILPS	International League of People's Struggle
IPW	Indonesia Procurement Watch
IRM	Ikatan Remaja Muhammadiyah (Muhammadiyah Youth Association)
ISIS	Institute for Social Institutions Studies
Jabodetabek	Greater Jakarta (Jakarta, Bogor, Depok, Tangerang Bekasi)

JATAM	Jaringan Advokasi Tambang (Mining Advocacy Network)
JIL	Jaringan Islam Liberal (Liberal Islamic Network)
JIMM	Jaringan Intellectual Muda Muhammadiyah (Muhammadiyah Young Intellectuals Network)
Jokowi	Joko Widodo (politician)
KAJS	Komite Aksi Jaminan Sosial (Action Committee for Social Security Reform)
KA-KBUI	Kesatuan Aksi Keluarga Besar Universitas Indonesia (Action Unit of the Extended Family of the University of Indonesia)
KAMMI	Kesatuan Aksi Mahasiswa Muslim Indonesia (Indonesian Muslim Students Action Front)
kampung berkelanjutan	sustainable urban village
kampung deret	stacked urban village
kampung susun	layered urban village
KASBI	Komite Aksi Serikat Buruh Indonesia (Committee of Indonesian Unions Action)
kebun	garden
keterbukaan	openness
KKN	korupsi, kolusi, nepotisme (corruption, collusion and nepotism)
KNPA	Komite Nasional Pembaruan Agraria (National Committee for Agrarian Reform)
KOBAR	Komite Buruh untuk Reformasi (Workers Committee for Reform)
Komisi Empat	Commission of Four
Komnas Difabel	National Difabel Commission
Komnas HAM	Komisi Nasional untuk Perlindungan Hak Asasi Manusia (National Human Rights Commission)
Komnas Perempuan	Komisi Nasional Anti-kekerasan terhadap Perempuan (National Commission on Violence against Women)
KPA	Konsorsium Pembaruan Agraria (Consortium for Agrarian Reform)
KPI	Kongres Perempuan Indonesia (Indonesian Women's Congress)
KPK	Komisi Pemberantasan Korupsi (Commission for the Eradication of Corruption)

KPRI	Konfederasi Pergerakan Rakyat Indonesia (Confederation of Indonesian People's Movements)
KSBSI	Konfederasi Serikat Buruh Sejahtera Indonesia (Confederation of Indonesian Prosperous Labor Unions)
KSP	Kantor Staf Presiden (Presidential Staff Office)
KSPI	Konfederasi Serikat Pekerja Indonesia (Confederation of Indonesian Trade Unions)
KSPS	Komunitas Swabina Pedesaan Salassae (Salassae Rural Self-Governing Community)
KSPSI	Konfederasi Serikat Pekerja Seluruh Indonesia (Confederation of All-Indonesia Workers Unions)
ladang	dry fields
lading	land for shifting cultivation
lahan sementara tidak digunakan	temporarily unused land
LBH	Lembaga Bantuan Hukum (Legal Aid Foundation)
LBH-APIK	Lembaga Bantuan Hukum–Asosiasi Perempuan Indonesia untuk Keadilan (Indonesian Women's Legal Aid Foundation for Justice)
LBT-INA	Lesbian, Bisexual, and Transgender Indonesia
LGBT	Lesbian, gay, bisexual, and transgender
LKiS	Lembaga Kajian Islam dan Sosial (Institute for Islamic and Social Studies)
LMND	Liga Mahasiswa Nasional untuk Demokrasi (National Student League for Democracy)
LP3ES	Lembaga Penelitian, Pendidikan, dan Penerangan Ekonomi dan Sosial (Institute for Economic and Social Research, Education, and Information)
LSAF	Lembaga Studi Agama dan Filsafat (Institute for the Study of Religion and Philosophy)
madrasah	Islamic day school
mafia peradilan	judicial mafia
MIFEE	Merauke Integrated Food and Energy Estate
MM	Majelis Mujahidin Indonesia (Indonesian Council of Holy Warriors)
MPBI	Majelis Pekerja Buruh Indonesia (Indonesian Workers Assembly)
MPR	Majelis Permusyawaratan Rakyat (People's Consultative Assembly)

MTI	(Masyarakat Transparansi Indonesia) Indonesian Anti-Corruption Society
MUI	Majelis Ulama Indonesia (Council of Indonesian Ulemas)
Musrenbang	Musyawarah Rencana Pembangunan (Development Planning Consultation Forums)
Nasyiatul Aisyiyah	Young Women's Association (Muhammadiyah)
NGOs	nongovernmental organizations
NKRI	Negara Kesatuan Republik Indonesia (Unitary State of the Republic of Indonesia)
NU	Nahdlatul Ulama (Ulama Revival)
OHANA	Organisasi Handicap Nusantara (Archipelago Handicap Organization)
P3I	Persatuan Pergerakan Petani Indonesia (Association of Indonesian Peasant Movements)
P3M	Perhimpunan, Pengembangan Pesantren dan Masyarakat (Pesantren and Community Development Association)
PAN	Partai Amanat Nasional (National Mandate Party)
Pansus	Panitia Khusus (Special Committee)
Papernas	Partai Persatuan Pembebasan Nasional (National Liberation Party of Unity)
PBB	Partai Bulan Bintang (Crescent Star Party)
PDI	Partai Demokrasi Indonesia (Indonesian Democratic Party)
PDI-P	Partai Demokrasi Indonesia-Perjuangan (Indonesian Democratic Party of Struggle)
Pekuneg	Tim Penerbitan Keuangan Negara (Team to Regularize State Finances)
pembaharuan	renewal
pemerataan	equality
Perhutani	Perusahaan Hutan Negara Indonesia (State Forestry Corporation)
Perlesin	Persatuan Lesbian Indonesia (Indonesian Lesbian Union)
Pertuni	Persatuan Tunanetra Indonesia (Indonesian Blind Union)
pesantren	Islamic boarding school

Pilkada	Pemilihan Kepala Daerah (district head elections)
PITL	Persatuan Insan Tani Lampung (Lampung Peasant Union)
PK	Partai Keadilan (Justice Party)
PKB	Partai Kebangkitan Bangsa (National Awakening Party)
PKI	Partai Komunis Indonesia (Indonesian Communist Party)
PKS	Partai Keadilan Sejahtera (Prosperous Justice Party)
PM	Pemuda Muhammadiyah (Muhammadiyah Young Men)
politik praktis	electoral politics, lit. "practical politics"
POPOR	Partai Persatuan Oposisi Rakyat (People's United Opposition Party)
PPAB	Paguyuban Petani Aryo Blitar (Aryo Blitar Peasant Association)
PPBI	Pusat Perjuangan Buruh Indonesia (Indonesian Center for Labor Struggle)
PPCI	Persatuan Penyandang Cacat Indonesia (Indonesian Union for the Crippled)
PPDI	Persatuan Penyandang Disabilitas Indonesia (Indonesian Disability Association)
PPP	Partai Persatuan Pembangunan (United Development Party)
PPR	Partai Perserikatan Rakyat (People's Confederation Party)
PRD	Persatuan Rakyat Demokratik (People's Democratic Association), later Partai Rakyat Demokratik (People's Democratic Party)
preman	thugs, gangsters, or vigilantes
pribumi	indigenous
Prolegnas	Program Legislasi Nasional (National Legislation Program)
PSHK	Pusat Studi Hukum & Kebijakan (Center for the Study of Law and Policy)
rakyat kecil	lower classes, lit. "little people"
RBSJ	Relawan Buruh Sahabat Jokowi (Worker Volunteers for Jokowi)

reformasi	reform
reformasi total	total reform
RT	rukun tetangga (subneighborhood association)
RTI	Rukun Tani Indonesia (Indonesian Peasant Association)
RW	*rukun warga* (neighborhood association)
SAPDA	Sentra Advokasi Perempuan Difabel dan Anak (Center for Advocacy for Women and Children with Disabilities)
SARA	*suku, agama, ras, antar-golongan* (ethnicity, religion, race, class)
Sarbupri	Sarekat Buruh Perkebunan Republik Indonesia (Plantation Workers' Union)
Satpol PP	Satuan Polisi Pamong Praja (public order police)
sawah	wet rice fields
SBMI	Serikat Buruh Medan Independen (Independent Workers' Union of Medan)
SBM-SK	Serikat Buruh Merdeka–Setia Kawan (Solidarity Free Trade Union)
SBSI	Serikat Buruh Sejahtera Indonesia (Indonesian Prosperous Labor Union)
SIGAB	Sasana Integrasi dan Advokasi Difabel (Place for Integration and Advocacy for People with Disabilities)
Siskamling	*sistem keamanan lingkungan* (neighborhood security system)
SMID	Solidaritas Mahasiswa Indonesia untuk Demokrasi (Students in Solidarity with Democracy in Indonesia)
SPI	Serikat Petani Indonesia (Indonesian Peasant Union)
SPJB	Serikat Petani Jawa Barat (West Java Peasant Union)
SPN	Serikat Pekerja Nasional (National Workers Union)
SPP	Serikat Petani Pasundan (Sundanese Peasant Union)
SPRI	Serikat Perjuangan Rakyat Indonesia (Indonesian Peoples' Union of Struggle)
SPSI	Serikat Pekerja Seluruh Indonesia (All-Indonesia Workers' Union)
SPSU	Serikat Petani Sumatera Utara (North Sumatra Peasant Union)

STaB	Serikat Tani Bengkulu (Bengkulu Peasant Union)
STAIN	Sekolah Tinggi Agama Islam Negeri (State Islamic Teachers' College)
STN	Serikat Tani Nasional (National Peasant Union)
TGPTPK	Tim Gabungan Pemberantasan Tindak Pidana Korupsi (Joint Team to Eradicate the Crime of Corruption)
TII	Transparency International Indonesia
Tim Delapan	Team of Eight
Tim Tastipikor	Tim Koordinasi Pemberantasan Tindak Pidana Korupsi (Coordination Team for the Eradication of the Crime of Corruption)
Tipikor	Pengadilan Tindak Pidana Korupsi (Anticorruption Court)
TPK	Tim Pemberantasan Korupsi (Corruption Eradication Team)
UNDP	United Nations Development Program
UPC	Urban Poor Consortium
USAID	United States Agency for International Development
WALHI	Wahana Lingkungan Hidup Indonesia (Indonesian Forum for Environment)
YLBHI	Yayasan Lembaga Bantuan Hukum Indonesia (Indonesian Legal Aid Foundation)
YPAC	Yayasan Pendidikan Anak Cacat (Foundation for the Education of Handicapped Children)
YTM	Yayasan Tanah Merdeka (Free Land Foundation)

Activists in Transition

INTRODUCTION: SOCIAL MOVEMENTS AND DEMOCRATIZATION IN INDONESIA

Thushara Dibley and Michele Ford

In 1998, thousands of students occupied the Indonesian parliament, sleeping rough at night, chanting slogans and singing songs demanding the resignation of the man who had led Indonesia for more than three decades. Their elation at President Suharto's announcement of his resignation on May 21 was echoed in the headlines of newspapers around the world. The activists who staged protests at this critical moment precipitated one of the most significant shifts in Indonesia's political landscape since independence. The ensuing transition was tumultuous, with race riots, threats of separatism, and destruction of public and private property. But before long the country had settled into a period of democratic consolidation, which continued without major incident until Prabowo Subianto, a retired general accused of human rights abuses and Suharto's former son-in-law, threatened a return to a more authoritarian form of government in his campaign for president in the 2014 election. The immediate threat to the country's formal commitment to democracy was averted when Prabowo accepted his narrow defeat to Joko Widodo (Jokowi), the serving governor of Jakarta. Along the way, however, Indonesia's political culture had shifted considerably—with the progressive voices that had been so influential in 1998 increasingly displaced by reactionary social movements and, in particular, conservative Islamic forces.

Activists in Transition responds to Della Porta's (2014, 363) call "to single out the effects of democratic transformations on social movements [and] the effects of social movements on those transformations." It focuses on social movements with progressive agendas because these, and not their conservative counterparts, have imagined and articulated a democratic vision for Indonesia. Studies of regime change have shown that progressive social movements disseminate ideas about democracy among the wider population and mobilize opposition to undemocratic regimes (Adler and Webster 1995; Collier and Mahoney 1997; Tilly 2001). Less attention has been paid to the fate of social movements once that regime change occurs. In Grodsky's (2012, 12) words, "Scholars and policymakers who focus on democratization have accumulated a wealth of information on how social movements arise [but the] question of 'what next?' has . . . been largely pushed to the side."

This collection explores what went before *and* the "what next," tracking the trajectory of social movements' engagement in the political sphere from the short-lived period of openness (*keterbukaan*) in the late 1980s–early 1990s and the twenty-year anniversary of the fall of Suharto's New Order in 2018. Close consideration of progressive social movements' different roles at different times over these three decades makes it possible to better assess their contribution to Indonesia's democratic transition, thus sharpening our analysis of the dynamic relationship between political elites and various social actors at times of social and political change. It also sheds light on the impact of democratization on those movements as they reinvent themselves in an attempt to maintain or increase their influence in a new democratic polity.

This introductory chapter begins this task by focusing on the collective contribution of progressive social movements to Indonesia's transition to democracy and their collective fate in the decades since, setting the scene for the case studies to follow. First, however, we must explain how we understand the relationship between social movements and democratization.

SOCIAL MOVEMENTS AND DEMOCRATIZATION

Social movements consist of networks involving a diverse range of actors, including individuals, groups, or organizations that may be loosely connected or tightly clustered. These networks are defined by "shared beliefs and solidarity," which form the basis of collective action that seeks to "promote or oppose social change" (Diani 1992, 8–11). Progressive social movements are those that espouse a vision of society that is open and inclusive, treats all its citizens with respect, and provides them with equal access to civil and political rights. The idea of a "progressive" movement is not without its problems, as it—like the concept of democracy itself—enshrines a rights-based paradigm that emerged from the West. Even setting this caveat aside, assessments of whether or not a movement can be considered progressive depends on the perspective from which that judgment is made.[1] Fundamentalist religious movements may promote social change, for example, by creating more legal and social space for adherents to practice their religion as they see fit. They are thus clearly social movements. But it is a relatively straightforward exercise to exclude them from the "progressive" category since they so often impinge on the ability of women, sexual minorities, and people of other faiths to access their civil rights. Other cases are less clear cut. For example, a local movement based on ethnic identity may be considered emancipatory by participants but chauvinistic or backward by others. While most of the social movements canvassed in this book focus on promoting the interests of a particular group defined by class, gender, or other elements of identity, all are progressive in the sense that they envisage an inclusive society rather than one that privileges particular groups.

Democratization, meanwhile, is a process through which a polity moves toward "a system of governance in which rulers are held accountable for their actions in the public realm by citizens, acting indirectly through the competition and cooperation of their elected representatives" (Schmitter and Karl 1991, 76). The trajectory of democratization depends on the historical, political, and social context of the country concerned, and is seldom linear. Dramatic moments of regime change, such as that experienced by Indonesia in 1998, are just one of many aspects of that trajectory. Such moments are preceded by a series of developments that lay the foundations for political upheaval and followed by a period during which democratic institutions are constructed and democratic cultures established. What is more, the attainment of meaningful citizenship is a process that occurs unevenly, can retreat, and requires persistent work to sustain even in established democracies (Grugel 2013). The work of maintaining advances toward meaningful citizenship is necessarily far more taxing in an emerging democracy like Indonesia.

In locating progressive social movements at the center of our analysis, we do not seek to privilege them to the exclusion of elite proponents of democracy (cf. Stepan 1997). Rather, we draw attention to this particular element of what Threlfall (2008, 932) describes as the "co-construction" of democratization by multiple actors, including powerful individuals and the "organized and non-organized masses." Nor do we seek to downplay the obstacles social movements face. Many have argued, following Hadiz and Robison (2014) and Winters (2014), that Indonesia is controlled by an oligarchy whose power base is rooted in predemocratic times—and even assessments that challenge the fatalism of such accounts acknowledge the ongoing influence of long-established political and economic elites (Ford and Pepinsky 2014a). There are also deep-seated features of Indonesia's political system that hinder democratic practice, among them clientelism, the failure of the rule of law, and the growing influence of conservative countermovements.

As Aspinall argues in the concluding chapter of this volume, it has proven difficult for progressive social movements to stand strong in the face of these challenges. Nevertheless, they have continued to fight for what Beetham (1999, 91) describes as the "basic" principles of democracy, namely "control by citizens over their collective affairs and equality between citizens in the exercise of that control."

PROGRESSIVE SOCIAL MOVEMENTS AS A DRIVER OF DEMOCRATIZATION

One feature of different democratic trajectories is the degree of involvement, and impact, of progressive social movements. Most relevant to the process of regime change are national social movements, which "make claims on authorities" primarily through "cumulative nonviolent action"—a category that includes "publications, meetings, marches, demonstrations, petitions, lobbying, and threats to intervene directly in formal political life" (McAdam, Tarrow, and Tilly 1996, 22). Cumulative action of this kind can generate alliances with members of the political class, credibly threaten to disrupt political processes or directly influence electoral outcomes, or generate pressure from external powerholders (McAdam, Tarrow, and Tilly 1996, 22). Where it is most successful, it can shift the power relations between challengers and authorities, alter policy directions, or provoke broader systemic change (Guigni 1999, xxiii). The latter may include change in political institutions or in the social or cultural domain. In short, social movements "not only challenge state structures but also aim at redefining the sets of social relations that presuppose such structures and the symbolic elements that justify them" (Guigni 1999, xxix).[2] All of these elements can play into—or impede—shifts toward a more democratic political system. Equally, there is no guarantee that social movements will achieve fundamental change in the political sphere even when they band together to make "explicit demands for democracy" (Tilly 1993, 22). Indeed, as Boudreau (2004, 30) reminds us, "Democracy movements rarely *themselves* bring down governments, and we should be wary of claims that equate democratization with strong pro-democratic-mobilization."

At the same time, it is important not to dismiss the contribution of progressive social movements to regime change, as the Indonesian experience attests (Aspinall 2005). Efforts to draw general conclusions about their contribution across different national contexts are relatively rare. In one such attempt, Rossi and Della Porta (2015,

18–24) draw on their assessments of developments in Latin America and Southern and Eastern Europe to argue that the role played by social movements evolves through different phases of the democratization process, namely resistance, liberalization, transition, and expansion. During the resistance phase, social movements develop underground networks that are critical to "undermining the legitimacy of the regime" (Rossi and Della Porta 2015, 18). These networks introduce and enact democratic values through their modes of interaction with one another and their constituents—in doing so, contributing to the creation of an alternative vision for the political culture, and thus undermining the authoritarian regime. In this way, as Rossi and Della Porta (2015, 18–19) argue, social movements become "effective promoters of democratic values and understandings that erode a non-democratic regime and set the necessary conditions for liberalization to take place."

The key characteristic of the next phase, liberalization, is an acceleration of change leading to "the perception among the authoritarian elites that there is no other way than to open the regime if they want to avoid civil war or violent takeover" (Rossi and Della Porta 2015, 21). As this period begins, social movement actors may engage in overt protest alone or in conjunction with their international allies. Equally, they may push back in less obvious ways that nevertheless undermine the regime. Where activists collectively gain momentum, political elites may be forced to make concessions, for example, by easing restrictions on oppositional organizations or taking a less punitive approach to demonstrations. As a consequence, social movements that previously had limited opportunity to organize or engage in public demonstrations experience a freeing of political space and new opportunities for public action. In this way, liberalization creates an environment in which social movements can exert further pressure on the regime as "organized society becomes more visible" (Rossi and Della Porta 2015, 21).

Increased social movement activity generates momentum and creates opportunities for key individuals and organizations to establish themselves as regime critics, in some circumstances culminating in the formation of a coalition for regime change. A successful *transition* generally requires the mobilization of a broad-based prodemocracy coalition with the power to trigger regime change. Once procedural democracy is achieved, this coalition may be demobilized. Alternatively, activists may continue to play a role in a fourth stage, which Rossi and Della Porta (optimistically) describe as *expansion.* Importantly, the success or failure of this phase is not measured by the conduct of free and fair elections, but rather by the "universal and effective application of citizenship rights, which transcend voting" (Rossi and Della Porta 2015, 24). These more robust indicators of democracy are particularly important for movements concerned with issues of identity and representation such as the movements for women's, gay and lesbian, or disability rights because they suggest that democratic consolidation is more accurately measured by the attitudes toward and treatment of all citizens, rather than just electoral procedures.

This framework provides a useful starting point because it offers a pathway for thinking about the relationship between the actions taken by social movements and phases of the broad trajectory of democratization. However, it suggests a degree of inevitability—reminiscent of Rostow's (1960) five stages of growth—that is belied by the messiness of the democratic project. For example, Rossi and Della Porta (2015) touch only lightly on the potential for breakdown in the democratization process. They indicate that the absence of a large coalition of social movements during the transition phase can make it difficult to achieve regime change because conservative forces or powerful elites opposed to democratization are able to derail the process. But their analysis does not account for contexts in which governments seek to contain social movements by creating opportunities for their participation in the policy sphere without committing to a broader process of democratization (Rodan 2018). Nor do they consider situations in which democracies that have entered into a period of consolidation then begin to regress. Social movements' experience of such situations is different from that in the resistance phase because they have already experienced success and have worked to adjust their institutional structures and strategies to the new demands of operating in a democracy. In the face of systemic changes associated with democratic regression, progressive social movements must again reassess their priorities, strategies, and institutional structures—and in many cases, their fundamental purpose—if they are to continue to mobilize successfully for social change.

Another limitation of the broad-brush approach taken by Rossi and Della Porta (2015) is that it fails to account for dynamics within individual social movements and in the relationship between individual social movements and the state. In transitional democracies, social movements must deal with a common set of challenges that may include excessive surveillance, the failure of the rule of law, or unnecessarily punitive requirements for the formation of social movement organizations or new political parties. However, the relative impact of these and other aspects of a country's political and social context on individual movements is different, as clearly evidenced in the case of Indonesia. For instance, the demands of the environmental movement were much more palatable to Suharto's government than those of the labor movement in the early 1980s (Ford 2009). Similarly, the rise of religious conservatism in the post-Suharto period is of much more significance to gay and lesbian activists than, for example, to activists in the anticorruption movement. The differential impact of broader political and social developments, as well as social movements' internal dynamics, account for the success or failure of particular movements to prosecute their cause.

ENGAGEMENT WITH A DEMOCRATIC STATE

shadow of authoritarian rule → substantive matters

In "what shape" (Boudreau 2013, 57) do social movements emerge from the experience of campaigning for regime change, and how do they engage with a newly democratic state? When the goal of procedural democracy is achieved, the focus of progressive social movements necessarily shifts. In the Philippines, Indonesia's neighbor, social movements experienced a fundamental change in orientation from systemic reform to more particularistic agendas after the ousting of President Marcos (Boudreau 2013). Reflecting on the reasons for this shift, Boudreau concludes that the broad-based democracy movement had

> a short shelf life once the dictatorship's most egregious violations of democratic process end. In the shadow of authoritarian rule, the right to free expression or assembly may seem luminous and sufficient. But procedural questions soon give way to substantive matters, and populations move from expectations that democracy will produce material benefits to more direct demands for those benefits. Pro-democracy coalitions then divide into blocs concerned with the *content* of politics. (Boudreau 2013, 58)

As the Philippines experience suggests, the new political arena in which social activists find themselves, while full of new possibilities, is also deeply challenging because it requires social movements to move beyond campaigning for regime change to the more complex and (sometimes) mundane negotiations involved in influencing policy once regime change has been achieved (Foweraker 2001, 848). In Indonesia, too, most progressive social movements found their goals much easier to define in the lead-up to the transition, when their collective focus was on bringing down an authoritarian regime, than after the moment of regime change. In the immediate aftermath of the fall of Suharto, students struggled to define their role in a context where their calls to purge Indonesia's political system of the New Order elite were not widely supported (Sastramidjaja, this volume). For its part, the labor movement shifted its emphasis from a narrow agenda focused on freedom of association and labor rights abuses to a broader range of issues including outsourcing and social security (Caraway and Ford, this volume).

In order to deal with their new reality, social movements develop new strategies and tactics. In some cases, mobilization continues to play an important role as democratization provides greater space for the airing of social movement concerns, or gives rise to new grievances (Friedman and Hochstetler 2002; Shin 2010). In other cases, social movements leverage more open decision-making processes to ensure their goals are reflected in governments' policy platforms (Ballard et al. 2005). In others still, social movement actors take advantage of the introduction of electoral competition, which opens up the possibility for them to reach agreements with parties or individual candidates based on their capacity to mobilize large blocks of voters—or, indeed, to participate directly in electoral politics.[3]

Indonesian activists have responded to these opportunities for direct political engagement in very different ways. Initially, many social activists avoided becoming directly involved. Over time, however, a subset came to see the electoral arena as important for social struggles. Of this latter group, some chose to stand as candidates within existing political parties while others decided to establish purpose-specific political vehicles. In some cases, activists in parliament have been able to make changes (such as the changes to quotas for women), but in many cases they have had limited influence and in a few instances have become involved in corrupt activities or become aligned with nondemocratic elites (Mietzner 2013). Others still worked outside the halls of power to influence policy and legislation. In the early days after the fall of Suharto, for example, nongovernmental organizations (NGOs) involved in environmental activism actively campaigned for the People's Consultative Assembly to pass a policy decision on agrarian reform, which ended up occurring in 2001 (Lucas and Warren 2003). More recently, as discussed in Dibley's chapter in this volume, disability activists played a critical role in ensuring that the disability law established during the New Order period was revised to better reflect global norms and practices.

Finally, regime change affects the ways in which international funding bodies interact with social movement organizations, sometimes leading to a decrease in resources available to a movement. With the advent of democracy, many of the NGOs that had spearheaded Indonesia's democracy movement lost much of their foreign funding. In cases where support is lost, NGOs and other donor-funded organizations can find themselves without the material resources to continue their social movement function (Grodsky 2012). Conversely, democratization can coincide or directly result in new international funding opportunities, which can contribute to new, more vibrant forms of activism. For example, disability organizations gained access to new sources of funding after Indonesia signed the United Nations Convention on the Rights of Persons with Disabilities.

In short, progressive social movement actors attempt to use the opportunities and resources available to them within the new political system to further their individual and collective agendas. Their success or failure depends on whether they have been able to develop a clear sense of their new goals and a new strategic repertoire through which to implement those goals in sometimes very challenging environments. Social movements around the world have coped with these changes in varying ways. Some adapt, even thrive, but others do not. The reasons for these variations are as diverse as the political contexts in which different social movements operate. What is important, though, is to recognize that this process of adjustment is a normal and necessary part of the development of a new democracy, which has consequences not only for the social movements concerned but also for the quality of democracy itself.

INDONESIAN SOCIAL MOVEMENTS AND DEMOCRATIZATION

The New Order regime was born of a moment of deep disruption, which saw the destruction of a vibrant social movement landscape dominated by the Left. Prompted by an attempted coup by a group called the September 30 Movement, Suharto, then in charge of the Army's Strategic Command, quickly seized political power in 1965 (Cribb 1990). The Indonesian Communist Party was blamed for the coup, prompting the mass murder of millions of suspected communists by vigilante groups supported by the military (Cribb 1990). The persecution of communists was further strengthened by legislation that outlawed Marxism-Leninism and that made it illegal for former political prisoners to participate in politics (Roosa 2006).

In order to cement its place in the Indonesian polity, the regime developed three key mechanisms of control: promoting Pancasila as a statist ideology, involving the military in civilian life, and amalgamating existing political parties and controlling the right to form mass organizations (Aspinall 2005). These strategies were a response not only to the specific threat of communism—which the regime invoked constantly—but to mass-based organizing more generally. The government achieved a more or less complete demobilization of society in the few short years between 1971 and 1975, reordering the political system and entrenching a series of "functional groups" for workers, peasants, fishers, youth, and women to contain the participation of constituencies formerly represented by independent social movements (Reeve 1985). For the next three decades, activists were forced to mobilize in fragmented and transitory pockets of political space not through "strongly institutionalized, deeply-rooted and resilient organizations" but rather "a kaleidoscope of small NGOs, action committees and informal networks" (Aspinall, this volume).

Developments during and after this period broadly align with the phases identified by Rossi and Della Porta (2015, 9). From the beginning of the New Order until the late 1980s—the period that aligns with Rossi and Della Porta's resistance phase—progressive activists opposed the regime by spreading ideas and practices about democracy. They maintained gentle pressure on the regime during this period, but engaged in relatively little public protest. This changed with the advent of keterbukaan in 1989. In this period of liberalization, social movements engaged in frequent demonstrations, contributing to increased awareness of ideas about, and practices of, democracy. This sustained wave of protest was, however, largely stifled when the Indonesian government retreated into more punitive approaches to social activism in the mid-1990s.

Social movements nevertheless maintained enough momentum to take advantage of instability wrought by the 1997–98 Asian financial crisis, which destroyed the legitimacy of the New Order. The impact of the crisis, and persistent protests against excesses of the regime, brought about Suharto's resignation in May 1998 and an end to authoritarianism. Indonesia subsequently entered a period of transition, the end of which was marked by the first direct election of an Indonesian president in 2004, which scholars heralded as marking its entry into democratic consolidation (Liddle and Mujani 2013; Mietzner 2015). However, following a short period of what Rossi and Della Porta (2015, 25) would describe as "expansion," Indonesia's democracy began to regress as a consequence of rising conservatism and declining space for the voices of progressive social movements.

RESISTANCE (1965–89)

Progressive social movements had to be resilient to survive the early years of the New Order. For many, resilience meant finding ways of dealing with the regime's changing levels of tolerance to their presence. This ability to adapt to their environment ensured their sustainability and laid the groundwork for future change (Aspinall 2005). For instance, after initially allowing students space to organize, the government dealt harshly with student protests in the late 1970s, silencing the student movement for a decade (see Sastramidjaja, this volume). In response, some student activists retreated from the public gaze, developing study groups focused on identifying "new solutions for the country's political, social, and economic problems" (Aspinall 2005, 121). Others expressed their opposition by joining NGOs, whose structures were better suited than mass movements to a harsh political climate in which the government and military had little sympathy or support for student activism. Similarly, after the labor movement was all but destroyed in the late 1960s, the handful of stalwarts who refused to be co-opted by the regime were joined by new allies in the left of the student movement, the Catholic and Batak Lutheran churches, and human rights–based NGOs, which, in turn, mobilized a new generation of worker-activists (Ford 2009). As these examples suggest, Indonesia's ban on mass-based organizing meant that many of the progressive social movements of this period were driven by middle-class activists, whose class position afforded them some protection from the regime.

A key tactic employed by NGOs in the 1970s was to package causes in ways that complemented government strategies rather than standing in direct opposition to the state (Hadiwinata 2003). From the 1980s, however, a new breed of NGO leaders critical of their predecessors' failure to "develop any effective theoretical framework or strategies for change" (Eldridge 1995, 38) emerged. Whether campaigning for gender equality, educating factory workers, or supporting peasant farmers, these activists were guided by the premise that the best way to challenge the authoritarian system was to empower the marginalized and advocate for their rights (see Anugrah, Rinaldo, and Caraway and Ford, this volume). Initially through their service and organizing work, and increasingly through public advocacy campaigns—which they used to gradually "shift the ground rules of politics" and push the state to concede to their demands (Aspinall 2005, 97)—this generation of NGO activists played a critical role in disseminating democratic ideas and practices throughout society. Among the most visible examples of this phenomenon was the campaign against Kedung Ombo, a World Bank–funded dam project that became a key focus for protest actions in the mid–late 1980s, which brought together environmental groups and agrarian activists concerned about the welfare of farmers who lost their land (Stanley 1994). While these kinds of land disputes did not threaten the New Order state directly, they "added to the mounting burden faced by the regime of maintaining its aura of legitimacy" (Aspinall 2004, 82). In introducing a focus on environmental justice, these groups laid bare the limitations of the New Order regime's developmentalist approach and proved that it was open to challenge.

LIBERALIZATION (1989–94)

Changes in geopolitics, and especially the end of Soviet isolationism, coincided with keterbukaan, which began in 1989 and lasted until mid-1994. This brief period of openness was prompted by growing tension within the regime between Suharto and the military (Crouch 1993) and pressure from foreign states less willing to accommodate authoritarian regimes as the Cold War drew to an end. During this period, controls on the press were relaxed and space became available for open public debate and widespread protest (Aspinall 1995, 25).

Social movements responded to these new opportunities by mounting a "push toward effective democracy" (Rossi and Della Porta 2015, 21). Students became increasingly focused on the needs of the poor and marginalized (Aspinall 2005, 123). They were joined in this endeavor by NGO activists and other progressive groups, whose shared aim was "empowering the powerless" (Heryanto 1988, 263). The student, labor, and land rights movements were particularly critical of the New Order's approach to human rights and the role of the military in this period. According to Aspinall (2005, 144), students had "a major impact on the politics of keterbukaan, especially by testing and expanding the political space for new forms of protest." Labor activists and their allies in the student and women's movements mounted a highly visible campaign against military intervention in the labor movement after Marsinah, a young worker activist in East Java, was raped, tortured and murdered, allegedly by the military, after participating in a strike in May 1993 (Ford 2003). Activists in the land rights movement also adopted a far more radical approach than it had taken in the early 1980s, openly resisting eviction and land grabbing by the state (Anugrah, this volume).

One tactic used to maintain pressure on the regime was to work with semi-oppositional forces within the regime (Aspinall 2005, 9). In the late New Order, the Indonesian Democratic Party (Partai Demokrasi Indonesia, PDI), with its direct links to Sukarno's descendants, played an important role in generating a mass base of opposition. Another critical factor was the extent to which activists could draw on support from their allies abroad. Rossi and Della Porta (2015, 22) explain that transnational alliances can have an impact on the ability of social movements to exert influence during a period of liberalization, as was certainly the case in Indonesia. Many of the NGOs that drove human rights activism in the 1990s received funding from international foundations and were backed by foreign governments keen to promote democracy in Indonesia. NGOs and other social movement actors also used their social movement connections to raise international awareness of restrictions on civil liberties and human rights abuses, in some cases forcing the government to act (Hadiwinata 2003; Dibley 2014; Ford 2009).

There were limits to how much the regime would tolerate, however. Keterbukaan ended abruptly in June 1994, when the government revoked the publishing licenses of the important news magazines *Tempo*, *Editor*, and *DeTik* following the publication of stories criticizing its purchase of secondhand warships from Germany (Romano 1996). From this time, many of the concessions made during this short period of liberalization were reversed in a return of repression that—while it was not immediately obvious—marked the beginning of Indonesia's transition to democracy.

TRANSITION (1994–2004)

Indonesia's transition to democracy was a decades-long process, which began in 1994 and extended past the point of regime change to Indonesia's first direct presidential elections in 2004. As Rossi and Della Porta observe (2015, 22), transition is necessarily characterized by "high uncertainty." However, their model does not account for situations in which liberalization is suddenly reversed, as in the Indonesian case, with the government's decision to wind back the freedoms it had introduced during keterbukaan. Ironically, this reversal played a decisive role in the process of transition since the return of repression engendered greater determination by social movements to push for change, giving Indonesian activists the courage to directly challenge the system in a way they had not been able to before.

A key force in this more frontal assault on the regime was the People's Democratic Association (Persatuan Rakyat Demokratik, PRD), which was formally established in 1994. Later known as the People's Democratic Party, the PRD consisted of students and former students who had been inspired by the work of exiled Indonesian author Prameodya Ananta Toer to organize workers in factories and other sectors as part of its ambition to build a mass movement (Lane 2008). For example, its labor wing, the Indonesian Center for Labor Struggle (Pusat Perjuangan Buruh Indonesia, PPBI), organized protests involving thousands of workers in industrial areas across Indonesia in the mid-1990s. At the same time, the PDI was slowly gaining momentum as an oppositional force. When Sukarno's daughter Megawati Soekarnoputri made a bid to become the leader of the party in 1993, she succeeded despite Suharto's lack of support. Her election signaled to radical student groups—including the PRD—that PDI could be a potential partner in its plans for the downfall of Suharto.

Over the ensuing years, leaders from within the PRD and other opposition forces began to work with individuals within PDI to create a large, very diverse movement for change (Aspinall 2005, 186–87). As Sastramidjaja (this volume) explains, the regime found this partnership to be "dangerously explosive," and both organizations were targeted in a violent crackdown in 1996 when government forces stormed the offices of Megawati's breakaway faction of PDI (Alliance of Independent Journalists 1997). The broader prodemocracy movement faced "a concerted crackdown on civilian dissent" in the lead-up to the May 1997 election (Aspinall 1997). The government's capacity to enforce repression was, however, disrupted by the onset of the Asian financial crisis, which saw the rapid devaluation of the rupiah in the second half of 1997 and increases in inflation, unemployment, and foreign debt. The spiraling economic situation sparked a total crisis, creating the conditions for social movements to make a final and successful push for regime change.[4]

According to Rossi and Della Porta (2015, 22), the initial stage of transition generally involves a prodemocracy coalition of "unions, political parties, churches and social movements" which "may push for social justice and the elimination of the reserved powers that limit the emerging democracy." In 1998 in Indonesia, the prodemocracy coalition consisted primarily of students, supported by academics, NGO activists, and middle-class women's groups, like the Voice of Concerned Mothers

(Suara Ibu Peduli), as well as some members of the political and religious elite (Aspinall 2005, 213–24). A wave of student protests reached a climax on May 12, when the military opened fire on students protesting at Jakarta's Trisakti University, killing four of the demonstrators. The shootings were followed by mass riots over two days in which shopping centers were destroyed, Chinese citizens were attacked, and more than a thousand people were killed (Aspinall 2005, 232). More student protests followed, accompanied by calls from everyone from stock exchange traders and journalists to major Islamic organizations, and even the youth wing of the ruling party, for Suharto to step down (Aspinall 2005, 232). These events triggered Suharto's eventual resignation on May 21 and, with it, the fall of the New Order.[5]

Between 1999 and 2004, the country reformed its political system. Transitional president B. J. Habibie immediately took steps to expand Indonesians' political freedoms through measures such as the introduction of freedom of association and freedom of expression, and the passing of a human rights law. His presidency, and the subsequent presidencies of Abdurrahman Wahid (1999–2001) and Megawati (2001–4), saw the liberalization of the party system and the introduction of competitive elections, culminating in the direct election of the president from 2004 (Crouch 2003; Liddle and Mujani 2006). While the political situation was not as volatile as it had been in 1998, these constant changes to the party system and election processes meant that the ground rules for politicians and social movements alike were in constant flux.

Another important political reform that dramatically changed the opportunities available to social movements was the massive process of decentralization initiated in late 1999 to shore up the new government's legitimacy and "forestall secessionist aspirations" following the loss of East Timor (Buehler 2010, 268–69). Laws passed in that year paved the way for the substantial devolution of power to provincial and district leaders and the restructuring of how government finances were allocated. In addition to "shatter[ing] the centralised state's monopoly over power and resources," decentralization opened the way for greater citizen engagement in public decision making (Antlöv 2003, 77–78). Equally, however, it created new challenges for almost every social movement, for example, contributing to "a resurgence of patriarchal attitudes" (Bessell 2010, 224).

As Rossi and Della Porta (2015, 23) explain, social movements may find it hard to adjust to the new circumstances as the period of transition evolves, depending on the characteristics of particular movements and of the political context prior to the transition. Indonesian social movements very much followed this pattern. The student movement, progressive Islamic groups, and the labor movement found the changes in the immediate aftermath of democracy difficult to navigate (Sastramidjaja, Fealy, and Caraway and Ford, this volume). For different reasons, the student movement and the progressive Islamic movement never really recovered. By contrast, after an initial period of little activity, the labor movement developed relatively effective strategies for leveraging a democratic and decentralized political system. For other movements, democratization had no immediate impact. As Wilson (this volume) demonstrates, the conditions of the urban poor, and consequently many of their everyday resistance strategies, changed little as a result of democracy either in the early 2000s or in the period since. Disability activism, on the other hand, was in such a nascent stage that democratization did not have any immediate effect, although the movement later benefited significantly from the opportunities offered by decentralization (Dibley, this volume). The women's, gay and lesbian, anticorruption, and land rights movements, meanwhile, found that the opportunities of democracy initially offered them a much more conducive environment in which to form cohesive movements, though their respective situations changed as time went by (Anugrah, Kramer, Rinaldo, and Wijaya and Davies, this volume).

A key factor contributing to the experience of social movements in the immediate aftermath of democratization was the role of foreign aid. Progressive social movements that became the targets of foreign aid in those early years of democracy tended to experience the most growth and consolidation in the immediate aftermath of regime change. The anticorruption movement is a key example. Prior to 1998, corruption was a key theme taken up by activists in different sectors opposing the Suharto regime; however, it was not until after 1998 that foreign donors directly funded organizations whose key goals and mission were to combat corruption (Kramer, this volume). This injection of foreign funding provided the movement with the infrastructure to pursue a strong anticorruption agenda in the early days of Indonesian democracy. As this example suggests, while donor assistance, or lack of it, is by no means a firm predictor of a social movement's performance, it can play a vital role in positioning some social movement actors to take advantages of the opportunities brought by democratization.

STAGNATION, NOT EXPANSION (2004–)

Indonesia's pathway to democracy became less clear after the election of President Susilo Bambang Yudhoyono in 2004. Yudhoyono served two terms as president, and was elected in a landslide in both elections. The strength of his electoral mandate, his commitment to parliamentary and judicial reform, and his efforts to limit military engagement in politics—as well as increased economic stability and declining rates of internal conflict—contributed to a sense that the country was undergoing a period of democratic consolidation (Mietzner 2015). In Rossi and Della Porta's (2015, 24) model, this period should have given rise to an opportunity for democratic "expansion." In the Indonesian case, however, 2004 is less a marker of consolidation than of stagnation (Tomsa 2010; Törnquist 2014; Mietzner 2015)—or even the beginning of a democratic recession. International leaders may have praised Yudhoyono for "Indonesia's apparent embrace of the universality of human rights," signaled by the signing of several international covenants (Berger 2015, 221). But this performance of engaging with global human rights discourse was little more than "lip-service" (Sidel 2015, 63), as during Yudhoyono's time in office the pace of reform slowed significantly, particularly in relation to corruption, the security sector, and electoral process (Mietzner 2015).

The response of social movements during this ten-year period was mixed. As noted earlier, the student movement never really recovered. There was increased student activity in the provinces, but the increasing privatization of higher education during this period left the movement struggling (Sastramidjaja, this volume). After some significant successes during the early years of *reformasi*, anticorruption activists found themselves working hard to defend gains made during Yudhoyono's presidency (Kramer, this volume). Other movements that did not fare well during this period included the progressive Islamic movement, the women's movement, and the movement for gay and lesbian rights, which have all struggled with rising religious intolerance. More successful were the movements for land rights and the rights of the urban poor, which managed to get their issues onto the policy table, though not necessarily achieving positive outcomes (Anugrah and Wilson, this volume). Disability and labor activists, meanwhile, had considerable success using existing structures to make concrete changes to policies affecting their constituents (Dibley and Caraway and Ford, this volume). This range of experiences suggests that the overall process of democratic stagnation plays out differently depending on the sector in which a social movement is active. In other words, it is not that social movements no longer have space to operate, but rather that democratic stagnation has affected social attitudes and political opportunity structures related to particular areas of concern.

The ongoing barriers to democratic "expansion" became increasingly obvious when Prabowo declared his candidacy in the lead-up to the 2014 presidential elections. The fear of the risks to democracy of a Prabowo government pushed many activists into the camp of Jokowi, who pledged to respect human rights and redress past abuses (Hearman 2016). As Jokowi's presidency proceeded, however, the progressive social movement actors that had supported him proved unable to hold him to account in areas including women's and labor rights, disability, sexuality, freedom of religion, and even economic empowerment (Muhtadi 2015). Restrictions on the freedom of association, freedom of expression, and freedom of religion continued to hamper citizens' right to live as they wish and activists' efforts to organize. The increasing prominence of conservative countermovements, but also structural changes under decentralization, placed additional pressures on women and minority groups. Members of minority Islamic sects, but also atheists, became an increasingly frequent target for religious extremists. There was a rise in the number of homophobic attacks (Yulius 2017). Labor activists, meanwhile, were subjected to increased surveillance and legitimate protest actions were met with criminal charges, while militias continued to break up gatherings to discuss the massacres of 1965. As Warburton (2016, 307) concludes, "Although the Jokowi administration [did not resurrect] the repressive tools of the New Order model" it had displayed "a growing impatience with liberal reform and an indifference towards human rights."

OUTLINE OF THE BOOK

As the case studies that follow demonstrate, progressive social movements have not only had quite different experiences of Indonesia's democratic trajectory, but also varying impacts on its outcomes, depending on their focus, internal structures, ability to mobilize resources, and engagement in the political sphere. Collectively, they have played a critical role over the last two decades in ensuring that different groups of citizens can engage directly in—and benefit from—the political process in a way that was not possible during the New Order. However, their efforts have had different outcomes, with some playing a decisive role in the destabilization of the regime and others serving as bellwethers of the advancement, or otherwise, of Indonesia's democracy in the decades since. Equally important, democratization has affected social movements differently depending on the form taken by each movement during the New Order period, their capacity to navigate the opportunities and challenges presented by regime change, and the actions of successive democratically elected governments but also of influential countermovements. As a consequence, some have lessened in significance while others have attained new levels of influence.

The specific movements examined in this volume are the student movement; the anticorruption movement; the labor movement; and movements consisting of agrarian smallholders, the urban poor, progressive Muslims, women, gay and lesbian activists, and people with disability. The first five of these movements contributed most to discrediting and, ultimately, directly challenging the authoritarian regime. Their experiences since 1998 have varied wildly, from that of the progressive student movement, which has largely dissipated, to that of the labor movement which, despite facing ongoing challenges, has adapted much more effectively to its new context. The vast differences in movements' trajectories demonstrate that it is not just the level of engagement of a movement prior to democratization that determines how a social movement responds to regime transition, but rather a far more complex set of factors involving institutional structures, resource opportunities, and policy decisions made by the new regime.

We begin with Yatun Sastramidjaja's account of the student movement, which traces its fall from political vanguard to "orphans of democracy." Heir to a long tradition of student struggle, student activists followed a similar path to student movements in other authoritarian societies, leveraging their privileged status to lead the campaign for democracy. From the late 1980s, they challenged the regime, fighting for land rights, organizing workers, and defying the government's bans on leftist political activity. Despite successive waves of repression, it was the students, too, who led the 1998 protests calling for Suharto's resignation and fundamental political reform. Suharto's resignation was, as Sastramidjaja argues, undoubtedly a victory for the so-called 1998 Generation. But, having failed to capitalize on the momentum they had generated, students quickly retreated from the political fray, with only the Islamic student movement making a place for itself in the new Indonesia. By 2004, what remained of the left of the student movement had been relegated to margins, while moderate reformists have moved into government or into other social movements, leaving just a few aging activists clinging to the more radical dreams of an earlier age.

One of the issues taken up by former members of the student movement has been the fight against corruption, which had emerged as a unifying theme in the prodemocracy movement in the New Order. In chapter 2, Elisabeth Kramer illustrates how the corrupt activities of Suharto, his cronies, and his family fueled antigovernment sentiment, even though the movement itself did not take form until after 1998. The new freedoms of Indonesia's reformasi era, combined with the backing of foreign donors, created space for the formation of new NGOs with the explicit mandate to oppose corruption. As Kramer explains, these NGOs played a central role in the formation of the Commission for the Eradication of Corruption (Komisi Pemberantasan Korupsi, KPK) in 2003 and the defense of it against attacks from 2009. The movement also developed a presence at a local level, in response to the proliferation of corruption as a result of decentralization. As she reveals, these local movements have had mixed success, struggling with a lack of resources. Ultimately, however, the most significant obstacle the anticorruption movement faces is the lack of support from the elite level, because without it the movement remains constrained by a political system that fosters corruption.

Unlike the student movement, the labor and the land rights movements were not central players during the actual moment of regime change. However, their actions in the preceding decade made a decisive contribution to the delegitimization of the regime, as Teri Caraway and Michele Ford demonstrate in chapter 3. Struggling to regain a foothold after the decimation of independent labor unions in the massacres of 1965 and repression in the decades that followed, worker activists and their middle-class allies nevertheless clawed their way back, raising awareness at home and abroad of the Indonesian government's unrelenting subjugation of labor rights in its search for economic growth and political stability. Having been forced to accommodate some of the labor movement's demands in the early 1990s, the government struck back, all but destroying the alternative labor unions that had emerged in the intervening years. As a consequence—and in contrast to many other democratic transitions—there was little evidence of worker mobilization in the immediate lead-up to the fall of Suharto. While continuing to grapple with the ongoing obstacles of low density of unionization among workers, organizational fragmentation, and political isolation, the labor movement has since asserted itself economically and politically.

Chapter 4 deals with land rights, which have long been a matter of contention in Indonesia. As Iqra Anugrah argues, a wave of peasant protests in the late Suharto period—and, in particular, a series of high-profile land disputes—not only gave rise to a series of regional peasant unions but also helped destabilize the regime. Like the labor movement, the peasant movement played little or no part in the actual moment of regime change. But, also like the labor movement, peasant movements have since worked to make use of the new political spaces made available to them by democratization. As the movement for land rights has evolved, it has been forced to broaden its repertoire of action from traditional modes of contentious politics, such as mass mobilization, to include tactics such as critical knowledge production, engagement in electoral politics, and a range of economic strategies. Anugrah concludes, however, that—despite its dynamism and some success in the policy arena—the movement failed to mount an effective challenge to the dominance of Indonesia's political and economic elites in this domain.

The final chapter in this first cluster examines the movement for the rights of the urban poor. As Ian Wilson explains in chapter 5, the urban poor played a significant role in the protests that brought down Suharto. Then, after 1998, some organizations emerged that supported the urban poor in their efforts to reform their local communities. But there was no coherent movement during the New Order, nor has there been since. Instead, the urban poor have had to look after themselves, engaging in the politics of the everyday and using defensive forms of action to protect their gains and respond to impending threats. The most significant change since democratization has been the recognition of the urban poor as a voting constituency. Nevertheless, in the absence of a political party with a particular and demonstrated interest in the politics of the poor, activism in support of the urban poor remains fragmented and confined primarily to individual rather than collective action.

The next three chapters focus on identity-based movements, which have been deeply affected by the rising conservatism that has characterized Indonesia's democratic recession. As these chapters reveal, the progressive Islamic movement, the women's movement, and the movement for gay and lesbian rights have all been forced to negotiate, with varying levels of success, the rise of conservative Islamic counter-movements. These cases illustrate the critical challenges faced by social movements that focus on aspects of personal identity that challenge the agendas of these conservative Islamic forces, which have been able to use Indonesia's democratic structures to their advantage. These movements were all able to achieve significant gains in the early stages of Indonesia's democracy. However, it was precisely these early successes that subsequently led to their persecution by conservative opponents.

One of the paradoxes of democratization is that the progressive Islamic movement—which had played such an important role in its genesis—quickly became a casualty of the increasing dominance of conservative Islamic forces. As Greg Fealy explains in chapter 6, liberal Muslim intellectuals and activists had drawn on religious teachings to popularize and validate political reform and human rights agendas from the late 1980s, thus preparing the way for Indonesia's majority Islamic community to embrace democracy as an alternative to authoritarianism. The wealth of progressive Islamic thought and action that marked those decades, has, however, fallen victim to the illiberal aspects of reformasi. Fealy concludes that while liberal Islam flourished in New Order Indonesia because it had the support of the regime, it was unable to leverage that success in the face of broader religiocultural and political changes from the early 2000s, which have been driven by, and favored, conservative Islamist forces.

In chapter 7, Rachel Rinaldo assesses the impact of the rise of these conservative Islamic countermovements on activism in support of women's rights. As she explains, women not only played an important role in the push for democracy but were able to see through significant reforms for women during reformasi. But the same conditions that have made it possible for progressive women activists, religious and secular, to make these gains contributed also to the rise of conservative Islamic groups whose values are directly threatened by a vibrant women's movement. Rinaldo argues that the movement's ideological divisions and its inability to mobilize a mass base—along with the changes brought about by decentralization—have made it difficult for the progressive women's movement to respond to more organized conservative forces.

In chapter 8, Hendri Wijaya and Sharyn Graham Davies examine the transformation of activism for lesbian and gay rights from an understated, but relatively secure, position in the heterosexist context of the New Order to a much more visible, but also vulnerable, movement. Lesbian and gay activists believed that democracy would improve their capacity to move beyond demands for inclusion and equal treatment to demands for acceptance, which initially proved to be the case. But democracy also created space for homophobic forces intent on eradicating public expressions of homosexual or queer identity. One reaction to this hostility—which reached the highest levels of government in 2016—was to retreat to the "safer" forms of activism characteristic of the New Order. As Wijaya and Davies demonstrate, however, activists have also responded by using digital media platforms to establish formal and informal networks and by reaching out to international organizations and to other Indonesian social movements with intersecting concerns.

The book's final case study focuses on the disability movement, a relatively new movement that has managed to draw on the increased availability of foreign funding to capitalize on the democratic structures now in place in Indonesia. In chapter 9, Thushara Dibley writes about how the disability rights movement, which was at best embryonic in the late New Order period, has developed momentum since the Indonesian government signed the United Nations Convention on the Rights of Persons with Disabilities (CRPD) in 2007. After that time, the availability of international aid to support activities related to disability contributed to the formation of a number of new organizations that were then well placed to respond to the opportunities that democratization offered. In particular, these organizations have been able to take advantage of the opportunities to influence policy at both the provincial and national levels. Their success, argues Dibley, highlights how Indonesian democracy offers inclusive and participatory processes for people with disabilities to have direct input into policy decisions.

In reflecting on the trajectories of these different movements, Edward Aspinall takes a step back to focus on the challenges they face in postauthoritarian Indonesia in the concluding chapter. Having acknowledged the advances social movements have made individually and collectively, he points to their structural weaknesses and failure to gain traction in the political arena as evidence of their enduring fragility.

This fragility, he argues, is a product of the patterns that continue to dominate Indonesian society, namely clientelism, the reliance of extralegal means to achieve political outcomes, and the ever-growing strength of rival political movements, which seek to mobilize the disenfranchised for different, and often antiliberal, ends. Aspinall contends that incrementalism is not sufficient in such circumstances if Indonesia's progressive social movements wish to prevail. Instead, he concludes, they must continue to strive for "root-and-branch transformation of the social order," with the goal of transforming Indonesia into a society based on ethical universalism, not particularism.

As the chapters in this book illustrate, democratization is "always and everywhere an unfinished process" (Beetham 1999, 159). Indonesia's road to democracy has been a long one, which progressive social movements have experienced in quite different ways. As they have transformed themselves, moreover, their actions have influenced the way that the democratization process has played out. Despite the increasing influence of conservative countermovements, Indonesia's democratic system offers progressive activists more opportunities to influence social attitudes and political outcomes than they had during even the most liberal years of the New Order. The outcomes of their efforts may have been uneven, but each one has continued to work to change the structures of Indonesian society in ways that make it more democratic, inclusive, and fair.

NOTES

1. Thanks to one of the anonymous reviewers for this point.
2. For a discussion of the tactics used by social movements in Southeast Asia, see Ford 2013.
3. As Escobar (1992) argues, distinctions between politically oriented and culturally oriented social movements are incremental, not absolute. This is especially true in emerging democracies where discrimination against different elements in society is enshrined in legislation or embedded in institutions or social practice. In such contexts, even social movements at the "cultural" end of that spectrum must engage politically.
4. For a general overview of the economic effects of the crisis see Hill 1999.
5. For early accounts of the events leading to the fall of Suharto, see Forrester 1998, and Schwarz 1999.

REFERENCES

Adler, Glenn, and Eddie Webster. 1995. "Challenging Transition Theory: The Labor Movement, Radical Reform, and Transition to Democracy in South Africa." *Politics and Society* 23 (1): 75–106.

Alliance of Independent Journalists. 1997. *Jakarta Crackdown*. Jakarta: Alliance of Independent Journalists, Asian Forum for Human Rights and Development, Institute for the Studies on Free Flow of Information.

Antlöv, Hans. 2003. "Not Enough Politics! Power, Participation, and the New Democratic Polity in Indonesia." In *Local Power and Politics in Indonesia: Decentralisation and Democratisation*, edited by Edward Aspinall and Greg Fealy, 72–86. Singapore: ISEAS–Yusof Ishak Institute.

Aspinall, Edward. 1995. "Students and the Military: Regime Friction and Civilian Dissent in the Late Suharto Period." *Indonesia* 59: 21–44.

——. 1997. "What Price Victory? The 1997 Elections." *Inside Indonesia* 51: 2.

——. 2004. "Indonesia: Transformation of Civil Society and Democratic Breakthrough." In *Civil Society and Political Change in Asia: Expanding and Contracting Democratic Space*, edited by Muthiah Alagappa, 61–96. Stanford: Stanford University Press.

——. 2005. *Opposing Suharto: Compromise, Resistance, and Regime Change in Indonesia*. Stanford: Stanford University Press.

Bachriadi, D. 2009. *Land, Rural Social Movements and Democratisation in Indonesia*. Bandung: Transnational Institute.

Ballard, Richard, Adam Habib, Imraan Valodia, and Elke Zuern. 2005. "Globalization, Marginalization and Contemporary Social Movements in South Africa." *African Affairs* 104 (417): 615–34.

Beetham, David. 1999. *Democracy and Human Rights*. Cambridge: Polity Press.

Berger, Dominic. 2015. "Human Rights and Yudhyono's Test of History." In *The Yudhyono Presidency: Indonesia's Decade of Stability and Stagnation*, edited by Edward Aspinall, Marcus Mietzner and Dirk Tomsa, 217–38. Singapore: Institute of Southeast Asian Studies.

Bessell, Sharon. 2010. "Increasing the Proportion of Women in the National Parliament: Opportunities, Barriers and Challenges." In *Problems of Democratisation in Indonesia: Elections, Institutions and Society*, edited by Edward Aspinall and Marcus Mietzner, 219–42. Singapore: Institute of Southeast Asian Studies.

Boudreau, Vincent. 2004. *Resisting Dictatorship: Repression and Protest in Southeast Asia*. New York: Cambridge University Press.

——. 2013. "Philippine Contention in the 'Democratic Transitions.'" In *Social Activism in Southeast Asia*, edited by Michele Ford, 56–71. London: Routledge.

Buehler, Michael. 2007. "Local Elite Reconfiguration in Post-New Order Indonesia: The 2005 Election of the District Government Heads in South Sulawesi." *Review of Indonesian and Malaysian Affairs* 41 (1): 119–47.

——. 2010. "Decentralisation and Local Democracy in Indonesia: The Marginalisation of the Public Sphere." In *Problems of Democratisation in Indonesia: Elections, Institutions and Society*, edited by Edward Aspinall and Marcus Mietzner, 267–85. Singapore: Institute of Southeast Asian Studies.

Collier, Ruth, and James Mahoney. 1997. "Adding Collective Actors to Collective Outcomes: Labor and Recent Democratization in South America and Southern Europe." *Comparative Politics* 29 (3): 285–303.

Cribb, Robert, ed. 1990. *The Indonesian Killings, 1965–1966*. Clayton, Victoria: Monash University.

Crouch, Harold. 1993. "Democratic Prospects in Indonesia." *Asian Journal of Political Science* 1 (2): 77–92.

——. 2003. "Political Update 2002: Megawati's Holding Operation." In *Local Power and Politics in Indonesia: Decentralisation and Democratisation*, edited by Edward Aspinall and Greg Fealy, 15–34. Singapore: ISEAS–Yusof Ishak Institute.

Della Porta, Donatella. 2014. *Mobilizing for Democracy: Comparing 1989 and 2011*. Oxford: Oxford University Press.

Diani, Mario. 1992. "The Concept of Social Movement." *Sociological Review* 40 (1): 1–25.

Dibley, Thushara. 2014. *Partnerships, Power, and Peacebuilding: NGOs as Agents of Peace in Aceh and Timor-Leste*. Houndmills: Palgrave Macmillan.

Eldridge, Philip J. 1995. *Non-Government Organizations and Democratic Participation in Indonesia*. Kuala Lumpur: Oxford University Press.

Escobar, Arturo. 1992. "Culture, Practice and Politics: Anthropology and the Study of Social Movements." *Critique of Anthropology* 12 (4): 395–432.

Ford, Michele. 2003. "Beyond the Femina Fantasy: The Working-Class Woman in Indonesian Discourses of Women's Work." *RIMA: Review of Indonesian and Malaysian Affairs* 37 (2): 83–113.

——. 2009. *Workers and Intellectuals: NGOs, Trade Unions, and the Indonesian Labour Movement*. Singapore: National University of Singapore Press/Hawaii University Press/KITLV.

——. 2013. "Social Activism in Southeast Asia: An Introduction." In *Social Activism in Southeast Asia*, edited by Michele Ford, 1–21. London: Routledge.

Ford, Michele, and Thomas Pepinsky, eds. 2014a. *Beyond Oligarchy: Wealth, Power, and Contemporary Indonesian Politics*. Ithaca: Cornell Southeast Asia Program.

——. 2014b. "Introduction: Beyond Oligarchy?" In *Beyond Oligarchy: Wealth, Power, and Contemporary Indonesian Politics*, edited by Michele Ford and Thomas Pepinsky, 1–10. Ithaca: Cornell Southeast Asia Program.

Forrester, Geoffrey. 1998. "A Jakarta Diary, May 1998." In *The Fall of Soeharto*, edited by Geoffrey Forrester and R. J. May, 24–69. Bathurst, UK: Crawford House.

Foweraker, Joe. 2001. "Grassroots Movements and Political Activism in Latin America: A Critical Comparison of Chile and Brazil." *Journal of Latin American Studies* 33 (4): 839–65.

Friedman, Elisabeth Jay, and Kathryn Hochstetler. 2002. "Assessing the Third Transition in Latin American Democratization: Representational Regimes and Civil Society in Argentina and Brazil." *Comparative Politics* 35 (1): 21–42.

Grodsky, Brian. 2012. *Social Movements and the New State: The Fate of Pro-Democracy Organizations When Democracy Is Won*. Stanford: Stanford University Press.

Grugel, Jean. 2013. "Introduction: Democratization—Charting a Path through Complexity." In *Democratization*, edited by Jean Grugel, xix–xlii. London: Sage.

Guigni, Marco. 1999. "How Social Movements Matter: Past Research, Present Problems, Future Developments. In *How Social Movements Matter*, edited by Marco Guigni, Doug McAdam and Charles Tilly, xiii–xxxiii. Minneapolis: University of Minnesota Press.

Hadiwinata, Bob. 2003. *The Politics of NGOs in Indonesia: Developing Democracy and Managing a Movement*. London: RoutledgeCurzon.

Hadiz, Vedi R, and Richard Robison. 2014. "The Political Economy of Oligarchy and the Reorganization of Power in Indonesia." In *Beyond Oligarchy: Wealth, Power, and Contemporary Indonesian Politics*, edited by Michele Ford and Thomas Pepinsky, 35–56. Ithaca: Cornell Southeast Asia Program.

Hearman, Vannessa. 2016. "No 'Magic Bullet.'" *Inside Indonesia* 123. https://www.insideindonesia.org/no-magic-bullet-2.

Heryanto, Ariel. 1988. "The Development of 'Development." *Indonesia* 46: 1–29.

Hill, Hal. 1999. *The Indonesian Economy in Crisis: Causes, Consequences, and Lessons.* St Leonards, UK: Allen and Unwin.

Lane, Max. 2008. *Unfinished Nation: Indonesia Before and After Suharto.* London: Verso.

Liddle, R. William. 2013. "Improving the Quality of Democracy in Indonesia: Toward a Theory of Action." *Indonesia* 96 (October): 59–80.

Liddle, R. William, and Saiful Mujani. 2006. "Indonesia in 2005: A New Multiparty Presidential Democracy." *Asian Survey* 46 (1): 132–39.

——. 2013. "Indonesian Democracy from Transition to Consolidation." In *Democracy and Islam in Indonesia,* edited by Mirjam Künkler and Alfred Stepan, 24–50. New York: Columbia University Press.

Lucas, Anton, and Carrol Warren. 2003. "The State, the People, and Their Mediators: The Struggle over Agrarian Law Reform in Post-New Order Indonesia." *Indonesia* 76: 87–126.

McAdam, Doug, Sidney Tarrow, and Charles Tilly. 1996. "To Map Contentious Politics." *Mobilization* 1 (1): 17–34.

Mietzner, Marcus. 2013. "Fighting the Hellhounds: Pro-democracy Activists and Party Politics in Post-Suharto Indonesia." *Journal of Contemporary Asia* 43 (1): 28–50.

——. 2015. "Indonesia: Democratic Consolidation and Stagnation under Yudhoyono, 2004–2014." In *Routledge Handbook of Southeast Asian Democratization,* edited by William Case, 370–83. New York: Routledge.

Muhtadi, Burhanuddin. 2015. "Jokowi's First Year: A Weak President Caught between Reform and Oligarchic Politics." *Bulletin of Indonesian Economic Studies* 51 (3): 349–68.

Reeve, David. 1985. *Golkar of Indonesia: An Alternative to the Party System.* Singapore: Oxford University Press.

Rodan, Garry. 2018. *Participation without Democracy: Containing Conflict in Southeast Asia.* Ithaca: Cornell University Press.

Romano, Angela. 1996. "The Open Wound: *Keterbukaan* and Press Freedom in Indonesia." *Australian Journal of International Affairs* 50 (2): 157–69.

Roosa, John. 2006. *Pretext for Mass Murder: The September 30th Movement and Suharto's Coup D'etat in Indonesia.* Madison: University of Wisconsin Press.

Rossi, Federico M., and Donatella Della Porta. 2015. "Mobilizing for Democracy: Social Movements in Democratization Processes." In *Movements in Times of Democratic Transition,* edited by Bert Klandermands and Cornelis van Stralen, 9–33. Philadelphia: Temple University Press.

Rostow, W. W. 1960. *The Stages of Economic Growth: A Non-communist Manifesto.* London: Cambridge University Press.

Schmitter, Philippe, and Karl, Terry. 1991. "What Democracy Is . . . and Is Not." *Journal of Democracy* 2 (3): 75–88.

Schwarz, Adam. 1999. *A Nation in Waiting.* Sydney: Allen and Unwin.

Shin, Kwang-Yeong. 2010. "Globalisation and the Working Class in South Korea: Contestation, Fragmentation and Renewal." *Journal of Contemporary Asia* 40 (2): 211–29.

Sidel, John. 2015. "Men on Horseback and Their Droppings: Yudhyono's Presidency and Legacies in Comparative Regional Perspective." In *The Yudhyono Presidency: Indonesia's Decade of Stability and Stagnation*, edited by Edward Aspinall, Marcus Mietzner, and Dirk Tomsa, 55–72. Singapore: Institute of Southeast Asian Studies.

Stanley. 1994. *Seputar Kedung Ombo*. Jakarta: Lembaga Studi Advokasi Masyarakat.

Stepan, Alfred. 1997. "Democratic Opposition and Democratization Theory." *Government and Opposition* 32 (4): 657–73.

Threlfall, Monica. 2008. "Reassessing the Role of Civil Society Organizations in the Transition to Democracy in Spain." *Democratization* 15 (5): 930–51.

Tilly, Charles. 1993. "Social Movements as Historically Specific Clusters of Political Performances." *Berkeley Journal of Sociology* 30: 1–30.

——. 2001. "When Do (and Don't) Social Movements Promote Democratization?" In *Social Movements and Democracy*, edited by Pedro Ibarra, 21–46. New York: Palgrave Macmillan.

Tomsa, Dirk. 2010. "Indonesian Politics in 2010: The Perils of Stagnation." *Bulletin of Indonesian Economic Studies* 46 (3): 309–28.

Törnquist, Olle. 2014. "Stagnation or Transformation in Indonesia?" *Economic and Political Weekly* 49 (50): 23–27.

Warburton, Eve. 2016. "Jokowi and the New Developmentalism." *Bulletin of Indonesian Economic Studies* 52 (3): 297–320.

Winters, Jeffrey A. 2014. "Oligarchy and Democracy in Indonesia." In *Beyond Oligarchy: Wealth, Power, and Contemporary Indonesian Politics*, edited by Michele Ford and Thomas Pepinsky, 11–34. Ithaca: Cornell Southeast Asia Program.

Yulius, Hendri. 2017. "The Dark Side of LGBT Awareness in Indonesia." *Jakarta Post*. http://www.thejakartapost.com/academia/2017/10/09/the-dark-side-of-lgbt-awareness-in-indonesia.html.

CHAPTER ONE

STUDENT MOVEMENTS AND INDONESIA'S DEMOCRATIC TRANSITION

Yatun Sastramidjaja

When Suharto resigned on May 21, 1998, amidst massive student protests, the student movement was widely acclaimed as the catalyst of this historic event. Suharto's reign had become untenable due to a string of political crises, exacerbated by the Asian financial crisis. Yet the public attributed his fall to the student movement, which had emerged as the heir to a long tradition of student struggle in Indonesia. This view resonated with historical memories of student political vanguardism that are lodged deep in the national consciousness. In 1998, these memories fueled the students' mobilizing power, and as students continued the struggle for "total reform" (*reformasi total*) in the following years, the public invested its hopes in their ability to push through the promise of structural change. Five years later, however, the students had lost their position in the limelight to other actors that were better equipped for the game of politics. Democratization had made the student movement irrelevant, and what remains of it has since struggled to forge a new identity for itself.

Not only in Indonesia, but throughout Asia, Africa, and Latin America, the role of students has long been recognized as one of political vanguard due to their prominent role in national liberation movements and their subsequent prominence in political reform movements against repressive regimes. Especially in authoritarian societies, where failing political institutions and muted civil societies created a political vacuum, students were often seen as the most suitable group to fill this vacuum due to their relatively privileged status, skills, and social capital, as well as the militancy seen lacking in older political and intellectual actors, who were often co-opted into the establishment and seemed too far removed from the common people (Baud and Rutten 2004; Emmerson 1968; Altbach 1989; Weiss, Aspinall, and Thompson 2012). As Weiss (2009, 517, 501) notes with regard to Southeast Asia, students are "*expected* to take a stand, and are respected for doing so by dint of their status as students," since their collective identity "bears a presumption of activism: the default in this case is for students, organized as such, to mobilize." For this reason, students can be specifically targeted for direct or indirect political suppression, although this further enhances their reputation as a potentially formidable political force.

Conversely, however, student movements generally lose their political influence once democratization sets in, as new freedoms of expression and organization reduce the need for students to speak out and act on behalf of "the people." Across Asia, a "real paradox of student mobilization," then, as Aspinall and Weiss (2012, 290) observe, is that "democracy may provide less fruitful a backdrop for its emergence and expression than authoritarianism." Yet, it is too soon to conclude, as Aspinall and Weiss (2012, 205) do, that the political role of students was "a product of particular political and social conditions that have now passed." Recent upsurges of student mobilization in Asia—such as the Sunflower Movement in Taiwan, the Umbrella Movement in Hong Kong in 2014, and the mass participation of students in the Bersih Movement in Malaysia—suggest that students still envisage and claim a national political role for themselves. In Indonesia, too, students continue to mobilize around various issues, although these student protests remain scarce and scattered and show few signs of consolidating into a national mass movement as in 1998. However, democratization did have an impact on the type of activism that students are drawn to, as the memory—and the myth—of student political vanguardism recede further into the past.

THE STUDENT VANGUARD

"Indonesia's student movement," writes Aspinall (2012a, 156), "was a child of authoritarianism, as much as it was its destroyer." Not only did it emerge and radicalize in response to authoritarianism but its nature and scope of action were the product of an authoritarian political culture that celebrated the student struggles of the past and delegitimized student activism in the present. While the "idea that students constituted a discrete political force, able to act as a cohesive unit . . . in defense of the nation, was always a myth" (Aspinall 2012a, 176), this myth was nurtured by the New Order regime and students alike. Provided they conformed to their historically recognized role, students had a limited license to voice the people's concerns, or so the euphemism for student protest went, "at least to a specific limit whose boundaries [were] never clear" (Heryanto 1996, n.p.); crossing these unclear boundaries subjected students to the same harsh repression as any other group in New Order society. This apparent contradiction between repression and recognition reflects the ambiguous relationship between the student movement and the regime, which can be traced to the birth moment of the New Order in 1966.

While students had played a key political role in Indonesia since the early twentieth century, it was the 1966 student movement that established "the idea that students represented an important political category with the capacity to save the nation in times of crisis" (Aspinall 2012a, 164). The 1966 student movement, like its successor, was born of authoritarianism, emerging from the deeply politicized and polarized climate of Sukarno's Guided Democracy. A key aspect of Sukarno's discourse was the revolutionary potential of students, which he framed as a historical duty to heed the "message of the people's suffering" (Sumohadiwidjojo and Mas 1988; Sastramidjaja 2020). While this discourse was meant to unite the postcolonial student body behind Sukarno's mass politics, it exacerbated tensions between the leftist students close to Sukarno and the allegedly "antirevolutionary" students of the Islamic Indonesian Student Association (Himpunan Mahasiswa Indonesia, HMI). HMI and other student organizations that felt marginalized by Sukarno's leftist politics had their revenge soon after the foiled coup of September 30, 1965, when they formed the anticommunist Indonesian Student Action Front (Kesatuan Aksi Mahasiswa Indonesia, KAMI). For months, KAMI staged aggressive mass demonstrations, attacking the Communist Party and its affiliates, then leftist elements in Sukarno's government, and finally Sukarno himself. The heroic image of this student struggle, against what they called the "tyranny" of Sukarno's government (Anwar 1980), provided the army, under Suharto's leadership, with the moral legitimacy to take power. In turn, the example of KAMI—with its tactics of creating an urban spectacle of protest, with masses of students wearing colorful campus jackets, marching through the city's arteries, yelling slogans, chanting songs, and waving university flags and banners—came to provide the performative repertoires and narrative script for future student movements.

Although KAMI was not only anticommunist but also antiauthoritarian, HMI's dominance in it, and the co-optation of its leadership in Suharto's government, effectively stifled any radical potential. As the story of the "1966 Generation" thus became the founding story of the New Order, the idea of student struggle was reconfigured into a historical myth about *past* achievements, implying that that struggle was completed. This myth was enshrined in the government-sponsored book *Indonesian Youth in the History of National Struggle*, published in 1984, which paints a heroic vision of the patriotic struggle of youth from the early twentieth century until 1966. As Suharto wrote in his preface, this history served as a lesson for the present—a reminder that youth had brought Indonesia independence and had given birth to the Order of Development, but also that they should learn from past mistakes to prevent a repeat in the future (Sastramidjaja 2020). The past mistakes to which he referred were the disruptive politics exemplified by the Communist Party and its allies and offspring, which had no place in the New Order.

These official accounts were instrumental in what Weiss (2009) calls the "intellectual containment" of student activism. But unlike the Malaysian case she refers to, where "normative delegitimation" of student activism was effected through its "historical erasure," in Indonesia the status of students in political mythology precluded complete silencing. Rather, the delegitimation of student protest occurred indirectly through allegations of impurity. While the regime claimed to acknowledge the moral integrity of students in voicing their concerns qua students, it also claimed that this integrity was readily diluted by manipulation by hidden nonstudent actors. This allegedly caused the "initially pure intentions" of students to degenerate into "anarchist" or "extremist" forms of disruption, aiding "subversive" or "communist" agendas, which justified repression (Sastramidjaja 2020).

It was to counter such allegations that students, following the lead of disaffected members of KAMI, presented themselves as a moral force. Students, they held, must remain "uncontaminated by the dirty and corrupting world of politics" (Aspinall 2012a, 154) in order to guard their capacity to take action against any ruler when needed. The moral force principle became an essential part of the collective identity of students, providing a persuasive legitimating frame for student protest by positioning students as "loyal critics" rather than opponents of the state (Budiman 1978; Sastramidjaja 2020). However, in declaring the students' distance from politics, it also legitimated the regime's contention that students should indeed steer clear from "practical politics," the New Order euphemism for activism. The student movements of the 1970s thus made themselves vulnerable to repression by remaining within the "moral" frame of student struggle, which precluded any form of activism outside the role of "loyal critic." They remained a child of the New Order—locked in a symbolic battle with the state within a self-centered bubble from which other actors were barred, as "the moral force idea also implies student separatism: the notion that students should not build alliances with other social or political groups who might pollute the students' agenda with their own interests" (Aspinall 2012a, 154).

This affected the issues they championed, their repertoires of action, and the scope and permissible bounds of their struggle, which was easily repressed once students attacked the main pillars of the New Order: the development policy, its military power base, and Suharto himself.

The regime's intolerance of student activism was demonstrated in its violent repression of student protests against wasteful government spending in 1972, and more dramatically in 1974 and 1978, when major student movements organized by university student councils criticized the government's development policy and, more boldly, in 1978, condemned the military dominance and Suharto's authoritarianism, calling for his resignation. The 1974 protests ended in massive riots, which effectively deterred street protest for years to come by affirming the regime's claim that protest incites anarchy. It also reinforced the separation between students and the underclass "masses" that were easily provoked. In 1978, the protests were quashed by overwhelming military force, with troops raiding and occupying the most active campuses. Hundreds of students were arrested, student leaders received lengthy prison sentences, student journals were banned, and student councils frozen. In the aftermath, a series of policies were implemented to curb political activity on campuses and generally keep a check on the student population through close surveillance.

This repression dampened overt student protest for a decade. But it had the unintended effect of driving student activists off campus and underground, where they began experimenting with alternative forms of activism. In the 1980s, informal discussion groups began to mushroom as an alternative channel for student criticism, where students discussed social, economic, and political issues based on banned leftist literature. Many students also became involved in grassroots NGO campaigns, which deeply affected their perceptions of their relationship to "the people," engendering a populist orientation that laid the basis for an emergent student Left. Meanwhile, campus-based proselytizing (*dakwah*) groups also began to flourish, representing a budding Islamic student movement that took advantage of the activist vacuum on campuses to take over student representative councils and generally increase their influence among the student population. But it was the student Left that pushed the long transition to democracy.

PUSHING THE LONG TRANSITION

Indonesia's political transition did not start in 1998, with Suharto's resignation, but in 1989, with the rise of student radicalism as an integral part, if not the engine, of a budding opposition movement. It ended around the 2004 elections, with the consolidation of a new status quo that signaled the student movement's decline. The transition began with a policy of "openness" (*keterbukaan*) launched in 1989 in response to domestic and international pressures for economic and political liberalization, which coincided with an intraregime conflict that created further opportunities for the reemergence and quick acceleration of student protests in the following years (Aspinall 1995). By the early 1990s, students in virtually all university towns were mobilizing around social justice and human rights issues, organizing themselves in ad hoc action committees that escaped campus controls (Aspinall 1993).

Student action in this period focused especially on land disputes in defense of disenfranchised communities, exemplified by the famous case of Kedung Ombo in Central Java where thousands of villagers had to make way for a prestigious dam construction, provoking a vigorous campaign by students and NGOs that lasted for two years (Aditjondro 1993). Such high-profile mobilizations contributed to the popularization of mass action among students and the populations they defended. Their populist orientation furthermore led students to develop new repertoires of activism, such as the "live-in" strategy of sustained community organizing, in which middle-class students lived among the communities they defended for periods of weeks or months—an experience that supposedly entailed "committing class suicide"—although this remained restricted to the most radical populist groups (Aspinall 1993; Sastramidjaja 2020). Other groups began attacking the regime more directly by staging small but bold demonstrations at the parliament or other government sites, targeting not only development projects that involved army interests but also New Order militarism. The more radical these protests became, the more they met with repression, including lengthy prison terms for some student activists. This not only further radicalized the students, but also helped to bring the student movement back into the spotlight.

This issue-based activism gave rise to solid activist organizations, but not all of them survived the end of the openness policy in 1994, especially where they relied on alliances with elite actors. For example, the Indonesian Student Action Front (Front Aksi Mahasiswa Indonesia, FAMI), which allied with Sri Bintang Pamungkas, a politician from the United Development Party (Partai Persatuan Pembangunan, PPP), disappeared when Pamungkas was sidelined and the student leaders were jailed. Affiliated groups continued to exist, but since their network was broken they could no longer engage in headline-grabbing action. Increasingly harsh repression—including the risk of abduction and torture by intelligence agencies, as happened in 1993 after a joint action with farmers in East Java—confronted other radical groups with the dilemma of whether to avoid provoking the regime further or to expand the strategy of mass mobilization (Lane 2008). In 1993, students favoring the latter strategy formed the Indonesian Student Solidarity for Democracy (Solidaritas Mahasiswa Indonesia untuk Demokrasi, SMID), which evolved into the People's Democratic Party (Partai Rakyat Demokratik, PRD), founded as a multisector union in 1994 and declared as a political party in 1996 (Miftahuddin 2004).

With its multisectoral strategy—including the mobilization of factory workers in a manner unprecedented in the corporatized New Order field of labor (Lane 2008; Ford 2009)—its controversial political demands, and its bold use of communist discourse and symbols, the PRD presented itself as a revolutionary force for systemic change, greatly transgressing the permissible bounds of student identity. At the same time, it precluded political marginalization by simultaneously pursuing a strategy of coalition building with reformist groups. By 1996 it was at the front of a major opposition movement, formed around its alliance with the Indonesian Democratic Party (Partai Demokrasi Indonesia, PDI) under the leadership of Megawati Soekarnoputri, Sukarno's daughter and the symbolic leader figure of the opposition. To the PRD, the PDI seemed an attractive partner for its loyal mass support base; to the regime, this alliance seemed dangerously explosive. On July 26, 1996, a regime-orchestrated leadership crisis in the PDI led to riots in Jakarta, which were instantly blamed on the PRD and landed key figures within its leadership in prison and further provided a pretext for the suppression of all opposition. Heightened surveillance on campuses further nipped all student protest in the bud.

Underground, though, student activists connected to the PRD and the former FAMI networks continued to consolidate their movement against Suharto's regime (Sastramidjaja 2020). Around the May 1997 elections, they managed to mobilize massive popular rallies against the state party Golkar and for Megawati and Sri Bintang Pamungkas (representing the PDI and the PPP, the only two other legal political parties) as alternative candidates for the presidency and vice presidency (Lane 2008). Sensing that the conditions were right, many targeted the upcoming session of the People's Consultative Assembly in March 1998 in an attempt to prevent Suharto's reappointment. They did not foresee the economic crisis that hit the country in late 1997, with devastating impact on the middle classes, which accelerated the process of Suharto's delegitimation and sparked an acute sense of urgency among the larger student population. Once this student population was called on—by activist peers and the general public—to live up to their historic reputation as defenders of the people in times of crisis, many thousands of students who had previously not been politically active were readily persuaded to join the first mass student movement since the 1970s, one more massive and militant than its predecessors due to the role of numerous smaller campuses across the country (McRae 1999; Aspinall 1999).

The 1998 student movement thrived on the image of a spontaneous student struggle, united behind the call for "total reform." But it was never a cohesive movement; a variety of organizations were mobilized and created in the course of the protest, some of which revived the moral force role, while others drew on the militant repertoires of the early 1990s. The moral force role was played by the university student senates that were still dominated by the HMI and other Islamic groups, and by the new Indonesian Muslim Students Action Front (Kesatuan Aksi Mahasiswa Muslim Indonesia, KAMMI), which was founded in March 1998 out of the campus-based dakwah movement, and allied with the self-styled spokesperson of the reform movement, Muhammadiyah chair Amien Rais. Exemplary of the radical image was the City Forum (Forum Kota, Forkot), a coalition based at private universities in Jakarta, also founded in March 1998. Forkot further exemplified the student movement's image of a "leaderless culture," assuming a form of collective leadership and refusing to put forward leading representatives or to ally with elite opposition leaders. This emphasis on student autonomy indicated that even the radical elements latched onto moral force principles, which augmented their heroic image. Beneath this image of a unified moral force, however, it was in fact the ideological and organizational diversity that allowed the student movement to garner support from virtually all elements in society, thereby creating opportunities for hitherto cautious critics to voice their disgruntlement with the regime by "standing behind the students."

This heroic image was further augmented by the students' increasingly daring demands and actions—calling for Suharto's resignation, while pushing to take the protest off-campus and onto the streets—and the regime's increasingly heavy-handed response. Violent clashes with security troops escalated on May 12, when students were killed at the elite Trisakti University, which was followed by days of riots in Jakarta and other cities, purportedly orchestrated by Suharto's son-in-law, Special Forces Commander Prabowo. By giving credence to the regime's warnings about the dangers of mass action, the riots put a damper on the students' efforts to build a people power type of movement, similar to that in the Philippines in 1986, to defeat the regime. While various other social groups participated in student protests in early May, the students proved not to be equipped to lead such a movement; hence, they proceeded with the script of student struggle. On May 19 masses of students started occupying the Parliament, by now supported by political leaders and the army. Together with students stationed at the gates, troops ensured that nonstudent grassroots groups were barred from the compound, despite objections from other student activists.

Suharto's resignation on May 21 could thus be framed as truly a "student victory." But while KAMMI and other Islamic student organizations gladly accepted Suharto's successor, B. J. Habibie, a patron of the Indonesian Association of Muslim Intellectuals, other student activists felt that this climax had come too soon, leaving them with little time to develop long-term strategies for the political transition. Suharto's exit was, rather, a quasi-victory that allowed New Order elites to remain in power without having to account for their crimes. These activists were determined to continue the struggle. However, for the "1998 Generation" as the student movement was called in the press—a category that implied accomplished victory, rather than providing a roadmap for mobilization—it was difficult to determine what kind of struggle this must be.

STRUGGLE IN TRANSITION

The lasting currency of the moral force myth complicated the students' political positioning, as engaging in "corrupting politics" remained anathema to the student identity. Thus, when Forkot and other groups began campaigning for a transitional government that would be purged from New Order elites, they maintained that students themselves should not be directly involved, since the student movement should remain an autonomous pressure group, using "a moral modus operandi" (Abdullah 1998, 51). Some students attempted to sidestep this issue by pressuring the most influential opposition leaders to draft a plan. But the moderate outcome convinced many that action was needed. During the special session of the People's Consultative Assembly in November 1998, students staged massive marches in Jakarta, demanding substantive political reform. The protests were not joined by KAMMI and other moderate elements, nor by opposition leaders, which left the students vulnerable to attacks from security troops and militia. But the students received unexpected support from thousands of Jakarta residents, who protected them from attacks or even joined the marches; to the students, this proved that the promise of people power was not a mere fantasy. The promise was shattered, though, with the deadly shooting of protesters on November 13, 1998. Different from the "Trisakti Tragedy" in May, the "Semanggi Tragedy," as the incident became known, did not become a political turning point, as the main opposition leaders remained silent. In October 1999, when Semanggi became the scene of another deadly clash during student protests against the emergency bill, the students again received little elite support. These experiences strengthened their conviction that politicians could not be trusted, further confirming the necessity of student struggle.

But the 1999 legislative elections brought political distraction and caused further division, as some groups supported the elections for strategic or pragmatic reasons while others dismissed it as a farce. Emblematic of the students' ambivalence on this matter was the PRD's slogan in the lead-up to the elections: "Boycott the elections, or vote PRD!" Conflicts were exacerbated as an effect of reentrenchment of patronage relations or strategic alliances with elite actors, although all student groups insisted on the principle of student autonomy. The ramifications were felt especially on the student Left, where many groups splintered over corruption issues and personalized conflicts—Forkot, once the leading organizational vehicle for militant students in Jakarta, is a case in point—or over strategic disagreements, as happened with the Action Unit of the Extended Family of the University of Indonesia (Kesatuan Aksi Keluarga Besar Universitas Indonesia, KA-KBUI, widely known as KBUI), which dissolved as a result (Sastramidjaja 2020). But the factional splits also opened the way for the formation of national activist organizations. The largest of these were the National Student League for Democracy (Liga Mahasiswa Nasional untuk Demokrasi, LMND), founded in 1999 by groups close to the PRD or the PDI, and the Indonesian Youth Struggle Front (Front Perjuangan Pemuda Indonesia, FPPI), founded in 2000 by Student Action Front for Reform and Democracy (Front Aksi Mahasiswa untuk Reformasi dan Demokrasi, Famred), the largest splinter group from Forkot, and groups from the former FAMI network close to Nahdlatul Ulama and the liberal Islamic parties. KAMMI, meanwhile, consolidated itself as the national organizational vehicle for the Islamic student movement. In many ways, then, the post-Suharto student movement continued the legacy of the student movements of the early 1990s, at least in ideological outlook. Still, they needed to develop new strategies suitable for the political conditions of the times.

Due to the volatile political climate, though, the students found little room to contemplate long-term strategies. They were repeatedly forced to respond quickly to political developments, falling back on older allegiances and enmities. This became apparent during the presidency of former Nahdlatul Ulama leader Abdurrahman Wahid (2000–2001), whose alleged involvement in a corruption case prompted mass protests against him, led by KAMMI and other Islamic groups allied to Wahid's arch rival Amien Rais, while FPPI, LMND, and other groups close to Wahid leapt to his defense. Months of bitter battle later, however, students on both sides had had enough of the escalation, realizing that the elite power struggle had diverted them from their longer-term goal of regime change. Public critics, too, noted that the students had made a "political blunder" by getting enmeshed in elite politics, which was deemed improper to the moral character of student struggle. But for the students, their political experiences of the past years precluded a return to the moral force identity, which by now appeared naïve. They recognized that much of the "success of the New Order regime" was achieved because it had "reduced the term 'political' into something dirty, haram, and taboo" (*Kompas*, March 11, 2001). Henceforth, they declared that they were in fact a political movement (precipitating the participation of former student activists in the 2004 elections, although this intent still remained unspoken). This discursive shift in the student movement was groundbreaking. The challenge was in putting it into practice.

By the time of Wahid's forced resignation in 2001, the students resolved to join forces to "destroy the old system," identifying Wahid's successor Megawati as the new common enemy. Once a symbol of the opposition, Megawati now represented the resurgence of the old regime, as she sided with the former New Order state party Golkar and the army, did little to tackle corruption, and proved intolerant to protest. Furthermore, her neoliberal economic policy hurt her own constituency among the urban poor, and represented a structural direction for Indonesia that did not sit well with the socialist, nationalist, and Islamic orientations within the student movement. In 2002, a broad activist coalition was formed in Jakarta that vowed to ignite a people power movement. Initiated by the PRD, and joined by leftist and Islamic student organizations, labor organizations, opposition figures and party leaders, and former student activists from the 1970s, 1980s, and 1990s, it was a remarkable coalition, meant to become an embryo for a new system of governance. Energized by a sense of promise, the coalition staged a series of actions and held numerous meetings to construct a proper discourse of revolution and determine a strategy and timeline needed to get there. But as it proved difficult to find common ground between the different groups involved—due to generational as well as ideological differences and diverging political interests—the coalition dissolved within five months (Sastramidjaja 2020).

Thereafter, student activists continued to forge tactical alliances among themselves and, spurred by the PRD, the larger antigovernment movement continued. But the student actions became increasingly smaller and more sporadic, while other opposition groups shifted their strategic focus to the 2004 elections. Occasionally there was still a flash of protest, such as the protests against price hikes in early 2003, which garnered broad public support and successfully led to government concessions. But the demonstrations staged on May 21 of that year to commemorate five years of reform received little press coverage. Even the repression of that day's student protest at the Parliament left the public cold. Public tolerance for disruptive student protest was evidently declining. As Lee (2016, 115) describes the sentiment: "As Generation 98 gets enfolded into nationalist history as one more wave of youth politics, appropriate for the past but not the present . . . Indonesians are impatient for the student movement to please leave already," for only when the students leave "will a new era be marked." This era arrived in 2004 when the Democratic Party leader, retired general Susilo Bambang Yudhoyono, won the presidential election, ushering in a new status quo that lasted throughout the decade of his administration. In this era of democratic consolidation, student vanguardism decidedly came to an end.

AGENTS OF CHANGE?

Despite the general public's growing intolerance of student protest, it recognized the student movement's contribution to the expansion of political space and freedoms. After the political restriction of the New Order, the era of reform has seen a burst of political participation and expression, in which the student movement led by example. Its clearest impact, then, on the nature of Indonesia's democratization was the establishment of a culture of protest—whether in the form of demonstrations or other repertoires of action that had long been the prerogative and defining feature of the student movement—which has since been adopted by a range of social and political movements. As a consequence, however, the student movement became merely one among many pressure groups, and in later years its mobilizational capacities paled compared to the colossal rallies staged by other social actors, and especially Islamic groups. Already in the first years of reform, the frequency of demonstrations in Jakarta led the public to characterize the democratic transition as "demo-crazy"—which indicated that the political value, meaning, and impact of protest were undergoing rapid inflation. This was also the effect of the fact that political elites, too, exploited the tactics of mass mobilization for their own purposes, which has contributed to the widespread impression that demonstrations are, more often than not, manipulated and paid for by "hidden actors," thus reviving a typical New Order argument. On the other hand, the culture of protest meant that the government could no longer ignore popular claims. It was forced to respond, whether repressively—in which case it was forced to reveal its authoritarian face, just as student protest had done during the New Order, with all its delegitimizing consequences—or more favorably with concessions, which demonstrated the efficacy and hence appeal of protest as a means of political pressure.

Throughout this long political transition, then, the student movement created opportunities for other social and political actors to assert their claims. Yet the progressive students themselves ultimately failed to leverage the new opportunities.

In part, this failure was due to the fact that many of the groups that emerged between 1998 and 2003 lacked a clear vision beyond the pamphlet ideology and shifting tactical alliances that marked their political existence. Only the Islamic student movement managed to consolidate an effective and stable position for itself within the post-Suharto political landscape. This was largely owing to the success of the Prosperous Justice Party (Partai Keadilan Sejahtera, PKS), which had emerged from the same campus-based dakwah movement as KAMMI, and has since been able to attract KAMMI activists and other highly educated, politically ambitious Muslim youth by offering them opportunities to develop a political career within the party (Hamayotsu 2011). Further, the Islamic students could build on a solid tradition of ideological socialization and long-term programs for transformation, derived from the time-honored Muslim Brotherhood tradition, which made them much less dependable on cycles of contention. Finally, on and off campus, the Islamic movement benefited from the faltering of the leftist and liberal elements of the student movement and civil society at large, which failed to present credible challenges to the structural conditions that underpinned the concerns of the larger population (Hadiz 2014). By contrast, it has become more difficult for progressive student organizations to regenerate in the normalizing atmosphere of democratization. LMND, FPPI, and several other groups that had emerged in the turbulent years of reform continue to exist. But they have led an increasingly marginalized existence, at least compared with the prominent political role they had played on the national stage in the heydays of mobilization.

Orphans of Democracy

The student movement seemed destined to become "history" from the moment it was labeled the 1998 Generation. The immortalization of the 1998 Generation—in photo exhibitions, monuments, archiving projects, popular movies, and other mnemonic devices—in effect immobilized the student movement, since the "very discourses that framed them as heroes of *reformasi*" bottled up "the students' historical agency" (Strassler 2005, 279). As a student activist noted in late 2002 during yet another "1998 Generation Reunion" at a fancy hotel, the student movement was "going in circles" and had not brought about the desired change; similar remarks were frequently made at activist meetings in later years. Yet, despite student activists' disappointment about the political outcome of their movement, and a growing sense that the student movement had become irrelevant, succeeding cohorts were still enticed to "continue the struggle."

From that time, befitting the spirit of decentralization that has marked Indonesia's democratization process, student activist organizations appeared to thrive especially in the regions, far removed from the center of national power on which previous student movements focused. In smaller university towns such as Makassar in South Sulawesi, Lampung in South Sumatra, or Banjarmasin in South Kalimantan, new generations of student activists still regularly stage protests, though mainly focused on local issues and mainly targeting local governments. Although these local groups remain connected to the national center through the national organizations they are part of, it seems that the "center" has lost its political meaning to them; after all, these new generations were not forged by the experience of New Order authoritarianism with its centralized power structures. For their part, the national organizations to which these provincial student groups belong are still modeled on the patterns of the past. Hence, in attempting to give substance to their role as legitimate actors with the right and reason to protest, they reenact the repertoires of struggle of the older student movement, even when these no longer have the desired effect in decentralized fields of contention, and even though, to the larger student population, these repertoires of action seem hopelessly outdated, making students less inclined to engage.

But there are also structural causes to the marginalization of student movements and their troubles of finding resonance among the larger student population. These include privatization and economic rationalization trends in higher education, which have intensified since democratization. While the rapid turnover of student cohorts and academic pressures generally hinder sustained participation, the push for neoliberal reform in higher education—spurred by structural adjustment policies that typically accompany democratization under the auspices of the IMF and the World Bank—further impairs the ability of students to exercise effective and meaningful political agency. Tighter curriculums, stricter requirements for student performance, shorter graduation periods, and other manifestations of neoliberal efficiency in higher education greatly diminish opportunities for political engagement, while rising tuition fees make the university less accessible to nonelite youth. As the experience of post-authoritarian Latin America shows, these types of reforms have proved detrimental to the mobilizational capacities of students, as they led to "divisive diversification" of the student body and diminished disposition toward activism generally, precipitating a loss of "the aura of national leadership, and the claim of serving as a national voice" (Levy 1991, 149). Likewise, in Africa, the historically derived status of students as "revolutionary intellectuals" was eroded following the privatization and diversification of higher education (Zeilig 2009). In Asia, too, the consequent "banalization of students' social status" sped up a "delegitimation of their political role," thus weakening their mobilizational potential "as a strategic political group" (Weiss, Aspinall, and Thompson 2012, 17). Consequently, the majority of students shun the intense and time-consuming type of radical activism of previous generations.

Student radicalism seems all the more out of place given the generally moderate character of postauthoritarian governments, which were brought to power, after all, by the conservative nature of the electorate itself (Levy 1991). This relates to the general pattern of a weakening Left, which to the public lost its credibility due to its faltering response to the neoliberal systems that took hold of postauthoritarian democracies, a faltering caused by the incapacitating fragmentation that has also marked the Indonesian Left (Aspinall 2012b). A complicating factor in Indonesia is the legacy of the New Order's demonization of the Left. The 1998 student movement made leftish radicalism fashionable among urban youth (Lee 2016), and leftist books that used to only circulate as shoddy copies among student activists are now readily available at mainstream bookstore chains, but the fact of the matter is that communism remains taboo. Any critical comment on the 1965 "communist" coup attempt and subsequent anticommunist massacres still risks repressive or violent response. For progressive activists, this limits the scope and impact of their criticisms, especially with regard to human rights. As many also realize, without tackling this final ghost of the New Order, more recent human rights crimes involving the army—including the abduction and disappearance of student activists and deadly shootings of student protesters in 1998—will remain unaccounted for.

To many activists, it became apparent in the early 2000s that the student movement might not be a suitable vehicle to effect systemic change since it lacks the strategic focus and the means necessary to give direction to structural processes. Hence, many activist students (as opposed to "student activists") have opted to join social movement organizations that seemed to offer more promising programs, including the numerous NGOs created by former student activists in fields such as human rights, legal aid, land disputes, labor, urban poverty, women's rights and gender equality, environmentalism, and indigenous culture. This diversification brought increasing competition for the student movement, thus further effecting its transformation from "vanguard" into "orphan" not only on the national political stage but also within the social field of "struggle." At the same time, the flourishing of alternative social movements and their capacity to attract educated youth disprove the notion of a structurally depoliticized student population; students have not turned their backs on activism. This latent resource meant that the student movement could regain strength when other conditions made it once more relevant.

REDIRECTED STRUGGLES

In the era of democratization, perhaps the greatest source of competition for student movements and other social movements alike is the attraction of the political arena. Again, former student activists of the 1990s led by example, entering formal politics as soon as the timing seemed right. During the 2004 and the 2009 elections, many either joined the "success teams" of political candidates as "activist brokers" (Aspinall 2014), or became legislative candidates for existing parties, apparently to use these parties' infrastructure and support base to influence the political system from the inside, with the "real means of power." Political compromise inevitably had a moderating effect on many of these activists-turned-politicians, and occasionally former activists failed to resist the temptations of power and became the corrupted figures they once fought. Shunned by their former comrades within and outside the government, they saw their political clout diminish. More detrimentally, the activist "infiltration" of parties across the political spectrum caused further fragmentation of the Left, which lost the capacity to mount a concerted political challenge and thereby lost its authority to new generations of student activists.

Nevertheless, as Mietzner (2013, 29) argues, "their presence in post-authoritarian [political] institutions has provided an important counterbalance to a political process otherwise marked by elite interests and a deeply rooted culture of patronage relationships." The difference that an activist counterbalance can make was demonstrated during the 2014 presidential elections, in which the very democratization process seemed to be at stake (Aspinall and Mietzner 2014). A return to authoritarianism suddenly seemed possible due to the candidacy of Prabowo Subianto, the former general who was allegedly behind the abduction of student activists, the Trisakti killings and subsequent riots in 1998, and other human rights crimes. To prevent his ascendancy, many former activists from the student Left, including former PRD members, and other former student activists who had not been politically active since the early 2000s, campaigned for Joko Widodo (Jokowi), then governor of Jakarta and an outsider to the political elite, who was backed by the now "activist-infiltrated" party PDI-P (the former PDI, with the added "P" for *perjuangan*, or struggle). During the campaign, the activist alliance or "Volunteer Team" behind Jokowi went "all out" with mass rallies, rock concerts, social media campaigns, and during and after the elections with a nationwide grassroots election monitoring movement.

Jokowi's term in office did not bring about the progressive changes his activist supporters had hoped for, mainly because the PDI-P and the government and bureaucracy at large were still dominated by a conservative establishment. In addition, progressive struggles had to contend with a conservative pushback represented by an increasingly belligerent Islamic movement (see Fealy, this volume), which in 2014 threw its support behind Prabowo, and around the 2017 gubernatorial elections in Jakarta showed its muscle by staging a concerted attack against the incumbent governor, Basuki Tjahaja Purnama (Ahok), a Christian of Chinese descent and ally of Jokowi, whose alleged "blasphemy" lost him the elections and eventually landed him in prison. This came as a shock to the progressive activists who had supported him, as well as to liberal-minded society at large, who felt this to be an attack not just on Ahok but on the very pluralist foundations of the Indonesian nation. Counterdemonstrations and solidarity actions were staged throughout the affair to "protect pluralism and peace," including by students from the established national organizations and the formal student executive bodies, who felt once again called on to defend the nation. These student groups demonstrated under banners such as Student Solidarity Action for the Unitary State of the Republic of Indonesia (Negara Kesatuan Republik Indonesia, NKRI), ironically, borrowing from New Order discourse, with such slogans as "Defend NKRI" that were once associated with authoritarian regional oppression.

But students were certainly not the only group that leapt to the nation's defense; neither did their actions strike the public as warranting special attention. Student protests received no more press coverage than the many other "pro-pluralism" actions staged by nonactivist middle-class groups, in Jakarta and other cities around the country. Many of these nonstudent actions made an impression by departing from traditional repertoires of protest, by mobilizing ad hoc through social media and using more optimistic, creative tactics such as cultural performances that demonstrated the nation's very strength in its pluralist nature. By comparison, the exclusive nature of student actions seemed inappropriate for the cause. As the controversy passed, however, nonstudent groups' flash of defiance also subsided, and ultimately it did little to halt the conservative pushback. Conservative forces remained unchallenged, since neither civil society groups nor progressive forces in the government were able to furnish a fundamental strategic response.

Forging a New Identity?

Thus far, no activist group has been able to confront the new challenges of democratization or to formulate a fundamental critique of the nature of Indonesia's democracy, because they remain entrenched in identities forged during the New Order. Students are no exception. Take, for example, this excerpt from an article posted in March 2016 on an online student platform by a member of the student executive body of the National University of Jakarta, who called on students to revive their historical duty as students:

> The student movement must learn from the struggles of the student movements of the past. Students . . . should not just mobilize in the virtual world with online petition movements, but mobilize in real action to make a statement. Besides engrossing themselves in theory, they should descend to the people through the live-in strategy and perform sociopolitical activities in order to create political awareness among the masses and a conviction of their strength. . . . STUDENT is a word full of significance, meaning, and hope that translates into change in the national order of Indonesia, Today and Tomorrow. Students must contribute to the people's struggle by forming a historical bloc through its role as *Agent of*

change, Iron Stock, Social Control, and Moral Force. The foremost task is to revitalize the "Struggle to defend the sovereignty of the Republic of Indonesia in this era of Mental Revolution [i.e. Jokowi's slogan]." Long Live Students!!! Long Live the People of Indonesia!!! (Fajrianto 2016)

In this statement, all the old narrative frames of student struggle are rehashed and recombined. It speaks of an impatient nostalgia for a past political relevance that the present student generation never experienced. However, current student activists are not the only ones experiencing such nostalgia. Almost two decades after overthrowing Suharto, in response to Ahok's conviction for blasphemy, former student activists of the "1998 Generation" have found a reason to resuscitate their dormant struggle. One striking example is the resurrection of the former action unit of the University of Indonesia, KBUI, a prominent element of the 1998 student movement that had disappeared after the 1999 elections. In May 2017, the former student leaders of KBUI held a press conference declaring their continued struggle: "Over the past 19 years since the start of reform, we see that the national political situation hasn't shown progress in realizing the agenda of reforms that KBUI fought for. KBUI feels the time has come to re-emerge and finish the unfinished task of struggle." Both for current and former student activists, then, nostalgia for the role of student vanguardism proves to be a mobilizing nostalgia. However, by falling back on the collective identity of "student strugglers"—an identity so intimately connected to authoritarian New Order conditions—they again risk making themselves irrelevant and their struggle unfit for the times.

Still, the desire for political relevance speaks of a real propensity for activism among present-day students. Perhaps it is only a matter of time before these impatient students find a narrative frame of activism that is more appropriate for the present. Campaigns promoting a pluralist society indicate one promising direction in which student activists might find new meaning and purpose, especially when focused on the vital larger questions of strengthening democratic citizenship in Indonesia—including questions of pluralism, inclusivity, participation, and openness, as well as unresolved human rights issues; indeed many students engage with these issues through discussions and other events.

CONCLUSION

It may be concluded that "democratization does indeed seem to have a radically dampening effect on student activism, or at least on the notion that students qua students constitute an important vanguard force" (Aspinall and Weiss 2012, 293). However, the obsolescence of the traditional frame of vanguardism might prove to be a blessing in disguise. During the New Order, public notions of student vanguardism created an illusory, unrealistic image of the student movement as a cohesive "moral force" capable of single-handedly defeating authoritarianism. This image augmented the student movement's mobilizing power but also made it vulnerable to repression and sped up its decline in the context of democratization. All things considered, it was despite as much as because of this image that the student movement had real influence on the political process that led to democratic reform. This was especially so between 1989 and 1996, when radical student activists transgressed the permissible bounds of student protest, and again in 1998, when students defied and eventually exhausted the regime's means of repression, which in both cases created opportunities for otherwise cautious opposition actors to assert their criticism and finally their rejection of the regime. Thereafter, persistent student action contributed to establishing a culture of protest that became a feature of Indonesia's democratization.

It was in this context of "demo-crazy" that the student movement lost its political relevance. No longer the only group with a special license to express criticism, students' demonstrations were soon overshadowed by those staged by other pressure groups. Their mobilizing capacities further diminished in the subsequent normalizing era of democratic consolidation fueled by neoliberal reforms in higher education, which led to increasing diversification of the student body and dwindling student interest in activism. Thus the student movement was truly "orphaned" by the conditions it had helped to create. It was perhaps for that reason that new generations of student activists have continued to cling to the legacy of their moral force identity—their one distinctive feature amidst a cacophony of political expression. This identity, however, has caused the student movement to keep "going in circles," as student activists also realized, and thereby to overlook new opportunities to reorient not just their strategies of struggle but the very foundation of their movement. Still, ongoing student protests, especially in the regions, show that a minority of students keep the potential of activism alive. This activism remains relevant for the enduring networks it establishes on and off campus, which sustain the strategic capacity of students outside wider cycles of contention and across generations (Crossley 2008; Ibrahim 2010) and can be quickly activated for mobilizational purposes—"when other conditions are right" (Weiss, Aspinall, and Thompson 2012, 12).

While the role of student movements in postauthoritarian Indonesia is an ambivalent one, this very ambivalence provides opportunities to adopt a more flexible attitude toward the contingencies and specific challenges of the times. For one thing, the decentralized experience of new generations of student activists suggests that student movements might do well to shed their obsession with national politics and search for more fruitful forms of cooperation between local struggles in the absence of other credible local actors; their specific skills, social capital, and embeddedness in multiple networks certainly make them suitable for such a role. In turn, such concerted student responses to local conflicts might provide promising cues for tackling the larger questions of citizenship. Above all, as Snellinger (2016, 28) argues with regard to the ambivalent position and limited influence of student activists in democratizing Nepal, one thing that still distinguishes them from other social and political actors is a capacity for "pragmatic enactments of hope." It is through a "strategic interplay between idealism and opportunism" in seizing the possibilities and tackling the challenges of changing political conditions that they contribute to "shaping democracy" in meaningful ways, thereby "demonstrat[ing] the generative nature of democracy as a radical ongoing process" (Snellinger 2016, 28). Similarly, the uncertain direction of Indonesia's democracy begs for the youthfully idealistic and politically capable pragmatic enactments of hope that student activism represents. Once student activists in Indonesia succeed in shedding the legacies of the New Order era, they might still prove their relevance in the ongoing process of democratization.

REFERENCES

Abdullah. 1998. "'Kesadaran' Menuju Reformasi Total." In *Suara Mahasiswa, Suara Rakyat: Wacana Intelektual di balik Gerakan Moral Mahasiswa*, edited by Alfian Hamzah, Musa Kazhim, and Muhammad Ikhsan, 41–52. Bandung: Remaja Rosdakarya.

Aditjondro, George J. 1993. *The Media as Development Textbook: A Case Study of Information Distortion in the Debate about the Social Impact of an Indonesian Dam.* Ph.D. diss., Cornell University.

Altbach, Philip G., ed. 1989. *Student Political Activism: An International Reference Handbook.* Westport, CT: Greenwood.

Anwar, Yozar. 1980. *Angkatan 66: Sebuah Catatan Harian Mahasiswa.* Jakarta: Sinar Harapan.

Aspinall, Edward. 1993. "Student Dissent in Indonesia in the 1980s." Working Paper 79, Centre of Southeast Asian Studies, Monash University, Clayton, Australia.

———. 1995. "Student and the Military: Regime Friction and Civilian Dissent in the Late Suharto Period." *Indonesia* 59: 21–44.

———. 1999. "The Indonesian Student Uprising of 1998." In *Reformasi: Crisis and Change in Indonesia*, edited by Arief Budiman, Barbara Hatley, and Damien Kingsbury, 212–37. Clayton: Monash Asia Institute.

———. 2005. *Opposing Suharto: Compromise, Resistance, and Regime Change in Indonesia.* Stanford: Stanford University Press.

———. 2012a. "Indonesia: Moral Force Politics and the Struggle against Authoritarianism." In *Student Activism in Asia: Between Protest and Powerlessness*, edited by Meredith L. Weiss and Edward Aspinall, 153–80. Minneapolis: University of Minnesota Press.

———. 2012b. "Still an Age of Activism." *Inside Indonesia* 107 (Jan–Mar). Accessed June 1, 2012. https://www.insideindonesia.org/still-an-age-of-activism.

———. 2014. "When Brokers Betray: Clientelism, Social Networks, and Electoral Politics in Indonesia." *Critical Asian Studies* 46 (4): 545–70.

Aspinall, Edward, and Marcus Mietzner. 2014. "Indonesian Politicsin 2014: Democracy's Close Call." *Bulletin of Indonesian Economic Studies* 50: 347–69.

Aspinall, Edward, and Meredith L. Weiss. 2012. "Conclusion: Trends and Patterns in Student Activism in Asia." In *Student Activism in Asia: Between Protest and Powerlessness*, edited by Meredith L. Weiss and Edward Aspinall, 281–96. Minneapolis: University of Minnesota Press.

Baud, Michiel, and Rosanne Rutten. 2004. "Introduction." In *Popular Intellectuals and Social Movements: Framing Protest in Asia, Africa, and Latin America*, edited by Michiel Baud and Rosanne Rutten, 1–18. Cambridge: Cambridge University Press.

Budiman, Arief. 1978. "The Student Movement in Indonesia: A Study of a Relationship between Culture and Structure." *Asian Survey* 18 (6): 609–25.

Crossley, Nick. 2008. "Social Networks and Student Activism: On the Politicising Effect of Campus Connections." *Sociological Review* 56 (1): 18–38.

Emmerson, Donald, ed. 1968. *Students and Politics in Developing Nations.* New York: Praeger.

Fajrianto, Rizky. 2016. "Napak Tilas Gerakan Mahasiswa dalam Era Pemerintahan Reformasi-Revolusi." *KanalMahasiswa.com*, March 28, 2016.

Ford, Michele. 2009. *Workers and Intellectuals: NGOs, Trade Unions and the Indonesian Labour Movement.* Singapore: NUS Press.

Hadiz, Vedi. 2014. "A New Islamic Populism and the Contradictions of Development." *Journal of Contemporary Asia* 44 (1): 125–43.

Hamayotsu, Kikue. 2011. "Beyond Faith and Identity: Mobilizing Islamic Youth in Indonesia." *Pacific Review* 24 (2): 225–47.

Heryanto, Ariel. 1996. "The Student Movement." *Inside Indonesia* 48: 10–12.

Ibrahim, Yousaf. 2010. "Between Revolution and Defeat: Student Protest Cycles and Networks." *Sociology Compass* 4 (7): 495–504.

Kraince, Richard. 2000. "The Role of Islamic Student Groups in the Reformasi Struggle: KAMMI." *Studia Islamika* 7: 1–50.

Lane, Max. 2008. *Unfinished Nation: Indonesia Before and After Suharto*. London: Verso.

Lee, Doreen. 2016. *Activist Archives: Youth Culture and the Political Past in Indonesia*. Durham: NC: Duke University Press.

Levy, Daniel. 1991. "The Decline of Latin American Student Activism." *Higher Education* 22: 145–55.

McRae, Dave. 2001. *The 1998 Indonesian Student Movement*. Clayton: Monash Asia Institute.

Mietzner, Marcus. 2013. "Fighting the Hellhounds: Prodemocracy Activists and Party Politics in Post-Suharto Indonesia." *Journal of Contemporary Asia* 43: 28–50.

Miftahuddin. 2004. *Radikalisasi Pemuda: PRD Melawan Tirani*. Depok: Desantara.

Sastramidjaja, Yatun. 2020. *Playing Politics: Power, Narrative, and Agency in the Making of the Indonesian Student Movement*. Leiden: Brill.

Snellinger, Amanda. 2016. "'Let's See What Happens': Hope, Contingency, and *Speculation* in Nepali Student Activism." *Critical Asian Studies* 48 (1): 27–49.

Strassler, Karen. 2005. "Material Witnesses: Photographs and the Making of Reformasi Memory." In *Beginning to Remember: The Past in Indonesia's Present*, edited by Mary S. Zurbuchen, 278–311. Singapore: Singapore University Press.

Sumohadiwidjojo, M. S., and R. Mas, ed. 1988. *Warisilah Api Sumpah Pemuda! Kumpulan Pidato Bung Karno di Hadapan Pemuda 1961–1964*. Jakarta: Haji Masagung.

Weiss, Meredith L. 2009. "Intellectual Containment: The Muting of Students in Semidemocratic Southeast Asia." *Critical Asian Studies* 41 (4): 499–522.

Weiss, Meredith L., Edward Aspinall, and Mark R. Thompson. 2012. "Introduction: Understanding Student Activism in Asia." In *Student Activism in Asia: Between Protest and Powerlessness*, edited by Meredith L. Weiss and Edward Aspinall, 1–32. Minneapolis: University of Minnesota Press.

Zeilig, Leo. 2009. "The Student-Intelligentsia in Sub-Saharan Africa: Structural Adjustment, Activism, and Transformation." *Review of African Political Economy* 36 (119): 63–78.

CHAPTER TWO

DEMOCRATIZATION AND INDONESIA'S ANTICORRUPTION MOVEMENT

Elisabeth Kramer

There is a compelling relationship between citizens' frustration with corruption and democratization as anticorruption concerns may spark dissatisfaction with undemocratic forms of government. Whether this then involves protestors taking to the streets and demanding the resignation of corrupt leaders or ongoing advocacy for better governance and accountability structures, it is evident that "anticorruptionism"—a term used to describe the "complex of resources," such as knowledge, people, money and symbols, that promote anticorruption ideals (Sampson, 2010, 262)—can be used to agitate for more democratic systems.

Idealized concepts of "democracy" have proven incredibly difficult to implement in reality. But these ideals underpin much of what the anticorruption movement hopes to achieve. In shifts from authoritarian regimes, these ideas manifest as a desire for increased participation coupled with transparency and responsiveness to citizens' needs and an end to corruption, misappropriation, and the waste of state resources (Doig, 2013). Democratization presents an opportunity to bring in policies that address these desires; however, as Johnston (2014, 1) asserts, "Corruption will continue—indeed, may well be the norm—until those with a stake in ending it are able to oppose it in many ways that cannot be ignored." Meanwhile, processes of democratization, and the path that democratization takes, give form to the opportunities and challenges facing the anticorruption movement. This path determines activists' capacity to secure transparency, accountability, and the implementation of reforms that police and prevent corruption.

Anticorruption protests, though stifled during the New Order, contributed to the broader movement for *reformasi* that forced Suharto's resignation in 1998. Moving in fits and starts, the anticorruption movement was far from cohesive or well-organized in New Order Indonesia—if it can be referred to as a "movement" at all. While a few small groups may have shared concerns about corruption, it would be an exaggeration to say that they formed a network, either formal or informal, or that they purposefully coordinated their collective actions. A handful of groups raised concerns about corruption during this time, but their actions were usually in isolation. Despite this lack of collectivity around the issue of corruption, anticorruption sentiment certainly existed and fed into the mass discontent that eventually spurred regime change in the late 1990s.

As democratization has unfolded, civil society-led anticorruption campaigns have become more prevalent and representative organizations have become more institutionalized. Prominent anticorruption NGOs now have a key role in public advocacy against corruption through direct lobbying of the government, public engagement, and local oversight projects. There is also an increasing number of grassroots efforts being made across Indonesia to address corruption at the local level. At the same time, reformasi saw the establishment of an independent anticorruption commission (Komisi Pemberantasan Korupsi, KPK), which entered the fold of the movement as an agitator for change from within government. However, political and economic elites continue to dominate government decision making, and while some seem happy to use anticorruption rhetoric when it suits their interests, corruption continues to thrive in the implementation of government projects and during elections. Key aspects of the democratic transition, such as decentralization, have facilitated higher levels of corruption (Hadiz 2003; Webber 2006). Moreover, regulations around political party financing have fostered a dependency on political donors and the private sector, while a lack of campaign oversight has led to soaring levels of "money politics" during electioneering (Aspinall and Sukmajati 2016). The anticorruption movement continues to demand fairer elections and more democratic government but has struggled to secure deep and genuine change due to these structural issues.

This chapter begins with a discussion of the history of anticorruption activism during the New Order and the early days of reformasi before discussing the opportunities and challenges leveled by Indonesia's democratic transition. Before 1998, protests were often triggered by concerns such as increases in the price of basic goods like food or fuel, but this discontent then fed into an underlying narrative that portrayed ordinary citizens as bearing the brunt of corruption. These protests were met with repression, including restrictions on student activity and prison sentences, though some instances did prompt lukewarm changes to policy. During this period, the anticorruption cause held widespread public appeal, but the movement was far from unified. This changed somewhat after reformasi, when the movement professionalized with the establishment of a dedicated group of nongovernmental organizations (NGOs) committed to fighting for transparency and accountability as well as the establishment of the KPK and a network of anticorruption courts (Pengadilan Tindak Pidana Korupsi, Tipikor). Since then, there have been numerous high-profile arrests and localized anticorruption programs have had some success in bringing corrupt individuals to justice. But, despite these advances, widespread corruption continues. This outcome is not entirely surprising, since postauthoritarian contexts also offer opportunities for new forms of corruption with new political elites coming to the fore (Harriss-White and White 1996). Whether the anticorruption movement has the capacity to temper these interests in the post-reformasi era is a question yet to be answered.

RESISTANCE AND REPRESSION

Moving through various political regimes over the last century, the issue of corruption has persisted in Indonesia as an issue and a rallying cry to demand political change. Records of official anticorruption efforts date back to the 1920s, when Governor-General Dirk Fock, who presided over the Netherlands East Indies from 1921 to 1926, commissioned investigations into corrupt officials who had accepted kickbacks or embezzled from the treasury (Wertheim 1963). Changing attitudes toward corruption were also linked to the rise of Indonesian nationalism and the independence movement (Smith 1971). As conceptualizations of "acceptable" and "nonacceptable" behavior among government officials altered, ideologies of equality and social justice also came to the fore, feeding into the argument for independence. However, anticorruption efforts were historically far from coordinated and the "movement"—like those in many other countries—was disparate, capturing a variety of actions across civil society, media, the government, and the international community (Moroff and Schmidt-Pfister 2010).

Setiyono and McLeod (2010) argue that the beginnings of an anticorruption movement first emerged in Indonesia in the mid-1960s as dissatisfaction with the government was channeled into often small-scale protests by disparate groups. Upon coming to power, Suharto was eager to build an image that would set his government apart from the previous regime, particularly in terms of combating corruption. Even the regime's name—the "New Order"—was intended to distance it from the previous era, which had become synonymous with elite extravagance and bureaucratic corruption (Feith 1994; Ricklefs 2001). Suharto projected these intentions early on through the establishment of the Team to Regularize State Finances (Tim Penerbitan Keuangan Negara, Pekuneg) to collect "incriminating material" related to the corrupt activities of members of the "Old Order" government (Crouch 1980, 296), and a Corruption Eradication Team (Tim Pemberantasan Korupsi, TPK), charged with investigating corruption cases and referring suspects for arrest and trial. However, government efforts to eradicate corruption during the early New Order were ineffective (van der Kroef 1971; Crouch 1980), and anticorruption sentiment began to gain momentum such that between 1965 and 1970 "there [were] few burning issues of comparable horsepower for opponents or critics of the regime" (Mackie 1970, 88). This is not to say that it was a new concern; there were frequent complaints about corruption during the Old Order, but it had been a relatively minor issue compared to the looming political conflict between the military and the Indonesian Communist Party (Partai Komunis Indonesia, PKI).

With Suharto in charge, and without the countervailing force of the PKI, opportunities for "dramatic self-enrichment" opened up for the military and the executive (Mackie 1970, 88). Moreover, the ubiquity of bribery and unofficial fees for government services ensured that the vast majority of Indonesians had direct experience of petty corruption among bureaucrats, the police, and other officials. Driven chiefly by student groups, but appealing also to members of the general public, antigovernment protests in the early New Order period threatened vigilante action against these "corruptors" (*koruptor*). A number of newspapers also published antigovernment pieces, including *Indonesia Raya* and *Nusantara*, as well as student publications such as *Harian Kami* and *Mahasiswa Indonesia* (Crouch 1980), bringing the issue to the attention of the public at a time when the cost of basic goods was rising. It was against this backdrop that on January 15, 1970, a wave of student protests erupted in Jakarta, taking the government to task not just for the increased cost of living but also for growing inequality and continued laxity in combating corruption (van der Kroef 1971).

The government responded to these protests by banning any demonstration conducted without official approval (Dahm 1971; van der Kroef 1971). In turn, students mounted sit-ins in a number of government offices, and student leaders issued manifestos declaring their disappointment with the government's lack of commitment to dealing with corruption and rising living costs (van der Kroef 1971). In an effort to appear as if he was accommodating student demands to address corruption within the government, Suharto announced the formation of the Commission of Four, charged with investigating the extent of the corruption in the government and providing recommendations for its eradication (Mackie 1970). In the same year, Attorney General Soegih Arto introduced a new anticorruption bill to the parliament, superseding the 1960 law that was deemed by many to be inadequate (van der Kroef 1971). Passed as Law No. 3/1971 on the Eradication of the Criminal Act of Corruption, the bill was welcomed by activists as it set out more specific procedures for defining and punishing corruption (Brata 2009). However, student activists were unhappy with the fact that the law would not be applied retroactively. More protests took place in subsequent weeks, calling attention to the government's reluctance to combat corruption, but parliament refused to meet their demands (van der Kroef 1971). In response, Suharto agreed to regular weekly meetings with student activists where they could present evidence of official corruption, but the arrangement was short lived (Brata 2009).

Suharto's wavering commitment to corruption eradication was also evidenced by his refusal to publicize the findings of the Commission of Four, which he summarily dismissed. In response, student groups stepped up their campaigning to highlight the ongoing negative impacts of corruption. An example of anticorruption activism during this period was the "Petition of October 24," signed in October 1973 by a group of students from the University of Indonesia, which outlined criticisms of the government, including rising prices, unemployment, corruption, abuse of power, and the lack of effective public participation in government decision making (Hansen 1975). Protests continued, culminating in the Malari Affair of 1974, when students staged mass protests during an official visit by the Japanese prime minister to Indonesia. Protesters' antigovernment rhetoric focused heavily on the perceived growing inequality between elites and ordinary people, and anger that elites were capitalizing on opportunities for self-enrichment at the expense of citizens (Surbakti 1999). The riots left eleven dead, two hundred seriously injured, and more than eight hundred under arrest.

The government responded with heightened vigilance toward dissent, stronger political repression and the suppression of public protest (Liddle 1996; Elson 2001). Suharto tried to pacify the anticorruption activists by amending foreign ownership laws to facilitate more business opportunities for Indonesians as well as embarking on a new development path by making "equality" (*pemerataan*) a guiding principle of Indonesia's new development policy, launched in 1978 (Surbakti 1999, 74). He also asked that associates "tone down excessive displays of wealth" in order to prevent provoking further anger (Vatikiotis 1993, 38). These measures dampened, but did not eradicate, public campaigns against corruption. Discontent continued to simmer, surfacing again in January 1978 with the publication of a manifesto issued by a group of students from Bandung demanding that Suharto step down as president. Titled the "White Book" (*Buku Putih*), the manifesto highlighted a number of corruption scandals to demonstrate that those in the government were "self-serving," "greedy," and ultimately should be removed (*Indonesia* 1978, 181). The government reacted immediately, banning the book, shutting down newspapers and rounding up student activists (Elson 2001). It also temporarily closed many leading universities and directed university leadership to "depoliticize" campuses (Aspinall 2005, chapter 5; Jackson 2013, 185–87). Those involved in writing the White Book were arrested and tried in January 1979 under the antisubversion laws.[1] The subsequent trials and crackdown on campus activism quashed the student movement, which had been a bastion of censure against the prevalence of corruption.[2] The banning of key newspapers and a new emphasis on the responsibility of the press to promote national stability also curtailed reporting of corruption scandals.

Although protest was stifled, Suharto recognized that perceptions of corruption could have a destabilizing effect on the regime. The government made periodic attempts to defuse the issue through arrests and trials of individuals, but those found guilty were mostly low- or mid-ranked bureaucrats (Cribb and Brown 1995; Liddle 1996). After several years of strict repression, however, Suharto found himself losing support from the military (Liddle 1992). Opening the floodgates for public criticism, retired general Sumitro, a former leader of the internal security agency (Badan Intelijen Negara, BIN), published an article in 1989 advocating more genuine parliamentary democracy (Bertrand 1996). More criticisms emerged following this publication, particularly from other former military personnel. Suharto attempted to rein in his critics by broadening political space, relaxing censorship, tolerating some political protests, and establishing a commission for human rights—a period that became known as "openness" (*keterbukaan*). In 1990, Sudomo, the coordinating minister for political affairs and security, announced that press licenses would not be revoked by his office and that army and information ministry officials would cease their practice of "informing" editors of which articles should not be published (Bertrand 1996, 326). However, while Suharto wished to portray his regime as "democratizing," the move was driven more by his conflict with some members of the military than by a genuine intention to welcome democracy.

Keterbukaan was short lived and repression reemerged in 1994 with the sudden closure of three major news magazines after they published a series of negative reports about a decision by the minister for research and technology to purchase East German warships (Robison and Hadiz 2004). The press had also begun to investigate a number of potentially embarrassing corruption scandals linked to Suharto's inner circle. This repressive turn fueled further antigovernment sentiment and galvanized the prodemocracy movement, with large-scale protests across Indonesia as a result of the press banning (Aspinall 2005). The reporting on corruption, and the subsequent government response, sparked the formation of a new activist coalition to protest the censorship, including "previously cautious intellectuals, artists, and others condemning the ban" (Aspinall 2005, 48). The prodemocracy sentiment generated during this brief period proved difficult to suppress, continuing to simmer until 1998.

THE DOWNFALL OF THE REGIME

Anticorruption sentiment played a pivotal role in the downfall of the regime, as the blatant wealth of Suharto's family and cronies grew increasingly obvious (Elson 2001). From the 1970s, Suharto's wife developed the nickname "Madame Tien Percent," referring to the share of profits she allegedly demanded from those granted business favors by her husband (Cribb and Brown 1995, 126). In the years that followed, Suharto's children were awarded contracts against the advice of the government's own ministers. By the early 1990s, the Suharto family assets were estimated at US $2–3 billion (Vatikiotis 1993). Suharto also created a network of supporters around him who were extremely wealthy, but also heavily dependent on him for business favors (Liddle 1996; Vatikiotis 1993).

Public concerns about corruption were intensified by the Asian financial crisis, when a dramatic devaluation of the rupiah caused the stock market to plummet, wiping out the savings of the middle class, leading numerous businesses to declare bankruptcy, and causing mass unemployment (Wie 2003). The Central Bank provided liquidity injections to failing banks whose owners had borrowed heavily to manage their global portfolios instead of using the funds to stabilize savings and reserves (Duncan and McLeod 2007). Soon after, the credibility of the government sank to new lows when it was revealed that the minister of manpower had used US $1.3 million from the workers' social insurance fund to pay for parliamentarians' accommodation and expenses while they were deliberating a new manpower law in 1997 (Bird 1998). Along with the instability generated by the financial crisis, these actions further fueled public discontent with the government at a time when many were affected by spiraling inflation and fears for the future.

Attempting to maneuver his way through the crisis, Suharto approved a 70 percent increase in the cost of fuel on May 4, 1998, sparking riots across the country (Bird 1999). Days later, soldiers opened fire on protesters, killing four students from Trisakti University and injuring several others (see Sastramidjaja, this volume). Public outrage at the deaths sparked riots in Jakarta and several other major cities. Enterprises owned by the Suharto family and Chinese-Indonesians were prime targets for arson and looting, with hundreds perishing in shopping mall fires (Siegel 1998; Aspinall 2005). Political elites also rebelled, with fourteen of Suharto's appointed cabinet members refusing to continue to serve under him. The military, under its chief, General Wiranto, withdrew its support for the president and Islamic leaders advised him to resign (Ricklefs 2001; Aspinall 2005). Suharto stepped down on May 21, 1998, and was replaced by Vice President Habibie until new elections could be held. Recognizing how pervasive anticorruption discourse had been throughout the protests against Suharto, the Habibie government immediately passed Law No. 28/1999 on the Establishment of a Commission to Examine the Wealth of State Officials (Komisi Pemeriksa Kekayaan Penyelenggara Negara, KPKPN), followed by Law No. 31/1999 on the Eradication of the Crime of Corruption (Butt 2011b; King 2004).

The Movement Consolidates

The collapse of the New Order regime facilitated more organized and sustained campaigns against corruption and advocacy for better governance. Civil society enjoyed new freedoms of association and changes in legislation allowed for open reporting on wrongdoing in the government. Foreign donors such as the World Bank, the Asian Development Bank, and the United Nations Development Program also offered their support, and several national aid organizations provided funding to stimulate good governance and transparency and to support the development of NGO watchdogs (Setiyono and McLeod 2010). Indonesia's media law was also redrafted in 1999, terminating the surveillance activities of the Ministry of Information, which had previously served as a proxy mechanism for censorship (Sen and Hill 2000). With support from foreign donors and a media that could now freely report on corruption, anticorruption activists had the chance to openly criticize the government and consolidate the movement.

As student activism declined in the wake of the New Order (see Sastramidjaja, this volume), NGOs with an explicit mandate to prevent and reduce corruption emerged as the new vanguard of anticorruption activity. Organizations formed in 1998 included Indonesian Corruption Watch (ICW), the Indonesian Anticorruption

Society (Masyarakat Transparansi Indonesia, MTI), and Indonesia Procurement Watch (IPW). The most prominent of these groups was ICW, an organization that was "midwifed" (*dibidani*) by the Indonesian Legal Aid Foundation (Yayasan Lembaga Bantuan Hukum Indonesia, YLBHI), one of Indonesia's oldest NGOs (Holloway 2001). ICW describes itself as committed to combating corruption through the "empowerment of the people to engage and actively fight against corrupt practices." It has developed a professionalized structure of investigators, campaigners, researchers, and monitors who monitor a range of institutions, including parliament, the judiciary, and the executive (ICW 2017). MTI, which also emerged during this period from an informal discussion group formed in late 1997, brought together students, retired government officials, journalists, bankers, academic, and entrepreneurs concerned with political issues in the New Order, but has a less formal structure (Setiyono and McLeod 2010). Over time, MTI evolved into a reporting body, hosting a website that publicizes corruption cases, whereas ICW and IPW continue to undertake sustained campaigns against corruption. Another prominent NGO, Transparency International Indonesia (TII) was formed in 2000. TII is a branch of the Transparency International network and focuses on providing governance training at the local level as well as lobbying for improved government oversight. These organizations have played a crucial role in keeping corruption cases in the media spotlight, lobbying government for better anticorruption legislation, and investigating suspected cases of corruption.

Collaboration between these NGOs has been important in sustaining the broader anticorruption movement. In 2001, they formed a membership alliance under the banner of the Movement against Corruption (Gerakan Anti-Korupsi, GeRAK) (Holloway 2001). In the same year, they formed an alliance with other interested groups, called Advocacy for a Corruption Eradication Commission (Advokasi untuk Komisi Anti-Korupsi, AKAK), to lobby parliament to pass laws that would facilitate the formation of an independent commission (Setiyono and McLeod 2010). Later, in the lead-up to the 2004 elections, these same NGOs participated in a broader alliance of NGOs called the Movement against Rotten Politicians (Gerakan Anti Politisi Busuk, GAPB) (Schütte 2009). The movement, which aimed to discourage the reelection of corrupt politicians, encouraged voters to reject parliamentary candidates with a history of corruption through a public campaign of rallies and concerts involving well-known musicians. The transition period also saw the increasing involvement of professional associations, Islamic organizations, labor organizations, women's organizations, lawyers and academics, resulting in an anticorruption movement that was "broader and more active . . . more sophisticated and tactical in its approach" (Setiyono and McLeod 2010, 351).

TAKING ON THE ESTABLISHMENT

As Johnston (1998) contends, real progress toward transparent and accountable government requires support from the highest echelons of political power. Despite strong public support for corruption eradication in the early reformasi period, the movement faced an uphill battle. Dick and Mulholland (2011, 65) assert that the state is an "arena for contestation" where "elite game[s] of power, wealth and status" play out. Who these elites are—and the exact nature of their relationship to one another—is a matter for debate (Ford and Pepinsky 2014). But while those vying for power and resources may not be working in unison, they certainly have little interest in revealing their activities through strengthened accountability mechanisms.

Recognizing the public desire for change, political leaders often highlighted the need for reform, but action was slow to follow. Official anticorruption efforts under early reformasi leaders Presidents Habibie (1998–99), Abdurrahman Wahid (1999–2001), and Megawati Sukarnoputri (2001–4) ebbed and flowed with promises of reform that were rarely fulfilled. For example, Abdurrahman Wahid set up a Joint Team to Eradicate the Crime of Corruption (Tim Gabungan Pemberantasan Tindak Pidana Korupsi, TGPTPK) as a stopgap measure while provisions could be made for the establishment of the national anticorruption commission under a law passed by Habibie. Wahid also signed Presidential Decree No. 44/2000 on the National Ombudsman Commission, a body tasked with receiving complaints from the public regarding the conduct and decisions of public officials (Sherlock 2002). However, he was impeached for corruption himself before these organizations could really establish themselves (Barton 2006; Liddle 2001). When Megawati took over as president, she was also accused of failing to address corruption (Crouch 2010). During her presidency the KPKPN was rendered ineffective because it required cooperation between the police and the Attorney General's office in order to prosecute corruption suspects and these two bodies were reluctant to collaborate. Megawati did nothing to encourage this relationship (Butt 2011b). By the time it was disbanded in 2004, the KPKPN had only reported eight officials to the police over five years.

The lack of political will to deal with corruption was especially apparent in the approach to prosecuting Suharto and his family (Hadiz 2000). With a new regime installed, the public had high hopes that Suharto and his associates would finally be punished for the corruption, collusion, and nepotism (*korupsi, kolusi, nepotisme*, KKN) that had come to "symbolise the social costs, inequities and abuses" of the regime (Hamilton-Hart 2001, 66). Pressure mounted to reopen the investigation into Suharto and charges were finally laid against the former president in August 2000 (Elson 2001). However, the charges were dropped in February 2001, when defense lawyers and the ruling judges agreed Suharto was too ill to face trial (Brown 2003). The only child of Suharto's to be tried was Hutomo Mandala Putra (Tommy) Suharto, who was sentenced to eighteen months imprisonment in late 2000 for swindling the State Logistics Agency (Badan Urusan Logistik, Bulog) out of approximately US $11 million (Crouch 2010).

Fears that the anticorruption framework established in the early years of reformasi was incapable of bringing political elites to justice led to renewed calls for an independent anticorruption commission. This institution would need to exist outside of the police and Attorney General's office, which were widely seen as corrupt and untrustworthy (Schütte 2012). NGOs focused first on the passage of new legislation that would provide the legal foundation for the commission and an associated court that specialized in hearing corruption cases (Setiyono and McLeod 2010). There was pushback against the commission from some legislators, but others elected on a reformist platform needed to establish their public credibility were supportive (MacIntyre 2003). Subsequent debates between those for and against the establishment of such a commission led to "a long gestation period" despite widespread public support (Crouch 2010, 228).

The UNDP-funded Partnership for Governance Reform in Indonesia and NGOs such as ICW and MTI played a key role in spurring public support for an anticorruption commission. The NGOs used examples from Hong Kong and Thailand to demonstrate the potential impact of an independent anticorruption institution in Indonesia. Through AKAK, they demanded that the new commission and an associated court be able to investigate and prosecute corruption cases without interference from the police or the Attorney General's office. The alliance created a working group with supportive legislators to develop a bill setting out the parameters of the new commission that could be put to the People's Representative Council (Dewan Perwakilan Rakyat, DPR). It also carried out a national survey on public opinions toward corruption and forwarded the results to the DPR (Setiyono and McLeod 2010). At the same time, NGOs issued regular press releases and appeared on national television to advocate for the independent commission, hoping that the media coverage would further drive public support and put pressure on the parliament to pass the legislation (Kramer 2013). Advocacy efforts directed public pressure toward DPR members who were seen as obstructing the process.

Law No. 30/2002 on the Commission to Eradicate the Crime of Corruption was passed by the legislature and signed by a reluctant Megawati in December 2002. This law paved the way for a new anticorruption body with wide-ranging powers, including the ability to wiretap suspects without prior approval from the Attorney General's office and to identify and prosecute suspects independently of the police. Following its establishment in 2003, the Commission for the Eradication of Corruption (Komisi Pemberantasan Korupsi, KPK) developed a reputation for tenacity after several successful convictions for corruption. It became one of Indonesia's most respected institutions and enjoyed strong public support (Butt 2011a). As Schütte (2012, 45) observes, the KPK has not only "managed to bring a number of high-office holders to justice," but also "revoked the perception of impunity for white collar crime in Indonesia." While it took some time for the KPK to gain momentum, the institution represented a crowning achievement for the anticorruption movement.

When Susilo Bambang Yudhoyono became president in 2004, it seemed that the anticorruption movement finally had a true ally in the highest echelons of power. Yudhoyono embarked on a much-lauded anticorruption drive, authorizing the KPK to investigate senior officials and parliamentarians and announcing new measures to "accelerate" the eradication of corruption (Crouch 2010, 217). During his first year as president, Yudhoyono signed off on investigations into fifty-seven officials (Crouch 2010, 218). The first Tipikor trial in April 2005 involving former Acehnese governor Abdullah Puteh was seen as a landmark (Crouch 2010). Following this, a slew of high-profile corruption cases were mounted, including some that Megawati had previously refused to approve. By September 2006, his anticorruption drive had led to the investigation and/or arrest of no less than seven governors, sixty-three district heads, and thirteen national parliamentarians (McGibbon 2006).

Yudhoyono steadfastly supported the KPK and anticorruption efforts throughout his first term in office (2004–9). Acknowledging the limited resources of the KPK and the Tipikor, he approved the formation of an additional body called the Coordination Team for the Eradication of the Crime of Corruption (Tim Koordinasi Pemberantasan Tindak Pidana Korupsi, Tim Tastipikor). Drawn from the Attorney General's office, the police, and the Finance and Development Board, the team answered directly to the president and brought cases to the ordinary courts instead of the anticorruption courts. It led some high-profile prosecutions, including a case against Megawati's minister of religion, who was charged and convicted of embezzling funds designated to assist

Indonesian citizens to undertake the pilgrimage to Mecca (Crouch 2010). However, Yudhoyono's second term (2009–14) was marred by corruption cases involving a number of high-profile political figures, including members of his own party.

Defending Progress

The democratic transition afforded the anticorruption movement more political space to agitate for better transparency and accountability measures and gave activists an opportunity to openly criticize corruption in public and via the media. But the movement was unable to rest on its laurels. Defending existing gains diverted efforts from making further gains in the anticorruption cause. NGOs, in particular, had an ongoing role in mobilizing support to defend the KPK, which was under constant political threat from elements within the government who were unhappy with the oversight power the institution wielded. From the late 2000s, there were a number of attacks against KPK officials and attempts to weaken the KPK itself. At their core, these attacks reflected the incomplete nature of reformasi, as elite interests endured and remained influential, particularly in the legislative and executive branches of government.

Having targeted several high-profile figures, the KPK itself became a target for those who wanted to preserve the status quo. The first prominent attempt to undermine the KPK was launched in May 2009 when Antasari, then chief of the KPK, was arrested for murder. Antasari was accused of ordering the assassination of a prominent businessman, Nasruddin Zulkarnaen, who was shot in the head on March 14, 2009 (Aspinall 2010; Butt 2011b). It was alleged that Antasari had been romantically involved with Nasruddin's wife, who, in turn, had decided to blackmail him. While the case against Antasari was far from ironclad (Butt 2011b), the South Jakarta District Court found him guilty and sentenced him to eighteen years' imprisonment. The case led to calls from some political elites to reduce the KPK's power, or to abolish it altogether (Aspinall 2010). While anticorruption NGOs did not defend Antasari personally, they made public statements claiming that his actions did not reflect the professionalism of the KPK itself.[3]

The anticorruption movement again mobilized to defend the KPK later in 2009 when activists accused other government bodies, including the national police and public prosecutor's office, of a high-level conspiracy to weaken the institution (Sukma 2009). The conflict stemmed from the Bank Century bailout, in which the head of the police force's criminal investigations unit, Susno Duadji, was accused of intervening on behalf of businessman Budi Sampoerna in return for a US $1 million kickback (Kurniadi 2009). The police responded by acting on allegations made by Anggoro Widjojo, a businessman who was being investigated by the KPK for bribing the head of the DPR's Forestry Commission (*Jakarta Post,* October 29, 2009), that KPK commissioners had accepted bribes to halt certain investigations. There was no evidence that these accusations referred to KPK deputy commissioners Bibit Samad Rianto or Chandra M. Hamzah, but the police used them to charge the pair with extortion (Butt 2011b).[4] In response, Yudhoyono formally suspended Bibit and Chandra, who were subsequently arrested in October 2009. A public outcry ensued when Susno Duadji likened the KPK's conflict with the police to a gecko fighting a crocodile (Aspinall 2010), an image subsequently adopted by civil society activists and the media in their support for the KPK.[5]

As the civil society movement to defend the KPK grew, it tested the anticorruption commitment of Indonesia's leaders and law enforcement bodies. The lack of response, especially from President Yudhoyono, was lambasted on social media, with the government accused of being complicit in weakening the KPK (Molaei 2015). Facing mounting criticism, Yudhoyono was forced to act, establishing an independent team, known as the "Team of Eight" (Tim Delapan), to investigate the allegations against Bibit and Chandra and the handling of the case by the police. The Team of Eight recommended that several senior police officers be dismissed (including Susno) and that the charges against Bibit and Chandra be dropped (Butt 2015). The acquittal of Bibit and Chandra represented a significant win for the anticorruption movement, as a guilty verdict would have undermined the integrity and independence of the KPK.

A third prominent attack on the KPK occurred in 2012 in relation to the "driving simulator case," in which former traffic police chief, Djoko Susilo, was accused of accepting bribes in return for the simulator contract. In late July 2012, the KPK raided the headquarters of the traffic police, outraging police leadership (*Jakarta Post*, August 1, 2012). The police later recalled police investigators seconded to the KPK and filed a civil lawsuit against it (*Jakarta Post*, October 27, 2012). Some investigators refused to comply, including an officer named Novel Baswedan (*Jakarta* Post, October 8, 2012), whom anticorruption NGOs rallied to support. Leveraging their networks and social media, anticorruption activists encouraged concerned citizens to come, in person, to the KPK office to prevent Baswedan from being arrested. To thwart attempts to storm the KPK building, where Baswedan took refuge, anticorruption activists staged a vigil around the office, blocking entrances and monitoring police activity (*Jakarta Globe*, October 6, 2012). President Yudhoyono was eventually compelled to side with activists and declared that the driving simulator case fell under the KPK's jurisdiction.

These attacks on the KPK were accompanied by attempts to roll back the provisions of the 1999 Anticorruption Law, which were also staved off through public backlash (Butt 2011a). Yet the KPK's investigative and prosecutorial powers remain under threat. In 2017, the DPR launched an inquiry into the KPK through a Special Committee (Panitia Khusus, Pansus), tasked with considering whether the KPK has a partisan agenda and whether the special power of investigation (such as the ability to undertake wiretapping and sting operations) has resulted in an abuse of power. While the inquiry was widely criticized by anticorruption NGOs (*Jakarta Post*, October 12, 2017), several lawmakers supported the investigation, including high-profile lawmakers such as Fahri Hamzah from the Prosperous Justice Party (Partai Keadilan Sejahtera, PKS) and Fadli Zon from the Great Indonesian Movement (Gerakan Indonesia Raya, Gerindra) Party, both renowned critics the KPK (*Kompas*, June 18, 2016; *Tempo*, July 4, 2017). Anticorruption activists responded by questioning the truth and motivation of such claims, which they describe as self-serving. For example, ICW Coordinator Adnan Topan Husodo asserted, "The last ten years have seen highly intense political maneuvers dampening the spirit of anticorruption. The attacks have mostly targeted the Corruption Eradication Commission . . . Instead of giving full support to the fight against corruption, in most graft cases, politicians have become the KPK's enemy" (*Jakarta Post*, June 13, 2017). These clear signals that not all of those in government wish to see a strong, independent commission investigating corruption notwithstanding, the traction gained by the anticorruption movement in its defense of the KPK proved that the movement was still able to mobilize people and resources at the national level.

In terms of its broader significance, the fact that this battle continues is a reflection on the democratic transition overall. Allegations that the KPK is partisan and that commissioners are prone to abuse of power have been interpreted by the anticorruption movement as deliberate attempts to undermine an institution that is essential for democratic progress. This is not to suggest that there are no reformists in Indonesian politics, nor that the public has no influence on the matter, as the KPK's ongoing existence and continued independence attests. However, the KPK—and the NGOs that protect it—continues to be the primary force in the battle against corruption within a government that has yet to fully internalize the processes and procedures needed to combat corruption from within.

DECENTRALIZATION AND BATTLING CORRUPTION IN THE REGIONS

Dismantling the centralized power structures of the New Order had been an important focus of the democratic transition, with relevant laws passed in 1999 and the program enacted in 2001. Offering more authority to provincial, regional, and local governments (theoretically) presented new opportunities for citizen oversight, accountability, and improved service delivery (Ahmad and Mansoor 2002). In the early days of reformasi, anticorruption NGOs supported decentralization, which they saw as a counterbalance to centralized New Order power structures that had fostered corruption during the regime (ICW 2017). Predictably, however, undertaking such a complex process in such a short space of time proved problematic. Within the new decentralization laws were contradictions in the roles and responsibilities of newly empowered regional and local government, which in many cases lacked the capacity to meet their new responsibilities (King 2004). Moreover, this newly endowed authority allowed for the creation of new, subnational patronage structures as local-level elites could now run for office and more easily leverage their positions for personal gain. As a consequence, the anticorruption movement also faces new challenges as a result of decentralization.

In some instances, decentralization has made it easier to fight corruption. Tomsa (2015, 215) writes of cases where local politicians have become an "unlikely anticorruption force" as they use corruption charges as a way to remove rivals. More generally, however, these new power structures have fostered new forms of corruption. As Hadiz (2004, 699) asserts, they have given rise to "newly decentralized, predatory networks of patronage." There are numerous examples of corruption cases linked to officeholders who rose through the structures set up to accommodate decentralization. The first landmark case involved the prosecution of Aceh governor Abdullah Puteh, who was sentenced to a ten-year jail term in April 2005 for misappropriating funds through the procurement of a helicopter purchased with state funds, for which Puteh paid more than four times the market rate (McGibbon 2006). In 2017, former Banten governor Ratu Atut Chosiyah was sentenced to eight years in prison and a US $18,774 fine for misappropriating the province's health budget, costing the state US $6 million (*Jakarta Post*, July 20, 2017). In 2016 alone, ICW documented 292 registered district-level corruption cases, leading to a loss of more than US $35.5 million and sixty-two village-level cases that led to a loss of more than US $1.3 million (*Kompas*, March 3, 2017). Corrupt practices are also commonplace in provincial and district elections, with candidates paying off party officials in return for nomination and in buying the votes of local citizens through cash or the distribution of goods (Choi 2004, 2007; Buehler and Tan 2007).

Cases such as these have prompted the formation of localized anticorruption groups. In parallel with the development of formal anticorruption NGOs, these citizen movements had sprung up as early as 1998 as people rallied together to challenge entrenched corruption. For example, in Cianjur, thousands of residents called on the local district head to resign because of alleged corruption related to various local government projects in 1998, and in Bekasi, just outside of Jakarta, thousands attended a rally calling for an end to illegal charges for the provision of public services. In Bandung, state schoolteachers protested against illicit levies on their salaries (Setiyono and McLeod 2010).[6] Sometimes these local groups work with support from national NGOs, but they are primarily driven by the desire to combat corruption within their districts. One prominent example is Garut Governance Watch (GGW), established in 2002. GGW has overseen budget expenditure, lobbied for investigations in suspicious activity, and enacted youth anticorruption programs. It has also developed links with local Islamic groups to build a relationship between Islam and the anticorruption movement (Djani 2012). The organization has drawn praise and support from ICW and KPK but, more significantly, has kept a spotlight on the activities of local public officials in Garut. As a result, there have been numerous arrests related to a range of corrupt activities, for example siphoning money from official budget spending (*Media Indonesia*, October 26, 2004) and co-opting funds from the social assistance (Jaringan Aspirasi Masyarakat, Jasmara) budget (*Tempo*, April 28, 2009).

While there have been positive stories like those of GGW, not all provinces or districts can boast similar success. National NGOs simply do not have the resources required to investigate large numbers of cases, and therefore their impact is limited. Furthermore, tackling the underlying normalization of corruption in the government, in both the legislative and executive branches, is much more difficult than simply prosecuting individual cases. True progress requires not only a shift in attitude from elites, but also in the underlying structures that continue to cultivate corruption—effective independent bodies to oversee elections, budgetary spending, and to constrain nepotism in government contracting would no doubt assist in reducing corruption further.

CONCLUSION

Indonesia has undergone a number of political transitions since independence; however, the issue of corruption has persisted throughout, both as a political concern and as a rallying cry for those dissatisfied with the government. Dissatisfaction with the New Order regime was, in part, driven by frustration among everyday Indonesians at the extravagances of elites. Public disaffection, intensified by corruption, played a core role in mobilizing people against the regime while at the same time provoking some of the regime's most severe antidemocratic activities. Ultimately, it bolstered the prodemocracy movement that called for, and eventually secured, Suharto's resignation.

The democratic transition has also had a profound impact on the anticorruption movement itself. Most obviously, the opening of political space led to a more institutionalized and vocal movement willing to openly criticize the deficiencies of the government. The reformasi period also saw the movement professionalize through the establishment of key civil society organizations and the creation of the independent anticorruption institutions within the government. Anticorruption rhetoric has since been "mainstreamed," and the movement has succeeded in influencing government policy (though the extent to which policies are followed is a separate matter). Indeed, as Törnquist (2006, 232) contends of corruption in Indonesia, "almost all concrete measures taken at the top-level [sic] have been due to civic pressure." Despite numerous elections and changes in president, this still holds true.

At the same time, the anticorruption movement operates in an unforgiving political context, trapped between an unyielding commitment to fighting corruption and failure to make significant changes to the structural concerns that embolden corruption in the first place. Despite its successes, the anticorruption movement thus continues to face an uphill struggle that is likely to persist in the absence of a deeper form of democratization. If elites, whose support is needed to safeguard democracy (Etzioni-Halevy 1990), are not on board, then the anticorruption movement has a Herculean task ahead. NGOs within the movement are aware of the importance of democratic representation and support political candidates who will be allies for the anticorruption cause. During the 2014 parliamentary elections, for example, a consortium of NGOs created an online register of electoral candidates, found at Bersih2014.net, that they believed would truly represent citizens' concerns and were against corruption. Yet while the effort was valiant, it did not significantly alter the influence of elite interests in the elections nor the prevalence of corruption, and the gravity of the issue continues to play out in scandal after scandal involving parliamentarians and ministers.

The stakes are high: support for democracy itself may wane if the war against corruption fails, since "anticorruption initiatives are seen as part and parcel of democratization" (Andersson and Heywood 2009, 33–34). If anticorruption efforts appear to be failing, then citizens may feel like democracy is a lost cause. There is no doubt that the anticorruption movement has contributed a great deal to Indonesia's democratic transition. Whether it, along with other civil society movements, has the capacity to impel a deeper form of democracy in Indonesia over the long term will ultimately determine whether this is a winnable war.

NOTES

1. The journal *Indonesia* published the defense statements from students on trial in April 1979. The accompanying editorial content was written anonymously, presumably to avoid persecution from the New Order regime.
2. Students were not the only group to critique the government for corruption. For example, in May 1980 a group of fifty prominent Indonesians, including retired army generals and former prime ministers, signed a petition known as "The Petition of 50" which was critical of Suharto and his manipulation of Pancasila, which they believed he was using to threaten political enemies. See Elson 2001, 231–32, for further details.
3. NGOs were reluctant to defend Antasari because of his previous "poor track record" as a public prosecutor (personal communication with the former director of the Indonesian Forum for Budget Transparency, Forum Indonesia untuk Transparansi Anggaran, FITRA), October 17, 2017. Furthermore, ICW's deputy director, Emerson Yuntho, stated at the time that ICW suspected Antasari of being influenced by political forces to prioritize certain cases, though he was unable to provide evidence of this (*Jurnal Nasional*, May 4, 2009).
4. A detailed description and analysis of the case against Bibit and Chandra, and the subsequent events of the indictment can be found in Butt 2011b.
5. The gecko (*cicak*) versus crocodile (*buaya*) analogy is an Indonesian equivalent of David and Goliath. In Aspinall's (2010, 113) view, the movement drew public support of the order of the protests seen in the lead-up to Suharto's resignation.
6. An excellent summary of these and other local anti-corruption movements that occurred following Suharto's resignation can be found in Setiyono and McLeod 2010.

REFERENCES

Ahmad, Ehtisham, and Ali Mansoor. 2002. "Indonesia: Managing Decentralization." IMF Working Paper 1–21. Washington DC: International Monetary Fund.

Alm, James, Jorge Martinez-Vazquez, and Dana Weist. 2004. "Introduction." In *Reforming Intergovernmental Fiscal Relations and the Rebuilding of Indonesia*, edited by James Alm, Jorge Martinez-Vazquez, and Sri Mulyani Indrawati, 1–14. Cheltenham, UK: Edward Elgar.

Andersson, Staffan, and Paul M. Heywood. 2009. "Anti-Corruption as a Risk to Democracy." In *Governments, NGOs and Anti-Corruption: The New Integrity Warriors*, edited by Luis De Sousa, Peter Larmour and Narry Hindess, 33–50. London: Routledge.

Anwar, Dewi Fortuna. 2010. "The Habibie Presidency: Catapulting Towards Reform." In *Soeharto's New Order and Its Legacy: Essays in Honour of Harold Crouch*, edited by Edward Aspinall and Greg Fealy, 99–118. Canberra: ANUE-Press.

Aspinall, Edward. 2005. *Opposing Suharto: Compromise, Resistance, and Regime Change in Indonesia*. Stanford: Stanford University Press.

———. 2010. "Indonesia in 2009: Democratic Triumphs and Trials." *Southeast Asian Affairs* 2010 (1): 103–25.

Aspinall, Edward, and Mada Sukmajati. 2016. "Patronage and Clientelism in Indonesian Electoral Politics." In *Electoral Dynamics in Indonesia: Money Politics, Patronage, and Clientelism at the Grassroots*, edited by Edward Aspinall and Mada Sukmajati, 1–38. Singapore: NUS Press.

Barton, Greg. 2006. *Gus Dur: The Authorized Biography of Abdurrahman Wahid*. Jakarta: Equinox Publishing.

Bertrand, Jacques. 1996. "False Starts, Succession Crises, and Regime Transition: Flirting with Openness in Indonesia." *Pacific Affairs* 69 (3): 319–40.

Bird, Judith. 1998. "Indonesia in 1997: The Tinderbox Year." *Asian Survey* 38 (2): 168–76.

———. 1999. "Indonesia in 1998: The Pot Boils Over." *Asian Survey* 39 (1): 27–37.

Brata, R. Arya. 2009. "Why Did Anticorruption Policy Fail? Implementation of the Anticorruption Policy of the Authoritarian New Order Regime in Indonesia, 1971–1998." In *The Many Faces of Public Management Reform in the Asia-Pacific Region*, edited by Clay Westcott and Bidhaya Bowornwathana, 123–53. Bingley, UK: Emerald.

Brown, Colin. 2003. *A Short History of Indonesia: The Unlikely Nation?* Sydney: Allen and Unwin.

Buehler, Michael, and Paige Tan. 2007. "Party-Candidate Relationships in Indonesian Local Politics: A Case Study of the 2005 Regional Elections in Gowa, South Sulawesi Province." *Indonesia* 84 (Oct 2007): 41–69.

Butt, Simon. 2011a. "Anti-Corruption Reform in Indonesia: An Obituary?" *Bulletin of Indonesian Economic Studies* 47 (3): 381–94.

———. 2011b. *Corruption and Law in Indonesia*. London: Routledge.

———. 2015. "The Rule of Law and Anti-Corruption Reforms under Yudhoyono: The Rise of the KPK and the Constitutional Court." In *The Yudhoyono Presidency: Indonesia's Decade of Stability and Stagnation*, edited by Edward Aspinall, Marcus Mietzner and Dirk Tomsa, 175–98. Singapore, ISEAS.

———. 2015. *The Constitutional Court and Democracy in Indonesia*. London: Brill.

Choi, Nankyung. 2004. "Local Elections and Party Politics in Post-Reformasi Indonesia: A View from Yogyakarta." *Contemporary Southeast Asia* 26 (2): 280–301.

——. 2007. "Local Elections and Democracy in Indonesia: The Riau Archipelago." *Journal of Contemporary Asia* 37 (3): 326–45.

Collins, Elizabeth Fuller. 2007. *Indonesia Betrayed: How Development Fails*. Honolulu: University of Hawai'i Press.

Cribb, Robert, and Colin Brown. 1995. *Modern Indonesia: A History since 1945*. New York: Longman.

Crouch, Harold. 1980. *The Army and Politics in Indonesia*. Ithaca: Cornell University Press.

——. 1993. "Democratic Prospects in Indonesia." *Asian Journal of Political Science* 1 (2): 77–92.

——. 2010. *Political Reform in Indonesia after Soeharto*. Singapore: ISEAS.

Dahm, Bernhard. 1971. *History of Indonesia in the Twentieth Century*. London: Pall Mall Press.

Dick, Howard, and Jeremy Mulholland. 2011. "The State as Marketplace: Slush Funds and Intra-Elite Rivalry." In *The State and Illegality in Indonesia*, edited by Edward Aspinall and Gerry van Klinken, 65–85. Leiden: KITLV Press.

Djani, Luky. 2012. "A Double-Edged Sword." *Inside Indonesia* 108. https://www.insideindonesia.org/a-double-edged-sword.

Doig, Alan. 2013. "In the State We Trust? Democratisation, Corruption, and Development." In *Corruption and Democratisation*, edited by A. Doig and R. Theobald, 13–36. London: Frank Cass.

Duncan, R., and McLeod, R. 2007. "The State and the Market in Democratic Indonesia." In *Indonesia: Democracy and the Promise of Good Governance*. Singapore: Institute of Southeast Asian Studies.

Eklof, Stefan. 2003. *Power and Culture in Suharto's Indonesia: The Indonesian Democratic Party (PDI) and the Decline of the New Order*. Copenhagen: NIAS Press.

Elson, Robert E. 2001. *Suharto: A Political Biography*. Cambridge: Cambridge University Press.

Etzioni-Halevy, Eva. 1990. "Exchanging Material Benefit for Political Support: A Comparative Analysis." In *Political Corruption: A Handbook*, edited by Arnold J. Heidenheimer, Michael Johnston and Victor T. Le Vine, 287–302. New Brunswick: Transaction Publishers.

Feith, Herb. 1994. "Constitutional Democracy: How Well Did It Function?" In *Democracy in Indonesia: 1950s and 1990s*, edited by David Bourchier and John Legge, 16–25. Melbourne: Monash University.

Fitzpatrick, Daniel. 2008. "Culture, Ideology and Human Rights: The Case of Indonesia's Code of Criminal Procedure." In *Indonesia Law and Society*, edited by Tim Lindsey, 499–514. Singapore: Federation Press.

Ford, Michele, and Thomas B. Pepinsky. 2014. "Introduction: Beyond Oligarchy?" In *Beyond Oligarchy: Wealth, Power, and Contemporary Indonesian Politics*, edited by Michele Ford and Thomas B. Pepinsky, 1–10. Ithaca: Cornell Southeast Asia Program Publications.

Hadiz, Vedi. 2000. "Retrieving the Past for the Future? Indonesia and the New Order Legacy." *Southeast Asian Journal of Social Science* 28 (2): 11–33.

——. 2003. "Reorganizing Political Power in Indonesia: A Reconsideration of So-Called 'Democratic Transitions.'" *Pacific Review* 16 (4): 591–611.

——. 2004. "Decentralization and Democracy in Indonesia: A Critique of Neo-Institutionalist Perspectives." *Development and Change* 35 (4): 697–718.

Hadiz, Vedi, and Richard Robison. 2014. "The Political Economy of Oligarchy and the Reorganization of Power in Indonesia." In *Beyond Oligarchy*, edited by Michele Ford and Thomas B. Pepinsky, 35–56. Ithaca: Cornell Southeast Asia Program Publications.

Hainsworth, Geoffrey. 2007. "Rule of Law, Anti-Corruption, Anti-Terrorism, and Militant Islam: Coping with Threats to Democratic Pluralism and National Unity in Indonesia." *Asia Pacific Viewpoint* 48 (1): 128–44.

Hale, Christopher D. 2001. "Indonesia's National Car Project Revisited." *Asian Survey* 41 (4): 629–45.

Hamayotsu, Kikue, and Ronnie Nataatmadja. 2016. "Indonesia in 2015: The People's President's Rocky Road and Hazy Outlooks in Democratic Consolidation." *Asian Survey* 56 (1): 129–37.

Hamilton-Hart, Natasha. 2001. "Anti-corruption Strategies in Indonesia." *Bulletin of Indonesian Economic Studies* 37 (1): 65–82.

Hansen, Gary. 1975. "Indonesia 1974: A Momentous Year." *Asian Survey* 15 (2): 148–56.

Harriss-White, Barbara, and Gordon White. 1996. "Corruption, Liberalization and Democracy: Editorial Introduction." *IDS Bulletin* 27 (2): 1–5.

Holloway, Richard. 2001. "Corruption and Civil Society Organisations in Indonesia." Paper read at International Anti-Corruption Conference (IACC), at Prague, Czech Republic.

ICW. 2017. "Tentang ICW." September 17. http://www.antikorupsi.org/id/icw.

Jackson, Elisabeth Yvonne. 2013. "'Warring Words': Students and State in New Order Indonesia, 1966–1998." Ph.D. diss., Australian National University.

Johnston, Michael. 1998. "Fighting Systemic Corruption: Social Foundations for Institutional Reform." *European Journal of Development Research* 10 (1): 85–104.

——. 2014. *Corruption, Contention, and Reform: The Power of Deep Democratization.* Cambridge: Cambridge University Press.

King, Dwight Y. 2004. "Political Reforms, Decentralization, and Democratic Consolidation in Indonesia." In *Reforming Intergovernmental Fiscal Relations and the Rebuilding of Indonesia*, edited by James Alm, Jorge Martinez-Vazquez, and Sri Mulyani Indrawati, 47–64. Cheltenham, UK: Edward Elgar.

Kramer, Elisabeth. 2013. "When News Becomes Entertainment: Representations of Corruption in Indonesia's Media and the Implication of Scandal." *Media Asia* 40 (1): 60–72.

——. 2015. "What's in a Symbol? Emerging Parties and Anti-Corruption Symbols in Indonesia's 2014 National Legislative Election Campaigns." Ph.D. diss., University of Sydney.

Kurniadi, B. Danang. 2009. "Anti-Corruption Rollback: The Recent Phenomenon of Anti-Corruption Stagnation in Indonesia." Paper read at Executive Corruption and Anti-Corruption Seminar, October 2009, at Australian National University.

Lavena, Cecilia F. 2015. "Book Review: Corruption, Contention, and Reform: The Power of Deep Democratization." *American Review of Public Administration* 45 (4): 494–95.

Liddle, R. William. 1992. "Indonesia's Democratic Past and Future." *Comparative Politics* 24 (4): 443–62.

——. 1996. *Leadership and Culture in Indonesian Politics*. Sydney: Allen and Unwin.

——. 2001. "Indonesia in 2000: A Shaky Start for Democracy." *Asian Survey* 41 (1): 208–22.

Liddle, R. William, and Saiful Mujani. 2005. "Indonesia in 2004: The Rise of Susilo Bambang Yudhoyono." *Asian Survey* 45 (1): 119–26.

MacIntyre, Andrew J. 2003. *The Power of Institutions: Political Architecture and Governance*: Ithaca: Cornell University Press.

Mackie, J.A.C. 1970. "The Commission of Four Report on Corruption." *Bulletin of Indonesian Economic Studies* 6 (3): 87–101.

McCoy, Jennifer L., and Heather Heckel. 2001. "The Emergence of a Global Anti-Corruption Norm." *International Politics* 38 (1): 65–90.

McGibbon, Rodd. 2006 "Indonesian Politics in 2006: Stability, Compromise and Shifting Contests Over Ideology." *Bulletin of Indonesian Economic Studies* 42 (3): 321–40.

Mietzner, Marcus. 2012. "Indonesia's Democratic Stagnation: Anti-Reformist Elites and Resilient Civil Society." *Democratization* 19 (2): 209–29.

——. 2015. "Dysfunction by Design: Political Finance and Corruption in Indonesia." *Critical Asian Studies* 47 (4): 587–610.

Molaei, Hamideh. 2015. "Discursive Opportunity Structure and the Contribution of Social Media to the Success of Social Movements in Indonesia." *Information, Communication, and Society* 18 (1): 94–108.

Moroff, Holger, and Diana Schmidt-Pfister. 2010. "Anti-Corruption Movements, Mechanisms, and Machines—an Introduction." *Global Crime* 11 (2): 89–98.

Ricklefs, Merle Calvin. 2001. *A History of Modern Indonesia since C. 1200*. 3rd ed. Stanford: Stanford University Press.

Robison, Richard, and Vedi Hadiz. 2004. *Reorganising Power in Indonesia: The Politics of Oligarchy in an Age of Markets*. London: Routledge Curzon.

Sampson, Steven. 2010. "The Anti-Corruption Industry: From Movement to Institution." *Global Crime* 11: 261–78.

Schütte, Sofie Arjon. 2009. "Government Policies and Civil Society Initiatives against Corruption." In *Democratization in Post-Suharto Indonesia*, edited by Marco Bunte and Andreas Ufen, 81–101. New York: Routledge.

——. 2012. "Against the Odds: Anti-Corruption Reform in Indonesia." *Public Administration and Development* 32 (1): 38–48.

Sen, Krishna, and Hill, David T. 2000. *Media, Culture, and Politics in Indonesia*. Oxford: Oxford University Press.

Setiyono, Budi, and Ross H. McLeod. 2010. "Civil Society Organisations' Contribution to the Anti-Corruption Movement in Indonesia." *Bulletin of Indonesian Economic Studies* 46 (3): 347–70.

Sherlock, Stephen. 2002. "Combating Corruption in Indonesia? The Ombudsman and the Assets Auditing Commission." *Bulletin of Indonesian Economic Studies* 38 (3): 367–83.

Sidel, James T. 1996. "Siam and Its Twin? Democratization and Bossism in Contemporary Thailand and the Philippines." *IDS Bulletin* 27 (2): 56–63.

Siegel, J. T. 1998. "Early Thoughts on the Violence of May 13 and 14, 1998, in Jakarta." *Indonesia* 66 (October 1998): 75–108.

Smith, T. M. 1971. "Corruption, Tradition and Change." *Indonesia* 11(April): 21–40.

Sukma, Rizal. 2009. "Indonesian Politics in 2009: Defective Elections, Resilient Democracy." *Bulletin of Indonesian Economic Studies* 45 (3): 317–36.

Surbakti, Ramlan. 1999. "Formal Political Institutions." In *Indonesia: The Challenge of Change*, edited by Richard Baker, Hadi Soesastro, J. Kristiadi and Douglas E. Ramage. Leiden: KITLV Press.

Tapsell, Ross. 2010. "Newspaper Ownership and Press Freedom in Indonesia." Paper read at Asian Studies Association of Australia Biennial Conference, July 5–8, 2010, at Adelaide.

Tomsa, Dirk. 2015. "Local Politics and Corruption in Indonesia's Outer Islands." *Bijdragen tot de taal-, land-en volkenkunde/Journal of the Humanities and Social Sciences of Southeast Asia* 171 (2–3): 196–219.

Törnquist, Olle. 2006. "Assessing Democracy from Below: A Framework and Indonesian Pilot Study." *Democratization* 13 (2): 227–55.

Tupai, Roy. 2005. *Chronology of Tommy Suharto's Legal Saga: From Playboy Defendant to Fugitive Murderer to Pampered Prisoner & Soon to Freedom.* Jakarta: Paras Indonesia.

van der Kroef, Justus Maria. 1971. *Indonesia after Sukarno.* Vancouver: University of British Colombia Press.

Vatikiotis, Michael R. J. 1993. *Indonesian Politics under Suharto.* London: Routledge.

Webber, Douglas. 2006. "A Consolidated Patrimonial Democracy? Democratization in Post-Suharto Indonesia." *Democratization* 13 (3): 396–420.

Wertheim, W. F. 1963. "Sociological Aspects of Corruption in Southeast Asia." *Sociologia Neerlandica* 2 (1963): 129–54.

"White Book of the 1978 Students' Struggle." *Indonesia* 25 (April 1978): 151–82.

Wie, Thee Kian. 2003. "The Indonesian Economic Crisis and the Long Road to Recovery." *Australian Economic History Review* 43 (2): 183–96.

Winters, Jeffrey. 2014. "Oligarchy and Democracy in Indonesia." In *Beyond Oligarchy: Wealth, Power, and Contemporary Indonesian Politics*, edited by Michele Ford and Thomas Pepinsky, 11–34. New York: Cornell University.

CHAPTER THREE

Indonesia's Labor Movement and Democratization

Teri Caraway and Michele Ford

Labor movements and their political allies played a decisive role in the democratization of early industrializing economies, a dynamic recognized by a long tradition of academic research (Bellin 2000; Rueschemeyer, Stephens, and Stephens 1992). However, much of the literature on later democratic transitions has focused on the role of elites in regime change, a fact that has drawn criticism among scholars of the labor movement (see, for example, Collier and Mahoney 1997). This tendency to neglect the role of labor movements in moments of political transition reflects both scholarly proclivities and the complex relationship between organized labor and the democratic impulse in late-developing countries (Bellin 2000). As Valenzuela (1989, 445) has noted, while "virtually all processes of redemocratization include a sharp increase in labour movement activation through strikes and demonstrations," organized labor may act to facilitate or impede political change. Whether or not the labor movement supports (re)democratization depends on a range of factors, including its strength in absolute terms and relative to capital (Barrett 2001; Valenzuela 1989), the characteristics of its institutions (Chu 1998), and its relationships with the state and the broader prodemocracy movement (Bellin 2000; Calenzo 2009).

Where a labor movement *does* play a significant role in the fall of an authoritarian regime, its contribution to regime change can take many forms. It may, for example, shape the oppositional agenda (Chu 1998), undermine the ruling party's legitimacy and thus destabilize the regime (Collier and Mahoney 1997), or directly trigger regime change through mass protest (Kraus 2007). Its capacity to contribute to democratic consolidation depends on a great many factors, some of which are related to its structures and prior experience (Buchanan and Nicholls 2003) or its ability to refashion its relationship with government and the ruling elites (Hamilton and Kim 2004; Lee 2006). In other circumstances, that capacity may hinge on the economic context of the transition and subsequent changes in that context, which may undermine formal improvements in the position of workers and their representative institutions (Alemán 2010; Calenzo 2009; Kraus 2007; Shin 2010; Valenzuela 1989).

While democracy presents new political opportunities for the working class, the economic crises and neoliberal reforms that accompanied most political transitions in the late twentieth century constituted a challenge for organized labor movements. Labor movements have fared differently in the wake of these political and economic transformations (Caraway, Cook, and Crowley 2015). In Eastern Europe, unions experienced a hemorrhaging of membership after the transition to democracy and a market economy (Crowley and Ost 2001). In Latin America, labor unions reclaimed collective rights denied to them under authoritarianism but were weakened by labor market reforms that undercut their organizational strength (Cook 2002). In the new democracies of Southeast Asia, unions emerged from authoritarianism weak, often deeply fragmented and without partisan allies, hampering their capacity to make gains (Caraway 2009; Ford and Gillan 2016). How labor movements responded to these challenges depended on authoritarian legacies and the specific features of the transition context (Caraway, Cook, and Crowley 2015). On balance, the assessment of labor scholars has been that globalization has trumped democratization, and that workers' movements are in decline.

The experience of the Indonesian labor movement presents some parallels and some contrasts with these general trends. In many countries, the story is one of resurgence during the transition followed by decline. In the repressive context of Suharto's Indonesia and an impotent official union, the labor-oriented nongovernmental organizations (NGOs) and self-styled alternative unions of the late Suharto years helped shape the oppositional agenda and destabilize the regime by undermining its legitimacy at home and abroad in the early–mid 1990s (Ford 2009). During this period, labor activists successfully internationalized labor abuses, raising awareness of how Indonesia's oppressive political environment undermined workers' labor rights. In response, the regime drove vocal labor activists underground. As a result, workers did not participate as an organized force in the antiregime protests that swept through Indonesia in the wake of the Asian Financial Crisis (Aspinall 1999). This legacy of exclusion affected the capacity of unions to seize new opportunities for political mobilization, both during and after the transition to democracy.

What is striking, however, is the increased visibility of labor after the moment of regime change. Small in size and without links to political parties, unofficial unions were poorly positioned to seize the opportunities presented by the collapse of the Suharto regime. Labor activists both within and outside of labor unions nevertheless exploited the greater political openness of the Habibie years to register new organizations and to engage in collective protest. Unions have demanded more favorable treatment for their members in the workplace. They have also pursued working-class interests in the political arena, persuading politicians at the local and national levels to adopt many proworker policies. In the process, they have challenged the deeply rooted belief that only educated elites have a right to engage politically.

This transformation was possible because labor activists managed to leverage fundamental changes within the political opportunity structure to shift the locus of the movement from outside mainstream labor unions to within them. Indonesia's fragmented unions also succeeded in putting aside their many differences to cooperate on many important policy issues, like social security, with impressive results. But, while these successes are quite remarkable, unions have most likely reached the limits of what they can accomplish without greater membership density, more effective collaboration, and an organic link to a programmatic party of the Left.[1]

LABOR ACTIVISM AND THE PUSH FOR DEMOCRACY

For most of Suharto's thirty-year reign, the most dynamic forms of labor activism were located outside labor unions. The New Order regime domesticated preexisting unions through exclusionary corporatist structures designed to control rather than empower workers (Ford 2009; Hadiz 1997). Outside official union structures, a small army of labor NGOs organized workers and advocated for worker rights at home and abroad. Closer international scrutiny put the spotlight on labor rights abuses in the early 1990s, creating an opportunity for activists and workers to contest low pay and labor rights violations, which in turn prompted a wave of labor mobilization. The Suharto regime responded initially by granting some concessions, but again repressed labor activism in its waning years. Labor activists emerged from the shadows only briefly, playing a minimal role in the protests that deposed Suharto just a few years later. Their activism nevertheless played an important role in undermining the ruling party's legitimacy and destabilizing the regime.[2]

STRUGGLING IN THE SHADOWS

The Indonesian labor movement was in a poor position to contribute to the push for democracy in the 1990s in terms of its strength relative to capital and to government, the characteristics of its institutions, and its relationship with the state. Although Indonesia's formal sector has always been small, labor unions held a privileged position during the first two decades of independence by virtue of their participation in the revolutionary struggle. However, the political space available to labor activists was seriously curtailed first by Sukarno's introduction of Guided Democracy in 1959 and then by the anticommunist purges of 1965 (Cribb 2002; Lev 1966). Powerful leftist unions were destroyed, leaving the labor movement all but decimated in the transition to the New Order. The centrist unions that had survived the purges were forced to merge in 1973 into a single national federation to which all unionized workers were to belong. Twelve years later, this federation was replaced by a single union, which—although subsequently restructured as a federation in response to international criticism—had lost what little remained of its independence (Ford 1999; Hadiz 1997).

The official union, the All-Indonesia Workers' Union (Serikat Pekerja Seluruh Indonesia, SPSI), was part of a broad suite of state-controlled "functional groups," the structures of which served as a means of control, not representation (Reeve 1985). Unions had access to check-off systems and some government funding, but played little role in workplace industrial relations. Importantly, also, their previously vigorous engagement in the political sphere was curtailed by an ideological approach to unionism that had no place for politics (see Ford 2010). State surveillance of attempts to work around these systemic barriers to freedom of association was overt and effective: reformists within the official union were marginalized; wildcat strikes and demonstrations broken up by the military; and worker-activists persecuted, imprisoned, or even killed. As a consequence, it fell to student groups and NGO activists—not unionists—to find ways to support and organize workers.

Deeply embedded in the broader democracy movement, these middle-class activists were committed to building independent worker organizations as part of the broader push for democracy. The first labor NGOs were established by disenchanted unionists and human rights activists between 1978 and 1985. By the time the regime fell in 1998, there were dozens of labor NGOs in Indonesia's main industrial regions, and even in some of its less industrialized cities and provincial towns. Many of these labor NGOs engaged in research or policy advocacy, or a combination thereof. They used media statements and public advocacy campaigns to expose labor abuses and to lobby the government and multinational corporations for increases in the minimum wage, for changes to legislation, and on issues such as the military intervention in labor disputes. They also documented the living and working conditions of factory labor, writing lengthy reports for dissemination in Indonesia and elsewhere. As it was illegal to form independent labor unions, other labor NGOs established community-based worker groups or cells of "guerrilla workers" within factories and provided logistical support and encouragement for strike actions. This work was dangerous: activists were shadowed by the National Intelligence Agency (Badan Intelijen Negara, BIN), visited in their homes and threatened, and sometimes even held by police overnight.

The government was all too aware of the potential impact of labor NGOs' research and advocacy work on perceptions abroad. As the minister for defense and security acknowledged, NGOs "influence international relations because they are extremely active in internationalizing issues and shaping public opinion" (Edi Sudrajat cited in *Kompas,* September 30, 1994). Yet NGOs' advocacy of labor rights was tolerated, if at times barely, by a regime increasingly concerned with its reputation with foreign states and foreign investors. Where the regime drew the line was on the involvement of NGOs and student groups in grassroots labor organizing, which threatened its capacity to control the masses. Forced underground, this work was necessarily limited in its scope and impact. It nevertheless played a vital role in convincing a core group of workers—the vast majority of whom had no exposure to independent unionism beyond cautionary tales about its dangers—that collective action offered the only chance to improve their working lives.

Challenging the Regime

Having struggled in the shadows, NGO activists and student groups became more openly confrontational from the late 1980s, when economic liberalization, interelite conflict, and the fall of the Berlin Wall forced the regime into a period of political "openness" (*keterbukaan*), which lasted from 1989 to mid-1994 (Aspinall 2005b). In the mid-1980s, Indonesia had shifted from an economic model that favored import substitution to one focused on export-oriented production (Hadiz 1997). Then, with the end of the Cold War, came a strengthening of connections between human rights and international aid and trade agendas, resulting in increased pressure on the regime. The government responded to these pressures by relaxing controls on civil society and being more tolerant of public expressions of dissent.

These developments created the conditions that allowed NGO activists to be more vociferous in their criticisms of the regime's labor rights record and more visible in their organizing activities. The pattern of underground organizing work that had dominated in the 1980s was first disrupted by human rights NGOs, who came together in collaboration with former labor union activists to establish the first of the alternative unions of the late New Order period. The organization known as the Solidarity Free Trade Union (Serikat Buruh Merdeka–Setia Kawan) was established by a group of NGO activists, human rights activists, and unionists in September 1990 (Bourchier 1994). Among its high-profile founders was Muchtar Pakpahan, a lawyer and labor NGO activist who later headed the second alternative union, the Indonesian Prosperous Labor Union (Serikat Buruh Sejahtera Indonesia, SBSI), established in 1992 after Setia Kawan's collapse. The inability of Setia Kawan and SBSI to register as labor unions meant that they, like the informal workers' groups sponsored by NGOs and student groups, were unable to openly engage in workplace organizing, let alone participate in collective bargaining or tripartite committees. Unlike those groups, however, the very existence of these alternative unions challenged the one-union policy head on, prompting the regime to take a stronger stance than it had against underground organizing, which in turn forced its record on labor rights further into the international spotlight. Workers also took direct action, mounting thousands of wildcat strikes in the early 1990s (Kammen 1997).

Setia Kawan was never officially banned, but SBSI was denied permission to hold its inaugural congress in 1993. Following this incident, and several cases where strikes were repressed or SBSI members were dismissed from workplaces, SBSI filed a complaint of violations of freedom of association with the International Labor Organization (ILO 1994). In the same year, as part of an NGO-led alliance called the Solidarity Forum for Workers (Forum Solidaritas untuk Buruh, Forsol Buruh), Pakpahan met with the team sent by the U.S. government to assess Indonesia's eligibility for ongoing Most Favored Nation status under its Generalized System of Preferences.[3] Recommendations from this review led to the restructuring of the state-sponsored union as a federation and the issuing of a ministerial decision in 1994 permitting the formation of nonaligned enterprise unions, but not recognition of SBSI as a legal union. Momentum continued to grow, and in April 1994 SBSI initiated strikes involving tens of thousands of workers from some twenty factories in Medan. The strike action quickly descended into ten days of wide-scale destruction and anti-Chinese violence. Dozens of strikers were arrested, including many from SBSI and some labor NGO activists, and at least one person was killed. Pakpahan was arrested on charges of inciting the violence and subsequently imprisoned, serving a number of months of his sentence before being released in response to international pressure. He was again imprisoned in July 1996 after the so-called July 27 Affair, when the headquarters of the Indonesian Democratic Party (Partai Demokrasi Indonesia, PDI) were stormed and prodemocracy activists arrested and held until the end of the New Order.

SBSI was joined in 1994 by the Indonesian Center for Labor Struggle (Pusat Perjuangan Buruh Indonesia, PPBI), the labor wing of the People's Democratic Association (Persatuan Rakyat Demokratik, PRD). Known from 1996 as the Democratic People's Party, the PRD was established by student activists seeking to pursue more radical mobilization tactics. Its stated aim was to pursue democratization based on "the sovereignty of the people" (PRD 1996). The PRD was not merely anticapitalist; it took an explicitly Marxist position regarding the role of the working class as the primary agent of change (PRD 1996). Unlike Setia Kawan and SBSI, PPBI did not seek registration as a union. Rather, it took a confrontational approach that centered on strike action, staging a series of high-profile public protests, including a series of strikes involving more than ten thousand workers from fifteen factories across Surabaya. The PRD was outlawed after the July 27 Affair, when PRD leaders and the head of PPBI were among those arrested (Alliance of Independent Journalists 1997).

Labor Contained

The government failed to eliminate the groundswell of worker opposition that SBSI and PPBI had represented in the crackdown of 1996. However, it did succeed in containing both organizations, leaving the independent labor movement in a greatly weakened state. Labor NGOs continued to engage in grassroots organizing and prosecute the labor movement's change agenda, for example, through a national campaign against Law No. 25/1997 on Manpower (Amiruddin and Masduki 1997). But without mass mobilization of the scale achieved by SBSI and PPBI in the mid-1990s, the collective power of the labor movement was much diminished in the final years of the New Order. The advent of *reformasi* (reform) in May 1998 found the labor movement reeling from aftereffects of the repression of 1996 and from the Asian financial crisis, which caused serious disruption in the economy in 1997–98, and ultimately led to regime change.

The collapse of the exchange rate and growing investor uncertainty had a serious impact on Indonesia's small formal sector. Secondary industry—where unions are concentrated—had experienced strong growth in the 1980s and 1990s, but real wages plummeted and more than a million manufacturing jobs were lost in 1997–98 alone (Manning 2000). In this climate, workers were understandably reluctant to engage in union activity for fear they would be sacked. It is not surprising, then, that organized labor did not drive the mass protests that triggered regime change. While industrial workers participated in the wave of demonstrations immediately prior to the end of Suharto's thirty-two-year reign, the mobilizations that ushered in the new regime were dominated not by labor but by students and the urban poor (Aspinall 1999; Törnquist 2004).

ORGANIZED LABOR IN TRANSITION

It took time for the labor movement to generate sufficient momentum to take full advantage of the opportunities presented to it by the new political context. Labor activists were quick to take up the opportunity to establish new unions, but they struggled to translate official recognition into strong collective bargaining agreements. Poorly functioning industrial relations institutions and unions' top-heavy structures and lack of experience with workplace collective bargaining meant that there was little change for ordinary workers in most workplaces, despite the rapid growth in the number of independent unions (Ford and Sirait 2016). Union officials had more success in mobilizing their membership outside of the factory gates to defend against policy reforms that unions opposed and to push for policies that benefited their membership.

Unions were slow to engage in the political arena, reflecting the depth of influence of the New Order's economic model of unionism among labor activists (see Ford 2005). Over time, however, the organized labor movement clawed its way in from the periphery to become a significant presence on the national stage, not only through policy advocacy but also through an increased engagement in electoral politics, where they have demanded a more programmatic approach to campaigning and even run union candidates for office. In the process, these unions refashioned their relationship with government and the ruling elites and demonstrated that the industrial working class can have a voice beyond the factory. Whereas unions used to sit on the sidelines, they are now a visible and vocal organized presence in local and national politics.

A NEW ORGANIZATIONAL LANDSCAPE

Organized labor was one of the first beneficiaries of democratization, as Habibie's new government responded within weeks of assuming office to international pressure to recognize workers' right to freedom of association.[4] This change in policy resulted in a rapid increase in the number of unions and the shift in the locus of activism from labor NGOs and student organizations, and their associated worker groups, to mainstream unions. With the recognition of freedom of association, the legacy union—now known as the Confederation of All-Indonesia Workers Unions

(Konfederasi Serikat Pekerja Seluruh Indonesia, KSPSI)—faced significant challenges to its monopoly. Soon after the transition to democracy, reformists supported by the international labor movement broke away to create a series of new unions, which in 2003 established the Confederation of Indonesian Trade Unions (Konfederasi Serikat Pekerja Indonesia, KSPI). Meanwhile, SBSI registered formally within weeks of the end of the New Order and later changed its name to the Confederation of Indonesian Prosperous Labor Unions (Konfederasi Serikat Buruh Sejahtera Indonesia, KSBSI).[5] These three mainstream confederations are the dominant players in contemporary labor politics in Indonesia.

In addition to these large national unions, smaller unions registered at the factory or regional level in Greater Jakarta, Medan, and Surabaya, many emerging out of the NGO-sponsored workers' groups and the PRD-supported networks of the late Suharto period. These included the Jakarta-based Workers Committee for Reform (Komite Buruh untuk Reformasi, KOBAR), which incorporated leftist unions and several groups formerly associated with Christian and human rights-based labor NGOs (Interview with KOBAR activist, February 1999). In 1999, these committees came together to establish the National Front for Indonesian Workers' Struggle (Front Nasional Perjuangan Buruh Indonesia, FNPBI), which finally achieved formal status in September 2000. Unlike other unions, FNPBI continued to rely on mass mobilization, campaigning on globalization and the increasing precarity of employment, rather than on "traditional" union concerns (Interview with FNPBI president, July 2003). Over time, however, FNPBI's focus on supporting the PRD in the political arena drained its resources, and before long it had all but disappeared (Interview with PRP activist, September 2016).[6]

NGO-sponsored unions that endured beyond the early years of reformasi include the Independent Workers' Union of Medan (Serikat Buruh Medan Independen, SBMI) and the Association of Independent Labor Unions (Gabungan Serikat Buruh Independen, GSBI), a Jakarta-based union that had its roots in factory-level organizations supported by Sisbikum. Of particular note, however, is the Committee of Indonesian Unions Action (Komite Aksi Serikat Buruh Indonesia, KASBI), which brought together a number of FNPBI affiliates and NGO-sponsored unions in Jakarta, Medan, and Surabaya in 2003 (Interview with KASBI activists, October 2006). On May Day 2008, KASBI transformed itself into a confederation—called the KASBI Confederation (Konfederasi KASBI)—which has grown in influence since that time. However, while KASBI and other smaller leftist unions have been active in the policy sphere, they remain relatively minor players on the national stage as a consequence of their failure to develop a large membership base in the factories and their lack of engagement in electoral politics.

Unions and Policy Advocacy

In the early years after the fall of Suharto, unions were most visible in the realm of policy advocacy. None of the major political parties—which differentiate themselves primarily by whether they are religious or nationalist (Aspinall 2005a; Mietzner 2008; Tomsa 2010)—espouse a proworker platform, so there was no obvious ally for unions. In the absence of institutionalized links to a particular party, the main venue through which unions have influenced policy is through collective mobilization. Initially, unions' efforts focused on issues pertaining to industrial relations such as labor law reform. Later the scope of their concerns expanded to include social protection measures such as universal healthcare. As unions adapted to the new political context, they began to complement street-based protest with other tactics such as lobbying and challenging government actions in court.

One key to unions' success in the policy arena was that Indonesia's fragmented unions collaborated across organizational divides to advance their shared policy interests (Caraway and Ford 2017). This collaboration was evident in their engagement with the labor reform process. After the ratification of ILO Convention No. 87, the government turned its attention to rewriting the Suharto-era legal framework governing industrial relations. As the government began to formulate the Trade Union Act, Indonesia was rocked by major protests in response to the revocation of a ministerial decree that provided very generous severance pay to workers (Ministerial Decree No. 150/2000). The unilateral revision of the decree by the Wahid administration unified Indonesia's divided labor movement in protests across the archipelago, forcing the government to reinstate the original ministerial decree. In mid-2002, unions flooded the streets once again in response to the second major labor bill, which contained many provisions that unions opposed. The Indonesian legislature responded by drawing unions and employers into bipartite negotiations to craft a compromise, which eventually became Manpower Law No. 13/2003. Although unions were divided in their assessment of the law, three years later they were united in the streets when the Yudhoyono administration announced its intention to revise the law in response to complaints by employers and the international financial institutions. Unions mounted large protests and succeeded in derailing the reform.[7]

These early mobilizations around labor law reform demonstrated that workers could influence policies that affected them through exercising their collective power in the streets. The threat of disruption led legislators to back away from policies that unions opposed. Once the dust from the labor reform battles settled, unions engaged in campaigns against the ongoing use of outsourcing, the introduction of privatization, reductions in fuel subsidies, and for the introduction of universal social security. Driven by the powerful Federation of Indonesian Metalworkers Unions (Federasi Serikat Pekerja Metal Indonesia, FSPMI), the campaign for universal healthcare involved thirty-three unions, federations, and confederations of varying size and influence. In addition, several union networks, many of which brought together small independent unions that grew out of the NGO-sponsored alternative labor movement of the late Suharto period, became involved. What become known as the Action Committee for Social Security Reform (Komite Aksi Jaminan Sosial, KAJS) also included farmers' and fishers' alliances, and high-profile NGOs, including the Trade Union Rights Center, Indonesian Corruption Watch, and the Urban Poor Consortium. While the campaign did not have universal support within the labor movement, it not only drove the passage of Law No. 24/2011 on Social Security Providers, but convinced legislators and others of the salience of the labor movement in the policy sphere.

KAJS used a broad range of tactics, which helped ensure the success of the campaign. It lodged a citizen's lawsuit, forged partnerships with individual politicians and academics, and attended parliamentary debates on the law, disrupting proceedings to make their opinions known (see Cole and Ford 2014). Ultimately, however, these tactics were underwritten by labor unions' capacity to stage large-scale demonstrations. Following a series of rallies across Indonesia, momentum peaked on May Day 2010, when some 150,000 workers marched in Jakarta (Tjandra 2014). Workers again marched on the parliament on July 29 to demand recommendations made by the relevant parliamentary commission be incorporated into a draft law (*Detik News* July 29,

2010). On May Day 2011, hundreds of thousands of workers demanded that the government immediately ratify the draft implementing law (*Hukum Online* May 1, 2011). The following month, hundreds of workers walked the 250 kilometers from Bandung to the Presidential Palace in Jakarta bearing a petition with fifty thousand signatures (*Antara News* June 20, 2011). Demonstrations ramped up as the deadline for the passing of the bill approached, culminating in a large demonstration on October 28, the last possible day of debate for the law. Some thirty thousand people gathered outside the national parliament, demanding that the law be passed (*Suara Pembaruan* October 28, 2011). Having learned that two factions were continuing to oppose it, protestors broke down the gate and entered the parliamentary complex. That night, protest turned into celebration when Rieke Diah Pitaloka and Ribka Tjiptaning emerged to announce that the bill had become law (*Detik News* October 28, 2011).

Campaigns on issues like social security helped develop a shared platform between the confederations at the national level, culminating in the declaration on May Day 2012 of the formation of the Indonesian Workers Assembly (Majelis Pekerja Buruh Indonesia, MPBI) by the three main confederations and a number of smaller labor unions. MPBI organized a series of mass actions including a national strike involving millions of workers in fourteen industrial districts across the country in October 2012 (Sundari 2012). Calling for the eradication of outsourcing and the low wage policy, it popularized the discourse of a "decent" standard of living, which became a core demand in the years to come. These efforts resulted in a number of concrete achievements including an expansion in the basket of goods used to calculate the decent living standard figure used in minimum wage setting and the strengthening of the anti-outsourcing provisions in the Manpower Law through Ministerial Regulation No. 19/2012 on the Conditions Under which Work Can Be Undertaken by Other Companies.

This very public alliance between the three main confederations brought the union movement a higher profile than it had enjoyed in decades. However, MPBI soon faltered as a consequence of interelite rivalries and disagreements around wages strategy, as well as fundamental differences in approach. After differences deepened further around the 2014 presidential election, when the confederations supported different candidates, their relationship was to some extent restored with the formation of a coalition called the Indonesian Labor Movement (Gerakan Buruh Indonesia, GBI) on May Day in 2015. This and other attempts to restore unity to the labor movement have failed to achieve the level of collaboration experienced during the heady days of MPBI. However, KSPI remained actively engaged in the policy sphere, tackling a broad range of industrial and social issues from better maternity leave provisions to the opposition to eviction of poor communities from government land in Jakarta and Law No. 11/2016 on Tax Amnesty.

MOBILIZING FOR THE MINIMUM WAGE

Unions' most consistent policy advocacy campaign focused on the annual minimum wage negotiations. In tandem with the democratization process, Indonesia undertook a dramatic decentralization of government functions. District and municipal governments came to play a dominant role on issues of deep concern to workers including the enforcement, or lack thereof, of national regulations pertaining to labor. Most important, they were made responsible for the annual minimum wage setting process, which typically begins mid-year when the representatives from the unions, the local branch of the employers' association, and the local government conduct market surveys to determine the cost of the basket of goods and services used to calculate the minimum decent standard of living. Once this information is gathered, the wage council recommends a figure to the district head or mayor, who then approves or adjusts this recommendation and then forwards it to the provincial governor for final approval.

This annual process created an opportunity for unions to work together to secure generous minimum wage increases for workers. Prior to the initiation of decentralized wage setting, real minimum wages plunged in the wake of the Asian financial crisis, only returning to precrisis levels in 2000. From 2000 to 2002, real increases averaged about 10 percent per year (Bird and Manning 2008). When the new decentralized system came into effect in 2002, however, unions had limited success in securing major gains for workers through the wage councils, and average minimum wage increases in Java's more than one hundred districts and municipalities hovered just above the inflation rate until 2013. During this period, real increases were too small in most localities to bring minimum wages into line with the minimum decent standard of living.[8]

Unions responded to this relative wage stagnation by mounting a campaign for a living wage in 2010. This campaign was initially carried out by local coalitions of unions and depended on mass collective mobilization, or the threat thereof, to achieve its goals. The peak of mobilization occurred in late 2011 and early 2012, producing some of the most disruptive mass protests of the democratic era. In the 2011–12 wage negotiation cycle, tens of thousands of workers brought the Batam free trade zone to a standstill after employers reneged on a promise to bring the municipality's minimum wage in line with the living wage standard. Soon after the wage negotiations were settled in Batam, mass protests took place in Bekasi and Tangerang, two major industrial areas near Jakarta. Workers there poured onto the toll roads to pressure the local and national governments to support large minimum wage increases (Caraway and Ford 2014). In Tangerang, the governor acquiesced to worker demands to match Jakarta's minimum wage, and in Bekasi, the national government pressured employers to concede to wage increases that they had challenged in court.[9]

The disruptive power of workers' collective mobilization and the normative resonance of worker demands for a decent living heightened concern about labor peace at the national level and produced important changes that opened the door to wage gains of an average of more than 44 percent in the industrial areas around Jakarta and Surabaya in the 2012–13 round (author calculations). With wages now equal to or greater than the living wage standard in these areas, unions needed a new strategy to maintain upward momentum. Unions began to question more systematically the adequacy of the government's definition of the living wage and called for increases in the minimum wage that far exceeded that level. MPBI formulated a national strategy for minimum wage negotiations and timed the national strike for October 3, 2012, just as minimum wages at the local level were intensifying. Unions faced little resistance from local governments in the areas where unions had engaged in major disruptions in 2011–12, though workers had to push harder in other industrial areas. As a consequence of this campaign, minimum wage increases in industrial areas that year averaged around 40 percent.[10]

One reason that unions were able to achieve such large wage gains is that they had learned to exploit the electoral vulnerability of incumbents. In mid-2005, district heads and mayors began to be directly elected. In contrast to the previous system of indirect elections by the local legislature, direct elections required candidates to appeal directly to voters. The advent of independent candidacies for executive positions further intensified political competition by creating a new route to executive power. The greater intensity of these executive races increased the incentive for candidates to engage with working-class voters in union-dense regions. In the Riau Islands, for example, the successful candidate in the province's first gubernatorial election entered a political contract with KSPSI, gifting a building to house its secretariat in return for union support (Ford 2014). In 2017, a candidate challenging the incumbent governor of Jakarta signed a ten-point political contract with thirteen unions that, among other things, promised to ignore a government regulation designed to limit minimum wage increases. Incumbents in several other industrial areas have also sided with workers in the minimum wage negotiations that preceded their reelection bids (Caraway, Ford, and Nguyen 2019).

In addition to leveraging local elections to their advantage, cooperation among unions in core industrial centers around Jakarta (Jabodetabek) and Surabaya (Ring 1) resulted in a form of pattern bargaining on minimum wages. In the Jabodetabek and Ring 1 metropolitan areas, unions exploited gains in neighboring districts to pressure local executives to side with them in the wage negotiations. When the governor of Jakarta signed off on a minimum wage that exceeded the level agreed to in Tangerang, workers demanded that the mayor keep his pledge that the minimum wage in the municipality would be equal to Jakarta. With some arm-twisting he finally agreed, and once the municipality increased its minimum wage, Tangerang district followed suit.[11] In the Ring 1 metropolitan area, the governor had declared that Surabaya must have the highest minimum wage. Concerned that Surabaya's mayor would propose a wage increase the unions deemed to be too modest, unions in Pasuruan district exploited their close relationship with the district head to preempt a decision in Surabaya by announcing a large increase, which in turn put pressure on Surabaya's mayor to agree to higher wages. This sort of maneuvering across jurisdictions was made possible by unions sharing information about the progress of negotiations with each other so that they could strategize effectively, and by the political allegiances that unions in some localities had established with directly elected executives.

So effective were unions in exerting pressure on local governments to raise minimum wages that the newly elected government of Joko Widodo (Jokowi) intervened in 2015 with a government regulation that mandated that minimum wage increases be determined by a set formula and not through negotiation, thus eviscerating the local wage councils. The use of executive authority to undermine national labor legislation was unsuccessfully contested by unions in the courts, leaving them with few options to contest the regulation. In the meantime, unions lost their most valued institutionalized means of shaping policy outcomes. The disruption of the annual wage negotiation cycle also had serious implications for unions' ability to exert political influence, as it undermined their ability to strike bargains with incumbents and challengers in district head, mayoral, and gubernatorial races.

UNIONS AS VEHICLES FOR POLITICAL PARTICIPATION

Unions' hard-fought policy wins at both the national and local levels were important not just in themselves but also because they created space for nonelite actors to engage in electoral politics. Unions' political experiments were at first driven by interest from mainstream political parties, which had identified the potential benefits of accessing the voting blocs they assumed unions controlled in union-dense locations (Ford and Tjandra 2007). Emboldened by these approaches, their growing mobilizational power, and early experiences backing winners in executive races, union strategists and branch leaders subsequently began to consider running union candidates in legislative races (Caraway and Ford 2014).

From an organizational perspective, representation in the executive arm of government or in the legislature offered the promise of more direct influence, which would mitigate the frequency with which unions had to engage in mass mobilization and through it the drain on union resources. Perhaps even more importantly, electoral politics was seen as a means to give working-class actors a stronger voice in Indonesia's democratic institutions, and not just on the streets. However, the absence of any prolabor parties meant that there was no straightforward way for unions to engage electorally. In the early transition years, there were several failed attempts to establish a labor-based party. In addition to PRD, SBSI had established a party in the lead-up to the 1999 election, which competed under various names in the next three elections. Some KSPSI leaders also tried to set up political parties before the 1999 and 2004 elections. Once registered, a party must win a certain percentage of the popular vote in national legislative elections in order to participate in the subsequent election, and none of these parties cleared the threshold (Ford 2005).

Having failed to establish a sustainable labor party as an electoral vehicle, unions seeking to engage directly in elections were forced to join forces with a mainstream party.[12] The first major efforts by unions to test the electoral waters by partnering with existing parties occurred in the 2009 national elections (Caraway and Ford 2014). The party that offered the best deal was the Islamist Prosperous Justice Party (Partai Keadilan Sejahtera, PKS). PKS went on to conclude agreements to run multiple candidates from two large federations, and fielded labor candidates for local office and nine seats in the national assembly from several different unions in union-dense electoral districts in the Riau Islands, Central Java, West Java, and Banten (Interviews, various years).[13] Unlike the National Workers Union (Serikat Pekerja Nasional, SPN), which made an exclusive arrangement with PKS, FSPMI allowed its cadres to run as candidates for a variety of parties (Ford 2014). Five years later, FSPMI was the only large union to mount a concerted political campaign in the lead-up to the 2014 national elections, fielding candidates for a variety of parties in a number of districts in East Java, West Java, Banten, and the Riau Islands (Interviews, 2013). While FSPMI and SPN were the only federations that made deliberate decisions to run labor candidates, a number of other unionists who were also party cadres ran for office in 2009 and 2014 without institutional support from their unions.

Most efforts to elect union cadres to legislative office foundered in part because unions failed to cooperate effectively across organizational lines (Caraway and Ford 2017). In many cases, candidates from different unions (even sometimes from the same union) competed against each other in the same electoral district (Caraway, Ford, and Nugroho 2015; Ford 2014). Even in cases where candidates from different unions were not running against each other, unions did little to help candidates from other unions. Nevertheless, a small handful of candidates with union backgrounds did win seats. Most union candidates who succeeded relied more on connections with their party or community ties for victory than on union support. But, among the victors in 2014 were two candidates from FSPMI who ran on their union identities for two different parties in the local legislative contest in Bekasi district. These candidates won because of the size of the membership base in Bekasi and the fact that they ran just one official FSPMI candidate in each of those electoral districts. These two candidates drew explicitly on their union background and FSPMI's organizational resources to win.

A logical extension of unions' electoral experiments has been to field candidates in local and provincial executive elections—a strategy that has been tried in Deli Serdang and Bekasi.[14] In Deli Serdang, Bambang Hermanto, a union official and former factory worker, ran in 2013 for deputy district head alongside an activist from the peasant movement with support from his union. Together the team collected copies of 76,306 identity cards—significantly more than the number required to pass verification (*Utama News* May 29, 2013). Other unions in the district agreed to support the campaign (Interview with Bambang Hermanto, December 2013). However, financial restrictions meant that key campaign strategies could not be implemented, and the team came eighth of eleven, gaining just 15,745 of the 545,777 votes cast. In 2017, FSPMI official Obon Tabroni ran as an independent candidate for district head in Bekasi. Having collected copies of almost double the required 135,000 identity cards, Obon qualified to compete in the race. Despite an energetic campaign, Obon placed third with about 18 percent of the vote, behind the incumbent and a former district head backed by coalitions of major parties but well ahead of the pair of candidates backed by another major party (Andryandy 2017).

In addition to fielding their own candidates, unions have also engaged in political bloc strategies in which they back a nonunion team running for executive office. Coalitions of unions have made public endorsements of candidates in executive races in Aceh, the Riau Islands, East Java, West Java, Banten, and Jakarta. In several of these cases, unionists extracted written political contracts from candidates. The most coordinated effort by unions to mobilize support for a nonunion candidate occurred in 2013, when a network of unions not only endorsed the prolabor PDI-P legislator Rieke Diah Pitaloka in West Java's gubernatorial race, but also actively campaigned on her behalf. Although she narrowly lost the race to the incumbent, she prevailed in the areas where unions were strongest (author calculations).

After years of testing the waters in these lower-level executive races, unions ventured into presidential politics in 2014. The major union confederations were split over their choice of candidate. The leaders of KSPSI and KSBSI backed Jokowi and formed an organization called Worker Volunteers for Jokowi (Relawan Buruh Sahabat Jokowi) to support his campaign (Ford and Caraway 2014). The mobilization on behalf of Jokowi, however, paled in comparison to KPSI's efforts in support of rival candidate, Prabowo Subianto, a former military officer with a record of human rights violations. KSPI agreed to back Prabowo after he signed a political contract on several issues of concern to unions. Echoing developments at the local level in some union-dense areas, Prabowo's willingness to sign this political contract showed that candidates for top political office considered labor to be a constituency worth cultivating. A number of KSPI affiliates, and especially FSPMI, campaigned for Prabowo in worker-dense areas in the lead-up to the election, and convinced many of its members to punch their ballots for Prabowo on election day.

CONCLUSION

As demonstrated in this chapter, the labor movement may have been minimally involved in the actual moment of regime change, but it played a pivotal role in the broader push for democracy by publicizing the plight of Indonesian workers among members of the international community and challenging the regime's attempts to contain the labor movement, and has since grasped the opportunities presented to it by democratization. Once dominated by labor NGOs and leftist student groups, the movement now consists of independent unions, which have achieved significant victories in economic and policy terms locally and nationally. And while their efforts in the electoral arena have met with mixed results, they forced candidates for executive office—including that of president—to consider, and in some cases to accommodate, the interests of industrial labor. These achievements are impressive given the unfavorable legacies of authoritarianism and the continued dominance of oligarchic actors in contemporary Indonesian politics (Hadiz and Robison 2014; Winters 2014).

What, then, are we to make of the nature of labor's incorporation in post-Suharto Indonesia? While the exclusionary corporatist system of the Suharto years is gone and its legacy fading, contemporary Indonesia has not embraced the inclusionary incorporation of labor actors favored by populist governments in Latin America or social democrats in Western Europe. Instead, unions have gained the rights to freedom of association, collective bargaining, and public assembly characteristic of more established democracies without organic links to a major political party with a proworker platform. With no direct access to the electoral arena via a labor or leftist party, unions offer their votes to the highest bidder in the electoral market, producing some strange bedfellows. These limitations notwithstanding, there is no doubt that the organized labor movement not only helped lay the groundwork for Indonesia's democratic transition, but has contributed to democratic consolidation by mobilizing for labor rights and by providing a conduit for working-class engagement in politics.

NOTES

1. This chapter was written as part of an Australian Research Council Discovery Project entitled "The Re-emergence of Political Labor in Indonesia" (DP120100654). Our thanks to Abu Mufakhir, who assisted with the 2016 round of interviews.
2. This section draws on Ford 2009.
3. The Generalized System of Preferences is a scheme providing import concessions for developing countries. The Indonesian campaign was initiated in 1987 by the American Federation of Labor-Congress of Industrial Organizations, Asia Watch, and the International Labor Rights Education and Research Fund. It involved lobbying the U.S. government to cancel Indonesia's access to Most Favored Nation status on the grounds of its unacceptable level of labor rights violations. After two short reviews in 1987–88 and 1989–90, the American Office of the Trade Representative initiated an extended review in August 1992. For details see Glasius 1999.
4. This subsection draws on Ford 2009.
5. For more details of these unions and their evolution, see Caraway 2008; and Ford 2009.
6. The PRD ran unsuccessfully in the 1999 elections, attracting just 78,730 votes. It sought to contest the 2004 elections as the People's United Opposition Party (Partai Persatuan Oposisi Rakyat, POPOR) but failed to complete the registration process (Ford 2009). It was reconstituted a third time in 2007 as the National Liberation Party of Unity (Partai Persatuan Pembebasan Nasional, Papernas), but again failed to contest the 2009 election.
7. For further analysis of these labor law reform episodes see Caraway 2004; Ford 2004; and Juliawan 2010.
8. Wage trends in urban and industrial areas outside of Java that had wage councils, such as Medan and Batam, show a similar pattern.
9. The employers won the case, which was a trigger for perhaps the largest of a series of protests in Bekasi in early 2012. Government intervention was key in pushing employers to accept the results of the wage negotiations, despite their victory in court.

10. Wage increases in 2013–14 and 2014–15 were more modest but still in double digits in real terms, and as wage increases moderated in industrial areas, they increased in nonindustrial areas.
11. For a more detailed analysis of this episode see Caraway and Ford 2014.
12. Independent candidacies are prohibited in legislative races.
13. Apart from PKS, only Gerindra ran a recognized labor leader for national legislative office in 2009 (Caraway, Ford, and Nugroho 2015).
14. In 2011, Dwijatmiko, the provincial head of one of the KSPSI factions, ran for governor as an independent candidate. Dwijatmiko was a businessman, however, and was not considered to be a legitimate labor candidate. FSPMI's leader in Purwakarta, Fuad BM, has registered as a candidate for the vice district head for the 2018 race with the Gerindra Party.

REFERENCES

Alemán, José. 2010. *Labor Relations in New Democracies: East Asia, Latin America, and Europe.* New York: Palgrave Macmillan.

Alliance of Independent Journalists. 1997. "Jakarta Crackdown." Jakarta: Alliance of Independent Journalists, Asian Forum for Human Rights and Development, and Institute for the Studies on Free Flow of Information.

Amiruddin, and Teten Masduki, eds. 1997. *RUU Ketenagakerjaan: Pantas Meresahkan Buruh.* Jakarta: Komisi Pembaharuan Hukum Perburuhan.

Andryandy, Tommi. 2017. "Neneng Hasanah Jadi Bupati Bekasi Lagi." *Pikiran Rakyat,* March 15. http://www.pikiran-rakyat.com/jawa-barat/2017/03/15/neneng-hasanah-jadi-bupati-bekasi-lagi-396311.

Aspinall, Edward. 1999. "Democratisation, the Working Class, and the Indonesian Transition." *Review of Indonesian and Malayan Affairs* 33 (2): 1–32.

——. 2005a. "Elections and the Normalization of Politics in Indonesia." *South East Asia Research* 13 (2): 117–56.

——. 2005b. *Opposing Suharto: Compromise, Resistance, and Regime Change in Indonesia.* Stanford: Stanford University Press.

Barrett, Patrick. 2001. "Labour Policy, Labour-Business Relations and the Transition to Democracy in Chile." *Journal of Latin American Studies* 33 (3): 561–97.

Bellin, Eva. 2000. "Contingent Democrats: Industrialists, Labor, and Democratization in Late-Developing Countries." *World Politics* 52 (2): 175–205.

Bird, Kelly, and Chris Manning. 2008. "Minimum Wages and Poverty in a Developing Country: Simulations from Indonesia's Household Survey." *World Development* 36 (5): 916–33.

Bourchier, David. 1994. "Solidarity: The New Order's First Free Trade Union." In *Indonesia's Emerging Proletariat: Workers and Their Struggles,* edited by David Bourchier, 52–62. Melbourne: Monash University.

Buchanan, Paul, and Kate Nicholls. 2003. "Labour Politics and Democratic Transition in South Korea and Taiwan." *Government and Opposition* 38 (2): 203–37.

Burgess, Katrina. 2010. "Global Pressures, National Policies, and Labor Rights in Latin America." *Studies in Comparative International Development* 45 (2): 198–224.

Calenzo, Gaetono. 2009. "Labour Movements in Democratization: Comparing South Africa and Nigeria." Fifth CEU Graduate Conference in Social Sciences, "Old Challenges in a New Era: Development and Participation." Budapest.

Caraway, Teri. 2004. "Protective Repression, International Pressure, and Institutional Design: Explaining Labor Reform in Indonesia." *Studies in Comparative International Development* 39 (3): 28–49.

——. 2008. "Explaining the Dominance of Legacy Unions in New Democracies: Comparative Insights from Indonesia." *Comparative Political Studies* 41 (10): 1371–97.

——. 2009. "Labor Rights in Asia: Progress or Regress?" *Journal of East Asian Studies* 9 (2): 153–86.

——. 2010. "Labour Standards and Labour Market Flexibility in East Asia." *Studies in Comparative International Development* 45 (June): 225–49.

Caraway, Teri, Maria Cook, and Stephen Crowley, eds. 2015. *Working through the Past: Labor and Authoritarian Legacies in Comparative Perspective*. New York: Cornell/ILR Press.

Caraway, Teri, and Michele Ford. 2014. "Labor and Politics under Oligarchy." In *Beyond Oligarchy: Wealth, Power, and Contemporary Indonesian Politics*, edited by Michele Ford and Thomas Pepinsky, 139–55. Ithaca: Cornell Southeast Asia Program.

——. 2017. "Institutions and Collective Action in Divided Labour Movements: Evidence from Indonesia." *Journal of Industrial Relations* 59 (4): 444–64.

Caraway, Teri, Michele Ford, and Oanh Nguyen. 2019. "Politicizing the Minimum Wage: Wage Councils, Workers Mobilization, and Local Elections in Indonesia." *Politics and Society* 47 (2): 1–25.

Caraway, Teri, Michele Ford, and Hari Nugroho. 2015. "Translating Membership into Power at the Ballot Box? Trade Union Candidates and Worker Voting Patterns in Indonesia's National Elections." *Democratization* 22 (7): 1296–1316.

Chu, Yin-Wah. 1998. "Labor and Democratization in South Korea and Taiwan." *Journal of Contemporary Asia* 28 (2): 185–202.

Cole, Rachelle, and Michele Ford. 2014. *The KAJS Campaign for Social Security Reform in Indonesia: Lessons for Coalitions for Social Change*. Singapore: Friedrich-Ebert-Stiftung.

Collier, Ruth, and James Mahoney. 1997. "Adding Collective Actors to Collective Outcomes: Labor and Recent Democratization in South America and Southern Europe." *Comparative Politics* 29 (3): 285–303.

Cook, Linda. 2010. "More Rights, Less Power: Labor Standards and Labor Markets in East European Post-Communist States." *Studies in Comparative International Development* 45 (2): 170–97.

Cook, Maria. 2002. "Labor Reform and Dual Transitions in Brazil and the Southern Cone." *Latin American Politics and Society* 44 (1): 1–34.

Cribb, Robert. 2002. "Unresolved Problems in the Indonesian Killings of 1965–1966." *Asian Survey* 42 (4): 550–63.

Crowley, Stephen, and David Ost. 2001. *Workers after Workers' States: Labor and Politics in Postcommunist Eastern Europe*. New York: Rowman and Littlefield.

Ford, Michele. 1999. "Testing the Limits of Corporatism: Reflections on Industrial Relations Institutions and Practice in Suharto's Indonesia." *Journal of Industrial Relations* 41 (3): 371–92.

——. 2004. "A Challenge for Business? Developments in Indonesian Trade Unionism after Soeharto." In *Business in Indonesia: New Challenges, Old Problems*, edited by M Basri and Pierre van der Eng, 221–33. Singapore: Institute of Southeast Asian Studies.

——. 2005. "Economic Unionism and Labour's Poor Performance in Indonesia's 1999 and 2004 Elections." In *Reworking Work: Proceedings of the 19th Conference of the Association of Industrial Relations Academics of Australia and New Zealand*, February 9–11, Sydney, vol. 1 refereed papers, edited by Marian Baird, Rae Cooper, and Mark Westcott, 197–204. Sydney: AIRAANZ.

——. 2009. *Workers and Intellectuals: NGOs, Trade Unions and the Indonesian Labour Movement*. Singapore: NUS Press.

——. 2010. "A Victor's History: A Comparative Analysis of the Labour Historiography of Indonesia's New Order." *Labor History* 51 (4): 523–41.

——. 2014. "Learning by Doing: Trade Unions and Electoral Politics in Batam, Indonesia, 2004–2009." *South East Asia Research* 22 (3): 341–57.

Ford, Michele, and Teri Caraway. 2014. "Rallying to Prabowo's Cause." *New Mandala*. May 5. http://www.newmandala.org/rallying-to-prabowos-cause/.

Ford, Michele, and Michael Gillan. 2016. "Employment Relations and the State in Southeast Asia." *Journal of Industrial Relations* 58 (2): 167–82.

Ford, Michele, and George Sirait. 2016. "The State, Democratic Transition and Employment Relations in Indonesia." *Journal of Industrial Relations* 58 (2): 229–42.

Ford, Michele, and Surya Tjandra. 2007. "The Local Politics of Industrial Relations: Surabaya and Batam Compared." Indonesia Council Open Conference, Melbourne, September 24–25.

Glasius, Marlies. 1999. *Foreign Policy on Human Rights: Its Influence on Indonesia Under Soeharto*. Antwerp: Intersentia.

Hadiz, Vedi. 1997. *Workers and the State in New Order Indonesia*. London: Routledge.

Hadiz, Vedi, and Richard Robison. 2014. "The Political Economy of Oligarchy and the Reorganization of Power." In *Beyond Oligarchy: Wealth, Power, and Contemporary Indonesian Politics*, edited by Michele Ford and Thomas Pepinsky, 35–56. New York: Cornell University.

Hamilton, Nora, and Sunhyuk Kim. 2004. "Democratization, Economic Liberalization, and Labor Politics: Mexico and Korea." *Comparative Sociology* 3 (1): 67–91.

ILO. 1994. "Case No. 1756 (Indonesia)—Complaint Date: 21-DEC-93." http://www.ilo.org/dyn/normlex/en/f?p=NORMLEXPUB:50002:0::NO::P500 02_COMPLAINT_TEXT_ID:2902930.

Juliawan, Benny Hari. 2010. "Extracting Labor from Its Owner." *Critical Asian Studies* 42 (1): 25–52.

Kammen, Douglas. 1997. "A Time to Strike: Industrial Strikes and Changing Class Relations in New Order Indonesia." Ph.D. diss., Cornell University.

Kraus, Jon. 2007. "Trade Unions in Africa's Democratic Renewal and Transitions: An Introduction." In *Trade Unions and the Coming of Democracy in Africa*, edited by Jon Kraus, 1–34. New York: Palgrave Macmillan.

Lee, Yoonkyung. 2006. "Varieties of Labor Politics in Northeast Asian Democracies: Political Institutions and Union Activism in Korea and Taiwan." *Asian Survey* 46 (5): 721–40.

Lev, Daniel. 1966. *The Transition to Guided Democracy: Indonesian Politics, 1957–1959.* Ithaca: Cornell Modern Indonesia Project.

Manning, Chris. 2000. "Labour Market Adjustment to Indonesia's Economic Crisis: Context, Trends, and Implications." *Bulletin of Indonesian Economic Studies* 36 (1): 105–36.

Mietzner, Marcus. 2008. "Comparing Indonesia's Party Systems of the 1950s and the Post-Suharto Era: From Centrifugal to Centripetal Inter-party Competition." *Journal of Southeast Asian Studies* 39 (03): 431–53.

PRD. 1996. "Manifesto Partai Rakyat Demokratik." Jakarta: Partai Rakyat Demokratik.

Reeve, David. 1985. *Golkar of Indonesia: An Alternative to the Party System.* Singapore: Oxford University Press.

Rueschemeyer, Dietrich, Evelyne Stephens, and John Stephens. 1992. *Capitalist Development and Democracy.* Chicago: University of Chicago Press.

Shin, Kwang-Yeong. 2010. "Globalisation and the Working Class in South Korea: Contestation, Fragmentation and Renewal." *Journal of Contemporary Asia* 40 (2): 211–29.

Sundari. 2012. "Buruh Siapkan Mogok Nasional Jilid Dua." *Tempo.* October 17. http://nasional.tempo.co/read/news/2012/10/17/078436265/buruh-siapkan-mogok-nasional-jilid-dua.

Tjandra, Surya. 2014. "The Indonesian Trade Union Movement: A Clash of Paradigms." In *Worker Activism after Reformasi 1998: A New Phase for Indonesian Unions?* edited by Jafar Suryomenggolo, 45–65. Hong Kong: Asia Monitor Resource Centre.

Tomsa, Dirk. 2010. "Indonesian Politics in 2010: The Perils of Stagnation." *Bulletin of Indonesian Economic Studies* 46 (3): 309–28.

Törnquist, Olle. 2004. "Labour and Democracy? Reflections on the Indonesian Impasse." *Journal of Contemporary Asia* 34 (3): 377–99.

Valenzuela, Samuel. 1989. "Labor Movements in Transitions to Democracy: A Framework for Analysis." *Comparative Politics* 21 (4): 445–72.

Winters, Jeffrey. 2014. "Oligarchy and Democracy in Indonesia." In *Beyond Oligarchy: Wealth, Power, and Contemporary Indonesian Politics,* edited by Michele Ford and Thomas Pepinsky, 11–34. New York: Cornell University.

CHAPTER FOUR

MOVEMENTS FOR LAND RIGHTS IN DEMOCRATIC INDONESIA

Iqra Anugrah

That democratization occurs partly due to popular pressure from below and paves the way for a greater exercise of popular agency is a well-rehearsed observation in the scholarship of democratization and social movements (Acemoglu and Robinson 2000; Rueschemeyer, Stephens and Stephens 1992; Tarrow 1994; Teorell 2010). Across the developing world, the rural lower classes, and particularly peasants, play an important role in this process. But how these dynamics unfold varies across contexts. In postreform China, peasant protests have been one of the main forms of opposition against the authoritarian capitalism of the current regime (Walker 2006). In Latin American countries with sharper class conflict and stronger authoritarian, oligarchical, or corporatist legacies such as Chile, Mexico, and Venezuela, the success of peasant movements has been modest (Enríquez 2013; Sandbrook et al. 2007, 147–74; Trevizo 2011). In more democratic Brazil, where decentralization has always been more extensive, its leading peasant movement has been able to push the state to accommodate peasant interests, especially with regard to the implementation of land reform (Wright and Wolford 2003). Closer to Indonesia are the examples from the Philippines and Thailand, where peasant movements have contributed to the deepening of democracy in rural areas after regime change (Lara and Morales 1990; Phatharathananunth 2006).[1]

It is important to look at the intersecting dynamics between agrarian politics and democratization because "rural democratization cannot be separated from the challenge of democratizing the state more generally" (Fox 1990, 1). In Indonesia, a wave of rural citizens' and peasant protests in the last decade of the authoritarian New Order (1966–98) contributed to the impulse for democratization (Lucas 1992). After the regime's collapse, new political spaces have opened for a more assertive advocacy of land rights by environmental, peasant, and indigenous people's movements. During this time, land rights activism has intensified and inevitably turned into a more organized social movement (Bachriadi, Lucas, and Warren 2013). The proliferation of land rights advocacy at the local level in the early years of the reform era has prompted a scaling up in the scope of activism to the national level and a diversification of strategies.

Democratization has also influenced the movement's agenda. While in the past it was typically associated with efforts to promote land reform either through direct action such as mass mobilization, occupation, or advocacy, in recent years there has been a push toward critical knowledge production on agrarian issues and grassroots economic organizing in the agricultural sector. This new concern is understandable given that the movement does not have a clear common framework for land ownership, use, and management after successful attempts of land reclaiming and occupation (Interviews with academics, peasants, and activists, 2016–17; and observations of KPRI regional and national conferences, December 2015–January 2016). This development has occurred in the context of a fragmented land rights movement, where many organizations and informal coalitions cooperate, but also compete, with each other.

Two key questions continue to loom large in this new democratic era. First, how do we assess the current state of the land rights movement? Second, to what extent can it influence agrarian politics and policy in postauthoritarian Indonesia? As this chapter shows, despite its organizational fragmentation the movement has nevertheless contributed to Indonesia's democratic consolidation by challenging local repressions, broadening political space, and pushing for the expansion of socioeconomic rights.

LAND RIGHTS ACTIVISM SINCE INDEPENDENCE

Land rights have long been a contentious issue in Indonesia. Like its Southeast Asian neighbors (Adas 1981; Scott and Kerkvliet 1973), Indonesia has history of peasant rebellions and left-wing revolts (Benda and McVey 1960; Kartodirdjo 1973; Williams 1990). With the exception of several notable small-scale social revolutions, such as the 1946 Three Regions Affair on the northern coast of Central Java (Lucas 1989), peasant activism in the postindependence period combined electoral engagement and mass mobilization. In electoral and parliamentary politics, the Communist Party of Indonesia (Partai Komunis Indonesia, PKI) was arguably at the forefront of peasants' rights advocacy. In terms of mobilizational politics, the Indonesian Peasants' Front (Barisan Tani Indonesia, BTI) and Plantation Workers' Union (Sarekat Buruh Perkebunan Republik Indonesia, Sarbupri)—two unions with close ties to the PKI— championed direct action (White 2016). Though led by peasants, other actors, including indigenous people, also participated in the struggle for land rights. One notable example is the Dompea movement in South Sulawesi Province, formed in 1954, in which members of the indigenous Kajang community sought to protect their land and cultural practices from the incursions of the puritan Darul Islam sect (Gibson 2000).

This struggle for land rights reached its peak during Guided Democracy (1957–66) when Sukarno issued the 1960 Basic Agrarian Law, asserting the social function of land and most importantly mandating land reform (Lucas and Warren 2013). Armed with this mandate, BTI and Sarbupri launched "unilateral action" (*aksi sepihak*), a campaign of mass mobilization and land occupation targeting large landholdings and plantations. This extensive land reform campaign was halted by the 1965 anticommunist pogrom. Haunted by the specter of rural class struggle, the New Order regime tamed peasant radicalism by entrenching state coercive apparatuses and promoting capitalist development in the countryside (Antlov 1995; Pincus 1996). Peasant mobilization was restrained and left-leaning unions banned. In their place the Indonesian Farmers' Harmony Association (Himpunan Kerukunan Tani Indonesia, HKTI) was established by the regime ostensibly to represent—but in fact control—peasants' interests in authoritarian-corporatist fashion (Samson 1974). Open expressions of opposition were constrained in rural areas, forcing subtler forms of resistance in the realm of everyday politics.[2] The regime also reversed the earlier policy of land reform, promoting large-scale investments, especially in state lands and forests, and keeping rural poverty in check through transmigration and agricultural modernization rather than addressing the structural imbalance in the access to agricultural means of production.[3] As a consequence, the absolute number of small landholders and landless peasants continued to grow (Bachriadi and Wiradi 2011)

Given this context, it is understandable that the mode of rural activism that emerged in the first two decades of the New Order was more moderate than that of the Old Order. During this period, nongovernmental organizations (NGOs) concerned with rural development such as Bina Desa; Mitra Tani; and the Institute for Economic and Social Research, Education, and Information (Lembaga Penelitian, Pendidikan, dan Penerangan Ekonomi dan Sosial, LP3ES) promoted an agriculture-based and people-centered rural economy (Aspinall 2005, 87–94; Muhtada 2008). These NGOs, and especially Bina Desa, became a training ground for many agrarian activists who later facilitated the formation of other land rights NGOs and movements (Focus Group Discussion with researchers from the Pusaka Foundation, August 2016). Nonetheless, their alternative view of rural development, albeit critical of the regime, was imbued with developmentalist and productivist biases, assuming for example that assisting peasants to improve the agricultural productivity of their farmlands was the best solution for rural poverty and inequality. In short, what they sought was moderate reform rather than a radical overhaul of the regime's vision of rural development.

From the 1980s, however, there was a monumental shift as branches of the Indonesian Legal Aid Foundation (Yayasan Lembaga Bantuan Hukum Indonesia, YLBHI) across Indonesia became more involved in land rights advocacy efforts, combining elements of legal advocacy, political organizing, and student activism (Bachriadi 2011, 121–53). In the late 1980s and early 1990s, several noteworthy land disputes, including the cases of Kedung Ombo Dam in Central Java and Cimacan Golf Course in West Java, received a great deal of attention from the press and the wider public due to the resistance of local peasants against forced eviction and seizure of their lands (Lucas 1992). Although not successful, such open resistance to the regime's policy exposed peasants and their allies—NGO and student activists—to the experience of challenging the regime more openly and sharpened their militancy. It also provoked different reactions within the ruling elites. While the majority preferred to maintain the status quo, some others were more sympathetic to the peasants' plight and helped their cause to some extent. But this dynamic was not a one-way street. As pointed out by Bachriadi (2011) and other scholars (Afiff et al. 2005) the more liberalized political atmosphere during the late authoritarian period also gave more opportunities for peasants and activists to openly voice their grievances.[4]

These episodes of conflict marked an attempt to build a wider alliance for land rights connecting peasants and villagers with urban-based activists (Bachriadi 2011).[5] Building on the efforts of student activists, who had channeled their activism in various study circles and action committees, activists from LBH and various NGOs worked to establish links with victims of land disputes in the early to mid-1990s. These efforts bore fruit with the formation of a series of local peasant unions, including the West Java Peasant Union (Serikat Petani Jawa Barat, SPJB), the North Sumatra Peasant Union (Serikat Petani Sumatera Utara, SPSU), the Lampung Peasant Union (Persatuan Insan Tani Lampung, PITL), and the Central Java Independent Peasant Association (Himpunan Petani Mandiri Jawa Tengah, HPMJT). At the national level, meanwhile, activists affiliated with the leftist Students in Solidarity with Democracy in Indonesia (Solidaritas Mahasiswa Indonesia untuk Demokrasi, SMID) formed the National Peasant Union (Serikat Tani Nasional, STN) in 1993, with the explicit aim of connecting peasants' struggles with what was to become the People's Democratic Party (Partai Rakyat Demokratik, PRD). In the following year, the Consortium for Agrarian Reform (Konsorsium Pembaruan Agraria, KPA) was established as a national coalition of peasant unions, agrarian movements, NGOs, and individuals for agrarian reform. Sympathetic to the militancy of many local unions and movements, KPA focused on advocacy campaigns and supported direct action.[6] Land also emerged as one of the main foci of the nascent environmental movement, especially the Indonesian Forum for Environment (Wahana Lingkungan Hidup Indonesia, WALHI) (Focus Group Discussion with Pusaka Foundation researchers, August 2016).

These deliberate efforts to address the issue of land rights (the main concern for rural Indonesians) and rebuild a new mass politics in Indonesia (the main aspiration of urban, middle-class activists) tested the limits of political dissent at a time when the regime was gradually and selectively liberalizing.[7] What happened during this period was a protracted process through which various modes of land rights activism, ranging from political and legal advocacy to the formation of land reform policy coalitions and peasant unions, emerged, overlapped, and coalesced with each other. This wave of activism contributed to societal pressure for regime change, serving as a foundation for cross-class alliances in rural areas and provincial towns. But its impact on democratization, though important, remained limited because of its rural base. But other social forces, such as student activists and communal elites, many of whom belong to religious organizations, forged the urban cross-class alliance that gave the final push to the dismantling of the authoritarian regime (Slater 2010). Along with other mass-based movements, most notably the labor movement (Ford 2009; Caraway and Ford, this volume), the movement for land rights undermined the stability of the regime. But the issue of land rights itself was subsumed into the larger issue of political and economic reforms at the moment of regime change, making the land question itself just a footnote in the demands of the prodemocracy coalition.

THE LAND RIGHTS MOVEMENT AND DEMOCRATIZATION

The fall of the regime and the process of democratization that followed in 1998 spurred a more assertive wave of land rights activism (Peluso, Afiff, and Rachman 2008). In addition to a newfound political openness, the increasingly promarket agrarian policy of the state and the unchecked rate of land dispossession contributed to the increasingly oppositional stance of the land rights movement. Both the rural dispossessed and their allies saw this opening as an opportunity to be seized, resulting in an upsurge in land rights activism that culminated in the formation of both local and national peasant unions across Indonesia in early 2000s (Bachriadi 2012).

Factors that influenced the movement's trajectory in the postauthoritarian period include organizational dynamics within the movement itself, local settings of agrarian politics, and the broader political economy, especially neoliberal penetration and oligarchic restructuring in local politics. Within this period, land rights movements and organizations fought some crucial battles and attained some key victories. But the democratic transition was also marked by internal disagreements, conflicts, and tensions within the movement itself, the genesis of which can be traced back to the early development of the movement under authoritarianism, and to broader patterns among Indonesian social movements. In general, the growing, but fragmented, land rights movement, with peasant unions and agrarian NGOs on the frontline, has been unable to push the state and the capitalist class to implement large-scale, nationwide land reform. The movement has had more success at the local level, winning land dispute cases after hard-fought battles and influencing local political dynamics in several regions.

THE CHANGING CONTEXT

No longer at the margins, agrarian issues have been brought to the policy table, thanks to sustained pressure from the movement. During the early years of democratic transition, possibilities for agrarian reform abounded due to political contingencies of that time, though it was only during the presidency of Susilo Bambang Yudhoyono (2005–14) that a clearer agrarian policy platform was delineated. Since then, various policies on agrarian reform and related issues have been formulated and implemented. Nevertheless, the main problem of an unequal agrarian structure, sustained by the dominance of big corporations, remains unaddressed.[8] This explains why the movement continues to maintain a critical distance from the state.

The early phase of *reformasi* saw policy changes pertaining to agrarian reform such as the strengthening of the National Land Agency (Badan Pertanahan Nasional, BPN) and the passing of Parliamentary Decree No. IX/2001 to bolster the mandate of agrarian reform (Rachman 2011). After the passing of the decree, which used the 1960 Basic Agrarian Law as a primary reference, there were high hopes for land reform. But this enthusiasm was short lived, as new policies proved difficult to implement at the local level, where local agrarian conflicts are widespread. This delicate situation was exacerbated by disputes surrounding commercial lease rights (Hak Guna Usaha, HGU) and the government's shifting focus to macroeconomic issues other than agrarian reform (Thorburn 2003; Tjondronegoro 2009). These issues created friction between agrarian activists and the state. One of the major tensions emerged in Yudhoyono's first term as president (2005–9) when the introduction of a policy of land title legalization effectively shifted the focus of agrarian reform policies to private land title registration for rural households without tackling the question at the heart of the issue, namely structural inequality in the ownership of, and access to, land. Yudhoyono's presidency also saw the introduction of agricultural policy that normalized and naturalized land dispossession under various guises such as the large-scale, corporate-oriented Merauke Integrated Food and Energy Estate (MIFEE) project for food security (Ito, Rachman, and Savitri 2014).

Yudhoyono's presidency saw an increase in agrarian conflicts, mostly sparked by land grabbing by state authorities or corporations. According to the data from KPA's 2014 year-end report, there were some 1,500 agrarian conflicts involving almost 1 million agricultural households and more than 6.5 million hectares of land in the period from 2004 to 2014. The same report also shows that while there were only 89 agrarian conflicts in 2009, by 2014 the number had increased to 472, or by more than five times in five years (KPA 2014). While the total area of agricultural land remained more or less the same between 2010 and 2014 at around 36–38 million hectares (Pusat Data dan Sistem Informasi Pertanian 2015), the share of employment in agriculture dropped significantly (World Bank's Jakarta Office 2016).[9] These numbers reveal the severity of agrarian conflicts in the postauthoritarian period.

This upsurge in agrarian conflict coincided with the decentralization of political power to districts and municipalities, which has significantly empowered local governments and provided new opportunities for the movement's advocacy efforts. This shift, combined with the localized nature of many agrarian conflicts, explains why land rights activism often takes place in the districts. Local land rights movements have some leverage and bargaining power with local governments, since local elites must respond to societal pressure in securing their interests, whether it is to stay in office or maintain investment levels. In contrast to those local successes, the achievement at the national level has been modest. With regard to the latter, the presidency of Joko Widodo (Jokowi), hailed as the people's president, initially gave a new hope for the deepening of agrarian reform. But despite a proagrarian reform platform, which included conflict settlement, land redistribution, land legalization, and social forestry, there was little change after he assumed the presidency (Ompusunggu 2016). While there is more political freedom to organize openly, in some regions peasants, indigenous people, and their allies continue to face harassment from various state authorities such as police, military officers, and hired thugs. In some of these cases, movement activists and members have continued to be labeled as troublemakers, or worse, communist sympathizers (Interviews with peasants and activists, December 2015–November 2016).

This is not to suggest that there has been no change. There is indeed a qualitative difference in terms of political openness in the postreform era that allows these movements to organize openly. Rural lower classes and their allies can now engage the state in different ways, leading to local accommodations ranging from the issuance of local regulations acknowledging the rights of indigenous (*adat*) communities to land redistribution after years of struggle (Interview with peasants and activists, 2016–17; see also Gaol 2016; Purnama 2016). In the view of many in the movement, however, despite the government's rhetoric of agrarian reform, in the two decades following regime change activists did not manage to achieve any substantive policy change relating to land ownership, land redistribution, or the targets or objects of land reform. As a consequence, activists and concerned rural citizens continue to rely on mass mobilization and direct action when engaging with the state.

A FRACTURED MOVEMENT

One of the most notable changes in the post-Suharto period has been the shift from a middle-class-oriented, liberal form of advocacy led by legal aid bureaus and NGOs to a social movement–based form of advocacy representing rural lower-class interests. Once typically seen as beneficiaries of activists' advocacy efforts, peasants and other rural poor now play a greater role in the movement with many assuming leadership positions at the local level, as practiced in many local peasant unions.[10] However, the dream to build a unified agrarian movement remains a herculean task.

Many peasant unions and alliances remain very localized.[11] However, others have worked to establish a nationwide agrarian movement. A key player is the Alliance of Indigenous People of the Archipelago (Aliansi Masyarakat Adat Nusantara, AMAN), which was established in 1999 to promote the interests of indigenous people, including their land rights. The formation of AMAN was a significant move, which coincided with the larger trend of indigenous revivalism in the post–New Order era (Bourchier 2007; Henley and Davidson 2007). In early 2000s, the consolidation of many local peasant movements led to the creation of the Federation of Indonesian Peasant Unions (Federasi Serikat Petani Indonesia, FSPI), which later became the Indonesian Peasant Union (Serikat Petani Indonesia, SPI). As part of this transformation, SPI required the local unions to restructure as branches of the national organization, prompting the withdrawal of leading several unions, including the Sundanese Peasant Union (Serikat Petani Pasundan, SPP). Another split, this time involving KPA, occurred in 2004 with the creation of the Alliance of Agrarian Reform Movement (Aliansi Gerakan Reforma Agraria, AGRA), which also aimed to pursue a more unified and collectivist peasant movement (Bachriadi 2011, 239–61, 280–87).[12]

In addition to SPI, AGRA, STN, and AMAN, major players in the postauthoritarian period included the Indonesian Peasant Association (Rukun Tani Indonesia, RTI), the Indonesian Peasant Alliance (Aliansi Petani Indonesia, API), and the National Committee for Agrarian Reform (Komite Nasional Pembaruan Agraria, KNPA). More recently, some big local unions such as SPP, the Bengkulu Peasant Union (Serikat Tani Bengkulu, STaB), and the Aryo Blitar Peasant Association (Paguyuban Petani Aryo Blitar, PPAB) joined the Association of Indonesian Peasant Movements (Persatuan Pergerakan Petani Indonesia, P3I), which is affiliated with the multisectoral Confederation of Indonesian People's Movements (Konfederasi Pergerakan Rakyat Indonesia, KPRI). The environmental movement has played a role in connecting this diverse array of local struggles. In the early years of the reform era, WALHI was heavily involved in numerous mass struggles for land rights in different places. Later, it supported the formation of many peasant and indigenous people's movements at the local level. Many WALHI cadres are also trained to give education on citizen activism, politics, and social analysis with critical or class perspectives for members and cadres of peasant and indigenous people's movements (Interview with the former director of the South Sulawesi Branch of WALHI, June 2016; Interview with an AGRA cadre, May 2016). Several key NGOs and think-tanks, including the Sajogyo Institute, the Agrarian Resource Center (ARC), the Mining Advocacy Network (Jaringan Advokasi Tambang, JATAM), the Free Land Foundation (Yayasan Tanah Merdeka, YTM), Sawit Watch, and the Pusaka Foundation, are also important partners for agrarian unions and movements (Focus Group Discussion with researchers from Pusaka Foundation, August 2016 and personal communication with activists, November 2016; see also Muhtada 2008).

These actors have different organizational bases and political tendencies. As evident in many cases, it is not always easy to bridge the gap between activists' political imagination and peasants' most pressing concerns, or for that matter the class differences between them (Bachriadi 2011; Sangaji 2007). Moreover, while there is indeed a genuine concern for the plights of indigenous people as marginalized communities, the crude and elitist nativism of local community leaders still influences the political articulation of the indigenous people's movement (Bourchier 2007; Li 2007a). In facing state and market forces, indigenous people tend to have very little bargaining power, even in fighting for their rights to govern their own customary forests—one of their primary bastions of livelihood and cultural autonomy (Rachman 2014; Savitri 2014). Despite the attempt to promote leftist ideas and introduce a more systematic form of organizing, activists must reconcile their respective organizing schemas with varying local contexts and real conditions on the ground. As a result, actual organizing methods on the ground do not differ greatly. At the local level, the movement also faces the challenge of educating its organizers as well as rank-and-file members on the importance of ideology, political organization, and solidarity economy.[13]

These organizational dynamics within and among different unions and organizations pose an additional challenge for the cohesiveness of the land rights movement. Fragmentation can take various forms such as disagreements, competing claims, and splits among different peasant unions and agrarian movements over organizational structure, autonomy of local branches and movements, membership base, and political orientation, not to mention the lure of opportunism for some activists, organizers, and movement members. This fragmentation is exacerbated by the political economic configuration at the local level. The democratic era has seen a devolution of power, which has created new space for advocacy. However, bureaucrats, business actors, and brokers continue to dominate local politics, leaving little room for social movement actors to intervene in local political contestations (Hadiz 2010; Johansyah 2017). Furthermore, in rural areas, a wide range of neoliberal schemes, such as microcredit and block grant programs, have paved the way for the so-called individual economic empowerment through inclusion in market citizenship (Carroll 2010, 180–207). All of this, combined with the enduring webs of patron-client relationships, make organizing efforts to build collective solidarity even harder. Why should a peasant community join or form a union when they can directly lobby the local parliament or district government to help them make their case for land recognition, for example (Interview with a peasant leader, May 2016)?

MOVEMENT STRATEGIES IN POST-SUHARTO INDONESIA

Political change and agrarian transformation have driven a significant shift in the movement's modes of activism in the post–New Order period. The movement has had to adapt to the new openings, which present both opportunities and challenges. Over time, the movement has become more organized, shifting its focus from disparate rural protests and advocacy coalitions to social movement organizations and peasant unions. At the same time, it faces the new challenge of confronting long-suppressed agrarian issues in the context of a decentralized political environment, a reality that has impelled the movement to improve its tactics.

The political settings under which the movement currently operates have allowed it to expand its scope of activism beyond advocacy approaches developed during the New Order era, leading to a diversification of the movement's strategies. Over time, the land rights movement has taken different approaches and strategies in advancing its struggle. Moving away from its early economistic concerns and focus on legal-oriented advocacy, the movement has taken on an increasingly political tone. More recently, it has also started to experiment with a variety of other strategies in the economic and cultural realms designed to back up the movement's political initiatives. However, mass mobilization continues to be the main weapon of the movement, whereas economic organizing, a rather recent concern, remains as an afterthought in many instances.

MOBILIZATIONAL STRATEGIES

In the early years of reformasi, peasants, indigenous people, and other elements of the rural population and their allies intensified their open, direct actions by turning to mass demonstrations and land occupation. The existing scholarship has documented these struggles in various regions such as North Sumatra (Afiff 2004; Situmorang 2003), South Sumatra (Collins 2007), Bengkulu (Bachriadi 2011), East Kutai (Urano 2010), West Java (Rachman 2011), Malang (Wahyudi 2005), Central Sulawesi (Li 2007b), and South Sulawesi (Tyson 2010), as a part of the national trend of agrarian activism (Rachman 1999; 2003). What is particularly striking about these mobilizational strategies is that, by employing them, peasants effectively challenge unequal power relations in everyday politics. Through these forms of "rightful resistance" (O'Brien 1996), peasants also uphold and expand the notion of the rule of law.

As part of its increasingly political orientation, the land rights movement has adopted a plethora of assertive and contestational strategies including mass demonstrations, land occupation, daily protests against officials and other people in power, and the burning of transgenic seeds. These direct actions also commonly incorporate cultural tactics such as theatrical acts and protest songs. The use of arts as a method of protest incorporates a wide range of narratives, ranging from the unity of peasants and indigenous people in their struggle for land rights (Gueta and Manga 2013), the importance of socially engaged arts and artists in peasants' struggle (Batubara and Mariana 2015), and the deployment of indigeneity, peasantness, and motherhood as an expression of insubordination (Anugrah 2016; Yulius 2016).

Peasants, indigenous people, and their middle-class allies scale up their activism and campaign on the national level as a measure of last resort, taken when local efforts prove inadequate. By raising the profile of local agrarian struggles and enlisting the help of sympathetic state and nonstate allies, activists hope to acquire more bargaining power with local elites. Typically, scaling up involves a national campaign and advocacy effort and the formation of many solidarity action committees, a common strategy since the early days of agrarian activism under the New Order. Recent agrarian conflicts that generated attention in national agrarian activist circles include cases in Tulang Bawang (Lampung), Sukamulya (West Java), and the Kendeng region of Central Java. In these most recent conflicts, national solidarity campaigns and networks were established to draw attention to the severity of these conflicts against big capital in Tulang Bawang and Kendeng and airport construction in Sukamulya. By rallying people to their cause, it is expected that peasants and activists can exert more pressure against the establishment to achieve their objectives.

In several cases the state has conceded, but these accommodations remain localized. It remains difficult for the land rights movement to push the state to turn the assets of big capital interests, such as the State Forestry Corporation (Perusahaan Hutan Negara Indonesia, Perhutani) and big corporations holding HGU rights, into objects for land reform. In other words, there have been no agrarian reform policies comparable to the populist land reform campaign under Sukarno, in terms of its extensiveness, swiftness, and socialist undertone, since 1998. Activists and the rural poor have wrung some concessions locally, but at the national level its capacity to influence the direction and implementation of land reform policy remains limited, indicating the absence of a radical change in the power structure of agrarian politics.

POLITICAL STRATEGIES

Softer, more diplomatic approaches, including policy advocacy and lobbying, are often used to balance these contentious tactics. A good example of this is the participation of agrarian movements and NGOs in agrarian law reform at both national and local levels (Lucas and Warren 2003). A key politico-legal victory was achieved in 2001 when SPP mobilized thousands of West Javanese peasants to stage a demonstration in favor of the Parliamentary Decree No. IX/2001, which as noted earlier strengthened the mandate of the 1960 Basic Agrarian Law (Afiff et al. 2005, 4–5).[14] In recent years, some activists have also taken up key positions in the state bureaucracy, such as in the Presidential Staff Office (Kantor Staf Presiden, KSP) and the National Human Rights Commission (Komisi Nasional untuk Perlindungan Hak Asasi Manusia, Komnas HAM). Yet, while the inclusion and participation of activists in key policy areas and political processes might suggest the deepening of proreform agendas right at the heart of the center of power (Mietzner 2013), in the case of the land rights movement, their influence remains limited in terms of agenda setting, with no major agrarian policy changes occurring since these movement actors joined the bureaucracy. While one can argue that legal reforms recognizing indigenous communities' ownership of customary land and promoting social forestry schemes represent some positive changes or even reforms, these policies have not addressed the inequality in landholding and ownership, the continuing dominance of big capital and local vested interests in land politics, or the contraction of democratic space for land rights advocacy for activists and the rural dispossessed.[15]

In addition to advocacy and lobbying, some peasant unions decided to expand their repertoire by participating in electoral politics. STaB pursued different electoral strategies, from supporting district head candidates with close connections to civil society to fielding its own candidates to participate in the local and national parliamentary elections (Bachriadi 2011). It also endeavored to build a new, social movement–based political party called the People's Confederation Party (Partai Perserikatan Rakyat, PPR) (Bachriadi 2011, 338). In addition, SPP experimented with participation in formal political channels at a smaller scale, lobbying local government officials and politicians at the district level and contesting in elections for the Village Representative Council (Badan Perwakilan Desa, BPD) seats in Garut (Afiff et al. 2005, 16–18). FPPB also chose to participate in village electoral politics, fielding cadres for village head elections in several villages in Batang District (Safitri 2010). AMAN, too, has repeatedly fielded cadres to contest for seats in local parliaments and the national senate as well as candidates for district heads, with modest success (Barahamin 2017; Gumanti 2016). This electoral strategy is not exclusive to the land rights movement. Labor, for instance, has also intervened in the electoral arena in various ways, including in collaboration with the peasant movement, as demonstrated by the experiment in the 2013 Deli Serdang District Head elections (Caraway and Ford, this volume).

The attempt to engage in formal politics and policymaking processes should, however, be viewed with some caution. First, the inclusion of agrarian movements, NGOs, and leading scholar-activists does not necessarily guarantee pro–land rights policies. If anything, as the history of several lower-class movements suggests (Piven and Cloward 1979), it is the daily expression of contentious politics that gives the rural poor leverage to make their case, negotiate with authorities, and get their demands implemented at the local level. Second, while electoral participation allows movement cadres to hone their political skills—and in some cases gain seats in parliament or other political offices—engagement in electoral politics has the potential to exhaust the energy of the movement too quickly, or worse, result in political adventurism. For example, some STaB cadres in North Bengkulu ran in local parliamentary elections on the party ticket of the People's Conscience Party (Partai Hati Nurani Rakyat, Hanura), a party of old elites and oligarchs led by Wiranto, a former New Order general with a reputation as a human rights violator (Interviews with peasants and activists affiliated with STaB, April 2017).[16]

The choice to participate in elections with a such a party is unlikely to help the movement to achieve its goals, let alone support broader prodemocratic agendas.

ECONOMIC STRATEGIES

As a part of the effort to realize its economic vision, the land rights movement has also expanded its strategies into the economic realm. The question that many peasant unions grapple with is what happens after land is reclaimed. Typically, problems include the distribution of reclaimed land, its recommodification or monetization, and maintenance of agricultural productivity. Peasant unions usually attempt to institute a solidarity economy model to avoid conflict between the needs of the community and individual peasant households after land reclamation. Technically this means not only distributing reclaimed land to individual households but also establishing a communal land for common agricultural production through which agricultural surplus can be generated and distributed collectively (Interviews with AGRA organizers, August 2016 and peasants and activists affiliated with STaB, April 2017).

A number of peasant unions have pursued different ways to establish a solidarity economy. One often-cited example is SPI's attempt to grow coffee on reclaimed land in Kepahiang in the province of Bengkulu (Sipayung 2016; SPI 2016). SPI members in the districts of Kepahiang and Rejang Lebong have been able to organize coffee production through a cooperative formed by SPI. Unlike typical cooperatives, which are structured as consumer cooperatives, this cooperative aims to organize production activities democratically. For some time, SPI has been able to maintain this attempt of democratic production and aims to increase its coffee production level and find a market to sell its coffee products (Personal observation of SPI discussions, April 2016). SPI has also been experimenting with organic farming as an economic strategy to improve peasant livelihood and political consciousness (Edwards 2013). While engaging with the market, it seeks to promote more sustainable farming practices based on family farmers as a strategy to counter neoliberalism. Another organization that promotes an organic farming strategy is the Salassae Rural Self-Governing Community (Komunitas Swabina Pedesaan Salassae, KSPS) in Bulukumba, which seeks not only to improve the quality of agricultural outputs and peasant livelihoods, but also to challenge the domination of big capital (Chandra 2014; 2016). Through organic farming, it is hoped that peasants will have the ability to control production by themselves, gradually lessening their dependence on big fertilizer corporations, and eventually develop their political consciousness (Interview with a KSPS/FPSS organizer, June 2016).

In addition to various attempts to engender democratic production, the land rights movement has attempted to establish a number of peasant cooperatives and credit unions. Such cooperatives, described as peasant-run collective enterprises (Badan Usaha Buruh Tani, BUBT) by the late Professor Sajogyo, an eminent rural sociologist, have been discussed by agrarian scholars and activists since late 1970s. Their basic aim is to involve landless and near-landless peasants in farming activities on land purchased, owned, and collectivized by the state through a democratic farming enterprise controlled and organized by the peasants themselves (Shohibuddin 2016). Credit unions have also gained popularity as an alternative financial institution to support farming activities and eventually a rural-based solidarity economy (Fernando et al. 2015). This is by no means an easy task. In the case of SPI's experiment in Kepahiang, for example, its coffee cooperatives have struggled to maintain their operations and accountability, causing members to withdraw (Interview with activists in Bengkulu, May 2017). In general, efforts to promote a solidarity economy have faced difficulties in maintaining and scaling up their operation. In a way, this is understandable as it was not until 2010 that the building of solidarity economy became a key strategy of the movement (Interview with a KPRI organizer, July 2017). Nonetheless, these alternative economic ideas at the very least add to the growing corpus of strategies of the contemporary land rights movement.

CONCLUSION

Standard structuralist arguments emphasize how democratization opens up what Tarrow (1994) calls political opportunity structures. No less important, however, is the impact of social movements on democracy. Social movements are widely understood to contribute to the deepening of democracy (Fung and Wright 2001; Gaventa 2006). But how exactly and in what ways a particular movement contributes to democratic deepening may differ across contexts. The Indonesian case illuminates the contribution of agrarian movements to democratization. It also confirms that the "peasant question" (Moore 1966)—that is, the question of how the modern state should treat its peasant population—remains relevant in the context of electoral democracy.

In light of this elaboration, how would we assess the role of the land rights movement in the process of democratization? During the New Order, the movement exerted limited, but nevertheless significant, pressure on the regime by challenging the limits imposed on dissent and on alternative political ideas and oppositional formations under authoritarianism. After the fall of Suharto, the movement has grappled with new political openings, which present opportunities and challenges. There is more room for marginalized rural populations to mobilize and influence agrarian discourses. Yet while some concessions have been made, the movement is still unable to mount a unified resistance against the state and the market, suffering as it does from the legacies of the New Order and the impact of patronage politics on the social movement landscape in postauthoritarian Indonesia. As a consequence, the movement cannot yet pose an effective challenge to the elites and its influence remains limited and at times token, confined to the agenda-setting stage of the elite-controlled political processes.

If we take agrarian reform—or land redistribution at the minimum—as a benchmark for land rights policy, we must conclude that no comprehensive agrarian reform agenda has been implemented at the national level. At the same time, the expansion of the movement's modes of activism and strategies, especially in the political and economic domains, has opened up opportunities for the advancement of the land rights struggle. Through these efforts, the movement has shaped discourses on agrarian politics. Its most important achievement has probably been to put agrarian reform back on the policy table. Its mobilizational strategies have also revitalized populist discourses regarding peasant livelihood. In terms of securing democratic transition and consolidation, it has been able to challenge what political scientists describe as local authoritarian enclaves (Gibson 2012; Sidel 2014). The movement has also challenged the discourse of Indonesian democracy by highlighting the rights and participation of marginalized rural populations beyond the liberal emphasis on civil and political liberties. At the very least, by keeping its repertoire of struggle alive, the movement has managed to insert rural concerns and social justice into debates about Indonesian democracy. In this way, it has contributed to the process of democratizing class relations by bringing concerns about agrarian and ecological justice, rural socioeconomic inequality, and the political rights of rural citizens to the table in an electoral democracy characterized by deep socioeconomic inequality.

NOTES

1. This chapter is a part of my dissertation project on the politics of elite-peasant relations in postauthoritarian Indonesia. Research for this chapter was made possible due to generous funding from the Transparency for Development Predoctoral Fellowship, the NIU Political Science Department Russell Smith Memorial Scholarship, the University of Sydney's Southeast Asia Centre Visiting Ph.D. Scholar Fund, and ENITAS Scholarship from the Institute of Thai Studies at Chulalongkorn University. I would like to thank the participants in the 2017 Activists in Transition Workshop and Sirojuddin Arif for their comments and suggestions on this chapter. All errors remain my own.
2. For an excellent discussion on this issue see Bertrand 1995.
3. Transmigration (*transmigrasi*) is essentially a population resettlement and redistribution program. Although this policy was initially implemented under the Dutch colonial administration, it was during the New Order period that transmigration was intensively promoted. The basic logic of transmigration is to resettle rural villagers from the heavily populated island of Java to the less-populated outer islands. This program continues. Although government and military officials who implemented this policy described it as a form of "land reform," it is best seen as one of the ways through which the New Order regime addressed the issue of rural poverty *without* disrupting the structure of rural landholding. On the dynamics of the New Order transmigration policy, see Hoshour 1997.
4. Of course, liberalization was selective. Some social forces and their aspirations—several elements of political Islam for instance (Liddle 1996)—were accommodated by the regime while others were ignored or repressed.
5. In my observation this pattern, that is, the use of case-by-case advocacy as a starting point to consolidate and form local peasant movements still continues.
6. During this period, the occasional deployment of anticommunist rhetoric and attacks by state security and paramilitary forces also hindered further development of the movement, especially when used against local peasant groups, which intensified their direct actions such as land occupations in mid-1990s, though KPA enjoyed a relative freedom in relation to advocacy.
7. In this context, liberalization can be defined as limited relaxation of the authoritarian regime's political grip and promotion of political pluralism within its framework (O'Donnell and Schmiter 1986). Democratization necessarily goes further.
8. Bear in mind that inequality in agrarian structure in Indonesia takes a very different form today. While the army used to be the primary land controller in the past, over time big state and private corporations and local village and community leaders play a more significant role as land controllers and owners.
9. This category includes wet rice fields (*sawah*), dry field (*tegal*), garden (*kebun*), land for shifting cultivation (*ladang*), and temporarily unused land (*lahan sementara tidak digunakan*).
10. For example, in the two peasant unions that I observed quite closely during fieldwork, AGRA Bulukumba and STaB, local peasant leaders actively participate in organizing their communities and occupy leadership positions in the unions. The increasing leadership role of local peasants in land rights advocacy is also visible in other local peasant unions and communities.
11. Thanks to Hanny Wijaya for this observation.
12. Internationally, SPI is affiliated with La Vía Campesina and AGRA is affiliated with the Asian Peasant Coalition (APC), which is a federation under the International League of People's Struggle (ILPS).
13. I witnessed this on several occasions during my field visits.

14. The decree has been a strategic tool for SPP, which uses it to justify its land occupations and increase its bargaining power vis-à-vis central and regional land management agencies. However, several peasant unions such as FSPI and AGRA criticized the decree and the decision to support it, seeing it as a Trojan horse for neoliberal policies.
15. On the ground, the legal reforms to protect adat forests and promote community participation in social forestry still faces various political, social, and administrative problems, from competing views regarding forest ownership and management to the lack of reliable records on community land (Sari 2018; Widodo 2018).
16. During fieldwork I also learned that this political maneuvering—joining a mainstream party—also happened with WALHI activists in other places.

REFERENCES

Acemoglu, Darren, and James A. Robinson. 2000. "Democratization or Repression." *European Economic Review* 44 (4): 683–93.

Adas, Michael. 1981. "From Avoidance to Confrontation: Peasant Protest in Precolonial and Colonial Southeast Asia." *Comparative Studies in Society and History* 23 (2): 217–47.

Afiff, Suraya. 2004. "Land Reform or Customary Rights? Contemporary Agrarian Struggles in South Tapanuli, Indonesia." Ph.D. diss., University of California, Berkeley.

Afiff, Suraya, Noer Fauzi Rachman, Gillian Hart, Lungisile Ntsebeza, and Nancy Peluso. 2005. "Redefining Agrarian Power: Resurgent Agrarian Movements in West Java, Indonesia." UC Berkeley Center for Southeast Asian Studies Working Paper, i–37.

Antlov, Hans. 1995. *Exemplary Centre, Administrative Periphery: Rural Leadership and the New Order on Java.* Surrey, UK: Curzon.

Anugrah, Iqra. 2016. "Cementing Dissent in Indonesia." *New Mandala.* May 2. http://www.newmandala.org/cementing-dissent-in-indonesia/.

Aspinall, Edward. 2005. *Opposing Suharto: Compromise, Resistance, and Regime Change in Indonesia.* Stanford: Stanford University Press.

Bachriadi, Dianto. 2011. "Between Discourse and Action: Agrarian Reform and Rural Social Movements in Indonesia Post-1965." Ph.D. diss., Flinders University.

———. 2012. "Fighting for Land." *Inside Indonesia.* https://www.insideindonesia.org/fighting-for-land.

Bachriadi, Dianto, Anton Lucas, and Carol Warren. 2013. "The Agrarian Movement, Civil Society, and Emerging Political Constellations." In *Land for the People: The State and Agrarian Conflict in Indonesia,* edited by Anton Lucas and Carol Warren, 308–71. Athens: Ohio University Press.

Bachriadi, Dianto, and Gunawan Wiradi. 2011. *Enam Dekade Ketimpangan: Masalah Penguasaan Lahan di Indonesia.* Bandung: Agrarian Resource Centre (ARC), Bina Desa, Konsorsium Pembaruan Agraria (KPA).

Badan Pusat Statistik. 2015. *Jumlah Perusahaan Perkebunan Besar Menurut Jenis Tanaman, 2000–2014.* September 3. https://www.bps.go.id/linkTabelStatis/view/id/1668.

Barahamin, Andre. 2017. "Berselancar di Parlemen." *Kumparan.* March 16. https://kumparan.com/andre-barahamin/berselancar-di-parlemen.

Batubara, Bosman, and Anna Mariana, eds. 2015. *Seni dan Sastra untuk Kedaulatan Petani Urut Sewu: Etnografi Wilayah Konflik Agraria di Kebumen.* Yogyakarta: Literasi Press.

Benda, Harry J., and Ruth T. McVey, eds. 1960. *The Communist Uprisings of 1926–1927 in Indonesia: Key Documents.* Ithaca: Cornell University Press.

Bertrand, Jacques. 1995. "Compliance, Resistance, and Trust: Peasants and the State in Indonesia." Ph.D. diss., Princeton University.

Bourchier, David. 2007. The Romance of Adat in the Indonesian Political Imagination and the Current Revival. In *The Revival of Tradition in Indonesian Politics: The Deployment of Adat from Colonialism to Indigenism,* edited by J. S. Davidson and D. Henley, 113–29. London: Routledge.

Carroll, Toby. 2010. *Delusions of Development: The World Bank and the Post-Washington Consensus in Southeast Asia.* London: Palgrave.

Chandra, Wahyu. 2014. "Belajar dari Kampung Organik di Desa Salassae." *Mongabay.* April 17. http://www.mongabay.co.id/2014/04/17/belajar-dari-kampung-organik-di-desa-salassae/.

——. 2016. "Kisah Sukses Para Petani Salassae Tebar 'Virus' Organik." *Mongabay.* August 30. http://www.mongabay.co.id/2016/08/30/kisah-sukses-para-petani-salassae-tebar-virus-organik/.

Collins, Elizabeth Fuller. 2007. *Indonesia Betrayed: How Development Fails.* Honolulu: University of Hawaii Press.

Dove, Michael R. 2006. "Indigenous People and Environmental Politics." *Annual Review of Anthropology* 35: 191–208.

Edwards, Nicola. 2013. "Values and the Institutionalization of Indonesia's Organic Agriculture Movement." In *Social Activism in Southeast Asia,* edited by Michele Ford, 72–88. London: Routledge.

Enríquez, Laura. 2013. "The Paradoxes of Latin America's 'Pink Tide': Venezuela and the Project of Agrarian Reform." *Journal of Peasant Studies* 40 (4): 611–38.

Fernando, Aditya, Hanny Wijaya, Hizkia Yosie Polimpung, and Myta Yesica. 2015. "John Bamba: CU Gerakan Adalah Alternatif terbaik Saat Ini Buat Gerakan Civil Society di Indonesia." *IndoProgress.* October 7. http://indoprogress. com/2015/10/john-bamba-cu-gerakan-adalah-alternatif-terbaik-saat-ini-buat-gerakan-civil-society-di-indonesia/.

Fontana, Lorenza Belinda. 2014. "Indigenous Peoples vs. Peasant Unions: Land Conflicts and Rural Movements in Plurinational Bolivia." *Journal of Peasant Studies* 41 (3): 297–319.

Ford, Michele. 2009. *Workers and Intellectuals: NGOs, Trade Unions, and the Indonesian Labour Movement.* Honolulu: University of Hawai'i Press.

Fox, Jonathon A. 1990. "Editor's Introduction-The Challenge of Rural Democratization: Perspectives From Latin America and the Philippines." *Journal of Development Studies* 26 (4): 1–18.

Fung, Archon, and Erik Olin Wright. 2001. "Deepening Democracy: Innovations in Empowered Participatory Governance." *Politics and Society* 29 (1): 5–41.

Gaol, Amy Lumban. 2016. "Lika-liku Jalan Penetapan Perda Masyarakat Adat Kajang." *World Agroforestry Centre.* February 26. http://www.worldagroforestry. org/news/lika-liku-jalan-penetapan-perda-masyarakat-adat-kajang.

Gaventa, John. 2006. "Triumph, Deficit or Contestation? Deepening the 'Deepening Democracy' Debate." IDS Working Paper 264. Brighton: Institute of Development Studies.

Gibson, Edward. 2012. *Boundary Control: Subnational Authoritarianism in Federal Democracies*. New York: Cambridge University Press.

Gibson, Thomas. 2000. "Islam and the Spirit Cults in New Order Indonesia: Global Flows vs. Local Knowledge." *Indonesia* 69 (April): 41–70.

Gueta, Rhoda, and Kathryn Manga. 2013. *Rising of the Landless: Landgrabbing in Bulukumba, South Sulawesi, Indonesia—The Case of PT Lonsum and the Indigenous People's Struggle to Reclaim their Land*. Quezon City: Asian Peasant Coalition.

Gumanti, Datu Usman. 2016. "Deklarasi Pencalonan Menuju Pilkada Tebo 2017: Datu Usman Gumanti, Calon Bupati Tebo dari Jalur Independen." In *Tegaknya Marwah Sumatera Kami: Sekarang Saatnya Politisi Berpikir Waras*, edited by Arief Wicaksono, Ambrosiuis Ruwindrijarto, Khalid Saifullah, Christian Bob Purba, and Laksono Adi Widodo, 15–56. Bogor: Samdhana Institute.

Hadiz, Vedi. 2010. *Localising Power in Post-Authoritarian Indonesia: A Southeast Asia Perspective*. Stanford: Stanford University Press.

Halim, Abdul. 2014. *Bukan Bangsa Kuli*. Jakarta: KIARA.

Hasan. 2016. "RRI: Persatuan Rakyat Bangun Partai Politik." *Suara Indonesia*. June 11. http://suaraindonesia-news.com/rri-persatuan-rakyat-bangun-partai-politik/.

Henley, David, and Jamie S. Davidson. 2007. "Introduction: Radical Conservatism— the Protean Politics of Adat." In *The Revival of Tradition in Indonesian Politics: The Deployment of Adat from Colonialism to Indigenism*, edited by Jamie S. Davidson and David Henley, 1–49. London: Routledge.

Hoshour, Cathy A. 1997. "Resettlement and the Politicization of Ethnicity in Indonesia." *Bijdragen tot de Taal-, Land- en Volkenkunde*, 153 (4): 557–76.

Ikhwan, Mohammed. 2007. *Ini Tanah Kami! Perjuangan Reforma Agraria di Bukit Kijang, Asahan, Sumatera Utara*. Jakarta: Federasi Serikat Petani Indonesia.

Ito, Takeshi, Noer Fauzi Rachman, and Laksmi A. Savitri. 2014. "Power to Make Land Dispossession Acceptable: A Policy Discourse Analysis of the Merauke Integrated Food and Energy Estate, Papua, Indonesia." *Journal of Peasant Studies* 41 (1): 29–50.

Johansyah, Merah. 2017. "Mewaspadai Ijon Politik Pertambangan dan SDA di Pilkada Serentak 2017." Public Presentation, Jaringan Advokasi Tambang (JATAM), Jakarta.

Kartodirdjo, Sartono. 1973. *Protest Movement in Rural Java: A Study of Agrarian Unrest in the Nineteenth and Early Twentieth Centuries*. Singapore: Oxford University Press.

KPA (Konsorsium Pembaruan Agraria). 2014. *Catatan Akhir Taun 2014: Membenahi Masalah Agraria—Prioritas Kerja Jokowi-JK Pada 2015*. Jakarta: Sekretariat Nasional Konsorsium Pembaruan Agraria.

Lara, Francisco, and Horacio. R. Morales. 1990."The Peasant Movement and the Challenge of Rural Democratisation in the Philippines." *Journal of Development Studies* 26 (4): 143–62.

Li, Tania Murray. 2007a. "Adat in Central Sulawesi: Contemporary Deployments." In *The Revival of Tradition in Indonesian Politics: The Deployment of Adat from Colonialism to Indigenism,* edited by Jamie S. Davidson and David Henley, 337–70. London: Routledge.

———. 2007b. *The Will to Improve: Governmentality, Development, and the Practice of Politics.* Durham, NC: Duke University Press.

Liddle, R. William. 1996. "The Islamic Turn in Indonesia: A Political Explanation." *Journal of Asian Studies* 55 (3): 613–34.

Lucas, Anton. 1989. *Peristiwa Tiga Daerah: Revolusi dalam Revolusi.* Jakarta: PT Pustaka Utama Grafiti.

———. 1992. "Land Disputes in Indonesia: Some Current Perspectives." *Indonesia* 53: 79–92.

Lucas, Anton, and Carrol Warren. 2003. "The State, The People, and Their Mediators: The Struggle over Agrarian Law Reform in Post-New Order Indonesia." *Indonesia* 76: 87–126.

———. 2013. "The Land, the Law, and the People." In *Land for the People: The State and Agrarian Conflict in Indonesia,* edited by Anton Lucas and Carrol Warren, 1–39. Athens: Ohio University Press.

Mietzner, Marcus. 2013. "Fighting the Hellhounds: Pro-Democracy Activists and Party Politics in Post-Suharto Indonesia." *Journal of Contemporary Asia* 43 (1): 28–50.

Moore, Barrington. 1966. *Social Origins of Dictatorship and Democracy: Lord and Peasant in the Making of the Modern World.* Boston: Beacon Press.

Muhtada, Dani. 2008. "Membela Petani: Refleksi atas Gerakan Mitra Tani Yogyakarta." *Quantum: Media Warta Dinamika BBPPKS Padang* 5 (10): 50–55.

O'Brien, Kevin J. 1996. "Rightful Resistance." *World Politics* 49 (1): 31–55.

O'Donnell, Guillermo, and Philippe C. Schmiter. 1986. *Transitions from Authoritarian Rule: Tentative Conclusions about Uncertain Democracies.* Baltimore: Johns Hopkins University Press.

Ompusunggu, Moses. 2016. "Jokowi's Agrarian Reform Agenda Stalls." *Jakarta Post.* October 24. http://www.thejakartapost.com/news/2016/10/24/jokowi-s-agrarian-reform-agenda-stalls.html.

Peluso, Nancy, Suraya Afiff, and Noer Fauzi Rachman. 2008. "Claiming the Grounds for Reform: Agrarian and Environmental Movements in Indonesia." *Journal of Agrarian Change* 8 (2–3): 377–407.

Phatharathananunth, Somchai. 2006. *Civil Society and Democratization: Social Movements in Northeast Thailand.* Copenhagen: NIAS Press.

Pincus, Jonathon. 1996. *Class Power and Agrarian Change: Land and Labour in Rural West Java.* New York: St. Martin's Press.

Piven, Frances Fox, and Richard A. Cloward. 1979. *Poor People's Movements: Why They Succeed, How They Fail.* New York: Vintage House.

Purnama, Feri. 2016. "Badega Mensyukuri Kemenangan Agraria." *ANTARA News Jawa Barat,* May 16. http://www.antarajabar.com/berita/58048/badega-mens yukuri-kemenangan-agraria.

Pusat Data dan Sistem Informasi Pertanian. 2015. *Statistik Lahan Pertanian Tahun 2010–2014.* Jakarta: Kementerian Pertanian.

Rachman, Noer Fauzi. 1999. *Petani dan Penguasa: Dinamika Perjalanan Politik Agraria Indonesia.* Yogyakarta: INSIST, KPA, and Pustaka Pelajar.

——. 2003. *Bersaksi untuk Pembaruan Agraria: Dari Tuntutan Lokal Hingga Kecenderungan Global.* Yogyakarta: Insist, KPA, and KARSA.

——. 2009. "Land Titles Do Not Equal Agrarian Reform." *Inside Indonesia.* October 18. https://www.insideindonesia.org/land-titles-do-not-equal-agrarian-reform.

——. 2011. "The Resurgence of Land Reform Policy and Agrarian Movements in Indonesia." Ph.D. diss., University of California, Berkeley.

——. 2014. "Masyarakat Hukum Adat Adalah Bukan Penyandang Hak, Bukan Subjek Hukum, dan Bukan Pemilik Wilayah Adatnya." *Wacana* 33 (16): 25–48.

Robison, Richard, and Vedi Hadiz. 2004. *Reorganising Power in Indonesia: The Politics of Oligarchy in An Age of Markets.* London: RoutledgeCurzon.

Rueschemeyer, Dietrich, Evelyn Huber Stephens, and John D. Stephens. 1992. *Capitalist Development and Democracy.* Chicago: University of Chicago Press.

Safitri, Hilma. 2010. *Gerakan Politik Forum Paguyuban Petani Kabupaten Batang (FPPB).* Bandung: Akatiga.

Samson, Allan A. 1974. "Indonesia 1973: A Climate of Concern." *Asian Survey* 14 (2): 157–65.

Sandbrook, Richard, Marc Edelman, Patrick Heller, and Judith Teichman. 2007. *Social Democracy in the Global Periphery.* New York: Cambridge University Press.

Sangaji, Arianto. 2007. "The Masyarakat Adat Movement in Indonesia: A Critical Insider's View." In *The Revival of Tradition in Indonesian Politics: The Deployment of Adat from Colonialism to Indigenism,* edited by Jamie S. Davidson and David Henley, 319–36. London: Routledge.

Sari, Sri Mas. 2018. "KLHK: Perhutanan Sosial Terkendala Kapasitas Masyarakat." March 11. http://industri.bisnis.com/read/20180311/99/748388/klhk-perhutanan-sosial-terkendala-kapasitas-masyarakat.

Savitri, Laksmi Adriani. 2014. "Rentang Batas dari Rekognisi Hutan Adat dalam Kepengaturan Neoliberal." *Wacana* 33 (16): 61–98.

Scott, James, and Ben Kerkvliet. 1973. "The Politics of Survival: Peasant Response to 'Progress' in Southeast Asia." *Journal of Southeast Asian Studies* 4 (2): 241–68.

SPI (Serikat Petani Indonesia). 2016. "Potong Distribusi, Petani Kopi SPI Bengkulu Pasarkan Langsung ke Konsumen." May 30. https://www.spi.or.id/8807-2/.

Shohibuddin, Mohamad. 2016. "Hadirkan Reforma Agraria yang Sejati dalam RUU Pertanahan: Urgensi Perluasan Kerangka Konseptual dan Operasional." *Epistema Institute Policy Brief* 4: 1–8.

Sidel, John Thayer. 2014. "Economic Foundations of Subnational Authoritarianism: Insights and Evidence from Qualitative and Quantitative Research." *Democratization* 21 (1): 161–84.

Sipayung, Helti Marini. 2016. "SPI Tingkatkan Kapasitas Petani Kopi Bengkulu." *ANTARA Bengkulu.* May 26. http://www.antarabengkulu.com/berita/37673/spi-tingkatkan-kapasitas-petani-kopi-bengkulu.

Situmorang, Abdul Wahid. 2003. "Contentious Politics in Toba Samosir: The Toba Batak Movement Opposing the PT. Inti Indorayon Utama Pul and Rayon Mill in Sosor Ladang-Indonesia (1988 to 2003)." M.A. Thesis, Ohio University.

Slater, Dan. 2010. *Ordering Power: Contentious Politics and Authoritarian Leviathans in Southeast Asia.* New York: Cambridge University Press.

Tarrow, Sidney. 1994. *Power in Movement: Social Movements and Contentious Politics.* New York: Cambridge University Press.

Teorell, Jan. 2010. *Determinants of Democratization: Explaining Regime Change in the World, 1972–2006.* New York: Cambridge University Press.

Thorburn, Craig C. 2003. "The Plot Thickens: Decentralisation and Land Administration in Indonesia." *Asia Pacific Viewpoint* 45: 33–49.

Tjondronegoro, Sediono. M. 2009. "A Brief Quarter Century Overview of Indonesia's Agrarian Policies." In *Land and Household Economy 1970–2005: Changing Road for Poverty,* edited by I. Wayan Rusastra, Sahat M. Pasaribu, and Yusmichad Yusdja, 21–35. Jakarta: Indonesian Center for Agriculture Socio Economic and Policy Studies (ICASEPS).

Trevizo, Dolores. 2011. *Rural Protest and the Making of Democracy in Mexico, 1968–2000.* University Park: Pennsylvania State University Press.

Tyson, Adam. 2010. *Decentralization and Adat Revivalism in Indonesia: The Politics of Becoming Indigenous.* Abingdon: Routledge.

Urano, Mariko. 2010. *The Limits of Tradition: Peasants and Land Conflicts in Indonesia.* Melbourne: Trans Pacific Press/Kyoto University Press.

Wahyudi. 2005. *Formasi dan Struktur Gerakan Sosial Petani: Studi Kasus Reklaiming/ Penjarahan atas Tanah PTPN XII (persero) Kalibakar Malang Selatan.* Malang: Penerbitan Universitas Muhammadiyah Malang.

Walker, Kathy Le Mons. 2006. "'Gangster Capitalism' and Peasant Protest in China: The Last Twenty Years." *Journal of Peasant Studies* 33 (1): 1–33.

White, Ben. 2016. "Remembering the Indonesian Peasants' Front and Plantation Workers' Union (1945–1966)." *Journal of Peasant Studies* 43 (1): 1–16.

Wickham, Trevor. 1987. "WALHI: The Indonesian Environmental Forum." *Environment: Science and Policy for Sustainable Development* 29 (7): 2–4.

Widodo, Kasmita. 2018. "Opini: Menagih Janji Perlindungan Hutan Adat." *Mongabay.* June 25. http://www.mongabay.co.id/2018/06/25/opini-menagih-janji-perlindungan-hutan-adat/.

Williams, Michael C. 1990. *Communism, Religion, and Revolt in Banten.* Athens: Ohio University Center for International Studies.

Wolf, Eric Robert. 1966. *Peasants.* Englewood Cliffs, NJ: Prentice-Hall.

World Bank. 2016. *Indonesia Economic Quarterly: Resilience through Reforms.* Jakarta: World Bank.

Wright, Angus, and Wendy Wolford. 2003. *To Inherit the Earth: The Landless Movement and the Struggle for a New Brazil.* Oakland, CA: Food First Books.

Yulius, Hendri. 2016. "The Kartinis of Kendeng: Using Motherhood as a Form of Resistance." *Indonesia at Melbourne.* April 20. http://indonesiaatmelbourne. unimelb.edu.au/kartini-of-kendeng-using-motherhood-as-a-form-of-resistance/.

CHAPTER FIVE

URBAN POOR ACTIVISM AND POLITICAL AGENCY IN POST–NEW ORDER JAKARTA

Ian Wilson

The poor have historically been at the forefront of struggles for democracy and regime change, though have not necessarily been its primary beneficiaries (Holzner 2010). The intertwining of democratization with neoliberal reforms has, in many cases, undermined the capacity and opportunities of the urban poor to mobilize and participate politically compared to other socioeconomic classes or served to reframe their participation and agency in ways that do not disrupt broader power relations, including those constitutive of poverty (Soss et al. 2011; Leal 2007). Social movement theory has often struggled to adequately conceptualize the political agency of the poor. As Das and Randiera (2015) note, a frequent assumption is that a fundamental divide exists between moments of "extra-ordinary" action, mobilization, and intensity, such as demonstrations, riots, or elections, and the everyday, which is identified with political passivity. For the urban poor, the everyday is defined by ongoing struggles to secure housing, sources of income, and access to essentials such as healthcare and clean water. Rather than being outside of politics or political action the everyday is, by nature of the poor's precarious position, the primary sphere of their political engagement and action.

Postauthoritarian Indonesia has seen increases in levels of urban poverty and income inequality, but also opportunities for the poor and their allies to organize and act politically in new ways.[1] Yet Indonesia has not experienced the emergence of coherent or broad-based social or political movements of the urban poor such as have occurred elsewhere (Hutchison 2007; Mainwaring 1987). Focusing on the Jakarta metropolitan area, home to one-fifth of Indonesia's urban population, this chapter posits that urban poor activism and political agency has, and continues to be, shaped and constrained by the specific conditions of urban life and the precarious circumstances and social relationships constitutive of poverty in contemporary Indonesia. I argue that urban poor agency and activism in Indonesia, both during and after the New Order, has manifested on two main fronts. The first is in the politics of the everyday. Poor people operate politically in everyday life on multiple levels, which requires managing complex relationships and arrangements, including those with the powerful, in order to hedge risk and encroach on spaces and opportunities formally denied them or otherwise made structurally inaccessible. The second is in what I refer to as defensive forms of action, which involves defending gains and responding individually or collectively to immediate threats to livelihoods, assets, and security. Such approaches can be confrontational, in the case of physical resistance to eviction, but still occur within, rather than fundamentally disrupting existing power relations. While defensive action is often collective, it rarely however leads to collective forms of organization. Bayat (2013) has articulated the concept of "social non-movements" to capture this "collective action of dispersed and unorganized actors" such as the poor who engage in claim making through direct action, rather than through pressuring the state for concessions.

The New Order severely curtailed possibilities for oppositional forms of political organization; however, a number of pro-poor organizations emerged toward the end of its reign.[2] These organizations approached the "problem" of urban poverty and the parameters of the political struggle of the urban poor in distinctly different ways, ranging from grassroots community organizing, legal rights advocacy, and continuations of leftist politics of the anti-Suharto student movement. The advent of decentralized electoral politics and regional autonomy that have become a hallmark of the post–New Order political landscape have presented new opportunities but also obstacles for the urban poor and their advocates. Electoral populism has resulted in some redistributive concessions targeting poor voters. Particularly in parts of the country identified as having high levels of poverty, "poor-oriented" policies and campaign promises, such as forms of government subsidized health care, education, and housing, are now standard. This has been, arguably, the main contribution of urban poor activism to Indonesia's postauthoritarian trajectory: the emergence of "the poor" as a recognized voting constituency and category of citizen requiring assistance.[3] More substantive kinds of reform or representation, however, have been ignored or co-opted, with the urban poor's engagement still deeply intertwined with patronage and brokerage politics and paradigms (Wilson 2016). With political parties having little social base among the urban poor, electoral politics has focused on the identification of "pro-poor" champions within political elites, with decidedly mixed results.

The New Order's War against the Poor

From the beginnings of the New Order, the urban poor in Jakarta presented a particular "problem" and source of unease for the regime. This problem was not, however, one of how to eliminate poverty but rather of managing populations considered to be a potential source of political instability and disorder. The regime considered the poor and the unplanned informal spaces, or *kampung*, in which many lived, as an unsightly impediment to the realization of its modernizing and developmentalist rhetoric, with the poor themselves lacking in so-called "urban rationality," as well as presenting a potential source and breeding-ground of crime and social and political unrest (Kusno 2004). The street is a specific social space with its own kind of politics, forms of organization, conviviality, and networks. During the Sukarno era, the streets were a locus for popular mobilization (Kusno 2010). The potential for informal kampung to be a generative site for social and political dissent, disturbance, and violence loomed large in the paranoid imagination of the New Order regime.

Government authorities dealt with the poor and the spaces they occupied in ways that significantly constrained their political agency. For example, the New Order regime introduced a vast neighborhood surveillance structure known as the "neighborhood security system" (*sistem keamanan lingkungan*, siskamling). Based on the military's territorial command structure, siskamling established networks of local security posts manned by a combination of local residents and registered security guards under the direction of the police. This surveillance system was combined with ongoing, though largely futile, efforts by the city's administration to "close" Jakarta to a constant stream of migrants from other parts of the country and to register its inhabitants, which nonetheless excluded certain categories of the poor from formal systems of governance (Kusno 2010). The heterogeneous, informal, and unregulated types of labor and livelihood on which many of the poor relied, such as driving pedicabs (*becak*), food vending, and street trading were subjected to criminalization and other forms of control by the state (Murray 1991). The 1988 Public Order law, for example, prohibited non–state sanctioned economic activity, deeming it illegal to sell goods or conduct business in streets, parks, or other public places except in areas designated by the governor, and became the primary legal instrument by which to "manage" informality. In practice these regulations were sporadically and patchily enforced, or deployed instrumentally to clear space for state or corporate developments.

Various forms of informal street work may have conflicted with the state's notion of a modern urban aesthetic and order, but it also relieved pressure on it for welfare and redistributive provisions and failures to generate employment, mitigating the potential transformation of economic hardship into political disturbance. The reality was that informal labor was the primary source of income for more than half of Jakarta's population (Blunch, Canagarajah, and Raju 2001). This disjuncture between a formal legalist and bureaucratic order and an informal reality resulted in complex parallel forms of governance, rent seeking, and patron clientelism involving the police, military, local officials, various local strongmen, traders, and businessmen through and with whom the poor were required to negotiate, if not placate. This often occurred at great peril and expense, in the form of merciless exploitation, violence, and insecurity, but also offered opportunities to find and consolidate a place in the face of formal and legal nonrecognition.[4] Authorities would periodically raid spaces occupied by the poor, disrupting any claims to permanency. Complex political economies would often emerge, involving regular or episodic payments by the poor to officials, the military, or gangsters in exchange for advanced warnings of impending raids, or the possibility of protection or exemption.

Similar patterns of informality and improvisation characterized the everyday politics involved in securing housing. It was estimated that by the early 1990s more than 60 percent of housing in Jakarta was on unregistered land (Leaf 1993). The development boom of the late 1970s saw the beginning of waves of dislocations of inner city kampung, changing the relationship between kampung and the emerging "modern" city. As Jellinek (1991, 171–72) describes, the growth of large-scale, capital-intensive enterprises and more centralized government bureaucracy made obsolete a range of small-scale income activities on which the poor depended, "squeezing" them both spatially and financially. With limited affordable or accessible housing, the poor made use of whatever space was available: unused government or commercial land, municipal facilities such as cemeteries or rubbish tips, railway sidings, river banks or fields. They were in many respects the city's pioneers and explorers, breaking new ground and "disrupting clearly delineated sectors, territories and policies" (Simone 2015, S15). As one long-term resident expressed it, "We settled these swamps, we transformed the forest into kampung. When we started living here no government came to claim this was state land. Only after we'd formed a community, built something positive, did they come and try and take it from us" (Interview with kampung resident, July 2015). Forced evictions, displacement, and relocations, often involving the military and police, were routine and used by government to "manage" the poor and their "illegal" occupation and use of urban space.

Despite the regime's willingness to use coercive force, the urban poor actively resisted displacements and evictions (Jellinek 1991). Residents of an informal settlement in Kampung Tanggul, for example, managed to postpone repeated attempts at removing them, beginning in 1991, through a combination of well-organized protests, assistance from nongovernmental organizations (NGOs), and bureaucratic incompetence, paving the way for eventual formal incorporation into the city's administrative structure in 2001 (Delmacius 2004). The Indonesian Legal Aid Institute was one of the few organizations that provided advocacy support for the poor (Murray 1991). With the law structurally hostile to the poor, this advocacy commonly involved efforts by NGOs at brokering a deal with authorities, such as forms of compensation or identifying alternative sites.

At moments the tensions, anomies and resentments generated by a city increasingly segregated by power and class erupted into opportunistic and targeted looting and violence. For example, in 1993, poor and working-class fans of Metallica, unable to afford entry to their concert, rampaged through elite neighborhoods in Jakarta's south, burning luxury car showrooms. These riots may have had a temporary pressure valve effect for those involved but were used by the regime to underscore its discourse that the poor and the kampung in which they lived were hotbeds of disorder, and hence required a firm disciplining hand. In July 1996, thousands of poor kampung youth destroyed police stations, banks, and government offices in a display of deep-seated animosity toward the regime provoked by its violent intervention in the leadership of the nominally oppositional Indonesian Democratic Party (Wilson 2015). This violence was seen by many as a turning point in the momentum against the New Order (Eklof 1999).

The economic crisis of 1997, which precipitated the political crisis that resulted in the removal of Suharto, caused a sudden and dramatic increase in the numbers of the poor and precarious in the capital. Street vendors, cart sellers, beggars, hustlers, drivers of public transport, and others seeking to make ends meet occupied public parks, private land, sidewalks, overpasses, intersections, and any available space. Those involved included the long-term poor, but also those more recently thrust into unemployment and poverty by economic collapse. The politics of the everyday took on a new intensity, and also desperation. In the midst of soaring food prices, the urban poor significantly bolstered mobilizations by student activists against the regime in 1998. Political alignments, however, were fragmented and often driven by instrumental concerns. While many urban poor joined proreform students, some of whom had been attempting to organize them politically, others were recruited into proregime militias mobilized by the military to counter street demonstrations. The 1998 May riots that precipitated the end of Suharto's rule saw kampung dwellers of all ages engaged in opportunistic looting, while others vented rage through rioting and social violence (Lane 2006). As one participant in the 1998 riots explained, "We hated the state and resented the rich, and took the opportunity to take the things that we'd been denied" (Interview, November 2015).

EVERYDAY AND DEFENSIVE POLITICS IN POST–NEW ORDER INDONESIA

In the wake of the unraveling of the New Order, the streets and neighborhoods of Jakarta became a renewed space of contestation between various social classes and interests. New organizations, networks, and alliances formed, and an invigorated sense of a right to the city prevailed. Protests against the city administration, previously a risky activity, occurred almost daily, and street vendors and informal settlers intensified their physical resistance to evictions by state authorities, stalling their displacement or forcing negotiations of some kind (Kusno 2010, 35). Many of the poor started to think differently about their circumstances and make new kinds of claims against powerful actors through street demonstrations, petitions, and new types of local organizations, and also by using new strategies to manage their everyday relations.

A whirlwind of claim making on the state, including by the poor, characterized post–New Order Jakarta. As Jakarta's "transition" governor Sutiyoso himself noted in a *Jakarta Post* article on November 11, 2002, between 1997 and 2002 there were more than forty-five hundred demonstrations against him. Sutiyoso in turn sought to regain control of the streets by rehashing some well-used repertoires. The administration launched new campaigns of forced evictions, displacements of the street economy, and harassment of the most vulnerable of the poor such as beggars, buskers, and sex workers (often under the mantle of "anti-thug" campaigns), while reviving New Order discourses that associated the poor with the city's perennial infrastructure woes such as flooding and traffic congestion.[5] Physical space was also altered, for instance, by the erection of barriers by the city administration to prevent vendors or squatters from setting up. The city's upper-middle classes, who were increasingly living within gated estates and apartments away from the poor, were particularly receptive to these kinds of interventions. The administration also increased the deployment and powers of public order police (Satuan Polisi Pamong Praja, Satpol PP) and worked to establish relationships with informal street authorities, such as a new generation of ethnic gangs and religious militias (Wilson 2015).

Using new technocratic language and rationales, post–New Order administrations have made efforts to formalize the complex informal arrangements and networks on which the poor rely. The urban poor have resisted these highly disruptive and limiting interventions. Efforts by Governor Joko Widodo (Jokowi) in 2013 to move street vendors in Tanah Abang into low-rent state-managed market buildings were widely hailed as an example of democratic good governance, but vendors uniformly considered these efforts a social and economic disaster (Ridwansyah 2014). Almost identical measures had been carried out by previous governors, going back to the 1970s (Murray 1991, 90). The urban poor's compliance with these measures has largely been opportunistic and seeking to limit risk, with many returning to more lucrative and flexible street-side vending after an inducement of a six-month rent free period expired (Interviews with vendors, December 2014).

As during the New Order, the urban poor have remained deeply enmeshed in local clientelist politics, but often with a greater degree of flexibility and leverage. Patrons and advocates may demand loyalty, but poor people are more likely to invest heavily in multiple relationships, and in some circumstances will prioritize personalized relations over contracts or even rights. For example, religious and ethnic militias and other social organizations routinely require an oath of exclusivist loyalty, but in practice many urban poor youths will be involved in a number of groups simultaneously, or will move in and out of groups on a regular basis. The more fluid context of post–New Order Jakarta has made contingent loyalties and "patron-hopping" far easier for the poor, and has meant that local patrons or brokers have greater pressure on them to deliver tangible outcomes to their clients if they wish to be able to mobilize them in significant numbers, the key to their own political capital. A more explicit emphasis on directly addressing the material needs of the poor, such as a program run by the ethnic militia the Betawi Brotherhood Forum (Forum Betawi Rempug, FBR) to find jobs for its members, is in some respects a reflection of this altered dynamic (Wilson 2015).

A core strategy the poor use is to encroach on services, utilities, and space otherwise denied them. It has been estimated, for example, that in 2010 up to 40 percent of Jakarta's residents were illegally or at least unofficially connected to the city's electricity grid (Arditya 2011). This syphoning is of course not the sole preserve of the poor, but is for the poor a form of both individual and often collective self-help. Campaigns launched by the city administration to clamp down on such practices have in some cases provided the opportunity for encroachers and long-term informal residents without tenure to convert illegal connections into legal ones, a victory of sorts against forms of infrastructural exclusion. The precarious tangle of power lines that crisscross the city in some respects mirror the complex social entanglements required by the poor to gain affordable access to utilities.

Another strategy of everyday resistance used by the poor has been to use or appropriate state-owned land. The intense marketization of space in Jakarta has resulted in an oversupply of high-end housing and retail developments with minimal government or private sector investment in low-income housing (Winarso, Hudalah, and Firman 2015). Informal use and appropriation of state-owned land can generate pressure on the government to selectively integrate informal settlements even if individual residents may not possess recognized land title. Legitimacy, of a sort, can accrue through continued occupation over time. There are multiple semiformal systems of land tenure in operation, and perceptions of how secure one is vary considerably (Simone 2015). While informality prevails and some of the poor prefer to live free from land taxes, fees, and government bureaucracy, recognition by the government is often a desired outcome depending on its terms. In particular, incorporation within the administrative structure as a neighborhood association (*rukun tetangga*, RT, or *rukun warga*, RW) enables residents to obtain Jakarta identity cards and subsequently potentially gain access to health, education, and other services, including the ability to vote.[6] It does not, however, provide any measure of protection from eviction. Shifts in government policies or local commercial arrangements can rapidly turn seemingly secure livelihood arrangements into insecurity, eviction, and even homelessness.

Despite the highly atomized nature of these kinds of "quiet encroachment" (Bayat 2013) at moments of mutual threat, most commonly forced evictions or displacements by government authorities, otherwise passive networks of solidarity connecting largely unrelated individuals can become active, engaging in protests, physical resistance, or collective lobbying. In 2010 for example, efforts by the city administration to remove unregistered buildings at the tomb of a local saint in Koja in Jakarta's north, resulted in wide-scale violent resistance by residents, allies from neighboring districts, and a number of religious vigilantes. Other defensive forms of politics that the urban poor deploy include maintaining invisibility, noncompliance, and calling on allies and powerful actors to intervene or provide protection. In the riverside neighborhood of Kampung Tongkol, for example, residents responded to the ongoing threat of eviction by voluntarily reducing the size of their homes to comply with government requirements for a maintenance road, planting trees, and cleaning the river, in doing so challenging representations of their community as a lawless slum (Interview with Kampung Tongkol residents, June 2016).[7]

Organizing the Unorganizable

In the post–New Order era, the urban poor and their advocates have engaged in a range of efforts to organize collectively around a shared identity and a set of issues such as tenure security, threats of eviction, access to health care, and the right to livelihood. These efforts have been on different spatial scales, from the neighborhood level to those attempting to develop citywide or even national networks and political movements. As during the New Order, formal pro-poor organizations have served an important brokering and advocacy role, in particular providing legal defense in response to threats of displacement and lobbying government for improved basic services and social protection. Often with well-educated middle-class leadership, pro-poor NGOs have also provided a representational bridge to political elites which has, with the advent of electoral politics, offered degrees of strategic leverage in seeking particularist concessions usually in return for promises of electoral or campaign support. Organizations such as the Urban Poor Consortium (UPC) and the Jakarta Citizens Forum (Forum Warga Jakarta, FAKTA) have also worked to conceptualize and articulate coherent pro-poor positions and develop alternate policy approaches in key areas such as housing.

The UPC was established by several social activists in 1997 inspired by the community activism praxis of U.S. community activist Saul Alinsky together with their respective experiences of living and working in the poorest parts of Jakarta. The UPC sought to build on existing self-help and self-organizing practices in Jakarta's kampung by drawing together a broad consortium of urban poor groups, communities, and sectoral cooperatives, such as becak drivers, fishermen, and street vendors. The UPC's vision is based on a "rights to the city" framework which asserts that fundamental rights (such as to housing, livelihood and basic services) should be politically realized and accessible to all, and that development processes in the city should be grassroots driven and bottom up, preserving and creating spaces that meet the needs and aspirations of local residents (Group discussion with UPC members, 2015). It constituted one of the first post–New Order coordinated efforts in Jakarta to advocate on behalf of the urban poor as a coherent group or class, rather than on an individual kampung or issue basis (Interviews with UPC activists, December 2014).

In the early 2000s, the UPC focused on protest actions and street mobilizations aimed at raising the profile of tenure insecurity, government harassment of street economy workers, access to health services, and the rising costs of basic goods. In 2001, for example, it was able to mobilize thousands of becak drivers in a protest against their banishment from central Jakarta districts. These activities were combined with efforts to build a broader citywide network by reaching out to poor communities and groups around Jakarta. This was a period of significant turmoil and realignments in Jakarta's street politics, and saw the UPC targeted by ethnic militias aligned to Sutiyoso, such as the FBR, which made operating in some parts of the city difficult. This was, in effect, a clash of competing claims not just as to *who* represented the poor, but how they could be represented in a democratizing Indonesia.

The introduction in 2007 of elections for governor and municipal parliament led to a strategic shift away from more confrontational forms of protest and street mobilizations for the UPC. The new approach had two parts. The first formulated and articulated alternate urban development models and visions, in the hope that greater access to formal power could enable policy influence. The introduction of some structurally circumscribed "participatory" governance frameworks, such as found in government multi-stakeholder development and budgeting consultation forums (Musyawarah Rencana Pembangunan, Musrenbang), also offered opportunities at the subdistrict level.[8] UPC activists and members collaborated with various allies such as urban planners and architects in formulating detailed plans for social housing such as the concept of "layered kampung" (*kampung susun*) and "sustainable kampung" (*kampung berkelanjutan*) as well as site specific proposals such as modifications to residential zoning or flood mitigation strategies not involving forced relocation.[9] In the second part, the UPC assisted poor neighborhoods in articulating, organizing, and advocating individually and collectively and in doing so reducing reliance on clientelism. For example, regular meetings of kampung women in Penjaringan facilitated by the UPC are used to identify local problems, such as bureaucratic hurdles in accessing health services, and then developing a plan of action. As one UPC activist explained, "There's often a tendency for kampung residents to follow a figure upon whom they project often unrealistic expectations, including hoping they'll do the struggling for them. We encourage kampung residents to self-organize and to self-advocate" (Group discussion with UPC activists, 2015). Through these kinds of approaches, the UPC has endeavored to generate "activist citizens." Using a consortium model, the UPC brought together a diverse range of disparate local groups, most operating at the kampung level. This structure enabled constituent members to come in to contact with a range of issues, people, strategies, and ways of living in the city that served to broaden their understandings of what it meant to be poor. It nonetheless faced difficulties in translating into a coherent citywide social movement for the same reasons, as the emphasis on heterogeneity creates difficulties among some residents in recognizing points of commonality.

FAKTA, established in the immediate post–New Order period, has been another advocate and organizational hub for Jakarta's poor. Initially it was intended as an "alternative city council" that would represent the interests of those "forgotten or ignored" by the regional government (Interview with Azas Tigor Nainggolan, chairperson of FAKTA, July 2014). FAKTA's objective has been to "empower" the poor to actively assert their rights as urban citizens, together with building links with middle-class and elite allies, be they in the bureaucracy, NGOs, the media, or political parties, with the goal of more inclusive forms of urban development and governance. As reported in a *Jakarta Post* article on February 12, 2007, during Sutiyoso's second period as governor (2002–7), FAKTA led a number of class actions against the administration's mismanagement of flood mitigation, together with routine demonstrations in the city center demanding an end to forced evictions. FAKTA's chairperson explained that the act of taking the government to court was important because it demonstrated that the urban poor could campaign for their rights through institutional channels, while simultaneously exposing the poor to the contradictions of institutionalized power. Like the UPC, FAKTA reduced its use of protest mobilizations post-2007 with greater emphasis on establishing dialogue with receptive bureaucrats and politicians and negotiating for better services on behalf of its stronghold communities. It has also worked on developing alternative policy, for example, advocating for improved public transport as a means of increasing mobility for the poor, drafting blueprints for eviction-free solutions to the low-cost housing problem as well as humane standard operating procedures for evictions (Forum Warga Kota Jakarta 2006). In this respect, it has emphasized the use of a personalist and advocacy approach as a means to extract concessions from political elites.

While both UPC and FAKTA have emphasized rights-based notions of urban citizenship, legal advocacy around key issues affecting the poor, and forwarding alternative visions of urban development and planning, the Indonesian Peoples' Union of Struggle (Serikat Perjuangan Rakyat Indonesia, SPRI) has followed more closely in the footsteps of the left-wing student politics of the anti-Suharto movement of the 1990s. The socialist People's Democratic Party (Partai Rakyat Demokratik, PRD) saw the urban poor as the "lumpen proletariat" with attempts at organizing them, according to one former member, "like herding cats" (Interview with former PRD member, 2012). The party did recruit a number of urban poor youth in the mid- and late-1990s, one of whom was Marlo Sitompul, an illiterate parking attendant. Gaining his political education and organizing skills from the party, Sitompul and others established SPRI, which was affiliated with the PRD until it split in 2011. As of 2017 it had thirty-four branches, the majority in Jakarta but also in Medan, Lampung, West and Central Java, and Flores (interview with SPRI activist, November 2016).

In contrast to what Simone (2013, 71) has called the "complex congealment" of the consortium and network structures of UPC and FAKTA, SPRI has focused on consolidating communities of support with the goal of forming a political vehicle for the poor to directly pressure the state. The state is considered to be the primary source, or at least facilitator, of poverty as a consequence of what SPRI argues is its abandonment of the pro-people and welfare stipulations of the 1945 Constitution. SPRI uses a strategy of targeted advocacy, mapping of local issues and interaction with existing local constellations of power, such as local strongmen, religious, or community figures. Helping the poor gain access to health services has been a central focus, resulting in the Ministry of Health formally recognizing their efforts. Alongside this advocacy, SPRI has provided its members with ideological education, such as critiques of neoliberal capitalism, theories of political change, and organizational skills with the hope this will aid in the coalescing of broader coherent forms of collective action and political organization by the poor.

The possibilities for the emergence of collective organization beyond the everyday, defensive or reactive, however, are limited by the conditions of precarious life and the heterogeneous livelihood strategies that evolve in response to it. These conditions constitute a significant challenge for pro-poor organizations seeking to mobilize the poor as a coherent group, transcendent of other social forms such as ethnicity or gender, irrespective of those organizations' ideology or strategic emphasis. While there is no shortage of localized action and mobilization, many of which are deeply embedded in kampung life and the dynamics of street economies, the heterogeneous economic and social practices and "entanglements" in which people have to engage in in order to generate livelihoods are not easily subsumed under codified notions of collective rights or coherent reform programs, particularly the types of consensual participation often reified in urban social movements (Simone 2013, 70). Ultimately for many of the poor, such organizations are one option among many that may be strategically or instrumentally useful at different times.

In terms of the ability to attract and maintain a large active membership, progressive and left-leaning groups such as UPC, FAKTA, and SPRI have frequently "lost" to reactionary groups who possess greater means to intimidate and also redistribute material gains, such as the FBR and the religious vigilantes, Defenders of Islam Front (Front Pembela Islam, FPI), whose ability to broker relations with powerful actors and provide forms of material relief or benefits have, often, more immediately met demands of everyday life, even if the poor's engagement is primarily instrumental (Wilson 2015). Such groups have also provided grievance narratives that have resonated with many of the poor, linking conditions of poverty and marginality to sectarian identity politics or populist conspiracy theory (Wilson 2016). In doing so, they have instrumentally co-opted anomie and resentments that may otherwise be directed elsewhere.

Activists described suspicion, or at least ambivalence, on the part of poor kampung residents when encouraged to engage in active solidarity with other neighborhoods also facing common threats, such as eviction (Interviews with UPC activists, July 2015). Despite the seeming similarity of structural and economic circumstances, these were often perceived as fundamentally different.[10] Class-based solidarity of this kind was also often seen as risky insofar as it could bring unwanted attention from the authorities or hostile groups, and shut doors to other possible courses of action by tying one's fate to others. The specter of allegations of communism has also served to undermine local efforts at collective organization and representation. Reactionary groups, such as the FPI, have regularly used claims of a resurgent Indonesian Communist Party (Partai Komunis Indonesia, PKI) as a means of attacking and delegitimizing liberal and progressive social movements, including those of the poor.[11] This has been further complicated by the deep intersection of the poor's lives with patronage and clientelist politics. As such, legalist and rights-based approaches have been perceived by many of the poor as not relevant, self-limiting, or of strategic value only at particular moments. For these reasons, at least a few urban poor allies concluded that if city- or even nationwide pro-poor changes were to be effected, it would need to come through elite political champions rather than a mass movement or collective organization.

ELECTORAL POLITICS AND JAKARTA'S POOR

As Aspinall (2013) has noted, despite deep continuities in the configuration of Indonesia's ruling elites and oligarchies into the post–New Order era, electoral politics has contributed to a much more dynamic political landscape in Indonesia in which the competition between a diverse array of elites, brokers, bureaucrats, and interest groups is intense. Far from being static, alliances, coalitions, and patronage relationships shift and change with great frequency. This dynamic has created a host of new opportunities for the poor and other socially marginal groups and offered spaces in which to maneuver. Some politicians have sought to strengthen their power through direct appeals to the poor as a constituency, in the form of populist welfare and health policy, short-term or limited redistributions or other forms of concession in return for electoral support or street-level mobilization. While such appeals indicate that various social interests beyond those of oligarchic elites, including those of the poor and marginal groups, can and do impact the form and content of policy, this process remains nonetheless deeply constrained. The poor have a relatively limited capacity to hold politicians accountable to election promises, and any coherent organizational vehicle such as a pro-poor political party or social movement is notable for its absence. In many respects, the urban poor's engagement with electoral politics in Jakarta has been characterized by tensions between an instrumentalist approach toward democracy driven by immediate needs and the desire for greater democratic representation that has, as an outcome, seen the democratic process become more deeply enmeshed in everyday life.

Due to its status as the Special Capital Region, it was not until 2007 that the first municipal parliament and governor elections were held in Jakarta. This was two years behind the rest of the country where district head elections (Pemilihan Kepala Daerah, Pilkada), despite not resulting in institutional power for marginalized social groups, did see some politicians attempt to court the popular vote with minimum wage increases and promises of subsidized health care (Aspinall 2013). Urban poor groups and advocates in Jakarta realigned and recalibrated their strategies to influence candidates to introduce both particularistic and programmatic policies beneficial to the poor in return for electoral support. For example, in the 2007 elections both UPC and FAKTA negotiated modest political contracts with each of the two main candidates, career bureaucrat Fauzi Bowo, and former national police commissioner Adang Daradjatun, in what was seen as an "experiment" in political lobbying (Interview with UPC activists, July 2015).[12]

Mass organizations such as FBR and FPI offered their services as brokers between political parties and the poor and working-class constituents they claimed to represent, in return for material concessions (Wilson 2015). The efficacy of these "traditional" forms of clientelism was challenged by a more open and fluid environment that enabled the poor to "patron-hop" and "maximize the harvest" as one described it, from a range of sources rather than remaining ostensibly loyal as was the case during the New Order (Interview with kampung youth, June 2013). This approach, according to some activists, reflected the poor's view of elections as an opportunity for short-term accumulation, without hope or expectation that the result would necessarily deliver tangible benefits or change. Electoral support for a candidate or party was often arbitrary or determined by affiliation with territorial or identity-based groups, with large numbers of the eligible not voting at all.[13]

Jokowi emerged on the Jakarta political scene in 2012, forwarded as a candidate for governor by the Indonesian Democratic Party of Struggle (Partai Demokrasi Indonesia Perjuangan, PDI-P), and paired with Gerindra politician Basuki Tjahaja Purnama. Jokowi was by then already well-known due to media coverage of his modest efforts at urban renewal as mayor of Surakarta, a Central Java city of half a million. Many commentators identified him as part of a new breed of reform-minded regional politicians, "clean skins" without close patronage or political ties to the previous New Order regime or its subsequent oligarchic reconfigurations, and with a commitment to "participatory" approaches.[14] He offered, in the eyes of urban poor activists, the possibility for significant social and political reforms and more direct lines of communication and influence.

As campaigning began, Jokowi's particular brand of everyman populism saw his popularity among kampung dwellers swell. His use of impromptu visits (*blusukan*), which were in reality highly stage managed meet-and-greets, captured the public and media's attention. As one kampung dweller explained, "He sat and talked to us in Javanese. It left a big impression on all of us" (Interview, December 2014). Winning the kampung vote, particularly in the densely populated north and south of the city, with its high concentrations of poor and working class, was identified by Jokowi's strategists as crucial (Interview with Jokowi presidential campaign advisor, 2014). The incumbent had strongholds of support through his close clientelist relations with Betawi mass organizations with roots in the city's kampung and liberally used discretionary city budget social assistance funds as a campaign slush fund to shore up this support (Wilson 2015).

Urban poor activists begun a dialogue with Jokowi in an attempt to broker a political contract, and he proved to be receptive, with regular meetings and an "open-door" policy (Interview with UPC activists, July 2015). Further guarantees were given by Jokowi that no evictions would take place unless alternative accommodation, such as subsidized rental apartments, was available, and that these would be, ideally, close to existing homes. The UPC was instructed to identify land that the city administration could then later purchase (Interview with UPC activists, June 2016). Alternative planning proposals, such as the "stacked kampung" (*kampung deret*) concept of riverside neighborhoods, as reported in *Tempo* on November 12, 2012, were also embraced by the candidate.

A three-point contract was negotiated, which aside from recognition of kampung dwellers' right to tenure and a disavowal of evictions, also emphasized amorphous "participatory" approaches to budgeting and city planning together with the importance of the informal sector street economy. At a ceremony for the signing of the contract next to the Pluit water catchment area, residents gave Jokowi a container of collected money, a symbolic reversal of the usual distribution of cash by candidates. According to one UPC activist, "This was extremely important, as it showed this was not politics as usual. We, the poor, were entrusting this candidate to work with us in achieving the goals we'd set together" (Interview with UPC activist, April 2017). With the contract signed, UPC and other urban poor groups mobilized their networks to campaign for Jokowi and Purnama, using door-to door discussions, street convoys, and music events. Photocopies of the contract were widely distributed. The overall electoral impact of this campaigning is difficult to assess; however, in UPC stronghold areas in the north of the city Jokowi won more than 70 percent of the vote, the highest of any district.

Within just months of the election victory, informal settlements in Pluit, the site of the contract signing, were subjected to forced eviction, albeit sweetened by rental apartments that came furnished and stocked with household appliances and food courtesy of corporate social responsibility donors. Discursively the promise of legalizing kampung disappeared entirely to be replaced by relocation of the poor to government-owned rental apartments. The UPC, as instructed by Jokowi, sought to identify areas of land that could be used to build alternative accommodation, but these were stifled at other levels of the city administration. In the one success in Muara Baru, kampung deret plans were discarded by the city administration in favor of generic apartment blocks. At the same time, direct access to the governor became increasingly difficult (Interview with UPC activists, July 2015).

The consequences of this betrayal were multiple. In some cases, local activists were accused by residents of the neighborhoods in which they worked of deception, and verbally and physically harassed (Interview with urban poor activist, July 2015). The active support base of the UPC also began to fragment. Jokowi's seeming about-face appeared to some as another all-too-familiar case of political elites, with the assistance of well-meaning NGO brokers, manipulating the hopes of the poor as a means to consolidate power (Interview with kampung activists, December 2014). When Jokowi announced his decision to run for the 2014 presidential elections, urban poor groups were faced with a dilemma as to how to position themselves. Despite breaking key contract promises, Jokowi sought the help of the UPC and others, telling activists that in order to fully implement his promises he required the executive power of the presidency. After intense internal debate, the UPC eventually committed to supporting Jokowi's presidential candidacy since he remained relatively accessible to activists and was the lesser of evils compared to his electoral rival, Prabowo Subianto (Interview with Gugun Muhammad, December 2016).

Jokowi still remained immensely popular in many of Jakarta's kampung, and a common view was that his backtracking was less due to ill intent than entrenched corrupt elites stifling his propeople (*pro-rakyat*) vision. As van Voorst (2014) has shown, many of Jakarta's poor voted against him in the presidential elections in order to *keep* him as governor. As tactical pragmatists, many preferred the idea of having an approachable politician like Jokowi (despite his flaws) close, as well as protecting them from his far more aggressive deputy, Ahok, who would later unleash a huge wave of evictions across the city (Wilson 2014). The lens through which he was perceived was still one framed by practices of patron-clientelism.

In the face of frustrated efforts at developing coherent mass organizations or movements, and the detachment of political parties from a grassroots social base, the identifying of electoral "champions of the poor" has been a key focus of many pro-poor activists and allies. This has also entailed a co-opting of the poor as voting blocks. A new breed of populism, embodied in the Jokowi campaign of 2012, moved beyond distributions of cash and favors to more substantive sets of policy demands and expectations reflecting some key concerns of the urban poor, as articulated via broker NGOs. Disappointment at the failure to realize many of these demands reaffirmed in some quarters the limited value of elections as a means to substantive pro-poor change, while for others it was understood as due to not yet finding the right elite champion. Some urban poor activists insist, however, that expectations and strategies have been fundamentally recalibrated. On the announcement of candidates for the 2017 governor elections, for example, several kampung prepared their own detailed political contracts, which any candidates wanting their support would be required to sign, bypassing brokers or intermediaries (*Kompas* 2016).

CONCLUSION

Poor people's politics are distinctive as they are highly constrained and defensive, instrumental, short term, and opportunistic, which are often the only effective strategies available to them, given their structural disadvantage. Perhaps what is most striking in looking at the politics of the urban poor from the New Order to post–New Order period is less the extent of change that has taken place as a part of broader processes of "democratization" in Indonesia than the extent of continuity. This continuity, in terms of the sustained focus on everyday survival and the defense of existing circumstances, is reflective of the broader conditions constitutive of poverty, that have remained largely unaffected, if not exacerbated, by the trajectories of Indonesia's postauthoritarian political transformation.

This transformation, as experienced by the urban poor has, however, undoubtedly offered new spaces and opportunities to negotiate, maneuver, and seek instrumental advantage. Patrons and advocates, on whom the poor often rely, frequently demand loyalty as a matter of course; however, the poor are more likely to invest heavily in multiple relationships simultaneously with progressives, reactionaries, and the police. Managing such diverse relationships is difficult and consumes energy, time, and resources but also leads to more risk-mitigating options in the face of insecurity and precariousness. In some circumstances the poor will prioritize personalized relations over contracts or even rights, including those ostensibly available within a democracy, taking advantage of spaces of opportunity, including elections and regime change, as they perceive these as opening up.

Invited, or at least accessible, spaces of "democratic participation," including that of electoral politics, are still largely constituted within existing power relations—so are less likely to empower poor people to demand transformative change that fundamentally disrupts power relationships, although these may serve a range of immediate everyday and defensive purposes. Where poor people have sought to make new claims against more powerful actors, such as the mobilizations by the poor against Jakarta's former governor, Basuki Tjahaja Purnama, in opposition to his evictions regimes, these have been politically co-opted and neutralized as power hierarchies have been reconstituted, or have manifested in limited clientelist representation (Wilson 2016).

Efforts at organizing in more traditional class-based social movements that would, in theory, provide a stronger foundation for making transformative claims on the state are countered—if not undermined—by the conditions of everyday life itself, marked by precariousness and heterogeneous livelihoods that make it difficult to mutually identify and establish the grounds for collective organization as "the poor." This is further compounded by institutional restrictions on electoral participation, such as high national thresholds for parliamentary representation, which serve to limit the number and diversity of political parties. Despite a large labor union movement, for example, Indonesia has yet to see anything resembling a labor party (see Caraway and Ford this volume). The momentum toward neoliberal market-based citizenship, a key component of state and donor "pro-poor" policy in post–New Order Indonesia, has served to further fragment and atomize the possibilities for collective action and organization. Where collective organization does take place, it has still tended to be highly localized, such as at the kampung level.

In their study of political leadership among the urban poor in Delhi, Das and Walton (2015) emphasize the importance of considering not just the ways in which democratization may or may not have served the poor, but how democratic politics is deepened by the poor's participation. Clearly Indonesian's postauthoritarian political transformation could and should serve Indonesia's urban poor far better than it has to date. For it to do so, broader structural transformations of the organization of power will need to take place. While this seems unlikely to occur anytime soon, the contribution of the poor to Indonesia's so-called democratic transition nonetheless remains significant, albeit in ways that do not capture headlines, or the attention of commentators and analysts. It is found in the countless ongoing everyday struggles of the urban poor to reclaim public space and amenities for themselves and others. In doing so, the urban poor articulate through direct action democratic forms of urban citizenship and solidarity, including reliance on plural forms of social networking and interaction with heterogeneous ways of life. All of this offers much in the way of democratic substance.

Notes

1. Defining poverty and "the poor" is politically and analytically fraught. There are no universal criteria for material deprivation. The complex, fluxing nature of precarious lives' makes frequently used government and donor indices for defining poverty, such as the World Banks US $1.25 per day, unhelpful if not deeply misleading. There is also no identifiable

social group of "the poor." It cannot be productively understood as a quantitative state, or reducible to particular demographics or forms of livelihood. For the purposes of this paper, poverty, drawing on Simmel 1965, is understood as the social relationships engendered by want. For a discussion of the analytical challenges in defining poverty, see Spicker 1999.

2. Reactionary, right wing, and criminal forms of social organization that have been popular among the poor and at times claimed to represent them, such as religious and ethnic militias, are discussed in detail elsewhere. See Wilson 2015.

3. According to Simmel, it is through being at the receiving end of ameliorative assistance that the "poor" are constituted as a sociological category, in the process binding them to a particular relationship with state and society (Das and Walton 2015). In policy terms, this is often reflected in paternalistic and policing orientated interventions by the state.

4. For an account of a gangster regime over street traders in Tanah Abang, see Wilson 2015.

5. See, for example, Human Right Watch's 2006 report on forced evictions under Sutiyoso.

6. RT and RW are the lowest levels of government administrative hierarchy.

7. See also Munk 2016.

8. The UPC made numerous representations to government departments, such as the Ministry for Social Affairs.

9. "Sustainable kampung," which draw on environmental sustainability paradigms, is based in the understanding that kampung constitute the primary form of housing in Jakarta and hence should be the starting point for the city's development rather than an impediment to it. See Forum Kampung Kota 2016.

10. For example, on grounds of the perceived status of land title, whether residents were owners or renters, recent arrivals, or long term, or even in terms of ethnicity. Open solidarity was also often seen as shutting out other possibilities

11. In September 2017, for example, a mob attacked the office of the Jakarta Legal Aid Institute, a key advocate of the poor and marginalized, after rumors were spread that it hosted a meeting of a reformed Indonesian Communist Party.

12. Political contracts emerged in the early 2000s with the beginning of regional elections as a means by which various social and interest groups sought to negotiate political change and hold elected politicians accountable.

13. Around 35.5 percent of eligible voters did not participate in 2007, more than the winning total of 33.7 percent. This increased to 37 percent in 2012. Nonparticipation rates have remained over 20 percent (*Suara Pembaruan*, July 12, 2012).

14. Examples of this view can be found in Otto and Ismar 2013.

REFERENCES

Arditya, Andreas D. 2011. "City Readies New Bylaw to Curb Electricity." *Jakarta Post*. September 30.

Aspinall, Edward. 2013. "Popular Agency and Interests in Indonesia's Democratic Transition and Consolidation." *Indonesia* 96: 101–21.

Bayat, Asef. 2013. *Life as Politics: How Ordinary People Change the Middle East*. Stanford: Stanford University Press.

Blunch, Niels-Hugo, Sudharshan Canagarajah, and Dhushyanth Raju. 2001. "The Informal Sector Revisited: A Synthesis across Space and Time." World Bank, Social Protection Discussion Series, Paper No. 0119.

Das, Veena, and Shalinie Randeira. 2015. "Politics of the Urban Poor: Aesthetics, Ethics, Volatility, Precarity." *Current Anthropology* 56 (S11): S3–S14.

Das, Veena, and Michael Walton. 2015. "Political Leadership and the Urban Poor." *Current Anthropology* 56 (S11): S44–S54.

Delmacius, Azas Tigor. 2004. "Partisipasi Politik Kaum Miskin Kota: Studi Kasus Advokasi Pengakuan Permukiman Warga Miskin di Dearah Penas Tanggal Jakarta Timur Tahun 1991 dan 2000." Masters diss., Universitas Nasional.

Eklof, Stefan. 1999. *Indonesian Politics in Crisis: The Long Fall of Suharto 1996–98*. Copenhagen: NIAS Press.

Forum Kampung Kota. 2016. "Kampung Susun Manusiawi Kampung Pulo." September 19. https://medium.com/forumkampungkota/.

Forum Warga Kota Jakarta. 2006. *Alternatif Penyelesaian Sengketa Pemukiman Miskin Kota*. Jakarta: Forum Warga Jakarta.

Harsono, Andreas. 2017. "Indonesia's Ban of Islamist Group Undermines Rights." Human Rights Watch. July 19. https://www.hrw.org/news.

Holzner, Claudio A. 2010. *The Poverty of Democracy: The Institutional Roots of Political Participation in Mexico*. Pittsburgh: University of Pittsburgh Press.

Human Rights Watch. 2006. "Condemned Communities: Forced Evictions in Jakarta." September 5. https://www.hrw.org/report/2006/09/05/condemned-communities/forced-evictions-jakarta.

Hutchison, J. 2007. "The 'Disallowed' Political Participation of Manila's Urban Poor." *Democratization* 14 (5): 853–72.

Jellinek, Lea. 1991. *The Wheel of Fortune: The History of a Poor Community in Jakarta*. Honolulu: University of Hawaii Press.

Kompas. 2016. "Anies Baswedan Tanda Tangani Kontrak Politik yang Diajukan Warga Tanah Merah." October 2.

Kusno, Abidin. 2004. "Whither Nationalist Urbanism? Public Life in Governor Sutiyoso's Jakarta." *Urban Studies* 41 (12): 2377–94.

——. 2010. *The Appearances of Memory: Mnemonic Practices of Architecture and Urban Form in Indonesia*. Durham, NC: Duke University Press.

Lane, Max. 2006. "The Urban Poor and the Proletariat in Mobilising Politics." September 14. http://blogs.usyd.edu.au/maxlaneintlasia/2006/09/the_urban_poor_and_the_proleta.html.

Leaf, Michael. 1993. "Legal Authority in an Extralegal Setting: The Case of Land Rights in Jakarta." *Journal of Planning Education and Research* 14: 12–18.

Leal, Pablo A. 2007. "Participation: The Ascendancy of a Buzzword in the Neo-Liberal Era." *Development in Practice* 17 (4/5): 539–48.

Lembaga Bantuan Hukum Jakarta. 2015. "Atas Nama Pembangunan: Laporan Penggusuran Paksa di Jakarta Tahun 2015." http://www.bantuanhukum.or.id/.

Mainwaring, Scott. 1987. "Urban Popular Movements, Identity, and Democratization in Brazil." *Comparative Political Studies* 20 (2): 131–59.

Munk, David. 2016. "Jakarta's Eco Future? River Community Goes Green to Fight Threat of Eviction." *The Guardian*. November 25. https://www.theguardian.com/cities/2016/nov/25/jakarta-kampung-tongkol-eco-future-river-community--green-to-fight-eviction-threat.

Murray, Alison J. 1991. *No Money, No Honey: A Study of Street Traders and Prostitutes in Jakarta*. Oxford: Oxford University Press.

Otto, Ben, and Andreas Ismar. 2013. "In Indonesia, a New Breed of Politician Is on the Rise." *The Wall Street Journal*. October 9. https://www.wsj.com/articles/in-indonesia-a-new-breed-of-politician-is-on-the-rise-1381284578.

Ridwansyah. 2014. "Balik ke Jalan, Relokasi PKL ke Blok G Gagal." *Sindo News*. August 18. http://metro.sindonews.com.

Rulistia, Novia D. 2012. "Electricity Theft a Silent Threat for Jakartans." *Jakarta Post*. April 17. http://www.thejakartapost.com/news/2012/04/17/electricity-theft-a-silent-threat-jakartans.html.

Safitri, Dewi. 2010. "Desakan Pembubaran Satpol PP Menguat." *BBC Indonesia*. April 15.

Simmel, Georg. 1965. "The Poor." *Social Problems* 13 (2): 118–40.

Simone, Abdou Maliq. 2010. *City Life from Jakarta to Dakar: Movements at the Crossroads*. New York: Routledge.

———. 2013. "Urban Water Politics in Jakarta." In *Jakarta: Architecture + Adaptation*, edited by Etienne Turpine, Adam Bobbette, and Meredith Miller, 61–101. Jakarta: Universitas Indonesia Press.

———. 2014. *Jakarta: Drawing the City Near*. Minneapolis: University of Minnesota Press.

———. 2015. "The Urban Poor and Their Ambivalent Exceptionalities: Some Notes from Jakarta." *Current Anthropology* 56 (Supplement 11): S15–S23.

Spicker, Paul. 1999. "Definitions of Poverty: Twelve Clusters of Meaning." In *The International Glossary on Poverty*, edited by Paul Spicker and David Gordon, 150–62. London: Zed Books.

Soss, Joe, Richard C. Fording, and Sanford Schram. 2011. *Disciplining the Poor: Neoliberal Paternalism and the Persistent Power of Race*. Chicago: University of Chicago Press.

Taylor-Robinson, Michelle M. 2010. *Do the Poor Count? Democratic Institutions and Accountability in a Context of Poverty*. University Park: University of Pennsylvania Press.

UN Habitat. 2015. "The Housing Crisis." September 12. http://www.unhabitat.org.

van Voorst, Roanne. 2014. "Hope, Cynicism, and Jokowi in a Jakarta Slum." *New Mandala*. April 16. http://www.newmandala.org.

Wilson, Ian. 2014. "Floods, Housing Security, and the Rights of Jakarta's Poor." *Jakarta Post*. February 8.

———. 2015. *The Politics of Protection Rackets in Post–New Order Indonesia: Coercive Capital, Authority, and Street Politics*. London: Routledge.

———. 2016. "Making Enemies out of Friends." *New Mandala*. November 3. http://www.newmandala.org.

Winarso, Haryo, Delik Hudalah, and Tommy Firman. 2015. "Peri-urban Transformation in the Jakarta Metropolitan Area." *Habitat International* 49 (October): 221–29.

CHAPTER SIX

REFORMASI AND THE DECLINE OF LIBERAL ISLAM

Greg Fealy

A striking paradox of Indonesia's post-1998 democratization is that the liberal Islamic movement, which had played such a pivotal role in creating favorable conditions for political reform, would ultimately fall casualty to it. Throughout the 1980s and 1990s, progressive Muslim intellectuals and organizations had been at the forefront of efforts to reform their country's authoritarian Suharto-led regime and bring about a new, more politically and religiously pluralist system. High-profile figures such as Abdurrahman Wahid, Nurcholish Madjid, Syafii Ma'arif, and Ulil Abshar-Abdalla, along with mass organizations like Nahdlatul Ulama (NU) and Muhammadiyah, argued that Islam provided a basis for liberalizing Indonesia. They drew on religious teachings and traditions to advocate for and popularize agendas built around notions of human rights, equality, and democracy. In so doing, they won broad legitimacy among Indonesia's majority Muslim community for the notion that Islam was not only compatible with democracy but, in fact, enjoined it. When Suharto's New Order teetered and fell in 1998, many of these same Muslim leaders played a crucial role in shaping the direction of the democratic transition. Some formed and led pluralist political parties, some played important advisory roles, and others used their powers of public commentary to press for a free and transparent system. By the early 2000s, the general consensus among scholars of Indonesia was that the speed and success of the democratic transition owed much to the advocacy of liberal-minded Islamic leaders and groups.

But within fifteen years of reformasi, the golden era of Indonesia's liberal Islamic movement was over and conservatism was resurgent, both politically and socially. Many of the most famous liberal thinkers had either passed away or been sidelined, and there seemed no emerging figures of comparable stature or intellect to replace them. Numerous progressive activists had gone into politics, some of whom largely abandoned their earlier agendas. Most of the nongovernmental organizations (NGOs) that had been prominent advocates of liberalism shrunk in size and profile, with many changing their strategies to pursue less controversial options. Mainstream organizations like NU and Muhammadiyah were now more cautious under the leadership of Islamic scholars who, though broadly sympathetic with the progressive cause, were not powerful advocates of it. At the same time, religious intolerance was rising, with increasing discrimination against and violence toward minorities by civil society groups and the state, and many politicians appearing more inclined to court rather than condemn sectarianism and other forms of undemocratic behavior.

Thus democracy has proven increasingly hostile to progressive Islam. This chapter examines the factors that led to its emergence and efflorescence during the

Suharto years and its decline over the past decade. To begin with, New Order authoritarianism favored religious liberalism. It suppressed political expressions of Islam, which it saw as a threat, while encouraging intellectual and spiritual activity that promoted pluralism and social harmony. Western aid also poured in to liberal NGOs and mass organizations from the late 1980s in the hope of speeding Indonesia's move to democracy. By contrast, reformasi saw the lifting of restrictions on more conservative forces. These turned out to be more adept at using the freedoms of democracy to reach out to and mobilize communities than progressive forces, giving them greater political clout. Liberal groups also made strategic mistakes in failing to take proper account of growing conservatism, leading them to pursue campaigns that proved counterproductive.

Several terms need careful definition for the purposes of this chapter. The most important of these is *liberal*. In Indonesia, as well as in the broader Islamic world, liberal commonly referred to those Muslims who promote reform of their faith and society through reinterpretation of Islamic texts with the aim of achieving greater freedom and equality. Particular issues of focus for liberal Muslims are democracy; quarantining religion from practical politics; the upholding of human rights, including those regarding gender and sexual orientation, religious, and ethnic minorities; environmental protection; and community empowerment (Kurzman 1999). From the late 1980s until the mid-2000s, the term *liberal* was widely used in Indonesian Islamic circles, especially by progressive intellectuals. Seminars, books, articles, and media programs often carried it in their titles, and many Islamic scholars were happy to be described as being liberal. There was even a subvariant within liberal Islam that identified itself as "Islam Kiri" (Leftist Islam). Drawing inspiration from the writings of the Egyptian academic Hassan Hanafi and Marxism, Islam Kiri was anticapitalist and called for moral revolution to address systemic poverty and oppression (Prasetyo 2004). But over the past decade, "liberal" has developed highly negative connotations and has largely fallen from use in mainstream Indonesian Islam, except as a pejorative. Indeed, many younger, conservative Muslims often associate liberalism with western decadence and promiscuity, regarding it as a threat to their piety. Despite its current unpopularity, I have retained the term because it best captures both the flavor of reforming Islam that flourished for several decades, as well as the more recent sharply adverse turn in public attitudes toward the very notion of liberalism.

Another significant and closely related term is *progressive*, which centers on the notion of improving or advancing society and politics usually through pursuit of greater openness and inclusion, as well as by enshrining universal rights. There is disagreement among scholars as to the similarity between "liberal" and "progressive," but many writers use the terms interchangeably (Duderija 2016). In Indonesia, "progressive" has become a less-loaded and stigmatizing alternative to "liberal," even though there is often little of substance to differentiate the two. In contemporary Indonesia, to call oneself a liberal Muslim is to invite ridicule and ostracism, but a small number of intellectuals and activists continue to use the term with pride.

The final term to mention is *Islamism*, which is usually taken to mean an opposing orientation in Islam to liberalism and progressivism. "Islamism" is defined here as the movement to bring Islamic principles into all aspects of life. For Islamists, correct adherence to Islam is not confined to the private sphere, it should also extend to the public sphere. This often involves advocacy of comprehensive application of Islamic law and the requirement that the state be based on Islam.

LIBERAL ISLAM DURING THE NEW ORDER

Since colonial times, scholars have characterized Indonesian Islam as more moderate and tolerant than other variants of the faith found in other regions. Much was written about the ability of Indonesians to blend Islam with preexisting religions to produce a form that was distinctive in the Muslim world. Attention was drawn to traditions of peaceful and harmonious coexistence of different religious communities across many areas of the archipelago (Formichi 2016).

But a genuinely liberal movement in Indonesian Islam, one which self-consciously developed and propounded new and innovative thinking about rights and equality using religious concepts and interpretations, did not begin to emerge until the early 1970s, when young intellectuals started to gain public attention and, sometimes, positions of influence within organizations based on their advocacy of religious and political reform. Many of these thinkers saw Islam as a means to critique the existing repressive system and to bring progress to society as a whole, whether ethically, socioeconomically, culturally, or politically. They sought to develop Islam's inclusive and universalist potential for transformation. Their political agendas were not related to electoral politics or specific policies but rather broader issues of creating a just and transparent system that could give freedom of expression and association to citizens, regardless of their faith (Barton 1996; Kurzman 1999).

At least four interlinked factors account for the rise of liberal Indonesian Islam from this period: the influence of international liberal Islamic discourses, particularly in the Middle East and some Western nations; the expansion of Indonesia's higher education sector and concomitant intensifying discourse within a growing Muslim intelligentsia; political conditions, particularly relating to suppression of Islamic politics but encouragement of cultural expressions of the faith; and the injection of foreign aid, especially from Western nations. Let me discuss each of these in turn.

INTERNATIONAL ISLAMIC LIBERALISM

New trends in Islamic thought, particularly from the Middle East and South Asia, have had a major impact on Indonesian Islam for more than two centuries. Indonesian students studying in Mecca and Medina in the late eighteenth and early nineteenth centuries were powerfully influenced by the severe revivalism that swept the Arabian Peninsula. When they returned to Sumatra to propagate what they regarded as a new and more pristine form of Islam, hostilities broke out with traditional Muslims, eventually leading to the Padri War (1803–37). Almost a century later, the reformist ideas of the Salafiyyah movement gave rise to major Islamic organizations such as Muhammadiyah, Persatuan Islam, and al-Irsyad. From the 1960s, explicitly liberal Islamic discourses began to attract the attention of Indonesian scholars and groups. The works of intellectuals such as Mohammad Arkoun, Hassan Hanafi, Abdullah Ahmed an-Naim, Fazlur Rahman, Rachid Ghannouchi, Ali Shari'ati, Fatima Mernissi, and Amina Wadud-Muhsin were studied in the original by Indonesian students abroad or were translated into Indonesian, allowing them to be accessible to a mass market. Their writings fired the imaginations of many younger Muslims who were eager to find new ways of understanding their faith and exploring its potential as a source of change. They wanted not just to comprehend the oeuvre of foreign liberalism but also to develop it further in ways that would be distinctively Indonesian (Hefner 2000; van Bruinessen 1996).

GROWING MUSLIM INTELLIGENTSIA AND ORGANIZATIONAL MOBILIZATION

Coincident with this external stimulus was a dramatic expansion in Indonesia's Islamic tertiary education sector. From the early 1960s, the government had begun establishing State Islamic Institutes (Institut Agama Islam Negeri, IAIN) and Teachers' Colleges (Sekolah Tinggi Agama Islam Negeri, STAIN) to meet the growing demand for degree and diploma programs for graduates from Islamic boarding schools (*pesantren*) and Islamic day schools (*madrasah*). By the late 1960s, IAIN and STAIN were producing large numbers of graduates with a strong grounding in Islamic studies. In addition to this, smaller numbers of *pesantren* students were completing courses in the "secular" state universities. The number of students studying abroad also grew dramatically from the 1970s, partly as a result of Indonesian government programs to "internationalize" their tertiary sector, and partly also due to foreign governments, particularly Canada, Australia, the United States, and Japan, offering scholarships to talented postgraduates. The overall result of this was a burgeoning, increasingly worldly, liberal Muslim intelligentsia (Latif 2008).

This new Islamic liberalism was initially known by the term "renewal" (*pembaharuan*), but by the 1980s it was more commonly referred to as "Cultural Islam," which underscored its counterpositioning to "Political Islam." Indeed, some of the sharpest critiques from the Pembaharuan/Cultural Islam Movement were of traditional political Islam. Liberal intellectuals accused Islamic parties and their leaders of failing to serve the interests of the Muslim community by pursuing agendas that created suspicion and hostility toward Islam and which in any case lacked sufficient electoral support to ever be realized. They particularly contested central pillars of Islamic political thought regarding the necessity to have a state based on Islam and the requirement for constitutional recognition of sharia law. Far better, they argued, for Muslims to concentrate on the intellectual, cultural, and spiritual aspects of the faith, than to continue to squander energy on futile sectarian politics (Barton 1996; Hefner 2000).

The Pembaharuan movement in its early days was focused on campuses but over time began to spread more widely across civil society as activists gained leadership positions in Islamic organizations or founded NGOs as platforms for their activities. The two preeminent figures within this movement were Nurcholish Madjid and Abdurrahman Wahid. Madjid, a graduate of IAIN Jakarta and the University of Chicago, was of mixed NU-Muhammadiyah background, and between 1966 and 1971 served as chairman of the Islamic Tertiary Students' Association (Himpunan Mahasiswa Indonesia, HMI). The most prolific and academically acute of all Indonesia's liberal thinkers, he founded the Paramadina Foundation in 1984, which became the leading liberal think tank for the next two decades (Kull 2005). Wahid was a graduate of Baghdad University and an NU blue blood. He was the grandson of NU's revered founder and the son of an NU chairman, who himself became chairman in 1984, a position he held until he became Indonesian president in 1999 (Barton 2002). Other influential liberals included: Djohan Effendi, also from the IAIN system, who became head of research at the Ministry for Religious Affairs; Dawan Rahardjo, a Muhammadiyah activist and academic; and Ahmad Syafii Maarif, another Chicago graduate, who served as Muhammadiyah chairman for seven years from 1998.

NU became the leading progressive mass organization in the late 1980s and 1990s, due in no small part to Wahid's charismatic personality and intellectual brilliance. Several of NU's organizational wings became focal points for liberal activism. Its young women's body, Fatayat, drove a wide array of women's and gender issues; its students' organizations served as platforms for reformist activists, and its development institute, Lakpesdam, acted as a nursery for research, scholarly discussion, and community programs. NU also spawned dozens of NGOs at the national and local level, including the Pesantren and Community Development Association (Perhimpunan, Pengembangan Pesantren dan Masyarakat, P3M), the Institute for Islamic and Social Studies (Lembaga Kajian Islam dan Sosial, LKiS), the Liberal Islamic Network (Jaringan Islam Liberal, JIL), the Institute for Social Institutions Studies (ISIS), and the Institute for the Study of Religion and Democracy (Lembaga Studi Agama dan Demokrasi, eLSAD). Within Muhammadiyah, its youth movements, the Muhammadiyah Youth Association (Ikatan Remaja Muhammadiyah, IRM), Muhammadiyah Young Men (Pemuda Muhammadiyah, PM), and its Young Women's Association (Nasyiatul Aisyiyah) took up aspects of the liberalizing agenda. Prominent intellectual Dawan Rahardjo established the Institute for the Study of Religion and Philosophy (Lembaga Studi Agama dan Filsafat, LSAF) and later Syafii Maarif founded the Maarif Institute to promote rights-based agendas. Younger intellectuals also established a Muhammadiyah counterpart to JIL called the Muhammadiyah Young Intellectuals Network (Jaringan Intellectual Muda Muhammadiyah, JIMM). It was not uncommon in these NGOs to find activists from NU and Muhammadiyah, as well as many other mass organizations, working together (Munawar-Rachman 2010).

REGIME POLITICS

Political factors also played a major role in the flourishing of liberal Islam from the 1970s. Within a few years of coming to power in 1966, Suharto's New Order regime set about systematically emasculating and marginalizing Islamic parties in order to ensure its own electoral vehicle, Golkar, secured large majorities. In 1973, Islamic parties were forced to amalgamate into a single party, the United Development Party (Partai Persatuan Pembangunan, PPP), which was in turn subject to constant manipulation and destabilization by the regime. As a result, the vote for Islamic parties never exceeded 29 percent during the thirty-two years of Suharto's rule. The regime, however, was not content to suppress political Islam. It also wanted to engineer within the Muslim community thinking and behavior that better aligned with the New Order's developmentalist agenda. It encouraged discourses that validated, or at the very least did not challenge, the regime and its policies; fostered social harmony and order; and endorsed the goal of rapid socioeconomic advancement.

In this context, the liberal Islam movement proved an attractive option for the New Order. Its theological criticisms of political Islam dovetailed with the regime's efforts to delegitimize Islamism, and its emphasis on the educational, cultural, and spiritual advancement of Islam was welcomed as contributing to national development. Not all aspects of the liberal agenda were to the regime's liking—it discouraged discussion of its own human rights failings and lack of democracy, for example—but it found the inclusiveness and nonconfrontational approach of the Pembaharuan/ Cultural Islam intellectuals broadly congenial. As a result, it supported liberal scholars and their organizations, provided they did not openly show dissent. Madjid's term as HMI chair was endorsed by the regime. More significantly, it allowed senior officials to attend his Paramadina seminars and workshops on Islamic issues, which served to popularize liberal thinking in elite Muslim circles. The New Order also quietly intervened in NU's 1984 congress to ensure that Abdurrahman Wahid would be elected chair. Numerous NGOs also enjoyed favored treatment from officials (van Bruinessen 1996). With this level of New Order facilitation, Islamic liberalism was able to grow and dominate debate about the role of Islam in society.

Despite regime support, tensions between the New Order and liberal scholars were not uncommon. The New Order pressured liberal Muslim leaders to endorse government policies and its political vehicle, Golkar, something that many were reluctant to do. Wahid, for example, was nominated by the government to fill one of the seats in the People's Consultative Assembly (Majelis Permusyawaratan Rakyat, MPR), reportedly without being consulted beforehand. He felt obliged to accept but was largely inactive in the role. For much of the 1980s and 1990s, there was mutual wariness between the regime and liberal Islamic groups (Barton 2002). Most liberal leaders avoided sharp or sustained criticism of the regime but nonetheless continued to press for reforms that the New Order rejected.

Relations between the New Order and a number of liberal Islamic groups were further complicated during the 1990s as the regime shifted strategy and began seeking political rapprochement with the Islamic community. After twenty-five years of striving to confine Islam to the religious sphere and limit its presence in the life of the state, the regime started granting concessions to Islamic sentiment and interests. It founded Indonesia's first sharia bank, relaxed restrictions on Muslim girls and women wearing headscarves, and began appointing devout Muslims to strategic positions in government. Senior officials became more diligent in their attendance of Islamic celebrations. Suharto set the tone for this new direction, as with so much of the regime's behavior. In stark contrast to his earlier well-known preference for heterodox Javanist spiritualism, Suharto undertook the pilgrimage to Mecca with his family and encouraged media coverage of his attention to pious devotions, such as studying the Qur'an or consulting with prominent Islamic scholars.

Perhaps the most significant initiative in the courting of Islamic support was the establishment, with Suharto's blessing, of the Indonesian Islam Intellectuals' Association (Ikatan Cendekiawan Muslim Indonesia, ICMI) in 1990. From the outset, ICMI was seen by many in the Muslim community as a means of influencing, and a vehicle for advancement within, the regime. Thousands joined the association within months of its founding. They came from a wide variety of backgrounds, including ministers, bureaucrats, ulema, senior ex-military officers, academics, scientists, politicians, and community leaders. Many, like Suharto, had not previously been known publicly as particularly devout. Tellingly, some critics of the government and prominent Islamists were welcomed into ICMI, a clear indication of the government's reaching out to those who would once have been persona non grata (Porter 2002).

The New Order's unexpected "Islamic turn" created a dilemma for many liberal Muslims. Some commended it because it allowed Islam to contribute substantively to the government and create a better society. But others believed that the regime's initiatives were driven by religiously insincere political motivations and that Suharto was looking for greater Muslim support after his relations with the military had soured. They worried that the New Order's Islamic concessions might result in the rise of illiberal trends, which could undermine their efforts to entrench tolerance and pluralism. ICMI became the most obvious site of contention among liberal groups. Nurcholish Madjid and Dawam Rahardjo joined the association and held prominent positions; Abdurrahman Wahid and Djohan Effendi refused. Wahid attacked it caustically, warning that this kind of state-sponsored Islam would harm Indonesia's tradition of religious neutrality and could lead to the type of violent sectarianism seen in countries such as Algeria and Pakistan. The regime retaliated against Wahid for his outspokenness and almost succeeded in orchestrating his removal as NU chairman at the organization's 1994 congress. After this, he toned down his criticisms of ICMI and became more compliant to government wishes so as to avoid further retribution. Despite Wahid's fears, it was evident by the mid-1990s that the regime would keep ICMI under tight rein. Although it did allow many devout Muslims an avenue into government, liberal influence on the association was minimal, as also was that of Islamists (Bush 2009).

FOREIGN FINANCIAL SUPPORT

The final element in the consolidation of liberal Islam was the availability of generous foreign aid. Particularly from the mid-1980s, Western governments began prioritizing programs that were seen as undergirding social and political reform in order to better prepare Indonesia for what was seen as its likely transition to democracy in coming years. A growing number of donors came to the view that Islam, and especially liberal Islamic groups, were valuable prospective partners in these reform programs. The Ford Foundation began funding NGOs such as P3M in the 1980s to undertake gender rights and mainstreaming projects as well as educational reform. In the mid-1990s, the United States Agency for International Development (USAID) commenced funding of an innovative Islam and civil society program through the Asia Foundation, which would direct funding to multiple partners for a wide range of programs, from interfaith dialogue, community development, exegetical and jurisprudential research, to religious rights and democratization advocacy. Among the grantees were Lakpesdam, LKiS, and eLSAD. Most controversial of all was JIL, which will be discussed in further detail below. Other aid agencies, such as the Canadian International Development Agency (CEDA), Britain's Department for International Development (DFID), and Australia's AusAID also later provided assistance.

No reliable figures are available for the total level of financial support from abroad but it is likely to have been tens of millions of dollars between the mid-1980s and the mid-2000s. The net effect of this flow of funding was to allow the rapid growth of liberal Islamic organizations and the development of ambitious programs to propagate progressive ideas. At its peak in the late-1990s and early 2000s, many dozens of Indonesian program officers and activists were employed at least part time on programs and many thousands of participants were involved in training sessions and workshops. Hundreds of books, journals, magazines, and pamphlets were produced, as also were syndicated newspaper columns and newspaper inserts. Radio programs and even, for a time, a national television program, were produced using largely foreign funds. The scale of these programs brought liberal messages to an audience of millions and helped to give progressive discourses far greater prominence than Islamist ones.

THE NEW ORDER'S FALL

When the New Order entered its death throes in April–May 1998, liberal Islamic leaders and groups did not play the decisive role that might have been expected in forcing Suharto from office. In fact, some champions of liberalism were ambivalent when it came to the New Order's collapse. Abdurrahman Wahid, for example, seemingly because of his own hopes that Suharto might anoint him as his successor, called on protestors to allow the president more time to resolve the regime's difficulties. The NU central board also disappointed many liberals by discouraging its members from joining the mass demonstrations and warning against unrest. By contrast, Nurcholish Madjid was invited by Suharto to mediate between the government and the protestors, which he sought to do in good faith, eventually urging Suharto to resign to avoid worse public disorder. One of the most effective leaders during this period was Muhammadiyah's chair, Amien Rais, a mercurial figure best known for his past Islamist views but who advocated pluralist democratic reforms in the run-up to Suharto's resignation. Rais's ability to provide leadership to the demonstrators on the streets made him an important player in the events that toppled Suharto. In the main, liberal groups welcomed the fall of the regime and many activists joined the mass demonstrations that precipitated it (Mietzner 2008; van Dijk 2001).

It should be noted, however, that Islamists also played a significant role. Muslim Brotherhood–inspired students' groups such as Tarbiyah and the Indonesian Muslim Students' Action Union (KAMMI) were as prominent as liberal Muslims in mobilizing against the regime. Like liberal groups, they insisted on a transition to democracy, albeit one with a more overt Islamic flavor (Furqon 2004). Islamists were soundly defeated by an array of political and religious forces that favored the continuation of a religiously neutral state and the revising of the constitution to strengthen civil rights but not include recognition of sharia law. All the major Islamic organizations supported retention of constitutional religious neutrality. The extent of the shift in thinking during the New Order period is apparent if we recall that in 1955, during Indonesia's first democratic election, all Islamic parties and most Islamic organizations supported the notion of an Islamic state and the inclusion of sharia in the constitution. This suggested that Indonesia's ensuing democratization process would be marked by relatively liberal values.

REFORMASI AND LIBERAL ISLAM

The New Order had, in many ways, provided an artificial environment within which the liberal Islamic movement operated. The regime prescribed promotion of religious tolerance and harmony through its educational system, its compulsory ideological training courses, and its public information campaigns, and dealt harshly with any person or group deemed to be pursuing sectarian causes. Indeed, anyone accused of fomenting religious tension or unrest could be prosecuted under laws which prevented the use of ethnic, religious or intergroup issues to create disharmony, known as the SARA (*suku, agama, ras, antar-golongan*) statutes. It also kept Islamist discourses on the need for an Islamic state and a sharia-based legal system largely from public view. Moreover, it fostered liberal Islam's efforts to popularize "secularized" religiosity in which faith was predominantly a matter of private belief and behavior rather than public, political activism.

This situation changed dramatically when Suharto resigned as president in May 1998. Within eighteen months of the New Order's collapse, most of the political restrictions that had characterized the regime's authoritarianism had been lifted, allowing far greater freedom of speech and association. More than one hundred new political parties were formed, the media was unshackled, and thousands of new social organizations sprang into existence. Free and fair elections were held in mid-1999, and by October of that year Indonesia had a new president chosen by a largely elected MPR. Although all this may have seemed consonant with liberal principles, in fact reformasi posed considerable challenges to progressive Islam. Liberal scholars and groups now had to compete in an open, vibrant, and increasingly clamorous discursive marketplace rather than navigate within the narrow, cautious, and relatively static confines of New Order–sanctioned public discussion.

Liberal Muslims were particularly concerned at the swift proliferation of Islamist civil society groups, media, and political parties. Some of these groups had long been active "underground" or cloaked their real orientation; others arose organically from loose networks of shared doctrinal orientation or were mobilized around charismatic figures. Among the soon-to-be prominent political organizations were the Justice Party (Partai Keadilan, PK), which was based on the nominally apolitical Tarbiyah movement; and the Crescent Star Party (Partai Bulan Bintang, PBB), a revival of the Masyumi party that had been banned in 1960. Hizbut Tahrir, a transnational movement, had a more uncompromising political agenda, which included rejecting democracy and seeking restoration of a global caliphate. Of more militant disposition were the Islamic Defenders' Front (Front Pembela Islam, FPI), a vigilante organization that campaigned against immorality by mobilizing among poorer Muslim communities around the greater Jakarta region; Laskar Jihad, a Salafist paramilitary movement formed to protect Muslims from attack by Christians; and the Indonesian Council of Holy Warriors (Majelis Mujahidin Indonesia, MMI), which had roots in jihadist groups such as Darul Islam and Jemaah Islamiyah. The Islamic media also sprouted quickly during this period. One of the most provocative publications was *Sabili*, a top-selling magazine in 2001–2 which contained sympathetic coverage of jihadist campaigns both domestically and internationally, but other publications such as *Jurnal Islam* and *Suara Hidayatullah* conveyed similarly uncompromising views (Fealy 2004; Platzdasch 2009).

Moreover, grassroots socio-religious dynamics were changing dramatically. In the last few years of the regime, sporadic interfaith clashes, sometimes with lethal results, had broken out in many parts of the country, suggesting mounting tensions. With the New Order's fall and the dismantling or downgrading of much of its security apparatus, religious violence rose alarmingly from late 1998, leading numerous observers to predict the possibility of Indonesia descending into a Balkans-like level of bloodshed and political fragmentation. The worst unrest occurred on the island of Ambon, in the southern part of Maluku Province from January 1999 and escalated into a major sectarian conflict. This spread to the northern region of Maluku in August of that year. The following year, Muslim-Christian violence broke out in the Poso area of Central Sulawesi. Peace agreements for the Maluku and Central Sulawesi conflicts were eventually brokered by the central government in 2002, and order was restored to both provinces. An estimated 5,000–7,500 people died in these eastern Indonesian conflicts between 1999 and 2002 and another 800,000 were displaced (Aragon 2007; Duncan 2005; Braithwaite 2010; McRae 2013). In many other parts of the nation, sectarian tensions simmered, leading to a high number of attacks on churches and mosques. Christian groups, for example, reported that some 362 churches were attacked in the first thirty-one months of reformasi, with at least 50 destroyed (Murphy 2001). More than a dozen mosques were also targeted. Dozens of Christians and Muslims perished in this communal violence (U.S. Department of State 2017).

These political and social developments gave rise to fears that a democratic Indonesia would end up being less tolerant and more sectarian than under Suharto's regime. If liberal groups chose not adapt to the new conditions, they risked not only marginalization but also Indonesia reverting to an uncivil sociopolitical culture. Debate among activists on how to respond revolved around several issues. The first and most divisive was whether they should become directly involved in politics or remain as civil society actors. Those in favor of political involvement argued that joining parties and becoming politicians was a legitimate way to represent their constituencies and give voice within formal politics to the liberal standpoint. To not get involved would be to cede influence to politicians who either did not care about liberal values or were hostile to them. The counterargument was that "practical politics" (*politik praktis*) would likely entail compromises on major matters of principle and would also expose liberal activists to a world awash with corruption and seedy deal making. How, they asked, would Islamic liberalism maintain its moral authority if many of its leading figures were caught up in unseemly political maneuvers?[1]

Many activists, including some of the most preeminent intellectuals, chose politics, the majority of whom ended up in two parties: the NU-affiliated National Awakening Party (Partai Kebangkitan Bangsa, PKB) founded by Abdurrahman Wahid; and the Muhammadiyah-oriented National Mandate Party (Partai Amanat Nasional, PAN) established by Amien Rais. Wahid's PKB had the largest number of liberal activists of any party. Among its ranks were Matori Abdul Djalil, Muhammad Hikam, Maria Ulfah Anshor, and Hanif Dhakiri, all of whom had long careers in liberal NGOs or were engaged in intellectual activities. Rais, as noted above, had fluctuated in his public positions between Islamist and sometimes sectarian stances on the one hand, to progressive, inclusive attitudes and behavior. He was well regarded in Islamist circles and was offered the chairmanship of two Islamist parties—PBB and the PPP—but rejected both in favor of creating a "rainbow" party with multifaith and multiethnic membership. Many Muhammadiyah activists of liberal disposition joined or supported PAN, including Rizal Sukma, Bachtiar Effendi, and Sandra Hamid. Smaller numbers of liberal activists could be found across other parties, though few enjoyed much influence. Nurcholish Madjid initially stayed aloof from party politics, but eventually decided to seek the presidential nomination for Golkar in 2003, a bid that ended in embarrassing failure for him. Ulil Abshar-Abdalla, who had also kept his distance from politics in the first decade of reformasi, joined the board of President Susilo Bambang Yudhoyono's Democrat Party in 2010, to the surprise of many of his colleagues, but failed in his attempt to win a parliamentary seat.

A great many other liberal leaders, such as Syafii Maarif, Masdar Mas'udi, Ahmad Suaedy, Djohan Effendi, Budhy Munawar-Rachman, Hairus Salim, and Farha Ciciek, eschewed parties and kept to social activism. Most NGOs from the New Order period remained active after 1998 and many enjoyed, at least during the early years of reformasi, increased foreign funding from governments keen to ensure that Indonesian democracy was not only characterized by electoral fairness but also inclusion and pluralism. Apart from continuing their earlier advocacy of liberal Islamic principles, many of these figures and groups were heavily involved in seeking to resolve the worsening interreligious conflict of the early 2000s and also lobbying national and local legislatures to ensure laws and regulations protected the rights of minority faith groups.

A second point of contention was the degree to which liberal activists should challenge conventional views and confront conservative forces that they saw as inimical to interfaith harmony and the upholding of rights. The bolder activists regarded an uncompromising agenda as the best way to stimulate discussion in the community and bring about change. They believed, not without justification, that some of the most cutting-edge thinking in the Islamic world was taking place in Indonesia and that they had a responsibility to bring its insights into the public domain. They might best be labeled the "vanguard" activists and intellectuals, who wanted to lead from the front of public discourse and policymaking. More cautious groups, perhaps best called "community-based" activists, worried that the public might not understand or care for the elaborate argumentation of their more adventurous scholars and that pushing the boundaries of debate too impatiently might lead to a backlash. Much better, they contended, to be more modest in one's objectives and emphasize concepts of tolerance and freedom that were easily grasped and implemented by ordinary citizens. The majority of NGOs opted for a lower-risk approach and avoided propounding topics that were likely to cause an adverse reaction. But several NGOs and liberal intellectuals pursued more audacious strategies, with controversial results, as will be discussed below.

LIBERAL ISLAM'S INFLUENCE ON REFORMASI

Appraising the impact of Islamic liberalism on post-Suharto Indonesia is a complex matter and opinion is divided among scholars and activists regarding how much the movement has achieved since 1998. Generalizations are indeed difficult, given the breadth of the liberal agenda, the diversity of experiences across regions and communities, and the changing political and social conditions over time. In the years immediately following the New Order's demise, liberal Islam contributed considerably to the creation of a substantially progressive political system. Liberal Muslim scholars and activists assisted in formulating the revision of laws and regulations that swept away much of the previous regime's structures of repression. By far the most significant success of liberal Islam was retention of the principle of religious neutrality in the constitution and concomitantly excluding any reference to Islamic law. In the MPR constitutional amendment sessions between 2000 and 2002, the three main Islamist parties—PPP, PBB, and PK—proposed that a clause be inserted obliging Muslims to observe Islamic law.[2] The proposal foundered and was not even put to a vote, after the parties realized it would receive an embarrassingly low level of support (Platzdasch 2009).

The failure of Islamists to rally support for constitutional recognition of Islam was historically important. Since Indonesia's creation in 1945, the place of Islam in the state had been among the most divisive issues to confront the nation. In the pre-independence draft constitution, Islamist parties had succeeded in inserting a clause stating that Islamic law must be implemented by adherents of the faith. This "sharia clause" was dropped from the constitution the day after independence in order to appease religious minorities who feared explicit reference to Islam would prejudice their rights. Islamic parties sought unsuccessfully to restore the sharia obligation in constitutional debates in 1957–59, when they gained a simple majority but not the necessary two-thirds majority to change the constitution. The resulting constitutional deadlock paved the way for President Sukarno to replace parliamentary democracy with the authoritarian Guided Democracy. In 1967–68, Islamic parties again sought inclusion of the sharia clause but were robustly rejected by the New Order. The failure of the 2002 sharia proposal showed how dramatically opinion within the Islamic community had shifted over three decades. PKB flatly opposed the sharia clause.

Moreover, all of the major Islamic mass organizations, including NU and Muham-madiyah, emphatically rejected the proposal and asserted that the religiously neutral character of the Indonesian state based on the principles set out in the Pancasila state ideology was final.

The preservation of a "deconfessionalized" constitution, which avoided termi-nology and concepts that might privilege a particular faith community, was a major victory for liberal Islam. It indicated that the decades-long liberal discourse opposing the Islamic state concept and constitutional sharia-ization had succeeded in changing the attitudes of a majority of Muslims. While a broad range of community groups endorsed this liberal agenda, primary credit for bestowing Islamic justification for such a progressive stance is due to the unstinting and eloquent advocacy of liberal Islamic intellectuals such as Wahid and Madjid, and the many Islamic organizations involved in promotion of core liberal ideas throughout the Suharto era.

But, despite their success constitutionally, progressive Muslim politicians had lim-ited influence on many other issues relevant to their cause. For example, many liberal activists greeted Abdurrahman Wahid's appointment as president in October 1999 with elation, but they were soon disappointed with his performance. Although Wahid espoused progressive values throughout the twenty-one months of his presidency, his erratic and impulsive style undermined any systematic pursuit of policy goals, and by the end of his controversial rule, his achievements were relatively few. He did succeed in gaining state recognition for Confucianism, according it the same status as Islam, Catholicism, Protestantism, Hinduism, and Buddhism. He also introduced a number of regulations strengthening religious rights and appointed numerous liberal activ-ists to strategic positions. PKB did, fairly consistently, support progressive agendas, including the protection of minority religious rights and criticism of proposals for greater sharia-ization (Bush 2009). PAN's record was patchier, reflecting some of the ambivalence that Amien Rais and senior party figures felt toward liberalism.

Democratization had at least two adverse consequences for liberal Islam. First, it deprived progressive Muslim NGOs of some of their most effective leaders and activists, as many were drawn into party politics and government positions. Some of these NGOs struggled to find competent replacements as the salaries and conditions they could offer were far below that available to politicians, political staffers, and senior bureaucrats. Second, progressive Muslim NGOs and activists found it increas-ingly difficult to gain media attention and compete against the strategies of Islamist groups. The growing popularity of television, with its emphasis on short, snappy, and entertaining content, disadvantaged many liberal commentators who preferred longer, more reflective discussions. Islamists proved especially adept at harnessing electronic media in presenting their views. They made innovative and highly effective use of websites and social media, presenting vivid images of Muslims under attack or fighting to defend themselves, and using emotionally charged language to galvanize audiences (Hasan 2006).

The most difficult issue of all for proponents of liberal Islam to address was the rising level of religious intolerance. The ten-year Yudhoyono presidency proved espe-cially problematic. A record number of blasphemy cases—seventy-eight in total—were prosecuted between 2004 and 2014, with all defendants being found guilty and jailed, usually for minor offences. This was also a period of unprecedented intimida-tion and violence targeting Ahmadiyah and the Shia. Ahmadiyah congregations were subjected to repeated attack across numerous provinces, especially after MUI declared it "deviant" in 2005 and called on the government to ban it. The Shia also came under increasing pressure since the mid-2000s. In most cases of vigilante violence against Ahmadis and Shias, the police were slow to act and, when prosecutions did occur, the judiciary usually handed down light sentences. The Yudhoyono government was also reluctant to intervene in disputes over the building of churches, despite the president's frequent declarations of his support for the principle of minority religious rights (Crouch 2012; Fealy 2016). While liberal intellectuals and activists condemned these trends in the media, many felt that their remarks gained little traction in the broader community, due either to indifference or a dislike or disdain for the minorities in question. The contrast with the New Order, when progressive groups enjoyed prominence in public discussions on religious rights, could not have been greater.

The Antiliberal Turn

The mid-2000s was a tipping point for community views toward liberal Islam. The ideas of progressive leaders and groups had been relatively well received, if not always accepted, across much of mainstream Islam up until this time. But from around 2004–5, general attitudes began to harden and become far less tolerant of liberal thinking and initiatives. By the end of that decade, *liberal* had become a taboo term in much of the Muslim community and only the most committed of intellectuals and activists would take it as a term of self-ascription. The reasons for this shift are multiple. As described above, Islamist movements were becoming far more effective than their liberal counterparts at harnessing the media and mobilizing mass support. Islamist attacks on and vilification of liberals grew more virulent in the early 2000s. Among other things, liberal groups that received USAID funding were accused of being minions of the CIA or peddlers of un-Islamic values. Perhaps more fundamentally, rapid socioeconomic change and globalization were generating more conservative preferences within the Islamic community, especially within large cities and the urban middle classes that had once been a primary audience for liberal intellectuals.

This "conservative turn" created increasingly conducive conditions for Islamists at the expense of liberals. But it is also arguable that some liberal Islam campaigns contributed to growing community hostility by pursuing agendas that alienated many of the mainstream organizations that had once been well disposed to it (van Bruinessen 2013). Among these were three particular developments emanating from vanguard groups within liberal Islam, which sparked a furious response from many sections of the Islamic community: the publication of *Fiqh Lintas Agama*; the release of a Counter-Legal Draft for the Compilation of Islamic Law; and JIL discourses on theological issues.

Fiqh Lintas Agama: Membangun Masyarakat yang Inklusif-Pluralis (Interfaith Jurisprudence: Developing an Inclusive-Pluralist Society) was funded by the Asia Foundation and published by Paramadina in 2004. Nurcholish Madjid is listed as the author but the book was in fact the work of a team of leading thinkers from within progressive circles, including Budhy Munawar-Rachman, Ulil Abshar-Abdalla, Komaruddin Hidayat, and Masdar Mas'udi (Interview with Budhy Munawar-Rachman, November 2016). It provoked almost immediate condemnation from a range of Islamic groups that saw it as an attempt to bridge jurisprudential differences between major faiths, thereby elevating the risk of Muslim apostasy. MUI declared that the book deviated from orthodox teachings and hard line Islamic preachers such as Hartono Ahmad Jaiz and Adian Husaini railed against it at public meetings and in their writings. Even eminent Islamic scholars such as Quraish Shihab rejected it as harmful (Jaiz 2002; Majelis Ulama Indonesia 2004).

The Counter-Legal Draft on the Islamic Law Compilation (Counter-Legal Draft–Kompilasi Hukum Islam, CLD-KHI)—also funded by the Asia Foundation—added further to the controversy surrounding *Fiqh Lintas Agama*, as it was seen as emerging from the same stable of liberal scholars. The CLD-KHI was prepared by a team within the Research and Development section of the Ministry of Religious Affairs, but the main author was Siti Masdah Mulia, a well-known feminist researcher. Among its recommendations were that men and women should have equal inheritance rights; polygamy be banned; and wives have equal rights to initiate divorce and reconciliation with their husbands. It caused a furor and forced the then religious affairs minister, Said Agil al-Munawwar, to withdraw his support for the document (White 2006, 348–59).

At the same time as these controversies were raging, antipathy toward JIL was mounting, not just among Islamist groups but also the mainstream Islamic organizations to which many JIL members were affiliated. A succession of JIL publications called into question conventional understandings such as the divine nature of Islamic law and the infallibility of the Prophet Muhammad (Harvey 2007). One of the most hotly disputed writings was Ulil Abshar-Abdalla's article, "Refreshing Our Understanding of Islam" (*Menyegarkan Kembali Pemahaman Islam*) in *Kompas* in 2002 (Abshar-Abdalla 2002). He wrote of Islam as a living organism, not an historical monument and criticized the wearing of Arab-style gowns, the proscription of interfaith marriage, and advocacy of *hudud* punishments such as caning, stoning, and amputation of hands. Most provocatively of all, he described Muhammad as a historical figure who required critical study and questioned the obligation to strictly follow all that the Prophet did and said. Several Islamist groups regarded Ulil's article as blasphemous and called for him to be tried (Muzakki 2007). And growing numbers of religious scholars outlawed JIL's ideas and texts.

Antiprogressive sentiment reached a peak in mid-2005 at the national assembly of MUI. A series of fatwa were issued that were to have long-term consequences for groups promoting progressive ideas, the most significant of which declared that "religious pluralism, secularism and liberalism" were "contrary to the teachings of Islam" and therefore prohibited (Fealy and Hooker 2006, 461–62). This fatwa was commonly known by the unattractive acronym of Sepilis, intended to give a decadent, syphilitic connotation to liberalism. Other fatwas renewed MUI's earlier call for the government to ban Ahmadiyah and also set out criteria for Muslims in assessing whether religious groups were deviant or not. With the release of these fatwas, conservative Muslims stepped up their condemnation of liberal Muslim NGOs, particularly JIL.

Within progressive NGO circles, JIL's reputation became toxic. Activists working at the grassroots complained that whenever they entered an Islamic school or sought to carry out community programs they were grilled by Islamic leaders about whether they were from, or supported, JIL. Repeatedly they were told that JIL's proponents were not welcome, and nor were those who espoused liberal thinking. The mounting antiliberal stigma marginalized JIL and led its American and Australian donors to curtail their financial support. The Asia Foundation withdrew funding in 2006 after growing vilification in the Islamist media and threats to attack its premises; foreign embassies cut their modest financial backing a few years later. Other religious NGOs were forced to alter their language in order to avoid being labeled "liberal" by the Islamic community.

Opinion within progressive circles these days regarding *Fiqh Lintas Agama*, the CLD-KHI, and JIL is divided. Many still praise the quality of the intellectual output of groups such as JIL and Paramadina and point to the continuing influence of their writings, particularly in Islamic universities, where future generations of Islamic leaders are being trained. They also bemoan the fact that Indonesia no longer possesses intellectually ambitious Islamic scholars with the daring to question cherished notions about their faith. But others felt that JIL, in particular, did significant damage to the reputation of all progressive groups, including those who had long-standing ties to grassroots communities. For example, when one senior activist from a progressive community-based NGO "retired" to his home village in rural Java to establish an Islamic boarding school, he faced protracted scrutiny and suspicion from Muslim leaders and was repeatedly asked to disavow any affiliation to JIL and its ideas. JIL provided the ammunition that allowed Islamists to counterattack in a devastating way. Whatever the brilliance of the ideas propounded by JIL and other vanguard scholars, the broader struggle to engender greater respect for rights and religious difference was set back considerably. It is difficult to avoid the conclusion that the programs of vanguard liberal thinkers exceeded the bounds of what the community could accept.

Conclusion

Liberal Islam has been much lauded by scholars and commentators who regard it as primarily responsible for Indonesia being, in their view, a moderate democratic Muslim-majority nation (Kunkler and Stepan 2013). Whether Indonesia is as moderate and tolerant as is often asserted is a matter of debate, as also is the issue of how much credit for its present democratic and pluralist system can be attributed to religious liberalism (Fealy 2016).

In a general sense, progressive mass Islamic organizations and NGOs have made a considerable difference to discourses and attitudes on rights, justice, and equality. The fact that Indonesia's constitutional basis as a religiously neutral nation is broadly accepted across Muslim society is due in no small degree to the advocacy of such a position by NU, Muhammadiyah, and many dozens of progressive researchers and activists. This maintenance of formal religious neutrality has been critical to upholding rights to religious freedom. Many of these same civil society groups have also highlighted rights abuses through their publications and media campaigns, lobbied policymakers for pluralist laws and regulations, and countered sectarian messages and actions. Without such activism, Indonesia would undoubtedly be a less tolerant country.

But it can also be argued that the pursuit of audacious, boundary-testing strategies, which sought to advance agendas that had little support in the community or directly challenged established majority viewpoints, has backfired, producing a more illiberal and conservative system. Democracy unleashed conservative forces within Indonesian society, and in particular within its Islamic community, which had been suppressed for more than three decades by the Suharto regime. In many ways, liberalism flourished because of Islamism's enforced marginalization by the state, and also because of financial support from Western nations keen to promote Islamic pluralism and democratization. Once these restrictions were removed in the late 1990s, the interaction between liberal and conservative forces soon came to reflect the more genuine strength of these opposing tendencies within Indonesia.

As a consequence, liberal Islam has lost much of its momentum and vibrancy. It has far fewer leaders and spokespeople who are able to command public attention, and certainly no young leaders of the eminence of Abdurrahman Wahid or Nurcholish Madjid have emerged to fulfill the role that the earlier generation did in national discussions on liberalism. Indeed, the very word *liberal* is now an unwelcome epithet, used more in denigration than in praise. This does not mean that Islamic liberalism will cease to play a role in future, but the golden era from the 1980s till the early 2000s is unlikely to be repeated.

NOTES

1. Much of the information in this section is drawn from my discussions with and observations of liberal Islamic NGOs and Islamic parties during the early reformasi period.
2. Amendments to the 1945 Constitution included clauses stipulating the independence of the judiciary, the right to freedom of religion, and the basic principles of electoral democracy, thus fundamentally altering what had previously been a document that privileged executive power.

REFERENCES

Abshar-Abdalla, Ulil. 2002. "Menyegarkan Kembali Pemahaman Islam." *Kompas*. September 18.

Aragon, Lorraine V. 2007. "Waiting for Peace in Poso." *Inside Indonesia* 70 (April–June 2002). https://www.insideindonesia.org/waiting-for-peace-in-poso.

Barton, Greg. 1996. "The Impact of New-Modernism on Indonesian Islamic Thought: The Emergence of a New Pluralism." In *Democracy in Indonesia: 1950s and 1990s,* edited by David Bourchier and John Legge, 143–50. Clayton, Australia: Centre of Southeast Asian Studies, Monash University.

——. 2002. *Gus Dur: The Authorised Biography of Abdurrahman Wahid.* Sydney: University of New South Wales Press.

Braithwaite, John. 2010. "Maluku: Anomie to Reconciliation." In *Anomie and Violence: Non-truth and Reconciliation in Indonesian Peacebuilding,* edited by John Braithwaite, Valerie Braithwaite, Michael Cookson and Leah Dunn, 37–41. Canberra: ANU Press.

Bush, Robin. 2009. *Nahdlatul Ulama and the Struggle for Power within Islam and Politics in Indonesia.* Singapore: Institute of Southeast Asian Studies.

Crouch, Melissa. 2012. "Judicial Review and Religious Freedom: The Case of Indonesian Ahmadis." *Sydney Law Review* 34 (3): 545–72.

Duderija, Adis. 2016. "Progressive Islam and Progressive Muslim Thought." *Oxford Bibliographies.* October 27. http://www.oxfordbibliographies.com/view/document/obo-9780195390155/obo-9780195390155-0230.xml.

Duncan, Christopher R. 2005. "The Other Maluku: Chronologies of Conflict in North Maluku." *Indonesia* 80 (October): 79.

Fealy, Greg. 2004. "Islamic Radicalism in Indonesia: A Faltering Revival?" *Southeast Asian Affairs*: 104–21.

——. 2006. "A Conservative Turn: Liberal Islamic Groups Have Prompted a Backlash." *Inside Indonesia* 87 (July–September 2006): 22–23.

——. 2016. "The Politics of Religious Intolerance in Indonesia: Mainstream-ism Trumps Extremism." In *Religion, Law and Intolerance in Indonesia,* edited by Tim Lindsey and Helen Pausacker, 115–31. London: Routledge.

Fealy, Greg, and Virginia Hooker. 2006. "Interactions: Global and Local Islam; Muslims and Non-Muslims." In *Voices of Islam in Southeast Asia: A Contemporary Sourcebook,* edited by Greg Fealy and Virginia Hooker, 411–80. Singapore: ISEAS.

Formichi, Chiara. 2016. "Islamic Studies or Asian Studies? Islam in Southeast Asia." *Muslim World* 106 (October 2016): 696–718.

Furqon, Aay Muhammad. 2004. *Partai Keadilan Sejahtera: Ideologi dan Praksis Kaum Muda Muslimin Kontemporer.* Jakarta: Teraju.

Harvey, Clare. 2007. "Muslim Intellectualism in Indonesia, The Liberal Islamic Network (JIL) Controversy." Honors thesis, Australian National University.

Hasan, Noorhaidi. 2006. *Laskar Jihad: Islam, Militancy, and the Quest for Identity in Post-New Order Indonesia.* Ithaca: Cornell University Press.

Hefner, Robert. 2000. *Uncivil Islam.* Stanford: Stanford University Press.

Jaiz, Hartono Ahmad. 2002. *Bahaya Islam Liberal.* Jakarta: al-Kaustar.

Kull, Ann. 2005. *Piety and Politics: Nurcholish Madjid and his Interpretation of Islam in Modern Indonesia.* Sweden: Lund University.

Kunkler, Mirjam, and Alfred Stepan, ed. 2013. *Democracy and Islam in Indonesia.* New York: Columbia University Press.

Kurzman, Charles. 1999. "Liberal Islam: Not a Contradiction in Terms." *ISIM Newsletter* 2 (1): 41.

Latif, Yudi. 2008. *Indonesian Muslim Intelligentsia and Power.* Singapore: ISEAS.

Majelis Ulama Indonesia. 2004. "Buku 'Fiqih Lintas Agama' Menyesatkan." Accessed December 1, 2017. https://catatanasrir.wordpress.com/2012/08/06/buku-fiqih-lintas-agama-menyesatkan/.

McRae, David. 2013. *A Few Poorly Organised Men: Interreligious Violence in Poso, Indonesia.* Amsterdam: Brill.

Mietzner, Marcus. 2008. *Military Politics, Islam, and the State in Indonesia: From Turbulent Transition to Democratic Consolidation.* Singapore: ISEAS.

Munawar-Rachman, Budhy. 2010. *Reorientasi Pembaruan Islam: Sekularisme, Liberalisme dan Pluralisme.* Jakarta: Lembaga Studi Agama dan Filsafat.

Murphy, Dan. 2001. "A Burned Church Can't Rebuild." *Christian Science Monitor.* March 21. https://www.csmonitor.com/2001/0321/p6s1.html.

Muzakki, Akh. 2007. "Accusations of Blasphemy." *Inside Indonesia.* July 15. http://www.insideindonesia.org/accusations-of-blasphemy.

Platzdasch, Bernhard. 2009. *Islamism in Indonesia: Politics in the Emerging Democracy.* Singapore: Institute of Southeast Asian Studies.

Porter, Donald J. 2002. *Managing Politics and Islam in Indonesia.* London: RoutledgeCurzon.

Prasetyo, Eko. 2004. *Islam Kiri: Jalan Menuju Revolusi Sosial.* Yogyakarta: INsist.

U.S. Department of State. 2017. *International Religious Freedom.* Accessed February 15. https://www.state.gov/j/drl/rls/irf/.

Van Bruinessen, Martin. 1996. *NU, Tradisi, Relasi-Relasi Kuasa dan Pencarian Wacana Baru.* Yogyakarta: LKiS.

———, ed. 2013. *Contemporary Developments in Indonesian Islam: Explaining the "Conservative Turn."* Singapore: ISEAS.

Van Dijk, Kees. 2001. *A Country in Despair: Indonesia between 1997 and 2000.* Leiden: KITLV.

White, Sally. 2006. "Gender and the Family." In *Voices of Islam in Southeast Asia: A Contemporary Sourcebook,* edited by Greg Fealy and Virginia Hooker, 273–353. Singapore: ISEAS.

CHAPTER SEVEN

THE WOMEN'S MOVEMENT AND INDONESIA'S TRANSITION TO DEMOCRACY

Rachel Rinaldo

Women's rights activism is often a critical part of democracy movements (Moghadam 2013), but democratic transitions have a mixed record when it comes to gender equality and women's rights. Indeed, research on democratic transitions in Latin America and Eastern Europe in the late 1980s and early 1990s found that women's parliamentary representation dropped; there were few improvements (and some regression) in areas of gender-related policy such as reproductive rights, maternity leave, and childcare; and in many cases, traditional gender expectations were strongly reasserted throughout society and by states (Haney 1994; Shayne 2004; Viterna and Fallon 2008). Recent research also finds that women's political representation often drops sharply with the advent of democratization, but over the long term, increasing democratic freedoms and additional elections tend to improve their political participation (Fallon, Swiss, and Viterna 2012).

The existence and quality of women's rights mobilization, as well as the movement's ability to frame issues successfully in order to garner public support matters greatly, but these are often not sufficient to ensure that a democratizing country moves in a more gender-egalitarian direction (Viterna and Fallon 2008; Walsh 2012; Htun and Weldon 2010; 2015). In fact, there are numerous factors that influence the outcomes of democratization for women. Pretransition political and institutional legacies can shape political culture in favorable or detrimental ways (Moghadam 2016) as does the relationship between religious institutions and the state (Walsh 2012; Htun and Weldon 2015). Whether the regime transition is complete or retains some aspects of authoritarianism also makes a difference (Viterna and Fallon 2008). State capacity—and willingness—to implement reforms matters when there are opportunities for policies or legislation that might empower women (Htun and Weldon 2010). These factors combine and intersect in different ways in different national contexts, illustrating that while support for democracy and women's mobilization are important, they do not necessarily ensure that a country takes a more egalitarian direction after democratization.

The struggle for women's rights after democratization can also be significantly influenced by the formation of countermovements, a factor that has not been considered as much by scholars of democratization. Social movement scholars find that progressive social movements very often face countermobilizations that can stymie potential reforms (Banaszak and Ondercin 2016). Such countermovements are often successful where marginalized groups have made gains (Meyer and Staggenborg

1996). As Hughes, Krook, and Paxton (2015) point out, this may be especially the case for women's rights activism, which has the potential to disrupt men's privilege. Scholars find that social movements interact with and shape each other, in what some have called "co-evolution" (Oliver and Myers 2002; Fetner 2008). This phenomenon has been seen in cases such as Poland, where following democratization in the 1990s, a lesbian and gay rights movement emerged in tandem with a religious countermovement. With strong backing from the Catholic Church, this countermovement succeeded in establishing a narrative that linked LGBT rights to external threats to national values (Ayoub 2014). As this chapter shows, countermobilizations may be a significant factor in the fate of social movements during and after democratization, as a more democratic political sphere allows for expanded political expression and facilitates competition and interaction between movements.

Indonesia is an especially interesting case study for democratization and women's empowerment because it is one of the few Muslim majority democracies and has a long history of women's mobilization. Women's activism emerged along with the nationalist movement in the 1920s and remained a force through to the 1960s, but along with other social movements, was subject to government suppression when the Suharto regime gained control in 1967. Nevertheless, a vibrant and diverse Indonesian women's movement arose in the 1990s and played an important role in the democracy movement. Since then, women's rights activists have achieved some crucial reforms but have also confronted unprecedented and complex challenges—notably, the rise of religious conservatism. Yet while democratization in Indonesia has produced important gains for women's rights, it has also empowered conservative countermovements that oppose much of the agenda of the women's rights movement. As a result, women's rights activists have increasingly found themselves on the defensive.

WOMEN'S ACTIVISM DURING THE NEW ORDER

The transfer of power to the Suharto regime and the subsequent New Order period (1966–98) left a lasting imprint on the Indonesian women's movement. The mass killings of communists and other regime opponents in 1965 that marked the beginning of this period were extremely destructive for women's organizing (Wieringa 2002). The regime repressed independent mobilization, especially of the Left. Millions of women were mobilized into state-controlled organizations that were depoliticized and promoted a domestic role for women (Suryakusuma 1996; Brenner 1998). Through the 1980s it was difficult for women to mobilize outside these state organizations. Initially, religious organizations were one of the only channels for women's activism. By the end of that decade, a few women from more privileged backgrounds had taken advantage of legal loopholes and a small political opening to establish NGOs, then a new institutional form. The regime's greater tolerance of religious organizations resulted in the emergence of a dynamic religious civil society that helped to fuel a unique blend of women's rights activism and reformist Muslim discourses, but that also generated an expanding network of more conservative Muslim activists that would become influential after 1998, when Suharto was compelled to step down (Hefner 2000; Sidel 2008; also see Fealy, this volume).

Throughout this period, the government sought to balance its international image against its domestic interests, and this created some space for the advancement of women's rights. Understanding this trajectory of government policy helps contextualize the decisions and strategies of women activists during the New Order period.

In the late 1970s, the government began responding to changing international norms regarding women. It created the Ministry for Women's Role in 1978 and ratified the Convention on the Elimination of all forms of Discrimination Against Women (CEDAW) in 1984 (Robinson 2008). Moreover, Indonesian women's workforce participation rate increased to nearly 50 percent by 1990 (Australia-Indonesia Partnership for Economic Governance 2017). Thus, while the regime was still promoting women's roles as housewives, women were increasingly working outside the house, including in the factories manufacturing goods for global export that helped to fuel Indonesia's economic boom in the late 1980s and early 1990s (Ford 2002). By the 1990s, some Indonesian bureaucrats were sufficiently influenced by transnational women's rights discourses that they began to use phrases such as women's empowerment and gender equality (Blackburn 2004; Robinson 2008). Some elements of the regime seemed open to women's education, jobs, and rights, yet the regime remained committed to the ideology of domesticity, particularly for middle-class women (Brenner 1998), and suppressed social movement activism more generally.

Women did not only engage in activism through donor-funded programs and NGOs supported by Western countries. Indeed, some of the earliest channels for women's activism in Indonesia were through religious organizations. In the 1980s, leading Muslim intellectuals began to explore ideas about democracy, human rights, and pluralism, arguing that such ideas were fully compatible with Islam. This intellectual ferment appears to have had global origins—many of the leading figures were educated overseas and influenced by Muslim reformists whose ideas were circulating internationally. It was not long before some of these figures, particularly Nurcholish Madjid and Abdurrahman Wahid, the long-time president of the large Muslim organization Nahdlatul Ulama, also began to make arguments in support of women's rights. The discourse of women's rights and gender equality soon spread to Muslim women's organizations (Hefner 2000; Robinson 2008; Brenner 2011).

Outside of religious organizations, repression drove many social movement activists underground and meant that NGOs became the primary institutional form for women's rights activism in the late 1980s and 1990s (Blackburn 2004; Aspinall 2005; Brenner 2011). Many of these women were inspired by attending the United Nations International Women's Conferences; visits to Australia and India, where they came into contact with feminists; as well as the expanding global women's movement. One of the first Indonesian women's rights NGOs was Kalyanamitra, which provided services and advocacy for victims of intimate partner violence. Another was the Indonesian Women's Legal Aid Foundation (Lembaga Bantuan Hukum–Asosiasi Perempuan Indonesia untuk Keadilan, LBH-APIK). The new organizations obtained funding from international sources such as UNICEF, Oxfam, and the Ford Foundation, all of which were starting to prioritize women's rights and equality. These NGOs focused on providing services desperately needed by women, but many staff members also saw themselves as building a foundation for a broader women's movement (Blackburn 2004; Robinson 2008).

A new generation of activists came up through the ranks of women's NGOs in the 1990s, some of whom established their own initiatives during this time (Ford 2002). These organizations argued for women's equality in both the public and private spheres. Their staff tended to be urban and highly educated. Many of the women's rights NGOs also took a more critical stance toward the government (Brenner 2005; Blackburn 2004). For example, Rifka Annisa, which provided counseling for women dealing with intimate partner violence, quickly began working toward policy change to address the problem of gender-based violence, in the process bringing a taboo subject into public view (Brenner 2011). Some NGOs espoused critiques of global capitalism—ideas that in the wake of the 1960s repression of the Left in Indonesia were still quite taboo. As the Suharto regime adopted more neoliberal economic programs many NGOs began to diversify and ally with lower-class women. Solidaritas Perempuan, for example, was established in 1990 to advocate for the rights of the increasing numbers of Indonesian women who were migrating overseas to as domestic workers. It also saw itself as part of a growing women's rights movement, and many of its early activists were especially critical of government economic policies that emphasized labor export, export-led production, and natural resource extraction (Ford 2002; Rinaldo 2013). These kinds of alliances between middle-class activists and poor women migrants have brought the issue of women's migration and labor exploitation to the forefront (Ford 2008). However, in the uncertain political environment of the 1990s, women's rights NGOs had to maneuver carefully. Although they were allowed to hold conferences and workshops, participating in demonstrations often resulted in assault or arrest at the hands of the military or the police (Rinaldo 2013).

In addition to the development of women's NGOs, women's religious activism also continued to grow in the 1990s. Many of the activists who participated in trainings run by the Ford Foundation during this period were part of a global trend for women to seek a more active role in the interpretation of Muslim teachings (Badran 2013). In the early 1990s, writings about Islam and gender equality by Middle Eastern feminists like Fatima Mernissi, Nawal el Saadawi, and Riffat Hassan were translated and published in Indonesian by NGO activists and became influential for many young people (Robinson 2008; Brenner 2011; Rinaldo 2013). Over the next decade, Indonesian activists also became aware of efforts by Muslim women scholars in the West, especially Asma Barlas and Amina Wadud, to produce egalitarian interpretations of the Quran. Many women activists' exposure to feminist ideas began with reading Middle Eastern Muslim women activists/scholars Fatima Mernissi and Nawal el Saadawi, whose works were circulating in the student underground. The Ford Foundation's gender trainings for Muslim women's organizations, some of which were conducted by the liberal Muslim activist Mansour Faqih, seem to have been especially influential. By the mid-1990s, organizations such as the Pesantren and Community Development Association (Perhimpunan Pengembangan Pesantren dan Masyarakat, P3M) had begun organizing workshops that combined critical reexaminations of Islamic texts with advocacy for women's rights. More established Indonesian Muslim women's organizations such as Fatayat, the women's division of Nahdlatul Ulama, were influenced by this trend. In their accounts, some Indonesian women's rights activists said that they began to think that the case for women's rights had to be made with religious grounding, and others commented that they were especially influenced by arguments that included religious frameworks (Interviews, September 2002 to July 2003).

Lies Marcoes, who worked for P3M as well as the Asia Foundation, and now runs her own NGO, believes that the ability for Indonesian secular and Muslim feminists to work together added a unique element to the Indonesian women's movement:

> I saw that there was a weakness to the secular feminist approach which is that they didn't know what to do with religion, they weren't brave enough to talk about *fiqh* [Islamic jurisprudence]. I felt that I had something that other activists

didn't, which was an understanding of theology, reinterpreting religious texts. How to read the Quran critically . . . We could help secular feminist friends, and vice versa. I think this convergence between feminists and Muslim friends made us distinctive, different from women's movements in other countries, even Malaysia. (Interview, June 2016)

Some women's rights activists in Indonesia, such as those involved in the NGO, Rahima, have continued to pursue a strategy of creating and disseminating egalitarian interpretations of Islamic texts, as well as training younger activists in such methods of interpretation. This strategy has helped to legitimize ideas about women's rights and gender equality among Muslims (Robinson 2008; Brenner 2011; Rinaldo 2013; 2014). For Marcoes, it was precisely this convergence between Muslim reformists and women's rights activists that made the Indonesian movement strong and less divided along religious–secular lines than the women's movements in many other Muslim majority countries.

The broader terrain of social movement activism also contributed to the dynamism of the women's movement in 1990s Indonesia. The women's movement grew alongside other social movements. Many women's rights activists spoke of the thrilling atmosphere of the emerging movement for democratic change, where they met activists from environmental, labor, and other social justice movements (Interviews, various years). Many of the human rights and women's NGOs founded in the late 1980s and early 1990s became important actors in the prodemocracy mobilizations. Moreover, the frequent mingling of the student movement and women's groups during this period brought about a new interest in gender and feminism among young people, and many student activists later worked for women's rights NGOs and/or Muslim women's rights organizations.

Alongside these social movements, another more conservative movement was developing momentum. The renaissance of progressive and liberal Muslim thinking was part of a broader Islamic revival in Indonesia that began in the 1980s, which included a far more conservative strain of Islamic thought that became particularly popular with underground student groups on university campuses. The Tarbiyah movement, as it became known, was influenced by the Muslim Brotherhood and Islamist thinkers from the Middle East, and its followers tended to espouse conservative views on gender and sexuality (see also Fealy, this volume). While they did not necessarily oppose women having education or working outside the house, they emphasized "natural" differences between men and women, argued against the liberalization of sexual mores, advocated much more conservative dress for women, and in some cases entered into arranged marriages. Tarbiyah activists formed a huge underground network that funneled members to new conservative organizations and political parties after 1998 (Van Bruinessen 2002; Sidel 2008; Machmudi 2006). While women's rights activists were aware of this movement, and many were to some degree influenced by it, they were not fully cognizant of its growing strength or its conservative politics until the late 1990s (Interviews, 2002–10).

The New Order era had a mixed impact and an enduring legacy for women's activism in Indonesia. Its repression made activism difficult and potentially dangerous, and resulted in more progressive activism being contained within NGOs, which were tolerated due to a combination of legal loopholes, their connections to the international community, and their strategy of employing the relatively neutral language of development. While the women's rights NGO community grew increasingly outspoken,

NGOs by their very nature are relatively small, tend to be led by middle-class elites, and do not constitute a mass movement (Alvarez 1999). Meanwhile, and especially as time went on, the Suharto regime became more tolerant of religious organizations. This fostered the growth of religious activism, including a unique and important blend of women's rights and Muslim reformism, but also helped much more conservative religious activists build networks that were not supportive of women's rights. Nevertheless, the activism of the 1990s brought together a wide spectrum of forces that culminated in the *reformasi* movement and fostered crucial cross-fertilizations between student, labor, environmental, and women's rights activists that still reverberate decades later.

Women's Activism in the Transition to Democracy

While the New Order era set the stage for women's activism with its repression of secular and Left social movements, it did not wholly determine how women's activism would develop in the transition to democracy. The trajectory of women's activism was also shaped by more contingent events. The key factors that were most influential from 1998 onward were the developing pattern of women's mobilization, the emergence of countermovement mobilization as a reaction, and political decentralization that has empowered conservative and illiberal actors.

Women played a prominent role, including in street demonstrations as the reformasi movement built through 1997 and early 1998. The Voice of Concerned Mothers (Suara Ibu Peduli) was one of the most visible groups organizing specifically as women—mobilizing to provide assistance to those affected by the ongoing financial crisis, as well as to assist demonstrators with food and water (Budianta 2003; 2006). Many younger women became involved in the movement through student organizations. Years later, many women described the electric atmosphere of the time, as they went between risking arrest on the streets and holing up in their rooms reading Xeroxed copies of forbidden foreign literature (Interviews, September 2002 to July 2003). It was during this period that many activists from Muslim student organizations encountered ideas about feminism and gender equality. Others, like Lies Marcoes, described the early reformasi period as being intellectually dynamic, a period of "progressive and extraordinary thought" that provided an ideal context in which to think about gender and Islam (Interview with Lies Marcoes, June 2016).

A key moment for the nascent women's rights movement was the mass rapes of May 1998 (Budianta 2003; Purdey 2006; Robinson 2008). As political tension peaked and security forces fired on student protestors in Jakarta and other cities, mass violence broke out. Mobs attacked both businesses and people in Chinese Indonesian areas. At least 168 women, mostly of Indonesian Chinese descent, were sexually assaulted. Women from a huge variety of organizations and religious backgrounds volunteered to assist the victims and push the police to investigate. In response, President Habibie created a committee in July 1998 to investigate the attacks, and then in October 1998 established the National Commission on Violence against Women (Komisi Nasional Anti-kekerasan terhadap Perempuan, Komnas Perempuan), which has become the primary national voice for women's rights. Though officially a state-supported organization, Komnas Perempuan remains close to the activist and NGO communities and acts as an umbrella group for women's rights activism (Van Doorn-Harder 2017). More than this, however, the mass rapes served as another galvanizing moment for many women activists and raised awareness about sexual assault. Despite the efforts of human rights and women's organizations, the government has never acted to prosecute anyone for these acts (Anggraeni 2014; Wargadireja 2017).

The period from 1998 to the early 2000s was also a fertile period for the establishment of new progressive NGOs devoted to women's rights. Among the more notable ones that emerged were Rahima, which promotes women's rights within an Islamic framework; the Indonesian Women's Coalition (Koalisi Perempuan Indonesia), a coalition of local women's groups that works on issues of gender equality and democracy; and Kapal Perempuan, which is particularly interested in women's rights and religious/ethnic pluralism. The proliferation of NGOs contributed to the professionalization of activism and the recruitment of activists from a wider variety of backgrounds, compared to the more elite activists of the 1990s (Rinaldo 2013). But it did not lead to the development of a broader grassroots movement. Although there are Indonesian women's rights NGOs that do attempt grassroots mobilization and community organizing, their efforts tend to be small scale. Moreover, the consolidation of women's rights activism within NGOs may have undermined the building of a mass movement because NGOs compete for donor funding and therefore usually specialize in particular issues or locations.

However, not all the Indonesian women activists emerging during reformasi were interested in women's rights. Young women who had been involved in the Tarbiyah movement and the conservative Indonesian Muslim Students Action Union (Kesatuan Aksi Mahasiswa Muslim Indonesia, KAMMI) helped to establish the Justice Party (Partai Keadilan, PK)—which was soon to become the Prosperous Justice Party (Partai Keadilan Sejahtera, PKS)—as well as the Indonesian branch of Hizbut Tahrir, both of which sought a greater role for Islam in the state, in Hizbut Tahrir's case, seeking the return of the Islamic caliphate. Unlike the women's rights NGOs and the women's groups associated with the major Muslim organizations, these women were involved in organizations that were not specifically oriented toward women's concerns, though they did aim to mobilize women in support of their broader cause. Many of these new activists were unsettled by the increasing successes of more progressive women's rights activism, as well as by what they felt to be too much liberalization of cultural norms related to gender and sexuality.

By 2001, it was clear that the women's movement included several distinct strands. While this is not unusual or necessarily a problem, in Indonesia these strands encompassed vast ideological differences. On the one hand, there were the generally secular women's rights NGOs such as Kalyanamitra, Solidaritas Perempuan, LBH APIK, and Kapal Perempuan. On the other hand, there were the increasingly energized women's divisions of the major Muslim organizations—Fatayat (Nahdlatul Ulama), Muslimat (Nahdlatul Ulama), and Aisyiyah (Muhammadiyah)—which generally had a good relationship with the women's rights NGOs. Then there was a new cohort of conservative Muslim women activists involved in emerging political parties such as PKS, and Islamist organizations such as Hizbut Tahrir and KAMMI (Kesatuan Aksi Mahasiswa Muslim Indonesia—Indonesian Muslim Students Action). Many women activists do not consider these last groups of activists to be part of the women's movement, but certainly they were women activists in the sense that they were women actors in the field of politics and often voiced critiques of women's rights agendas. Thus, the major distinction that emerged in the women's movement by the end of the reformasi period was not a religious–secular divide, but rather, a conservative–progressive divide (Rinaldo 2013).

The conservative–progressive distinction was initially not that apparent, as the women's movement united around the Anti–Domestic Violence Law, which still stands as one of the most important victories for women's rights in Indonesia's history. Beginning in 1999, women's rights activists began proposing a national plan to eradicate violence against women. At the time, the Indonesian Criminal Code contained penalties only for physical abuse of wives, and these were rarely applied due to widespread belief that domestic violence was a private issue (Eddyono et al. 2016, 36). Women's rights activists produced a draft anti-domestic violence bill, which recognized multiple forms of intimate partner violence, including marital rape (Eddyono et al. 2016). Activists reached out to diverse organizations and communities in formulating and discussing the proposed bill, especially to women members of parliament. The Ministry of Women's Empowerment supported the bill, but initially, the powerful Ministry of Religious Affairs opposed it and President Megawati seemed to be ambivalent (Eddyono et al. 2016, 40). Activists intensified their efforts, and with the 2004 elections approaching, declared that they would not support Megawati if she opposed the bill. Megawati finally changed her position, and Law No. 23/2004 on the Elimination of Domestic Violence was passed in September with the support of most of the political parties in parliament, including women representatives from PKS. It was a huge victory for women's activism in Indonesia, but it marked the last time that the movement coalesced around a common goal.

THE CONSERVATIVE BACKLASH

Democratization has had many benefits for the women's rights movement. The democratic public sphere provides much greater access to women activists, both to engage with the state apparatus and to bring their arguments to the public (Interviews, February–March 2008). The women's movement used these new opportunities to achieve several very significant gains. In addition to the Law on the Elimination of Domestic Violence (2004), women's rights activists were the leading advocates for a number of new laws mandating child protection (2002), a gender quota for political parties (2008 and 2012), the criminalization of trafficking in persons (2007), and the ratification of the UN Convention on the Rights of Migrant Workers and their Families (2012). The movement also made a significant contribution to the election of the reformist Joko Widodo (Jokowi) for president in 2014, a campaign that involved many civil society activists, particularly women.

Women's rights activists are, however, not the only beneficiaries of a more democratic and open public sphere. As Adriana Venny of Komnas Perempuan explained, "Democracy is moving along well, but there are some people who take advantage of it for a different agenda" (Interview, June 2016). Since 2004, progressive women activists have faced an increasing challenge from those who do not support the women's rights agenda, including conservative women activists. One of the first and most conspicuous examples of this was the struggle over Law No. 44/2008 on Anti-Pornography and Pornographic Acts. Although there had been efforts to create legislation on pornography in the 1990s, there was renewed attention to this issue after 1998 as media became much freer and deregulated, and with the rise of the Internet there was a widespread perception that pornography was increasingly available and that pop culture was becoming overly sexualized. The moral panic reached a peak in 2003 with the national controversy over pop singer Inul Daratista, who was condemned for her sexy dancing style and revealing outfits, spurring antipornography campaigners into action, particularly within PKS (Robinson 2008; Allen 2009; Rinaldo 2012). Although there were already statutes criminalizing sexually explicit images, the new campaigners were pushing for a broader definition of pornography, which included public performances that incite sexual desire (Tedjasukmana 2008)

The Anti-pornography bill proved to be a divisive issue for the Indonesian women's movement, with some activists proudly supporting free speech and art, and others concerned about the impact of pornography on women (Van Wichelen 2010). The key concern of women's rights activists who opposed the bill was that it sanctioned conservative interpretations of Islam that render women's bodies as immoral. Moreover, the controversy over the bill took up a great deal of the attention of women's rights activists during 2004–8, taking time away from other causes, such as reproductive health and rights, reforms to benefit the many women who work as domestic workers, or simply doing more to mobilize women outside major cities. But despite strong campaigning against it by women's rights and anticensorship activists, religious conservatives succeeded in passing the bill in 2008, with the support of some Muslim women's groups such as Aisyiyah (Allen 2009; Rinaldo 2012). Although the law is unevenly enforced, it has led to a number of high-profile prosecutions of celebrities and politicians. More recently, with the prosecution and jailing of Jakarta's Christian governor on blasphemy charges, increasing crackdowns on the LGBT community (see Wijaya and Davies, this volume), and an initiative to criminalize sex outside marriage, it appears that conservative religious actors are driving the national agenda, leaving women's rights activists increasingly on the defensive.

Concern about rising religious conservatism has fostered increased collaboration between secular and religious women's rights activists. More secular women's rights activists in Indonesia now frequently ask a progressive Muslim scholar to attend a training or speak at a conference. Some of these scholars are themselves women, a development enabled by the increasing trend for Indonesian Muslim women to attend Islamic universities and receive formal training in theology (Van Doorn-Harder 2017).[1] However, religious–secular collaboration has not helped women's rights activists achieve the goal of reforming, for instance, Law No. 1/1974 on Marriage, which many believe instills gender inequality at the heart of family life by mandating that men are heads of household and women are responsible for the family (Mahmood 2016).

Collaboration between secular and religious women's rights activists has also not been successful in preventing the conservative backlash. In 2004, a team led by Muslim female scholar Musdah Mulia, who was then working for the Ministry of Religion, produced a substantial revision of Islamic family law that called for the banning of polygamy, equal inheritance rights for men and women, equal rights to initiate divorce, among other things (Robinson 2008). What became known as the Counter-Legal Draft was based on reinterpretations of Islamic law, a strategy that is very much within the tradition of Indonesian Islam. However, it provoked an immediate angry reaction among both conservative and mainstream Muslim organizations and was immediately buried (Cammack, Bedner, and Van Huis 2015; also Fealy, this volume). While the backlash had been building since the 1990s, the moral panic around pornography and the controversy around the Counter-legal Draft provided issues around which conservative religious actors could mobilize. In the following years women's rights activists continued to try to amend the Marriage Law, but they have had difficulty building consensus even among women's organizations, with the issues of polygamy and same-sex marriage being major obstacles (Van Wichelen 2010; Eddyono et al. 2016).

One of the reasons that women's rights activists' efforts to achieve their aims has stalled is that the movement is not well enough represented in parliament and the bureaucracy. Women's rights activists do have some political connections, which has helped them exert more influence than their small numbers might suggest. After 1998, a number of veterans of the women's movement and civil society including Eva Sundari, Nursyahbani Katjasungkana, Rieke Dia Pitaloka, and Maria Ulfah Anshor entered the realm of formal politics (Mietzner 2013). Their work has been crucial in the major legislative efforts supported by women's rights activists. Among these achievements has been the adoption of a gender quota in 2003 and its subsequent strengthening in 2008 and 2012. Law No. 10/2008 required political parties to include at least 30 percent women candidates, and the electoral commission was required to verify that parties had carried out this commitment. This quota has contributed to a significant increase in the percentage of women legislators in the national parliament from 8.6 percent in the 1999 elections to 17.32 percent in the 2014 elections; however, this percentage is still lower than the global average of 19 percent, and far lower than many of the other countries that have adopted quotas (Shair-Rosenfield 2012; Hillman 2017; Prihatini 2018). Yet, while the gender quota was a measure that women's rights activists had long pushed for, it has not resulted in the major political parties prioritizing measures to empower women.

The activists who are involved in formal politics do nevertheless serve as a bridge between the women's movement and the state (Mietzner 2013), and they have helped to pass progressive legislation such as ratifying the Convention on the Rights of Migrant Workers (2012). But their numbers may not be enough to provide a strong counter to morality legislation such as the Anti-pornography Law, which gives lawmakers a chance to prove their religious credentials, nor are they sufficient to push for significant new legislation or policy changes. Compared to countries with democratic transitions that have been more egalitarian, such as South Africa, the Indonesian women's rights movement is not especially well connected to formal politics. For example, in South Africa, the women's rights movement historically had influence within the main opposition party, the African National Congress (ANC), and at the time of the transition, activists, politicians, and academics created the Women's National Coalition (WNC), which collaborated with women inside the trade unions, the ANC, and other organizations (Walsh 2012). According to Walsh, despite the social conservatism of the previous authoritarian regime, during the transition political parties and elites in South Africa came to support measures supported by the WNC, including reforms to promote women's equality in the workplace and measures to eradicate violence against women. Currently, women hold 35 percent of seats in South Africa's national legislature, making it one of the top countries in the world for women's representation in politics (Women in National Parliaments n.d).

Initially, with the victories of the legislation on child protection and domestic violence, it looked like Indonesia might follow in the steps of South Africa. But since 2004, it has become clear that the women's rights movement in Indonesia is relatively small and underfunded, and lacks influence in the corridors of power. It does not compare well to the institutions in which conservative individuals tend to be ensconced, such as PKS—which even with the downturn in its fortunes, still has the ability to mobilize large numbers of supporters—or an extremist movement like the Islamic Defenders Front (Front Pembela Islam, FPI), which claims 200,000 members and branches in twenty-eight provinces (Varagur 2017). The trend toward religious conservatism in Indonesia has strengthened these conservative parties and organizations, as well as institutions like the state-supported Council of Indonesian Ulemas (Majelis Ulama Indonesia, MUI), which has become something of a vanguard for conservative Islam in recent years. Moreover, it has meant that the rank and file of the traditional Muslim organizations such as Nahdlatul Ulama and Muhammadiyah are growing more conservative. Importantly, however, the role of the state throughout these changes has not been neutral. Conservative actors are often willing to mobilize a powerful religious discourse that stigmatizes anyone who disagrees with them as an unbeliever or immoral, and in many cases, they have the backing of the military, police, or powerful elites. Indeed, as Aspinall (2010) argues, in its bid for stability, the democratic state has sought to incorporate Islamists. While such co-optation seems to have indeed brought Muslim conservatives into the democratic fold—for example, PKS has moderated many of its stances, and even many hardline Islamists have embraced electoral politics—the government has shown much less concern for appeasing moderates and progressives, because they are less of a threat. Muslims with more conservative politics are better represented in state ministries, including the powerful Ministry of Religion, than are progressive Muslims. These dynamics help to explain why a fairly well mobilized women's movement has had such difficulty confronting the challenge of rising religious conservatism.

DECENTRALIZATION AND PATTERNS OF WOMEN'S RIGHTS MOBILIZATION

Imbalances between progressive and conservative forces are particularly evident at the local level, where women's rights organizations have little presence, as women's rights activists themselves have long recognized. As A.D. Eridani of the Muslim women's rights NGO, Rahima, explains, one of the most significant challenges for the women's movement is the "disconnect" between the national movement and women's needs at the village level. However, she notes, villages can be difficult for women's rights activists to access as they tend to be quite socially conservative (Interview, June 2016).

This divide between urban women's rights advocates and rural women has been exacerbated by decentralization, which proved to have unanticipated consequences for progressive activism. One of the major sources of disenchantment with the Suharto regime was its extreme centralization of administrative authority. After his election as president in 1999, Abdurrahman Wahid quickly moved to decentralize authority by giving greater administrative autonomy to provincial governments. The new system came into effect in 2001, and provincial governments rapidly took on greater authority and responsibilities. This initiative had widespread support, although some women activists were concerned that the potential resurgence of customary law (*adat*) in certain regions could compromise women's empowerment. But what they did not foresee was that local authority might be used to impose new local ordinances inspired by conservative interpretations of Islamic law.

Decentralization has given conservatives (often allied with secular parties) much more opportunity to control local provinces and regions, because they are better organized at the local level and often have inroads with the police and military (Budianta 2006; Buehler 2013; Buehler and Muhtada 2016). For example, in 2009, the city of

Tasikmalaya passed a bylaw, "Community Values Based on Muslim Teachings," and began planning to enact it in early 2012 with an ordinance requiring Muslim women to wear headscarves (Suwarni 2012). As foreign news media noted, the timing of the implementation was close to an election, in which the mayor, who represented a secular political party, was facing challengers (Hussain 2012). Indeed, since 2009, Tasikmalaya has become a stronghold of the United Development Party (Partai Persatuan Pembangunan, PPP), a conservative Muslim political party that has supported many of the controversial bylaws (Widhiarto 2014). Despite strong criticism from national women's rights activists and progressive Muslims, soon after the election, according to a Christian news service, the new mayor, Budi Budiman of PPP, announced plans to continue implementing Sharia-based laws due to the strong backing he received from local Muslim leaders (Hariyadi 2012).

Perhaps the most significant concern for women's rights advocates in the last fifteen years, then, is the unprecedented power of local governments, granted through decentralization and regional autonomy, to discriminate against women and minorities (Budianta 2006). The Tasikmalaya bylaw is just one of no fewer than 422 local bylaws legislating moral and religious behavior adopted between 1998 and 2013 (Buehler and Muhtada 2016). According to a report published by Komnas Perempuan in 2016, at least 389 of these bylaws discriminate against women and/or minorities (Putra 2017). Such laws may impose criminal sanctions on women through regulations on prostitution and pornography, institute gendered dress codes and religious standards, and place restrictions on women's mobility such as barring them from being outside at night without a male guardian. Although most of these policies are loosely inspired by conservative interpretations of Sharia, they were in many cases sponsored by secular political parties aiming to boost their Islamic credentials. Yet while they exist in twenty-eight provinces, the six provinces in which they are largely concentrated are East Java, South Kalimantan, South Sulawesi, West Java, West Nusa Tenggara, and West Sumatra—all provinces with a history of activists pushing for a state governed by Islamic law, suggesting that Islamist activists have benefited from decentralization (Buehler and Muhtada 2016).

The architecture of the women's rights movement has not made it easy for activists to grapple with these complex challenges. Prominent women's rights NGOs are relatively small, and their central offices tend to be located in Jakarta or Yogyakarta. Certainly, there are many women's NGOs outside the major cities, but they tend to be small, lacking financial resources, and often issue specific (Eddyono et al. 2016).[2] By contrast, the women's wings of the Muslim mass organizations have potentially much larger grassroots bases. With branches in cities, towns, and villages across the country, Fatayat claims a membership of at least 3 million (Rinaldo 2013). However, its membership is largely informal and volunteer based, so these numbers are likely an estimate of potential adherents rather than actual members. Moreover, Nahdlatul Ulama is ideologically divided and its influence in the country is greatly diminished due to competition from other religious organizations and political parties (van Bruinessen 2013). Though Fatayat's leadership has generally been supportive of women's rights, its local branches tend to focus mostly on less controversial issues such as health care, helping poor women formally register their marriages, and providing information and services to prevent trafficking. Meanwhile, Aisyiyah, the younger women's group of Muhammadiyah, claims some 15 million members in branches across the archipelago, though similar to Fatayat these numbers may not be accurate (McKay 2016). Although Aisyiyah has done much to promote female leadership, the organization has tended toward a somewhat more conservative interpretation of women's rights (Van Doorn-Harder 2006). Nationally, Aisyiyah also departed from most women's rights activists by supporting the pornography bill.

Komnas Perempuan and other women's rights activists have kept close track of such bylaws and have staged regular campaigns to make the public aware of them and their discriminatory content. They have also published important research documenting the effects of such regulations. Nevertheless, the attempts of women's rights activists to legally challenge these bylaws, for example, campaigning for the Constitutional Court to rule them unconstitutional, have been unsuccessful.[3] In early 2017, in a major defeat for reformist activists, the Constitutional Court ruled that the central government does not have the authority to revoke such bylaws (Butt 2017).

CONCLUSION

The women's movement was a critical part of Indonesia's reformasi movement, and women's rights activists have had major successes since the era of democratization began in 1998. Major legislation they have fought for has been passed, and women's political representation has increased. Women are becoming more active in public life and are more accepted as leaders in a variety of arenas. Collaboration between secular and religious activists has been a significant factor in these advances, as has a more open public sphere. Indeed, Indonesia continues to have one of the most dynamic civil societies of any Muslim majority country. Yet women's rights activists have had difficulty confronting the rise of religious conservatives.

As I have shown in this chapter, the key factors influencing the fate of women's rights activism during Indonesia's democratization have been the pattern of women's rights mobilization, countermovement mobilization, and political decentralization. Although the Indonesian women's movement has been vibrant since the 1990s, and has deep historical roots, women's mobilization has been ideologically divided, and the more progressive side of the movement has been increasingly subsumed into NGOs. As women's rights activists became more visible and had important legislative achievements in the early democratization period (1998–2004), and the broader culture was increasingly influenced by more liberal views of gender and sexuality, religious conservatives mounted a strong pushback. This backlash, often seen in response to progressive social movements, has been most successful at the provincial level, where the women's movement lacks strength (Budianta 2006). Women's rights activists have had difficulty responding to this challenge because of their ideological divisions and lack of a mass base, and because the state has been increasingly willing to defer to conservative forces. Moreover, as religiously conservative actors and institutions become more tightly linked to the state, it may become more difficult for women's rights activists to demand reforms that might provoke religious opposition, even when those reforms are religiously framed (Htun and Weldon 2010).

By contrast, while the actual numbers of committed religious conservatives may not be that large, they certainly have greater numbers and more grassroots organization than women's rights activists, and they have often garnered support from secular politicians seeking to bolster their moral credentials. While women's rights activists may very well have quiet public support, the voices of Muslim conservatives as well as a small number of extremists are amplified in Indonesian public life.

In this newly democratized context, the proponents of the backlash against women's rights have the emotional energy of defending "tradition" and "religion" on their side. This has resulted, most notably, in the passing of a law that defines pornography so expansively that it is now being used to crack down on the activism of sexual minorities as well as censorship of social media. It has made the climate hostile to proposed reforms to the Marriage Law, and women's rights activists have had little success challenging local bylaws that institute dress codes and/or mobility restrictions for women. A proposed Gender Equality bill, moreover, has remained stalled in parliament (Yamin 2012). Indeed, authoritarian and intolerant actors have seized the national agenda with the goal of criminalizing same-sex and extramarital sexual activities. While a petition for this was rejected by the Constitutional Court in December 2017, the provisions on sex outside marriage are part of a revision to the criminal code now under consideration by parliament (Bevins 2018). Although these provisions seem to be targeted mostly toward the LGBT community, they could have significant consequences for women, as pregnancy in an unmarried woman would be a highly visible sign of engaging in extramarital sex.

In sum, as scholarship on democratization and women's rights since the 1980s has shown, democracy does not automatically empower women (Fraser 1990; Viterna and Fallon 2008; Walsh 2012; Moghadam 2016). The experience of women's rights activists in Indonesia illustrates how democratization can empower countermovements and/or backlash against progressive reforms. Although this is a common theme in the literature on women's rights and democratization, the case of Indonesia shows that when women activists or other social justice oriented reformers lack grassroots strength, their opponents may be better poised to capitalize on decentralized democracy. This indeed may be a central tension for young democracies—in an era of rising conservative populism, the democratic apparatus can empower those who mobilize strongly to impose an illiberal agenda.

Notes

1. Such collaboration between religious and secular women activists is unusual. In Muslim majority countries like Egypt, Tunisia, Turkey, and Pakistan, the feminist movement is largely secular. Only in a few other instances, mainly in Iran, Malaysia, and Morocco, has there been significant collaboration between Muslim and secular women activists (Mir-Hosseini 2006; Salime 2011; Basaruddin 2016).
2. One exception is Solidaritas Perempuan, which has an unusual structure that includes a secretariat with paid workers in Jakarta, as well as satellite "communities" around the country. Yet although it has larger numbers than most Indonesian NGOs, based on the attendance rate at their 2008 national congress, there may be fewer than five hundred people actively engaged in the organization (Field notes, July 2008).
3. Several activists reported that the judiciary has become increasingly influenced by conservative interpretations of Islam, so that the courts are not necessarily friendly ground for human rights activists (Interviews, June 2016).

References

Allen, Pam. 2009. "Women, Gendered Activism, and Indonesia's Anti-Pornography Bill." *Intersections: Gender and Sexuality in Asia and the Pacific* 19. http://intersections. anu.edu.au/issue19/allen.htm.

Alvarez, Sonia. 1999. "Advocating Feminism: The Latin American Feminist NGO 'Boom.'" *International Feminist Journal of Politics* 1 (2): 181–209.

Anggraeni, Dewi. 2014. *Tragedi Mei 1998: Lahirnya Komnas Perempuan*. Jakarta: Kompas Publishers.

Aspinall, Edward. 2005. *Opposing Suharto: Compromise, Resistance, and Regime Change in Indonesia*. Palo Alto, CA: Stanford University Press.

——. 2010. "The Irony of Success." *Journal of Democracy* 21 (2): 20–34.

Australia-Indonesia Partnership for Economic Governance. 2017. "Women's Economic Participation in Indonesia." Accessed February 13, 2018. https://www.monash.edu/business/cdes/research/publications/publications2/Womens-economic-participation-in-Indonesia-June-2017.pdf.

Ayoub, Phillip M. 2014. "With Arms Wide Shut: Threat Perception, Norm Reception, and Mobilized Resistance to LGBT Rights." *Journal of Human Rights* 13 (3): 337–62.

Badran, Margot. 2013. *Feminism in Islam: Secular and Religious Convergences*. London: Oneworld Publications.

Banaszak, Lee Ann, and Heather L. Ondercin. 2016. "Explaining the Dynamics between the Women's Movement and the Conservative Movement in the United States." *Social Forces* 95 (1): 381–409.

Basaruddin, Azza. 2016. *Humanizing the Sacred: Sisters in Islam and the Struggle for Gender Justice in Malaysia*. Seattle: University of Washington Press.

Berg, Livia. 2015. "Women's Pathways into Parliament: The Case of Indonesia." Master's Thesis, Lund University, Sweden.

Bevins, Vincent. 2017. "Once Tolerant Indonesia Moves to Outlaw Gay—and Extramarital—Sex." *Washington Post*. February 9.

Blackburn, Susan. 2004. *Women and the State in Modern Indonesia*. New York: Cambridge University Press.

Brenner, Suzanne. 1998. *The Domestication of Desire: Women, Wealth, and Modernity in Java*. Princeton, NJ: Princeton University Press.

——. 2005. "Islam and Gender Politics in New Order Indonesia." In *Spirited Politics: Religion and Public Life in Contemporary Southeast Asia*. Ithaca, NY: Cornell University Press.

——. 2011. "Private Moralities in the Public Sphere: Democratization, Islam, and Gender in Indonesia." *American Anthropologist* 113 (3): 478–90.

Budianta, Melani. 2003. "The Blessed Tragedy: The Making of Women's Activism during the Reformasi Years." In *Challenging Authoritarianism in Southeast Asia: Comparing Indonesia and Malaysia*, edited by Ariel Heryanto and Sumit K. Mandal, 145–77. London: Routledge Curzon.

——. 2006. "Decentralizing Engagements: Women and the Democratization Process in Indonesia." *Signs: Journal of Women in Culture and Society* 31 (4): 915–23.

Buehler, Michael. 2013. "Subnational Islamization through Secular Parties: Comparing Shari'a Politics in Two Indonesian Provinces." *Comparative Politics* 46 (1): 63–82.

Buehler, Michael, and Dani Muhtada. 2016. "Democratization and the Diffusion of Shari'a Law: Comparative Insights from Indonesia." *Southeast Asia Research* 24 (2): 262–182.

Butt, Simon. 2017. "Constitutional Court Lets Local Governments Off the Leash." *Indonesia at Melbourne blog*. July 4. http://indonesiaatmelbourne.unimelb.edu.au/constitutional-court-lets-local-governments-off-the-leash/.

Cammack, Mark, Adriaan Bedner, and Stijn van Huis. 2015. "Democracy, Human Rights, and Islamic Family Law in Post-Soeharto Indonesia." *New Middle Eastern Studies* 5: 1–25.

Eddyono, Sri Wiyanti, Estu Fanani, Dini Anitasari Sabaniah, Yurra Maurice, Haiziah Ghazali, Juni Warlif, Sisillia Velayati, and Farha Ciciek. 2016. "When and Why the State Responds to Women's Demands: Understanding Gender Equality Policy Change in Indonesia." United Nations Research Institute for Social Development. Accessed February 12, 2018. http://www.unrisd.org/80256B3C005BCCF9/(httpAuxPages)/695474BA6D066870C1257FF60053961A/$file/Indonesia%20claims%20making%20report.pdf.

Fallon, Kathleen M., Liam Swiss, and Jocelyn Viterna. 2012. "Resolving the Democracy Paradox: Democratization and Women's Legislative Representation in Developing Nations, 1975–2009." *American Sociological Review* 77 (3): 380–408.

Fealy, Greg. 2007. "A Conservative Turn." *Inside Indonesia*. July 15. http://www.insideindonesia.org/a-conservative-turn.

Fetner, Tina. 2008. *How the Religious Right Shaped Lesbian and Gay Activism*. Minneapolis: University of Minnesota Press.

Ford, Michele. 2002. "Responses to Changing Labour Relations: The Case of Women's NGOs in Indonesia." In *Women and Work in Globalising Asia*, edited by Dong-Sook S. Gills and Nicola Piper, 90–111. London: Routledge.

——. 2008. "Women's Labor Activism in Indonesia." *Signs: Journal of Women in Culture and Society* 33 (3): 510–15.

Fraser, Nancy. 1990. "Rethinking the Public Sphere: A Contribution to the Critique of Actually Existing Democracy." *Social Text* 25/26: 56–80.

Haney, Lynne. 1994. "From Proud Worker to Good Mother: Women, the State, and Regime Change in Hungary." *Frontiers: A Journal of Women Studies* 14 (3): 113–50.

Hariyadi, Mathias. 2012. "West Java: New Tasikmalaya Mayor Plans to Implement Sharia." *AsiaNews*. November 20. http://www.asianews.it/news-en/West-Java:-new-Tasikmalaya-mayor-plans-to-implement-Sharia-26400.html.

Hefner, Robert. 2000. *Civil Islam: Muslims and Democratization in Indonesia*. Princeton, NJ: Princeton University Press.

Hillman, Ben. 2017. "Increasing Women's Parliamentary Representation in Asia and the Pacific: The Indonesian Experience." *Asia and The Pacific Policy Studies* 4 (1): 38–49.

Htun, Mala, and S. Laurel Weldon. 2010. "When Do Governments Promote Women's Rights: A Framework for the Comparative Analysis of Sex Equality Policy." *Perspectives on Politics* 8 (1): 207–16.

——. 2015. "Religious Power: The State, Women's Rights, and Family Law." *Politics and Gender* 11: 451–77.

Hughes, Melanie M., Mona Lena Krook, and Pamela Paxton. 2015. "Transnational Women's Activism and the Global Diffusion of Gender Quotas." *International Studies Quarterly* 59 (2): 357–72.

Hussain, Zakir. 2012. "Tasikmalaya Softpedals on 'Headscarf for all.'" *Straits Times*. June 19. http://eresources.nlb.gov.sg/newspapers/digitised/issue/straitstimes20120619-1.

Machmudi, Yon. 2006. "The Rise of Jemaah Tarbiyah and the Prosperous Justice Party." Ph.D. Diss., Australian National University.

Mahmood, Shahirah. 2016. "Contextualizing the Global and Remaking the Local: Islam and Women's Rights in Indonesia." Ph.D. diss., University of Wisconsin-Madison.

McKay, Laura Jean. 2016. "Aisyiyah: 99 Years of Women's Empowerment." *Development Policy Center Aid Profiles*. http://devpolicy.org/aidprofiles/2016/09/13/aisyiyah-99-years-of-womens-empowerment/.

Meyer, David S., and Suzanne Staggenborg. 1996. "Movements, Countermovements, and the Structure of Political Opportunity." *American Journal of Sociology* 101: 1628–60.

Mietzner, Marcus. 2013. "Fighting the Hellhounds: Pro-Democracy Activists and Party Politics in Post-Suharto Indonesia." *Journal of Contemporary Asia* 43 (1): 28–50.

Mir-Hosseini, Ziba. 2006. "Muslim Women's Quest for Equality: Between Islamic Law and Feminism." *Critical Inquiry* 32 (4): 629–45.

Moghadam, Valentine. 2013. "What Is Democracy? Promises and Perils of the Arab Spring." *Current Sociology* 61 (4): 393–408.

——. 2016. "Women and Democracy after the Arab Spring: Theory, Practice, and Prospects." In *Empowering Women after the Arab Spring*, edited by Valentine Moghadam and Marwa Shalaby, 193–215. New York: Palgrave Macmillan.

Oliver, Pam, and Daniel Myers. 2003. "The Coevolution of Social Movements." *Mobilization: An International Quarterly* 8 (1): 1–24.

Prihatini, Ella S. 2018. "How Can Indonesia Increase the Number of Women Legislators?" *The Conversation*. January 24. https://theconversation.com/how-can-indonesia-increase-the-number-of-women-legislators-90446.

Purdey, Jemma. 2006. *Anti-Chinese Violence in Indonesia, 1996–1999*. Honolulu: University of Hawaii Press.

Putra, Lutfy Mairizal. 2017. "Komnas Perempuan Nilai Kemendagri Masih Akomodasi Perda yang Diskriminatif." *Kompas*. August 2, 2017. http://nasional.kompas.com/read/2017/02/08/21035141/komnas.perempuan.nilai.kemendagri.masih.akomodasi.perda.diskriminatif.

Rinaldo, Rachel. 2012. "Religion and the Politics of Morality: Muslim Women Activists and the Pornography Debate in Indonesia." In *Encountering Islam: The Politics of Religious Identities in Indonesia*, edited by Hui Yew-Foong, 247–68. Singapore: ISEAS Press.

——. 2013. *Mobilizing Piety: Islam and Feminism in Indonesia*. New York: Oxford University Press.

——. 2014. "Pious and Critical: Muslim Women Activists and the Question of Agency." *Gender and Society* 28 (6): 824–46.

Robinson, Kathryn. 2008. *Gender, Islam, and Democracy in Indonesia*. London: Routledge.

Salime, Zakia. 2011. *Between Feminism and Islam: Human Rights and Sharia Law in Morocco*. Minneapolis: University of Minnesota Press.

Shair-Rosenfield, Sarah. 2012. "The Alternative Incumbency Effect: Electing Women Legislators in Indonesia." *Electoral Studies* 31: 576–87.

Shayne, Julie. 2004. *The Revolution Question: Feminisms in El Salvador, Chile, and Cuba*. New Brunswick, NJ: Rutgers University Press.

Sidel, John. 2008. *Riots, Pogroms, Jihad: Religious Violence in Indonesia.* Ithaca, CA: Cornell University Press.

Suryakusuma, Julia. 1996. "The State and Sexuality in New Order Indonesia." In *Fantasizing the Feminine in Indonesia,* edited by Laurie J. Sears, 92–119. Durham, NC: Duke University Press.

Suwarni, Yuli. 2012. "Tasikmalaya to Make Muslim Women Wear Headscarves." *Jakarta Post.* June 5. http://www.thejakartapost.com/news/2012/06/05/tasikmalaya-make-muslim-women-wear-headscarves.html.

Tedjasukmana, Jason. 2008. "Indonesia's New Anti-Porn Agenda." *Time.* November 6. http://content.time.com/time/world/article/0,8599,1857090,00.html.

van Bruinessen, Martin. 2002. "Genealogies of Islamic Radicalism in Post-Suharto Indonesia." *Southeast Asia Research* 10 (2): 117–54.

——, ed. 2013. *Contemporary Developments in Indonesian Islam: Explaining the "Conservative Turn."* Singapore: ISEAS Press.

Van Doorn-Harder, Pieternella. 2006. *Women Shaping Islam: Reading the Quran in Indonesia.* Champaign: University of Illinois Press.

——. 2017. "Gender, National Identity, and Nation-Building: Komnas Perempuan and Koalisi Perempuan Indonesia." *Contending Modernities.* January 25. http://contendingmodernities.nd.edu/field-notes/gender-national-identity-and-nation-building/.

Van Wichelen, Sonja. 2010. *Religion, Gender, and Politics in Indonesia: Disputing the Muslim Body.* London: Routledge.

Varagur, Krithika. 2017. "Indonesia's Moderate Islam Is Slowly Crumbling." *Foreign Policy.* February 14. http://foreignpolicy.com/2017/02/14/indonesias-moderate-islam-is-slowly-crumbling/.

Viterna, Jocelyn, and Kathleen M. Fallon. 2008. "Democratization, Women's Movements, and Gender-Equitable States: A Framework for Comparison." *American Sociological Review* 73: 668–89.

Walsh, Denise. 2012. "Does the Quality of Democracy Matter for Women's Rights? Just Debate and Democratic Transition in Chile and South Africa." *Comparative Political Studies* 45 (11): 1323–50.

Wargadireja, Arzia Tivany. 2017. "Indonesia's Mass Rape Victims Are Waiting for Justice that May Never Come." *Vice.* May 21. https://www.vice.com/en_nz/article/vv5jab/hundreds-of-women-were-raped-during-the-may-98-riots-will-they-ever-see-justice.

Widhiarto, Hasyim. 2014. "Islamic Parties Find a Home in Tasikmalaya." *Jakarta Post.* January 6. http://www.thejakartapost.com/news/2014/01/06/islamic-parties-find-a-home-tasikmalaya.html.

Wieringa, Saskia. 2002. *Sexual Politics in Indonesia.* London: Palgrave Macmillan.

Women in National Parliaments. n.d. Accessed February 12, 2018. http://archive.ipu.org/wmn-e/classif.htm.

Yamin, Kafil. 2012. "Islamists Stall Gender Equality Bill." *InterPress Service.* May 9. http://www.ipsnews.net/2012/05/islamists-stall-gender-equality-bill/.

CHAPTER EIGHT

THE UNFULFILLED PROMISE OF DEMOCRACY: LESBIAN AND GAY ACTIVISM IN INDONESIA

Hendri Wijaya and Sharyn Graham Davies

Democracy is built on the principle that minority groups, including lesbian and gay groups, merit social justice, equal representation, and participation (Macgillivray 2000). The transition to democracy thus often correlates with an increase in lesbian and gay activism and the granting of basic human rights (Drucker 2015). We see, for instance, same-sex marriage laws resulting from democratic regime change in Argentina (Brown 1999), Brazil (Green 1999), and South Africa (Gevisser 1995; Palmberg 1999). By contrast, in 2013, India's democratic Supreme Court reinstated a colonial-era ban on homosexual sex (Encarnación 2014, 91), proving that democracy does not guarantee lesbian and gay rights (Flores et al. 2015). It would seem, though, that democracy is a fundamental prerequisite to lesbian and gay rights given that no nondemocratic nation accords substantive rights to lesbian and gay citizens (Encarnación 2014).[1]

What, then, is it about democracy that enables lesbian and gay rights to emerge? This chapter analyzes the influence of lesbian and gay rights activism on democracy and democracy's influence on that activism. It argues that democracy enabled lesbian and gay activists to assert rights claims and demand acceptance of sexual and gender diversity while—*at precisely the same time*—their increasing visibility and influence provoked a constriction of democratic principles and a rise in homophobia never witnessed during authoritarian rule. As a result of this conservative backlash, lesbian and gay Indonesians, as sexual subjects, are being actively excluded from participatory democratic processes in a more targeted and punitive way than ever before.

LESBIAN AND GAY ACTIVISM IN NEW ORDER INDONESIA

There was little overt lesbian or gay activism during the New Order period (1966–98), and no activists publicly demanded either negative rights (for instance, the right not to be discriminated on the basis of sexuality or gender) or positive rights (for instance, the right to same-sex marriage). However, grassroots activists were quietly but passionately paving the way for the development of lesbian and gay organizations that were to emerge in post-1998 Indonesia. As we explore below, activists in the predemocratic era focused on two key ways to support lesbian and gay Indonesians. The first was through naming sexual desire as something that could identify an individual. The second was through the development of small activist groups, which, once democracy emerged, were able to take advantage of foreign funding and assistance to push for nationwide acceptance of gender and sexual diversity.

Naming Desire

During Indonesia's New Order period, lesbian and gay activists rarely attracted state or religious attention for two reasons. First, homosexuality was not considered a particular threat to state stability and so the state saw no advantage in drawing attention to the private sexual activities of homosexual couples despite its focus on the private sexual activities of unmarried heterosexual couples, which were considered threatening to state stability (Davies 2015). Second, lesbian and gay activists strategically submerged their activities under a heteronormative frame perceived by officials as nonthreatening. The lack of persecutory attention did not mean, of course, that Indonesia supported homosexuality; rather, New Order Indonesia was a heterosexist, rather than homophobic, society and, as such, national instability was positioned as potentially resulting from nonmarital heterosexuality. Within this gendered constellation, Suharto consolidated power by positioning himself as father of the nation and proposing the family principle (*asas kekeluargaan*) to frame heterosexuality as the proper symbol of citizenship (Bennett 2005; Blackburn 2004; Brenner 2011).

Although New Order Indonesia did not consider homosexuality a direct threat to its stability, lesbian and gay activists knew that any direct confrontation with the state would jeopardize their nascent movement and indeed even individuals themselves. As long as lesbians and gay men publicly conformed to the family principle, ideally through heterosexual marriage, institutions of power largely ignored private sexuality. Lesbian and gay activists thus saw little advantage in encouraging people to come out or to eschew heteronormativity. Indeed, heterosexual marriage and children offered rewards to lesbian and gay Indonesians that in some ways offset the lack of sexual freedom. Through marriage, lesbians and gay men could have children and create familial bonds while at the same time pursuing fulfilling private sexual and homosocial/homoerotic relationships. In these ways, lesbian and gay activists variously "dubbed" Western notions of homosexuality to produce meanings and subjectivities appropriate in an Indonesian context (Boellstorff 2003).

In order not to draw government attention, human rights language, which was perceived by many activists as an inappropriate Western import, was rarely publicly deployed during the New Order. Indeed, up until the 1990s, activism remained largely limited to local settings and there was yet to be significant international influence in terms of the promotion of Indonesian lesbian and gay rights (Offord 2011; Altman and Symons 2016). Further, rather than organizing protests in public and demanding rights, lesbian and gay activists focused on small-scale public education, awareness raising, and network formation to increase social acceptance of lesbian and gay Indonesians and to instill a sense of self-worth among lesbians and gay men themselves.

While strategic conformity to heteronormativity meant that much lesbian and gay activism was carried out under the government's radar, awareness of homosexuality as an identity grew as the New Order progressed. In the 1980s, lesbian and gay activists began to selectively tap into Western media, such as gay magazines, to promote the idea that sexual desires and practices could define a person's identity

(Boellstorff 2005; 2007). Activists also drew on locally made films featuring lesbian and gay characters to enable discussion of lesbian and gay identities (Munir 2016; Murtagh 2013). For instance, Murtagh (2013) showed how gay men "queered" the endings of even homophobic films cut short by censor boards to imagine gay protagonists kissing or falling in love. Mainstream media also began disseminating (mostly unfavorable) information about lesbian and gay Indonesians in newspapers, news magazines, and women's magazines. For instance, two stories about lesbians were covered in 1981, inciting a torrent of coverage discussing notions of love, belonging, citizenship, and what constituted normal/abnormal sexuality (Blackwood 2007).

Influenced by the West's focus on sexology and psychoanalysis, media coverage during this time in Indonesia centered on speculation over the cause of homosexuality, on the supposed link between homosexuality and disease (e.g., HIV), and on possible cures for homosexuality. Mainstream media coverage thus shaped lesbian and gay activism by compelling activists to reassure lesbian and gay Indonesians that their sexual desire was normal and healthy. In short, while these stories perpetuated homophobia, coverage enabled lesbian and gay activists for the first time to promote the idea that sexual desire could be named and that it could form the basis of an individual's identity. This naming of desire propelled an emerging lesbian and gay rights movement, which would later get into full swing in a newly democratic Indonesia.

AN EMERGING MOVEMENT

Coterminous with raising awareness of an identity that could be formed around sexuality, and through drawing inspiration from activists in Asia and the West, Indonesian lesbian activism began slowly to appear in the mid-1980s. The first lesbian activist network to appear was a short-lived initiative called the Indonesian Lesbian Union (Persatuan Lesbian Indonesia, Perlesin), which organized social events that encouraged lesbians to mingle with everyday members of Indonesian society. It was hoped that interaction with others would help reduce the stigma against lesbians (Blackwood 2010; Wieringa 1987 and 1999). In 1984, a small lesbian organization called Sappho emerged in Jakarta to provide psychological support to lesbians through regular face-to-face meetings. An explicit aim of these meetings, according to one of its cofounders, was to enhance lesbian confidence and boost their own self-acceptance (Agustine 2008). In the early 1990s, lesbian activists drew inspiration from the Asian Lesbian Network and formed Chandra Kirana, an organization whose members envisaged would bring lesbian women together from across the archipelago (Davies 2010; Gayatri 2015). Another lesbian organization, Suara Srikandi, also developed around this time. It accessed foreign health funding in order to expand its outreach and enable members to travel to national and international conferences. Very little is known about these early lesbian activist groups, however, as fear of persecution and harassment meant they had to keep their activities largely concealed (Blackwood 2010; Wieringa 1997). Nevertheless, there was certainly lesbian activism going on in the 1980s, and it was these activist seeds that would develop into more vocal rights groups once Indonesia moved toward democracy in the late 1990s.

In contrast to lesbian activism, gay activism was more public and sustained during the 1980s. In 1982, Dede Oetomo and other gay Indonesian men formed the group Lambda Indonesia. Lambda Indonesia had four key aims: to connect gay men across Indonesia; to connect gay Indonesians with gay activists internationally; to instill feelings of self-worth and respect; and to counter misinformation about homosexuality in the media and among the general public. While Lambda Indonesia's strategies were influenced to some degree by the Western gay rights movement, it did not prioritize a human rights agenda or promote individual sexual freedom (Oetomo 2003). Instead, it drew on Indonesia's history of sexual diversity to show that homosexuality was not irreconcilable with Indonesian culture. In its activist work, Lambda Indonesia focused on education and information dissemination. For instance, it disseminated information through articles in their zines about gender diversity and traditional male same-sex sexual practices such as *gemblak* in Java, *kawe* in Borneo, and *mairil* in Islamic boarding schools (Lambda Indonesia 1982).[2] There was at this time some tension between Lambda and lesbian organizations, with members of the latter feeling rather sidelined (Saskia Wieringa, personal communication, September 2017).

When Lambda Indonesia disbanded in 1986 Dede Oetomo established GAYa NUSANTARA, which remains the longest running gay rights organization in Indonesia. GAYa NUSANTARA brought lesbian and gay activists together from across Indonesia, providing them with a sense of community and empowering them to advocate for the acceptance of sexual diversity. Once democratic regime change occurred in Indonesia in 1998, GAYa NUSANTARA proved to be one of the key players, alongside other groups such as Arus Pelangi, advocating for lesbian, gay, bisexual, and transgender rights. Indeed, in 2012 Dede Oetomo progressed to the final stage of selection for the post of commissioner in the National Human Rights Commission (Komisi Nasional Hak Asasi Manusia, Komnas HAM), as did *waria* (transwoman) activist Mami Yuli. This achievement suggests that Indonesian lesbian and gay rights activism was paying dividends, though neither Dede nor Mami Yuli were ultimately chosen for the position. Dede was later to comment that Indonesia was still not ready to have an openly gay man in such a position of power (personal communication, July 2014).

THE MOVEMENT BROADENS

From the somewhat shaky beginnings of the lesbian and gay movement outlined above, progress was made. From the late 1980s and into the 1990s, lesbian and gay activists in Indonesia received increasing assistance from Western activists, academics, and international organizations. In particular, Indonesia received large amounts of money in response to the HIV/AIDS epidemic. This money proved useful for gay activists who used men's health as an umbrella under which they worked with gay men to reduce the spread of HIV (Oetomo 2003). Yet while growing alignment between Indonesian gay activists and Western sexual discourse invigorated Indonesian identity politics, lesbian and gay activists in Indonesia remained primarily committed to supporting health and well-being. Moreover, activists avoided the use of a human rights discourse, knowing that this would potentially draw critical government attention to their activities. Advocating for sexual health was an acceptable form of activism; claiming sexual rights was not.

Increasing lesbian and gay activism prompted the development of the Indonesian Lesbian and Gay Congress, which was held in 1993, 1995, and 1997. Activists involved in these successive congresses had a number of aims, including raising awareness about homosexuality; publishing newsletters and pamphlets focusing on homosexuality; promoting healthcare; consolidating smaller organizations; and expanding the burgeoning movement to include more members, particularly lesbian and transgender members (Oetomo 2003). Of particular concern to activists was tackling the threat of HIV/AIDS. Activists encouraged members to set up telephone hotline services and conduct health outreach programs to disseminate information on HIV/AIDS. They were also concerned about mental health and promoted counseling to increase the resilience of lesbian and gay Indonesians, and used arts and sports to foster positive relationships between lesbian and gay people and general society (Oetomo 2003). These congresses enabled lesbian and gay activists to develop strong national coordination and to establish unified strategies to increase acceptance of lesbian and gay Indonesians. Members of the first congress also went on to form the National Coordination Body of the Indonesian Lesbian and Gay Network. This network included a number of representatives from lesbian and gay organizations, and they began to welcome transgender Indonesians as a crucial part of the movement. The congresses and the Lesbian and Gay Network were signs of both the growing strength of lesbian and gay activism and that this activism was pushing Indonesia toward a democratic style of governance. Activist members of these groups were later able to use spaces opened up by democratic reform to further push for lesbian and gay acceptance.

In response to the growing voice of lesbian and gay activists, the Indonesian government periodically felt the need to emphasize its commitment to heterosexuality (Offord 2011). Just a year after the first Indonesian Lesbian and Gay Congress, the minister of population told the 1994 International Conference on Population and Development in Cairo that Indonesia would not support a declaration acknowledging moves to accept same-sex marriage. That same year, the minister for women's affairs stated that lesbianism was not part of Indonesian culture or state ideology. In 1997, a senior Muhammadiyah figure declared homosexuality in conflict with Indonesian culture and religion (Blackwood 2010). Notably, however, while these statements were made by individuals at the highest levels of power, they did not translate into any systematic state or religious persecution. Paradoxically, it was only in the democratic period that such statements by senior officials began to be reflected in policy.

In sum, lesbian and gay activism prior to democratic reform in Indonesia pushed the idea of a democratic state that would recognize the right of people of all sexualities and genders to have equal representation and participation. By striving for inclusion and equal treatment, and not demanding particular rights attached to sexual identity, lesbian and gay activists pushed the movement forward without being perceived as threatening to the state. These successful moves were also made possible by an emerging global discourse of lesbian and gay rights—which ironically provided fertile ground for religious fundamentalist groups to emerge as the main opponent of lesbian and gay activism in postauthoritarian Indonesia.

ACTIVISM AND DEMOCRACY

The advent of democracy initially enabled lesbian and gay activists to publicly lay claim to social inclusion and acceptance. The forced resignation of President Suharto and the subsequent opening of democratic political space provided lesbian and gay activists with the ability to push the movement forward. The activities of lesbian and gay activists in the previous two decades had laid the groundwork for the nascent movement, and key activists, such as Dede Oetomo, Aan Anshori, Nursyahbani Katjasungkana, Gayatri, and Agustine, were well positioned to take advantage of new opportunities. The transition also saw the ratification of domestic and international laws concerning human rights, particularly laws officially guaranteeing freedom of expression and freedom of the media (Davies, Stone, and Buttle 2016). Lesbian and gay activists were able to take advantage of these laws to stake a claim in civil society (Boyte 2010). Moreover, it was not just lesbian and gay activists who used newfound freedoms to try and increase acceptance of lesbian and gay Indonesians. Heteronormative Indonesians also began to advocate for lesbian and gay rights.

GROWING THE MOVEMENT

From the early stages of democratic reform, Indonesian lesbian and gay activists developed strong institutional and personal relationships with international supporters. As part of this process, Western lesbian and gay rights discourse began to increasingly influence how lesbian and gay Indonesians perceived themselves and their sexuality (Altman and Symons 2016). Lesbian and gay activists became part of organizations like the International Lesbian, Gay, Bisexual, Trans and Intersex Association (ILGA), which is an influential international advocacy network, and also part of the International Gay and Lesbian Human Rights Commission (Agustine 2008; Gayatri 2015). These international collaborations proved incredibly fruitful for sharing knowledge and experience, opening access to multiple forms of support to sustain local activism, and forming transnational activist networks.

One example of international collaboration is the formulation of the Yogyakarta Principles. While no Indonesian lesbian or gay activists were involved in the drafting process, the development of the Yogyakarta Principles on the Application of International Human Rights Law in relation to Sexual Orientation and Gender Identity did bring attention to sexuality in Indonesia. The Yogyakarta Principles were developed at a meeting in Indonesia in 2006, and it sought to encourage the use of international human rights law standards to address the abuse of the rights of lesbian, gay, bisexual, and transgender people. Not only did democratic reform provide space to help develop the Yogyakarta Principles, but the development of the Yogyakarta Principles *in* Indonesia provided activists with concrete tools to lobby the Indonesian government to recognize and protect the rights of lesbian and gay Indonesians. Although not binding, the Yogyakarta Principles provided for the first time a legal framework for lesbian and gay activists in Indonesia to push the movement forward at a national level. Moreover, this ratification tied Indonesia into complying with the International Covenant on Civil and Political Rights.

That Indonesia hosted the signing of the Yogyakarta Principles showed a possible way in which lesbian and gay activists were influencing the shape of its democracy. Moreover, in contrast to preceding years when activists avoided human rights language that might be seen as confrontational by the government, in the democratic era lesbian and gay activists publicly argued that the state had a responsibility to protect people regardless of sexual orientation or gender identity.

There is, of course, another side to the above argument and that is that the Yogyakarta Principles, with its attendant human rights language, was actually detrimental to local lesbian and gay activism. Indeed, many lesbian and gay activists in Yogyakarta now speak in scathing terms about the process, noting that only international lawyers and foreign activists were involved in the process and that grassroots communities were actively excluded (personal communication with lesbian and gay activists, August 2017). While these criticisms are valid, and more sensitivity is certainly needed when incorporating international agendas into Indonesian contexts, international collaborations have had positive impacts on the lesbian and gay rights movement, as shown below.

Alongside increasing international collaboration, an influx of funding and technical assistance from human rights and development organizations were being earmarked for lesbian and gay rights organizations. This funding and assistance resulted in the growing influence of lesbian and gay organizations in Indonesia. Some groups, such Arus Pelangi, used this funding to focus on policy and legal advocacy strategies to force government bodies to develop policies protecting lesbian and gay people (Davies 2010). Other groups, such as Suara Kita and the Ardhanary Institute, worked on improving portrayals of lesbian and gay Indonesians in mainstream media, while other groups focused on cultural activism by making films and hosting film screenings and book discussions (Febriyanti 2015). One example of where a gay couple was shown as a central and normative part of everyday life can be found in Nia DiNata's 2003 box office hit film *Arisan* (Maimunah 2011; Murtagh 2013). A key impact of the screening of films containing lesbian and gay themes was that activists began discussing terms such as *queer*. As Maimunah (2010) notes, film festivals, particularly ones such as the Q! Film Festival (discussed later), played a significant role in the growth of lesbian and gay activities. Indeed, the films provided a site around which discussions about sexuality were opened up and moved from a personal discussion to a political one.

The transition to democracy also provided increased space for activists to come together and build networks not only among themselves but also with non–lesbian and gay organizations (Human Rights Watch 2016). For instance, lesbian activists developed a solid working relationship with feminist activists during the early years of democracy. The National Commission on Violence against Women (Komisi Nasional Anti-kekerasan terhadap Perempuan, Komnas Perempuan) supported lesbian activists in lobbying the government to prioritize human rights (Komnas Perempuan 2017). In 1998, the Indonesian Women's Congress (Kongres Perempuan Indonesia) joined forces with lesbian group Sektor 15 to push human rights issues (personal communication with Saskia Wieringa, September 2017). Further, as many lesbians experienced discrimination in the workplace, lesbian and feminist activists came together to champion the protection of lesbian workers. Lesbian and feminist activists also facilitated public discussions and raised awareness of sexual diversity through social media postings and by presenting lectures at various universities. In addition, lesbian and gay groups came together with human rights groups to mark events such as the International Day against Homophobia and Transphobia. Gay, lesbian, and transgender activists also actively formed collaborations. For instance, activists formed the national LBT-INA (Lesbian, Bisexual, and Transgender Indonesia) network to bring a range of people together to share their experiences and expertise with the goal of increasing social acceptance of gender and sexual diversity (Alicias-Garen and Ranggoaini 2015).

While the transition to democracy saw lesbian and gay activists focus attention on identity politics, HIV/AIDS remained a key site of activism, particularly for gay men. Working under the banner of HIV prevention continued to offer activists a way to promote inclusion while avoiding the prejudice still associated with lesbian and gay activism. Moreover, public health issues made it possible for activists to reach poor gay men and men who have sex with men in rural locations where people did not necessarily identify as gay and thus would not think to become involved in gay activism. Groups such as the GWL-INA Network were thus established to coordinate national HIV/AIDS care and to unite gay and transgender activists in the fight for health care and social inclusion. GWL-INA actively promoted the use of condoms and clean needles to help reduce the spread of HIV. Further, it provided training and capacity building for local gay, men who have sex with men, and transgender people to prevent HIV transmission. While GWL-INA worked mainly on HIV prevention, it also worked more broadly. For instance, in 2016 it held a training workshop for police officers in Solo to teach them about issues of gender and sexuality and sensitive policing (Human Rights Watch 2017).

As this section has shown, lesbian and gay activists pushed to make Indonesian democracy accountable for protecting sexual and gender rights and, in the process, shaped a form of democracy that could have been a showcase of acceptance and inclusion. In the decade following democratic reform, lesbian and gay activists increasingly released public statements protesting negative government reports concerning homosexuality. Activists held peaceful protests to raise awareness about the harms caused through discrimination against lesbian and gay Indonesians and to shame the government into fulfilling its obligation to protect all citizens regardless of sexual orientation or gender identity. The demands made by lesbian and gay activists sought to extend the state's responsibilities toward sexual minority groups and to shape a democratic Indonesia that provided a safe place for all citizens regardless of sexuality or gender. But it was not only progressive activists that used and shaped Indonesian democracy; it was also used and shaped by conservative and religious hardliners.

The Rise of Hatred

Above we have seen how democratic reforms were utilized by lesbian and gay activists to advance rights-based claims and also how activists shaped the form of democracy Indonesia initially took. Yet as Encarnación (2014) notes, adversaries of the lesbian and gay community can also use democracy to undermine lesbian and gay rights, which is what transpired in Indonesia during the decades that followed (Katjasungkana and Wieringa 2016).

In order to understand how Islamic conservatives came to have such power in relation to sexuality, a slight detour into history is needed. When President Suharto forcibly took over power from President Sukarno in 1966, he set about consolidating his authority in part by repressing Islam. Worried that if left unchecked Islamic groups would unite and threaten his rule over the country, Suharto kept a tight rein on the expression of Islam for most of his tenure. In the waning years of the New Order, however, his attitude toward Islam shifted (Wichelen 2010). Due to his deteriorating relationship with powerful military commanders, on whom the regime relied, Suharto reconciled with Islamic organizations in the hopes of increasing his support base. The expansion of Islamic television programs, increased funding for Islamic schools, and the annulment of prohibitions on veiling were among important policies aimed at restoring the relationship in the mid-1990s. While relaxing state repression did not automatically enable Islamic politics to flourish, reconciliation did provide a platform for Islamist groups and dakwah movements to articulate moral concern. Moreover, this new environment of relative freedom provided fertile ground for Islamist politics to develop and to dominate the political agenda after 1998 (Robinson 2015). We see this development with the growing support of Islamist parties such as the Prosperous Justice Party (Partai Keadilan Sejahtera, PKS).

Indonesia's democratic era also witnessed a significant rise in the number and influence of religious, indeed vigilante, groups. The most vocal, the Islamic Defenders Front (Front Pembela Islam, FPI), paid particular attention to lesbian and gay activists, and FPI members quickly began undermining the movement by associating lesbian and gay activism with supposed moral decadence, western hegemony, and the conversion of youth and children to homosexuality. FPI held street demonstrations and openly attacked lesbian and gay activities before 2010, but it was really only from this date that attacks grew in scale and ferocity. The growing aggression of FPI was made clear in 2010 when a lesbian and gay book launch was disrupted by FPI members (Maimunah 2008a). In the same year, the conference of ILGA Asia, which was held in Indonesia, was violently disrupted by FPI members (Marching 2010). FPI members then stormed the hotel where delegates were staying, forcing any lesbian and gay people out of the hotel. The police, who were on standby, merely looked on as the aggressions took place (Poore 2010).

Claiming that it was defending state and religious morality, FPI also pressured the national government into regulating sexuality (Marching 2010). As a result of such pressure and the increasing visibility of lesbian and gay activism both domestically and internationally, in the early 2000s the Ministry of Justice and Human Rights considered amending the Criminal Code to penalize homosexuality for the first time in Indonesia's history (Offord 2011). With growing public support for regulating sexuality, in 2008 the government passed Law No. 44/2008 concerning pornography. While the law prohibits the depiction, production, and distribution of pornography, not sexual acts per se, it describes anal and lesbian sex as deviant, and so frames homosexuality as impermissible. Although the law does not criminalize gay and lesbian activism, such activism could be interpreted as distributing pornography, which became a criminal offence. This heightened state of punitive surveillance undermines Indonesia's democracy.

The rise of Islamist vitriol denigrating homosexuality worked in tandem with democratization to enable provinces to implement draconian laws against lesbians and gay men (Eldridge 2002; Coen et al. 2009; Robinson 2011). For instance, shortly after Aceh was granted special autonomy in 1999, it implemented sharia law, which provided a basis for the local government to control the sexual conduct of its citizens (Yulius 2015). Further, in October 2015, Aceh implemented the Qanun Jinayat, an Islamic criminal code bylaw, which specifically penalizes homosexual acts among both Muslims and non-Muslims (Simanjuntak 2015). Other provinces also used democracy to enact discriminatory laws. In 2002, South Sumatra implemented Regulation No. 13/2002 on the Eradication of Immoral Behavior, which described anal sex between men as immoral. In 2004, in Palembang, the City Ordinance No. 2/2004 on the Eradication of Prostitution conflated homosexuality with prostitution. As prostitution is illegal in the province, homosexuality became illegal by association (Allen 2007). In May 2017, gay men were flogged in Aceh for alleged homosexual acts and 140 men were arrested for being in a "gay sauna" (Lamb 2017). Regulating homosexuality meant lesbian and gay activists had to be increasingly careful about their activities. Democracy also enabled groups such as the Islamic profamily group, the Family Love Alliance (Aliansi Cinta Keluarga), to pursue legal steps toward criminalizing homosexuality at a national level. In 2016, the Family Love Alliance proposed that the Constitutional Court revise the existing penal code to criminalize male same-sex sexual relationships, which are currently only illegal when they involve people under the age of eighteen. The Family Love Alliance argued homosexual practices must be made illegal to ensure same-sex marriage never becomes legal in Indonesia. It also claimed that making homosexuality illegal would stop the spread of HIV, despite clear evidence that the fastest growing rate of HIV is among married heterosexual women who contract HIV from their husbands (Najmah, Davies, and Andajani 2017).

This homophobic rhetoric and action reached an unprecedented level in 2016 (Boellstorff 2016; Davies 2016; Human Rights Watch 2016). Looking to garner support from Muslim voters, government officials, including the minister of social affairs and the minister of women's empowerment and child protection, made public comments that reeked of homophobia (Human Rights Watch 2016). Given the turmoil, it was no surprise that the media picked up on stories of violence and discrimination, framing homosexuality as a contagious disease and a mental health disorder that threatened the moral fiber of young people and indeed Indonesia's entire culture. Policymakers subsequently mooted plans to amend the 2002 broadcasting law and ban lesbian and gay "appearance and behaviors" from advertisements and programs on TV and radio. Lesbian and gay activism was further constrained when the Indonesian government told international agencies, including the UN Development Program, to stop channeling funding to lesbian and gay organizations. President spokesperson Johan Budi publicly stated that there was no place for lesbian and gay activism in Indonesia. While the government stopped short of criminalizing lesbian and gay activism, the promise that democracy would open space for lesbian and gay activism remained unfulfilled.

RESPONDING TO INCREASING HOMOPHOBIA

While the climate for lesbian and gay activism was certainly restricted as Indonesia's experiment with democracy continued, the persecutory environment did not stop the movement outright. Rather lesbian and gay activists found a variety of ways to either challenge homophobia or work within its parameters to push the movement forward, including reframing activities in less threatening ways, collaborating with like-minded groups, making use of the media, and deploying United Nations protocols.

First, lesbian and gay activists refocused their efforts in ways that would be perceived as less threatening by government, religious groups, and general society. For instance, activists avoided using terms such as *lesbian* or *gay*, and they linked their activities to socially acceptable projects such as addressing sexual and gender-based violence (cf. Chua 2014). For example, a lesbian organization called the Ardhanary Institute collaborated with the mainstream One Vision Alliance (Aliansi Satu Visi) to address bullying at schools. By using terms such as "gender and sexual diversity" and "sexual orientation and gender identity," rather than lesbian or gay, Ardhanary worked with One Vision Alliance, often in high schools, to combat homophobia in ways that did not cause general alarm (Wieringa, Hidayana, and Pakasi 2012).

Second, in responding to an environment of increasing homophobia, activists sought to bring lesbians and gay men together alongside various institutions to advocate for tolerance of sexual and gender diversity; a similar tactic was utilized by labor unions, which collaborated across organizational divides to advance shared policy interests (Caraway and Ford this volume). Indeed, the call by the Family Love Alliance in 2016 to criminalize homosexuality and sex outside marriage unified prodemocracy organizations, women's groups, and other social movements to fight against these moves. Komnas Perempuan and Komnas HAM, along with other human rights organizations, also came together as a collective, showing how Indonesian democracy could work to support lesbian and gay activists and that lesbian and gay activists could demand more from Indonesian democracy. This collective reframed the issue from being one about homosexuality to one being about human rights and privacy.

Lesbians, bisexual women, and transgender women were also recognized as part of the mandate under Komnas Perempuan. Further, Komnas HAM recognized the lesbian, gay, bisexual, and transgender community as a minority group that needed protection (Komnas HAM 2016).

Tapping into transnational networks further provided lesbian and gay activists with access to international conferences and training workshops that enhanced advocacy skills, as well as providing emotional, financial, and strategic support. Information and knowledge exchange further strengthened and solidified lesbian activism, especially concerning the promotion of identity politics. A vivid account of the deployment of identity politics is seen in the use and distribution of the sexual orientation and gender identity model in public discussions, publications, training guidelines, and online articles that increasingly challenged heterosexual models and promoted diversity of sexual and gender identity and expression (Arus Pelangi 2016). An earlier example of unity is found when, in response to the violent disruption of the International Gay and Lesbian Association Conference by religious hardliners, activists developed Forum LGBTIQ Indonesia in 2010 (UNDP USAID 2014). The forum drew together various lesbian, gay and transgender organizations from across the archipelago to combat discrimination (personal communication with forum members, March 2016). As this drawing together suggests, while democratic reforms have proven on balance negative for the lesbian and gay movement, the resultant conservative backlash did often unify previously dispersed activist groups to promote a more inclusive society.

Third, the increasingly hostile situation faced by lesbian and gay activists in the democratic era worked to encourage the use of media platforms to establish formal and informal networks (cf. Fajar and Crosby 2012). The Internet, not strictly regulated by the government, provided space for the expression of homophobic sentiment, but it also was perceived to offer privacy and thus some ability for lesbian and gay activists to evade religious and state control. These activists used social media and blog sites to increase awareness of lesbian and gay issues and posted personal coming-out stories, created entertaining websites, and disseminated information about sexual and gender diversity. By 2017, though, the government had begun cracking down on Internet sites and indeed blocked online dating sites used primarily by lesbians and gay men (Listiorini and Davies 2017). While democracy had initially enabled the creation of media freedom, within two decades the government was again controlling the media, which had a detrimental impact on lesbian and gay activism.

In addition to using the Internet, publications, movie screenings, and public discussions, often held in collaboration with universities, also enabled activists to support lesbian and gay people and expand knowledge of sexual and gender diversity without necessarily drawing the attention of homophobic conservatives. Other innovative ways were also found to deflect homophobic attacks. For example, since it began operating in 2010, the Q! Film Festival had been targeted by religious vigilante groups to the point that screenings were cancelled in various cities. In order to avoid raids, activists thus advertised programs clandestinely by direct text or instant messaging (UNDP USAID 2014). Potential danger was always present though and so in 2015 the Q! Film Festival was held at a Christian theology school in Jakarta. Islamic vigilante groups did not attack the event because religious intolerance would, in theory, have sparked a mandatory police response.

Fourth, and finally, the failure of the democratic state to protect lesbian and gay Indonesians inspired lesbian and gay activists to expand their advocacy through engagement with international organizations. One strategy deployed in an attempt to force the Indonesian government into action was using existing mechanisms available through United Nations protocols. For instance, lesbian, gay, and other human rights activists came together to compile and submit a list of transgressions perpetrated on lesbian and gay Indonesians to the 2017 United Nations General Assembly Universal Periodic Review, which is a process of the Human Rights Council (Human Rights Watch 2017). The submission revealed the extent of state failure, and activists hoped that member countries of the General Assembly would subsequently pressure Indonesia to protect the rights of its lesbian and gay citizens—this was also a tactic used somewhat successfully in respect to Indonesia's ill-treatment of children in prison (Davies and Robson 2016). What we see here is that while Indonesian democracy failed lesbian and gay citizens, activists were able to still use democratic means to push the government to address issues of human rights failings.

Conclusion

Lesbian and gay activism is often most successful when it resonates with dominant cultural views. For instance, activists in neoliberal societies position lesbian and gay people as modern capitalist consumers in order to make successful rights claims (Lee 2016). In societies where romantic love is valued, lesbian and gay activists assert that same-sex marriage should be legalized to ensure people's right to marry for love (Tobin 2015). While lesbian and gay activists in one society might find public action effective (Currier 2009), in others covert action may be more feasible (Kurzman 1996). For example, lesbian and gay activists in the United States openly challenged state and federal marriage laws (Encarnación 2014), while activists in China strategically supported state interests to avoid antagonizing the government all the while covertly seeking to make small gains for lesbian and gay citizens (Hildebrandt 2013). Similarly, in Singapore, lesbian and gay activists sought small changes without challenging heteronormativity (Chua 2014). Lesbian and gay activism is thus most likely to succeed in democratic nations when it resonates with society's cultural and political norms (McAdam 1996; Puri 2016; Snow and Benford 1992).

Lesbian and gay activists in Indonesia have consistently attempted to frame their activism in ways that resonated with dominant cultural views. Prior to democratic reform, activists worked within the remit of heteronormativity to effect small but significant change, mostly around reassuring lesbian and gay Indonesians that they had self-worth. During this time, it was not considered important to "come out" as belonging to a particular sexual identity. Rather the movement focused on improving the lives of lesbian and gay Indonesians at the everyday level, ensuring access to like-minded people, self-acceptance, and information about sexuality and health care. When Indonesia initiated democratic reform in 1998, lesbian and gay activists worked hard to capitalize on previous advances. Through endeavors such as activating Indonesia-wide networks and building on the groundwork laid down over the previous two decades, lesbian and gay activists were able to sculpt a form of Indonesian democracy that would welcome participation from all sectors of society. Lesbian and gay activism thus helped lay the foundation for democratic reform and shape the form of democracy Indonesia initially took. From the 1970s to the 1990s lesbian and gay activism was largely conducted clandestinely and promoted inclusion by aligning with cultural norms rather than asserting lesbian and gay identity, yet there was increasing recognition that a truly democratic Indonesia could only be one that enabled the participation of all members of society, including lesbian and gay Indonesians. Lesbian and gay activism thus enabled the circulation of knowledge about sexuality that countered heteronormativity, and it expanded the notion of democratic citizenship to include sexuality and gender as bases for social recognition and acceptance.

Indonesia's transition to democracy brought hope to many, including its lesbian and gay community, of a more just future. Attendant reforms promoted media freedom, growth in civil society organizations, increased international collaboration and funding, and a sense of a global struggle for lesbian and gay rights. However, democracy has also allowed religious hardliners and political conservatives, whose voices were constricted under Suharto, to incite intolerance against lesbian and gay people. Lesbian and gay activists were positioned as a threat to national security and in need of overt regulation. Left unchecked, conservative elements of Indonesian society utilized democratic reforms to launch bitter and aggressive attacks on Indonesia's lesbian and gay community. These conservative forces provoked a retraction of democracy and threatened the stability of the democratic regime. The repression of lesbian and gay activities forced activists to reconfigure strategies to push the movement forward while avoiding direct attack from religious and political conservatives. Activists collaborated with non–lesbian and gay organizations, and drew on international and regional resources. Activists focused on immediate concerns, such as health, and used creative educational strategies to promote lesbian and gay welfare. Activists also developed ways to conduct activism while strategically acquiescing to social norms (cf. Chua 2014; Lee 2016; Oswin 2014).

Since 1998, lesbian and gay Indonesians have worked hard to strengthen Indonesia's democratic process and institutions. Initially lesbian and gay activism increased the legitimacy of Indonesian democracy by enabling lesbian and gay citizens to participate in civil society and political processes. Ironically, though, two decades on, democracy has permitted the very violation of lesbian and gay rights that it was supposed to protect. It is thus difficult to conclude that democracy has been a boon for lesbian and gay rights. Rather, democracy has proved a double-edged sword, on the one hand bringing awareness to the struggle for lesbian and gay rights but on the other permitting overt discrimination against lesbian and gay Indonesians.

Notes

1. Thanks to the editors, Michele and Thushara—and particularly to Michele who read numerous versions of this chapter and gave incredibly instructive feedback. Thanks also to Dede Oetomo and Saskia Wieringa for much and then some. We also thank the other contributors who offered feedback on an early draft at a workshop at the University of Sydney in February 2017, and especially Sonja van Wichelen. We dedicate this chapter to all the LGBT activists and their allies working toward making Indonesia a more tolerant place.
2. A number of other gay networks developed in the 1980s and 1990s but these were short lived.

References

Agustine, R. R. 2008. "Rahasia Sunyi: Gerakan Lesbian di Indonesia." *Jurnal Perempuan* 58: 59–72.

Alicias-Garen, Maria, and Jahja Ranggoaini. 2015. "Hivos: External Evaluation of LGBT Program Final Report." Unpublished Hivos report.

Allen, Pam. 2007. "Challenging Diversity? Indonesian's Anti-Pornography Bill." *Asian Studies Review* 31 (June): 101–15.

Altman, Dennis, and Jonathan Symons. 2016. *Queer Wars*. London: Polity Press.

Arus Pelangi. 2016. Available at: http://aruspelangi.org/rumah-belajar-pelangi/.

Aspinall, Edward. 2009. *Islam and Nation: Separatist Rebellion in Aceh, Indonesia*. Stanford: Stanford University Press.

Bennett, Linda Rae. 2005. *Women, Islam, and Modernity: Single Women, Sexuality, and Reproductive Health in Contemporary Indonesia*. London: RoutledgeCurzon.

Blackburn, Susan. 2004. *Women and the State in Modern Indonesia*. Cambridge: Cambridge University Press.

Blackwood, Evelyn. 2007. "Regulation of Sexuality in Indonesian Discourse: Normative Gender, Criminal Law, and Shifting Strategies of Control." *Culture, Health and Sexuality* 9 (3): 293–307.

——. 2010. *Falling into the Lesbi World: Desire and Difference in Indonesia*. Honolulu: University of Hawai'i Press.

Boellstorff, Tom. 2003. "Dubbing Culture: Mass Media and Lesbi/Gay Subjectivities in Indonesia." *American Ethnologist* 30 (2): 225–42.

——. 2005. *The Gay Archipelago: Sexuality and Nation in Indonesia*. Princeton: Princeton University Press.

——. 2007. *A Coincidence of Desires: Anthropology, Queer Studies, Indonesia*. Durham, NC: Duke University Press.

——. 2016. "Against State Straightism: Five Principles for Including LGBT Indonesians." *E-International Relations*. http://www.e-ir.info/2016/03/21/against-state-straightism-five-principles-for-including-lgbt-indonesians/.

Boyte, Harry C. 2010. *Everyday Politics: Reconnecting Citizens and Public Life*. Philadelphia: University Pennsylvania Press.

Brenner, Suzanne. 2011. "Private Moralities in the Public Sphere: Democratization, Islam, and Gender in Indonesia." *American Anthropologist* 113 (3): 478–90.

Brown, Stephen. 1999. "Democracy and Sexual Difference: The Lesbian and Gay Movement in Argentina." In *The Global Emergence of Gay and Lesbian Politics*, edited by Barry D. Adam, Jan W. Duyvendak, and Andre Krouwel, 110–32. Philadelphia: Temple University Press.

Chua, Lynette J. 2014. *Mobilizing Gay Singapore: Rights and Resistance in an Authoritarian State*. Singapore: National University of Singapore Press.

Coen, J., G. Holtzappel, and Martin Ramstedt, eds. 2009. *Decentralization and Regional Autonomy in Indonesia: Implementation and Challenges*. Leiden: Institute of Southeast Asian Studies.

Currier, Ashley. 2009. "Deferral of Legal Tactics: A Global LGBT Social Movement Organization's Perspective." In *Queer Mobilizations: LGBT Activists Confront the Law*, edited by Scott Barclay, Mary Bernstein, and Anna-Maria Marshall, 21–37. New York: New York Press.

Davies, Sharyn G. 2010. "Activism: Homosexuality and Queer Identity Movements—Southeast Asia." In *Encyclopedia of Women and Islamic Cultures*, vol. 6, edited by Suad Joseph, 654–59 Leiden: Brill Academic.

——. 2015. "Sexual Surveillance." In *Sex and Sexualities in Contemporary Indonesia: Sexual Politics, Health, Diversity and Representations*, edited by Linda Rae Bennett and Sharyn G. Davies, 10–31. London: Routledge.

——. 2016. "Indonesia's Anti-LGBT Panic." *East Asia Forum* 8 (2): 8–11.

Davies, Sharyn G., and Jazz Robson. 2016. "Juvenile (In)justice: Children in Conflict with the Law in Indonesia." *Asia-Pacific Journal on Human Rights and the Law* 16 (2): 24–41.

Davies, Sharyn G., Louise M. Stone, and John Buttle. 2016. "Covering Cops: Critical Reporting of Indonesian Police Corruption." *Pacific Journalism Review* 22 (1): 185–201.

Drucker, Peter. 2015. "Gay Normality and Queer Transformation." *Zapruder World: An International Journal for the History of Social Conflict*. http://www.zapruderworld.org/gay-normality-and-queer-transformation.

Eldridge, Philip J. 2002. *The Politics of Human Rights in Southeast Asia*. London: Routledge.

Encarnación, Omar. 2014. "Gay Rights: Why Democracy Matters." *Journal of Democracy* 25 (3): 90–104.

Fajar, Ricky Muchammad, and Alexandra Crosby. 2012. "Online Networking and Minority Rights: LGBT Communities Use Social Media to Organise Despite Threats of Violence." *Inside Indonesia* 110 (Oct–Dec). https://www.insideindonesia.org/online-networking-and-minority-rights-2?highlight=WyJuZ XR3b3JraW5nIiwibmV0d29yayIsIm5ldHdvcmsnIiwibWlub3JpdHkiLCJtaW5vciI sIidtaW5vciIsIm1pbm9ycyciLCJvbmxpbmUiXQ%3D%3D.

Febriyanti, Kiki. 2015. *Calalai—In-betweeness: A Documentary*. 40 minutes. Recorded in Indonesia.

Flores, Andrew, Jody L. Herman, and Christy Mallory. 2015. "Transgender Inclusion in State non-Discrimination Policies: The Democratic Deficit and Political Powerlessness." *Research and Politics* (Oct-Dec): 1–8.

Ford, Michele, and Lynne Parker, eds. 2008. *Women and Work in Indonesia*. London: Routledge.

Friedland, Roger. 2011. "The Institutional Logic of Religious Nationalism: Sex, Violence, and the Ends of History." *Politics, Religion, and Ideology* 12 (1): 65–88.

Gayatri, B.J.D. 2015. "Selarung Gerakan Lesbian dalam Epidemi Kebencian: Awal Advokasi SOGIE (Sexual Orientation, Gender Identity and Expression) di Nusantara." *Jurnal Perempuan* 20 (4): 8–47.

Gevisser, Mark. 1995. "A Different Fight for Freedom: A History of South African Lesbian and Gay Organisation from the 1950s to the 1990s." In *Defiant Desire: Gay and Lesbian Lives in South Africa*, edited by Mark Gevisser and Edwin Cameron, 14–88. New York: Routledge.

Green, James N. 1999. *Beyond Carnival: Male Homosexuality in Twentieth-Century Brazil*. Chicago: University of Chicago Press.

GWL-INA. 2012. *The GWL-INA: The History and Developments of the Network of Gay, Transgender, and Men Who Have Sex with Men in Indonesia*. http://www.afao.org.au/library/topic/transgender/GWL-INA-final-12-june-2012.pdf.

Hefner, Robert. 2000. *Civil Islam: Muslims and Democratization in Indonesia*. Princeton, NJ: Princeton University Press.

Hildebrandt, Timothy. 2013. *Social Organizations and the Authoritarian State in China*. Cambridge: Cambridge University Press.

Howard, Richard S. 1996. "Falling into the Gay World: Manhood, Marriage, and Family in Indonesia." Ph.D. diss., University of Illinois.

Human Rights Watch. 2016. "'These Political Games Ruin our Lives': Indonesia's LGBT Community under Threat." http://www.hrw.org/1-91.

——. 2017. "Human Rights Watch Submission to the Universal Periodic Review of Indonesia." September. https://www.hrw.org/news/2017/04/28/human-rights-watch-submission-universal-periodic-review-indonesia.

Katjasungkana, Nursyahbani, and Sakia E. Wieringa. 2016. "Creeping Criminalisation: Mapping of Indonesia's National Laws and Regional Regulations that Violate Human Rights of Women and LGBTIQ People." New York: OutRight Action International.

Komnas HAM (Komisi Nasional Hak Asasi Manusia). 2016. *Upaya Negara Menjamin Hak-Hak Kelompok Minoritas di Indonesia: Sebuah Laporan Awal* (State Efforts in Protecting Minority Rights in Indonesia: An Initial Report). Jakarta: Komnas HAM.

Komnas Perempuan. 2017. *National Commission on Violence Against Women*. http://www.komnasperempuan.go.id/tag/lgbt/.

Kurzman, Charles. 1996. "Structural Opportunity and Perceived Opportunity in Social-Movement Theory: The Iranian Revolution of 1979." *American Sociological Review* 61 (1): 153–70.

Lamb, Kate. 2017. "Indonesian Police Arrest More than 140 Men at Alleged Gay Sauna Party." *The Guardian*. May 22. https://www.theguardian.com/world/2017/may/22/indonesian-police-arrest-more-than-140-men-at-alleged-gay-sauna-party.

Lambda Indonesia. 1982. "Homoseks: Siapa Dia?" In *G: Gaya Hidup Cerita*, vol. 1 (August). Lambda Indonesia: Solo.

Lee, Charles. T. 2016. *Ingenious Citizenship: Recrafting Democracy for Social Change*. Durham, NC: Duke University Press.

Listiorini, Dina, and Sharyn G. Davies. 2017. "Online Dating Apps Blocked." *Inside Indonesia*. April 18. http://www.insideindonesia.org/online-dating-apps-blocked.

Macgillivray, Ian. 2000. "Educational Equity for Gay, Lesbian, Bisexual, Transgendered, and Queer/Questioning Students: The Demands of Democracy and Social Justice for America's Schools." *Education and Urban Society* 32 (3): 34–49.

Marching, S. T. 2010. "ILGA dan Anak Itik (ILGA and Duck)." *Bhinneka* 6 (Special Edition: ILGA), 18–25. https://issuu.com/bhinneka/docs/bhinneka-ilga2010/2.

McAdam, Doug. 1996. "Conceptual Origins, Current Problems, Future Directions." In *Comparative Perspectives on Social Movements: Political Opportunities, Mobilizing Structures, and Cultural Framings*, edited by Doug McAdam, John D. McCarthy, and Mayer N. Zald, 23–40. New York: Cambridge University Press.

Munir, Maimunah. 2008a. "Indonesian Queer: Non-Normative Sexualities in Indonesian Film, 2003–2006." M.A. thesis, University of Sydney.

——. 2008b. "Indonesia's Q! Film Festival: Young Indonesians Are Using an Alternative Film Festival to Promote Awareness of Sexual Diversity."

Inside Indonesia 93 (July–Sept). https://www.insideindonesia.org/indonesia-s-q-film-festival-2.

——. 2010. "Indonesian Queer and the Centrality of Heteronormative Family." *Asian Cinema* 21 (2): 114–34.

——. 2011. "Queering the Epistemology of 'Coming Out': The Representation of Male Same-Sex Relationship in Nia Dinata's Arisan." *Jati* 16 (December): 113–29.

——. 2016. "Sex and Sexualities in Contemporary Indonesia: Sexual Politics, Health, Diversity and Representations." *Sex Education* 1 (4): 1–3.

Murtagh, Ben. 2013. *Genders and Sexualities in Indonesian Cinema: Constructing Gay, Lesbi and Waria Identities on Screen.* London: Routledge.

Najmah, Sharyn G. Davies, and Sara Andajani. 2017. "HIV-Positive Mothers Left Behind." *Inside Indonesia.* https://www.insideindonesia.org/hiv-positive-mothers-left-behind.

Oetomo, Dede. 1996. "Gender and Sexual Orientation in Indonesia." In *Fantasizing the Feminine in Indonesia*, edited by Laurie J. Sears, 259–69. Durham, NC: Duke University Press.

——. 1997. "Ketika Sharon Stone Berbahasa Indonesia (When Sharon Stone Speaks Indonesian)." In *Bercinta Dengan Televisi: Ilusi, Impresi, dan Imaji Sebuah Kotak Ajaib* (In Love with Television: Illusions, Impressions, and Images from a Magical Box), edited by Deddy Mulyana and Idi Subyandy Ibrahim, 333–37. Bandung: PT Remaja Rosdakarya.

——. 2000. "Masculinity in Indonesia: Genders, Sexualities, and Identities in a Changing Society." In *Framing the Sexual Subject: The Politics of Gender, Sexuality, and Power,* edited by Richard Parker, Regina Maria Barbosa, and Peter Aggleton, 46–59. Berkeley: University of California Press.

——. 2001. "Gay Men in the Reformasi Era: Homophobic Violence Could be a By-Product of the New Openness." *Inside Indonesia* 66 (April–June). https://www.insideindonesia.org/gay-men-in-the-reformasi-era-2.

——. 2003. *Memberi Suara Pada yang Bisu.* Yogayakarta: Pustaka Marwa

——. 2016. "Q&A: Dede Oetomo on the LGBT Panic." Indonesia at Melbourne. http://indonesiaatmelbourne.unimelb.edu.au/interview-dede-oetomo-on-the-lgbt-panic/.

Offord, Baden. 2011. "Singapore, Indonesia and Malaysia: Arrested Development!" In *The Lesbian and Gay Movement and the State*, edited by Manon Tremblay, David Patternotte, and Carol Johnson, 135–52. UK: Ashgate.

Oswin, Natalie. 2014. "Queer Time in Global City Singapore: Neoliberal Futures and the 'Freedom to Love.'" *Sexualities* 17 (4): 412–33.

Palmberg, Mai. 1999. "Emerging Visibility of Gays and Lesbians in Southern Africa: Contrasting Contexts." In *The Global Emergence of Gay and Lesbian Politics*, edited by Barry D. Adam, Jan Willem Duyvendak, and André A. Krouwel, 266–92. Philadelphia: Temple University Press.

Poore, Grace. 2010. "LGBT Activism Under Attack in Surabaya, Indonesia. Part One." International Gay and Lesbian Human Rights Commission. http://iglhrc.wordpress.com/2010/04/01/threats-to-lgbt-in-surabaya-part-1/.

Puri, Jyoti. 2016. *Sexual States: Governance and the Struggle over the Antisodomy Law in India.* Durham, NC: Duke University Press.

Robinson, Kathryn. 2011. "Sawerigading vs. Sharia: Identities and Political Contestation in Decentralised Indonesia." *Asian Journal of Social Science* 39 (2): 219–37.

———. 2015. "Masculinity, Sexuality, and Islam: The Gender Politics of Regime Change in Indonesia." In *Sex and Sexualities in Contemporary Indonesia: Sexual Politics, Health, Diversity and Representations*, edited by Linda Rae Bennett and Sharyn G. Davies, 51–68. London: Routledge.

Simanjuntak, Hotli. 2015. "'Qanun Jinayat' Becomes Official for All People in Aceh." *Jakarta Post*. October 23. http://www.thejakartapost.com/news/2015/10/23/qanun-jinayat-becomes-official-all-people-aceh.html.

Snow, David, and Robert Benford. 1992. "Master Frames and Cycles of Protest." In *Frontiers in Social Movement Theory*, edited by Aldon D. Morris and Carol McClurg Mueller, 133–55. New Haven: Yale University Press.

Tobin, Brian. 2015. "'First Comes Love, Then Comes Marriage': Allaying Reservations Surrounding Marriage Equality and Same-Sex Parenting in Ireland." *Irish Journal of Family Law* 18 (1): 9–27.

UNDP USAID. 2014. *Being LGBT in Asia: Indonesia Country Report*. Bangkok. http://www.asia-pacific.undp.org/content/dam/rbap/docs/Research%20&%20Publications/hiv_aids/rbap-hhd-2014-blia-indonesia-country-report-english.pdf.

Wichelen, Sonja van. 2010. *Religion, Politics, and Gender in Indonesia: Disputing the Muslim Body*. London: Routledge.

Wieringa, Saskia. 1987. *Uw Toegenegen Dora D. Reisbrieven*. Amsterdam: Uitgeverij Furie.

———. 1997. "Jakarta's Butches: Transgendered Women or Third Gender?" Symposium conducted at the meeting of the Beyond Boundaries: Sexuality across Culture, Amsterdam.

———. 1999. "Desiring Bodies or Deviant Cultures." In *Female Desires: Women's Same-sex Relations Crossculturally*, edited by Saskia Wieringa and Evelyn Blackwood, 206–30. New York: Columbia University Press.

Wieringa, Saskia, Irwan Hidayana, and Diana Pakasi. 2012. "Mainstreaming Sexual Diversity in SRHR and HIV Programs in Indonesia." Report prepared for Dance4life and RutgersWPF.

Yulius, Hendri. 2015. "Sexuality, Censorship, and Dangdut." *Indonesia at Melbourne*. http://indonesiaatmelbourne.unimelb.edu.au/sexuality-censorship-dangdut/.

Zook, Darren. 2010. "Disability and Democracy in Cambodia: An Integrative Approach to Community Building and Civic Engagement." *Disability and Society* 25 (2): 149–61.

CHAPTER NINE

DEMOCRATIZATION AND DISABILITY ACTIVISM IN INDONESIA

Thushara Dibley

In late 2014, a group of disability activists gathered at the offices of the National Human Rights Commission. Joining the activists were representatives from the commission, legal drafters from the national legislature, and staff members from an NGO that specialized in legal issues. They were discussing the latest draft of the new national disability law, which had recently been returned to the activists to review after having been revised by a committee within the legislature. The process was highly participatory, with everyone who wished to speak being given the opportunity to state their case. The commitment of everyone around the table to working toward a draft that would be acceptable to all the stakeholders was clear, with officials from the legislature and the human rights commission discussing how to phrase the articles of the law in a way that would meet the spirit of what the activists were hoping for as well as the administrative requirements of the government. This was one of many such meetings held between 2012 and 2016, when the new national disability law was passed, and was a gathering that would not have been possible twenty years earlier, during the authoritarian New Order period in Indonesia.

This chapter tracks the ways in which disability rights activists have successfully leveraged changes to Indonesia's political system since the fall of Suharto to campaign for new disability laws based on the United Nations Convention for the Rights of Persons with Disabilities (CRPD) at the provincial and national levels. As it demonstrates, activists have taken full advantage of democratization, which has coincided with shifts in international norms related to disability, to secure policy change. Yet while the passing of provincial and national laws on disability paint a more optimistic picture about the effectiveness of social movements in disability than in other domains, concerns still remain about the implementation of these laws.

DISABILITY ACTIVISM DURING THE NEW ORDER

Disability activism during the New Order was almost nonexistent, even in the mid- to late 1990s when there was a general increase in political activity. Disability was seen as an issue of welfare in Indonesia during this time, a trope that contributed significantly to the lack of political activity around disability rights.[1] This view was compounded by the political environment, which made it nearly impossible for activists in any sector to directly influence the discourse used by the government to frame policy. The dominance of the welfare-based perspective also contributed to the idea that Indonesians with disabilities were victims, vulnerable and in need of assistance (Thohari 2013), an idea that shaped not only attitudes toward disability, but also the institutional structures that were established to support people with disabilities.

During the New Order, the government created a range of organizations for people with disabilities. A number of these organizations were established on the basis of disability type, including the Indonesian Movement for the Welfare of the Deaf (Gerakan untuk Kesejahteraan Tuna Rungu Indonesia, Gerkatin), established in 1981, and the Indonesian Blind Union (Persatuan Tunanetra Indonesia, Pertuni), established in 1966. There were others that were organized as peak representative bodies, including the Indonesian Disability Association (Persatuan Penyandang Disabilitas Indonesia, PPDI), established in 1987, and the Indonesian Association of Women with Disabilities (Himpunan Wanita Penyandang Disabilitas Indonesia, HWDI), established in 1997.[2] These organizations had close links to government ministries and national-level institutions engaged in social welfare. For example, HWDI was established with the direct support of the Ministry of Social Affairs (HWDI n.d.), and the websites of both Gerkatin and HWDI point to their close connection to the Indonesian National Council for Social Welfare (Dewan Nasional Indonesia untuk Kesejahteraan Sosial, DNIKS) (Gerkatin 2008; HWDI n.d.). The close connection that these organizations had to the state was consistent with the New Order government's approach to engaging with other types of citizens in Indonesia, which was to establish mass-based organizations with the purpose of depoliticizing groups of people with shared interests and values. The effect of this approach is still evident in the way some of these disability organizations continue to describe themselves. For example, the Gerkatin website explicitly states that the use of the word *gerakan*, or "movement," in the name of the organization does not have a "political" meaning, but rather reflects the "spirit of struggle amongst deaf Indonesians" (Gerkatin 2008).

The institutional structures of the disability organizations established at this time were similar to the structures of other New Order style mass organizations. Each of the disability organizations had headquarters in Jakarta and branches in other parts of the country. The organizations offered membership to constituents, and in theory, members were required to pay a fee that would help finance the organization, with a small proportion going to the branch and the remainder being directed to the head office. In practice, very few people with disabilities were able to pay the fee. Without resources, the ability of these institutions to support their members was limited. The lack of resources also affected the relationships between the headquarters and the branches, which often operated as independent entities. These problems have continued until the present time, significantly limiting the ability of these national-level organizations to engage and mobilize their grassroots constituents (Colbran 2010; PNPM Special Program on Disability 2015). This lack of dynamism and the restrictive political environment meant there was little incentive or possibility for them to work together to develop joint campaigns, or even have a sense of being part of a unified movement.

Despite the limitations of these disability organizations, groups such as Gerkatin and HWDI were an improvement on the types of institutions engaged with disability prior to the New Order. According to an activist from Yogyakarta, they were at the very least "organizations *of* the disabled," made up of people with disabilities. This was a step in the right direction, compared with organizations established during the 1950s, which were "organizations *for* the disabled," established by nondisabled people such as the Foundation for the Education of Handicapped Children (Yayasan Pendidikan Anak Cacat) (Interview with Setyo Adi Purwanta, December 2014). Nevertheless, the New Order associations were focused primarily on finding and bringing together people with disabilities under one umbrella, rather than on mobilizing them or campaigning for changes on their behalf. Gerkatin, for instance, states that the main reason it was established was to bring together a number of support groups for the deaf that existed in different parts of Indonesia (Gerkatin 2008). More than three decades later, this continues to be what members of Gerkatin identify as one of its main achievements (Focus Group Discussion with Gerkatin, December 2014). Many of the other activities that these organizations undertook during the New Order—including distributing mobility aids to people with disabilities, running training workshops, organizing meetings among members, and hosting religious events—were focused on service provision, rather than direct advocacy (Interview with Luluk Ariyantiny, June 2017). On one hand, this was a result of receiving direct funding from the government for operational costs, which limited the advocacy role that these organizations could take, while on the other hand, the political environment at the time was too oppressive to engage in any other way (Interview with Luluk Ariyantiny, June 2017; Interview Bahrul Fuad, June 2017).

The lack of disability activism in Indonesia during the New Order period was also related to the marginal position of disability rights globally at the time. Disability rights were not a priority for transnational activist communities or international aid organizations. The first international frameworks around disability established in the 1970s—the Declaration on the Rights of Mentally Retarded Persons and the Declaration of Rights of Disabled Persons—were based on the medical model of disability (Kanter 2003). It was not until the 1980s, when the World Program on Action Concerning Disabled Persons was established, that the "first statement on the equalization of opportunities for people with disabilities" was made by the United Nations (Kanter 2003, 256). This statement became the platform for the United Nations Decade for Disabled Persons (1983–93), during which the idea of the social model of disability began to emerge.

Although steps were taken by the United Nations toward the development of a specific platform for addressing the rights of people with disabilities, an international consensus on how to address the rights of people with disabilities was not reached until the Convention on the Rights of People with Disabilities was adopted in 2006. Up until this time, it was supposed to be the case that other human rights conventions were to address the rights of people with disabilities, but in practice this rarely happened (Kayess and French 2008). As a consequence, there was little to no aid available for disability rights projects and limited transnational networks into which activists could connect (Kayess and French 2008). The majority of funding and activism in support of disability rights was concentrated within domestic disability rights movements in the global north (Grech 2009).

It was only in the 1990s that a small number of activists began to mobilize around disability rights in Indonesia. In 1991, Indonesia's first disability NGO, called the Institute of Research, Empowerment, and Development for People with Different Abilities (Dria Manunggal), was established in Yogyakarta. This organization began as a discussion group among people with disabilities who were trying to understand their structural marginalization. Dria Manunggal looked to the disability movements in other parts of the world—such as the United States and India—as well as to other social movements, such as the women's movement and environment movement, for ideas about how to organize constituents and to drive social change (Interview with Setyo Adi Purwanta, December 2014). Its founders were particularly influenced by ideas emerging from the United States and the United Kingdom about a social model of disability, which was gaining considerable traction among disability activists world-wide (Interview with Setyo Adi Purwanta, December 2014; Thohari 2013). The ideas underpinning the social model of disability were the basis on which these activists formed the organization.

One of Dria Manunggal's early contributions to change in Indonesia was to cam-paign for Indonesia's first law on disability, Law No. 4/1997 on the Handicapped. Setyo Adi Purwanta, one of the organization's founders, explained that before the law was passed he submitted a draft of a law to the government based on his understand-ing of the social model of disability. While the New Order regime was open to imple-menting a disability law, the draft presented by Dria Manunggal was severely edited before being passed. The name of the law reflected its overall tone, which assumed that people with disabilities were defective and required support and assistance (Edwards 2014). Its content focused on how education and health services would be tailored to meet the needs of people with disabilities, rather than on disability rights, leading to it being described as a "charity-based" law by activists, scholars, and other observers of Indonesian disability policy (Edwards 2014). The law was a disappoint-ment for activists from Dria Manunggal, but the experience underscored the need for disability activists to learn how to pursue policy changes, skills that would become increasingly important after Indonesia's moment of democratic change.

The other major contribution that Dria Manunggal made to the movement was to provide a mentoring role to a new generation of disability activists in Indonesia. Until the 1990s, very few disability advocates thought of themselves as activists, and there was little cross-fertilization of activist strategies between disability activism and other forms of social activism. This changed with the participation of people with disabilities in the democratization movement in Yogyakarta. The personal friendship between Purwanta, and the country director of Oxfam at the time, Mansour Fakih, helped shape the institutional focus and approach of Dria Manunggal. Through Fakih, Purwanta met other NGOs funded by Oxfam and learned from them about advocacy and organizing. These skills and networks were shared with students with (or with-out) disabilities in Yogyakarta who volunteered at Dria Manunggal. Some of these volunteers also became involved in the prodemocracy movement in the late 1990s. Like Purwanta, their involvement in activism gave them exposure to activists from different sectors where they learned advocacy skills and organizational strategies that they were able to apply after the fall of the New Order regime.

OPPORTUNITIES OF DEMOCRATIZATION

When the New Order regime fell in 1998, a number of important changes occurred that affected the disability movement. The end of authoritarian rule in Indonesia was marked by the resignation of Suharto, president of Indonesia for thirty-two years. His successor, B. J. Habibie, oversaw a period of change commonly referred to as *reformasi*, or the period of reform (Aspinall and Fealy 2003). A number of important changes to the political structure were introduced that led to greater freedoms in Indonesian society, such as the release of political prisoners, greater freedoms for the press, and the opportunity for competitive elections (Crouch 2000). These changes contributed to an opening up of public space to Indonesian citizens, which had a significant impact on the opportunities available to disability activists.

As part of a series of measures to shift power away from the central government, Indonesia underwent a process of political decentralization. Decentralization meant that decisions about policy were no longer made exclusively at the national level, offering activists new pathways through which they could provide direct input into the legislative process and executive decision making. Under laws passed in 1999, decision-making processes were devolved to the local level, providing those at the district and municipality levels greater political authority, and thereby offering more locally based policymakers as targets for their advocacy (Buehler 2010; Aspinall and Fealy 2003).

These changes, coupled with laws on legislative drafting, local governance, and participatory planning passed in 2004, made law-making processes more open to citizen participation (Antlöv and Wetterberg 2011). Changes made to the structure and composition of the national legislature meant that elected representatives debated and decided on legislation, providing individual citizens some indirect input into the decisions about laws and policies. Decentralization meant this input could also be made to local legislatures empowered to influence policies and laws at the provincial and district levels. More significantly, the processes by which laws are developed now involve debate and consideration by commissions, which are the working units of the legislature. These commissions engage with the public—in fact, it is stipulated in the DPR procedural rules (2014) that community members must be able to easily access bills and draft legislation as part of the consultation process (Sherlock 2010).

Importantly, Indonesia's transition to democracy coincided with an increase in international pressure to establish a convention that recognized the rights of people with disabilities. In March 2000, the first global NGO Summit on Disability was held in Beijing, leading to the Beijing Declaration of Rights of People with Disability in the New Century. This statement marked the beginning of the campaign for a specific convention on the rights of people with disabilities that was based on the social, rather than medical, model of disability (Kanter 2003). The campaign, which centered on the failure of the Millennium Development Goals to refer specifically to people with disabilities (Kayess and French 2008), gained support because it emphasized how a convention could act as a framework for formally recognizing disability rights as a human rights issue. Those involved in the campaign argued that the establishment of a convention could help raise awareness of the challenges faced by people with disabilities and thereby protect them from potential harm by offering a better framework for monitoring whether the rights of people with disabilities were adequately protected. Of critical relevance for the disability movement in Indonesia, efforts to establish a convention also increased the attention and resources from international human rights and development organizations (Kanter 2003). The process culminated with the unanimous adoption of the CRPD by the United Nations General Assembly on December 13, 2006.

As in many other countries around the world, the CRPD provided a platform for activists in Indonesia to campaign for changes to their disability laws. Indonesia signed the convention in 2007, among the first countries to do so, and ratified it four years later in 2011 (Asrianti 2011). The signing of the CRPD helped activists to lobby for policy change consistent with the social model of disability, offering them a framework for proposing changes to the 1997 National Disability Law. The CRPD also paved the way for more international funding for disability-related activities around the world, including in Indonesia where organizations such as the Disability Rights Fund (DRF), the Australian Department of Foreign Affairs and Trade, and the International Labor Organization all began new programs related to disability (DFAT 2015). International disability NGOs, such as Handicap International and the Christian Blind Mission (CBM), which had operated in Indonesia prior to the signing of the CRPD, increased their emphasis on the question of rights where previously their programs had been more focused on accessibility and service provision (CBM 2015; Suprobo 2011).

Responding to New Opportunities

Disability activism has become more publicly visible in Indonesia in a variety of ways that illustrate activists' responses to the democratization process. Media coverage and discussion of issues relating to the rights of people with disabilities increased during election campaigns in 2004, 2009, and 2014 (Kurniawan 2004; Lutfia 2012; Osman 2011; Pasandaran 2008). While these campaigns led primarily to changes to the accessibility of voting booths rather than substantive debates around disability policy, they were a direct response to the changes that came about as a result of democratization. Disability activists have also run campaigns focused on issues of infrastructure and accessibility. For instance, activists have engaged in high-profile disputes with some domestic airlines about ensuring that people with disabilities are not discriminated against when traveling (Siagian 2013). Others have organized media-friendly "outings" around Jakarta to highlight how inaccessible the city is to people with certain disabilities (Dewi 2013). The main focus of disability activists since the ratification of the CRPD, however, has been campaigning for Indonesian legislation about disability to change so that it better aligns with the UN convention.

One of the most significant actions that activists have taken has been to push for changes to legislation about disability. The issue was one that activists felt was important for a long time, but the ratification of the CRPD was a major driver of campaigns for legislative change. Two major campaigns that involved aligning legislation with the CRPD were those run in support of the Provincial Regulation of the Special District of Yogyakarta No. 4/2012 about the Protection and Fulfillment of the Rights of People with Disabilities (the Yogyakarta disability law) and the Law No. 8/2016 concerning People with Disabilities (the national disability law). The Yogyakarta disability law was the first regulation in Indonesia based on the social model of disability. It was passed just over a year after the CRPD was ratified. The campaign for the national law took longer, not being passed until five years after the ratification of the CRPD. The campaigns were run by different parts of the movement, and their respective processes highlight the diverse ways in which disability activists have responded to the changes brought about by democratization.

Campaigning for the Yogyakarta Disability Law

Yogyakarta, where some of the most active and well-known disability organizations, including Dria Manunggal, are based, has been a hub of disability activism since the late 1990s. Two of the most active and prominent organizations in Yogyakarta—the Place for Integration and Advocacy for People with Disabilities (Sasana Integrasi dan Advokasi Difabel, SIGAB) and the Center for Advocacy for Women and Children with Disabilities (Sentra Advokasi Perempuan Difabel dan Anak, SAPDA)—were established by former Dria Manunggal volunteers. The experience of their young founders within Dria Manunggal, participating in political protests as part of the democratization movement, and their observations of how the larger disability bodies operated, led them to establish organizations based on thematic issues rather than on disability types.

Founded in 2003, SIGAB is particularly concerned with the structural marginalization of people with disabilities and their discrimination in terms of opportunities for education, health, employment, legal protection, and access to information. SIGAB's program is diverse, with activities including the formation of a model "inclusive" village, data collection and analysis, and advocacy, but with a particular focus on legal protection and advocacy for people with disabilities (SIGAB 2013). SAPDA was founded in 2005 to fill a particular niche in disability activism in Yogyakarta, namely, advocacy on behalf of women and children with disabilities. Again, reflecting the principles they acquired through Dria Manunggal, its founders felt it was important to find a way of engaging with disability that intersected with other sectors rather than focusing exclusively on disability (SAPDA 2016). In addition, they had observed that organizations lobbying for policy change at the national level tended to overlook the needs of people at the district level, and wanted to be sure that their efforts were going to make a difference to people living in and around the city. Another active disability NGO in Yogyakarta is the Center for Improving Qualified Activity in Life People with Disabilities (CIQAL). CIQAL was established in 2002, with an initial focus on economic empowerment. The organization also engages in advocacy work, but its key activities continue to involve training and support for people with disabilities to gain employment. The founders of this organization were members of the local branches of the membership-based mass organizations established during the New Order who felt that the problems with the legal structure of the local branches meant they were unable to take any action. In addition, like their colleagues from SAPDA and SIGAB, they believed it was important that people with different disabilities work together, rather than being siloed in separate organizations.

SIGAP, SAPDA, and CIQAL played a key role in the campaign for the Yogyakarta disability regulation. This regulation was not simply a response to the ratification of the CRPD but part of their longer-term agenda. Disability activists in Yogyakarta had been campaigning since 2005 to get the provincial government to enact legislation that would eliminate discrimination against people with disabilities (*Detik News*, January 24, 2005). They argued that the laws the provincial government passed did not consider the specific needs of people with disabilities, leading to their systematic discrimination. Activists were particularly concerned about issues of workplace discrimination and the lack of accessibility of public places. At this stage, however, Indonesia had not yet even signed the CRPD, making it difficult for these activists to make a case for their proposed changes. The signing of the CRPD by Indonesia in 2007 offered these activists an opportunity to better focus their campaign. SIGAB decided in 2008–9 to organize training for local government officials in Yogyakarta to raise their awareness of the new international framework. One of the unexpected results of this awareness-raising exercise was that the government officials themselves proposed that Yogyakarta should develop a provincial regulation about disability based on the CRPD. According to SIGAB activist, Muhammad Yoni Yulianto, the activists were excited about this proposition, but were unsure how seriously to take these government officials (Interview, December 2014).

It took almost a year before the campaign started in earnest. In 2010, the activists from Yogyakarta established a network called the National Disability Commission (Komnas Difabel).[3] Those activists had worked with Purwanta from Dria Manunggal and had heard his stories about the challenges of campaigning for the 1997 disability law. As a consequence, they recognized that the process was one that was likely to take a long time and would require collaboration with a range of organizations involved with disability in Yogyakarta as well as with a number of different government officials (Interview with Muhammad Joni Yulianto, December 2014). They opened up their network to a broad range of people with an interest in disability. The first action taken by Komnas Difabel was to bring together activists from around Yogyakarta to officially celebrate International Disability Day for the first time. They needed a theme for their campaign and decided to focus on campaigning for the Indonesian government to ratify the CRPD and campaigning for the provincial government of Yogyakarta to develop a provincial law based on the convention (Interview with Muhammad Joni Yulianto, December 2014).

The CRPD was ratified within a few months of this event, and the activists were well positioned to move quickly to push for a provincial law. According to Broto, who worked for the Yogyakarta Social Affairs Office (Dinas Sosial DIY) and who was closely involved in the process, they met three to four times a week to ensure the draft was completed (Interview, 12 December 2014). Muhammad Joni Yulianto and other individuals involved in the team report that the process went smoothly. The committee divided the work between organizations according to their skills and interests and made sure that they consulted regularly with the disabled people's organizations with which they worked (Interviews with Rofah Mudzakir and Supartini, December 2014). Part of their success was due to the fact that the activists had built a strong relationship with a range of different stakeholders who were pivotal to the process. The activists actively engaged with the Yogyakarta Social Affairs Office over the years. They had also cultivated relationships with academics interested in disability issues as well as key individuals within the office such as the head of Rehabilitation and Socialization of People with Disabilities and the person in charge of policy research for the Social Affairs Office. Their engagement with these individuals around other policy issues meant they were well placed to work collaboratively with them on the provincial law (Interviews with Rofah Mudzakir and Supartini, December 2014).

While the process of drafting and passing the law went smoothly, the activists faced significant resistance from other offices within the provincial government to the ideas that they had a role to play in the implementation of the new law. Traditionally in Indonesia, disability-related services have been the domain of the Social Affairs Office at the provincial level and the Ministry of Social Affairs at the national level. The activists believed that in order for the new law to be consistent with the CRPD, its implementation had to be cross-sectoral. This proposition not only challenged the understanding that other provincial agencies had about who was responsible for disability related issues, but also required these agencies to identify funding sources for the areas in which they were expected to be involved. As a consequence, although the law was passed quickly, its implementation has been weak, and activists have continued to lobby the provincial government to enact the legislation (Ridarineni 2015).

Campaigning for the National Disability Law

The campaign for the national disability law was more complex and drawn out, in part because there were more stakeholders involved in the process, and in part because of the characteristics of the disability movement in Jakarta. The National Human Rights Commission (Komnas HAM) started the drafting process in 2011 (Komisi Nasional Hak Asasi Manusia 2015). It sought input from one or two activists from the national-level disability organizations based in Jakarta and the Ministry of Social Affairs. But there was little engagement with other activists, including those who had been actively involved in the process of drafting the provincial disability law in Yogyakarta (Interviews, Jakarta and Yogyakarta, December 2014). The draft was submitted to the Legislative Committee (Baleg DPR) in early 2013 (Interview with Nurul Saadah Andriani, December 2014).

At around the same time, and unknown to the first group, a second draft was compiled and submitted to the national legislature by a working committee made up of a number of senior people from the Jakarta-based disability organizations. When it became clear that there were two drafts, Komnas HAM encouraged the groups to combine them.[4] With the assistance from the Centre for the Study of Law and Policy (Pusat Studi Hukum dan Kebijakan, PSHK), Komnas HAM established a working group of representatives from a range of Jakarta-based disability organizations to author the draft that became the basis for the current law. In late 2013, this law was included in the national legislation program for 2014, which put considerable pressure on the working group to finalize the draft so it could be deliberated before the end of the legislature's term, which ended that year. In May 2014, activists from Yogyakarta and other parts of Indonesia were invited to provide feedback on the draft at a meeting in Jakarta in early May 2014. As part of their preparation, SIGAB, SAPDA, and another disability organization called the Archipelago Handicap Organization (Organisasi Handicap Nusantara, OHANA) organized a workshop to gather feedback from disability organizations in Central Java (Indo 2014; Utami 2014). Once the feedback was collected they worked with senior disability activists and academics to compile the information in a format that was presentable to the national working group (Wijaya 2014).

It took another two years of negotiating and lobbying before the law was enacted. During this hiatus, activists from Jakarta and other parts of the country made use of different strategies in their continuing campaign for the law to be passed. These strategies not only highlighted the strengths and weaknesses of the movement, but more critically showed how activists were able to make use of the changes to Indonesia's political structures to deliberate issues related to disability. In the months following September 2014, while the law was debated, activists from Jakarta and Yogyakarta used the media to urge the legislature to pass the new legislation quickly (Afandi 2014; Wulandari 2014).

It became clear during this period that the activists in Jakarta were much better placed to follow up their calls for action with direct engagement with members of the legislature. For example, in January 2015, the working group in charge of drafting the law arranged a meeting with members of the legislature to keep the law on the agenda (Pusat Studi Hukum dan Kebijakan Indonesia 2015). In March, the head of the draft law working group, Ariana Soekwano, was quoted in the media again pushing for the legislation to be passed (*Republika*, March 12, 2015). In the same month, she met with the nine factions within the legislature, while other members of the working group met with the minister for social affairs to keep pressure on the legislature to pass the new law (Pusat Studi Hukum dan Kebijakan Indonesia 2015). More meetings took place between the working group and legislators in May and June 2015 as it became clear that the version the working group had presented would be heavily edited (Febiyanto 2015). As this chain of events suggests, while the national groups engaged in minimal consultation with activists in other parts of the country—or with members of their respective organizations—this type of direct engagement with national-level policymakers was possible because these activists were located in close physical proximity to those decision makers.

It was not until the middle of 2015 that disability activists from other parts of Indonesia, including branch members of the national organizations involved in the working groups drafting the law and activists from other sectors, began to engage with the campaign for the national law. Throughout July and August, the national-level disability organizations continued to campaign for the law to be passed before International Disability Day on December 3. They engaged activists from other sectors to support the campaign, leading to a rally of five hundred people in Jakarta in mid-August (Anwar 2015b and 2015a; Nurcaya 2015). From late August, disability activists from other parts of Indonesia gradually became involved in the campaign to pass the law. In late August, for example, in response to concerns that some parts of the law were too "Jakarta-centric," SAPDA organized a meeting to discuss the proposed law with representatives from the districts (Arief 2015). In mid-October, activists from PPDI and HWDI in North Sumatra marched to the provincial legislature to demand that changes be made to the law before it was passed to ensure the law was cross-sectoral, and not just focused on the Ministry of Social Affairs (*Menara News*, October 13, 2015). In early December, protestors in Surabaya organized a petition to urge the immediate passing of the draft legislation (Wicaksono 2015).

The final struggle that activists faced in their campaign was about the formation of a National Disability Commission. Disability advocates believed a national commission was necessary to ensure independent oversight of the implementation of the law and the fulfillment of rights of people with disabilities; however, the government did not want to commit to forming one.[5] In a press release issued in February 2016, President Joko Widodo indicated that the commission was unlikely to be developed as part of the law (Parawansa et al. 2016). Activists mobilized quickly, issuing a press release on the same day responding to the president's comments and reaffirming their commitment to the development of the commission (Soekanwo et al. 2016). Their cause was picked up by Desy Ratnasari, a member of Komisi VIII (the commission responsible for seeing the legislation through), who gave a speech defending the need for a National Disability Commission to ensure that people with disabilities were guaranteed full rights in the areas of public facilities, education, health, and employment (Commission VII DPR 2016). On March 10, the government and the legislature reached an agreement that the draft legislation would include the formation of a national commission for disability rights (Global Disability Watch 2016). A week later, on March 17, 2016, the new disability law was passed.

The passing of the law marked a huge success for disability activists, demonstrating how systems established in postauthoritarian Indonesia have created pathways for activists to have direct input into policy. Nevertheless, like the Yogyakarta disability law, implementation of the national law has been extremely slow. By mid-2018, more than two years after the law was passed, no regulations had been successfully implemented, despite considerable debate between policymakers and activists about how to put the ideas outlined in the law into practice (Nursyamsi 2017a and 2017b). Some of the key points of contention demonstrated a distinct lack of understanding on the part of Indonesian policymakers about the principles underlying the national law, particularly around the importance of involving a range of ministries rather than just the

Ministry of Social Affairs. This delay in implementation is unsurprising in the context of Indonesia where the implementation of progressive laws is regularly drawn out (Butt 2013). Nevertheless, it does indicate that while mechanisms exist for activists to directly influence policy, democratization in Indonesia has yet to compel policy-makers to ensure that policy and practice are consistent.

CONCLUSION

Over the last two decades, disability activism has undergone a significant transformation in Indonesia. Prior to the fall of Suharto, advocates for people with disability focused primarily on lobbying government for funding for welfare payments. Democratization, which coincided with changes in the global movement for disability rights, opened up new opportunities for disability activists to influence discourse and policy related to disability in Indonesia. A range of new disability advocacy organizations, including SIGAB, SAPDA, and CIQAL, have emerged over the last decade. These organizations have introduced new modes of activism and ideas into the movement, opened up disability activism to a range of new actors, and as a result, have contributed to a new vibrancy to disability activism in Indonesia. The energy and new ideas brought to disability activism by these organizations has had a substantial effect on laws and policies related to disability in Indonesia.

In Jakarta, disability activists used their access to policymaking processes to campaign for the national disability law. They did so in collaboration with experts from other sectors to develop a draft disability law and then followed this process up by putting pressure on the government to pass it through direct lobbying, the media, and public protest. Elsewhere, activists made strategic use of the opportunities provided by decentralization to lobby for changes at the local level in a way that would not have been possible during the New Order. These efforts included advocacy for the Yogyakarta disability law based on the CRPD, passed four years before the new national disability law. By pushing for this law, Yogyakarta-based activists were able to meet the needs of their local constituents without being beholden to the agenda and pace of mobilization of the disability activists working on the national law, most of whom were in Jakarta. This achievement built confidence among the activists, strengthened their credibility among international donors and their local community, and raised the profile of the movement more broadly.

In making it possible for activists to influence public policy in these ways, democratization brought to light differences in strategy, agenda, and skill between organizations within the movement. National organizations based in Jakarta tended to draw on repertoires of action that reflected their New Order roots, using their close proximity to decision makers at the national level to push for their agenda and to work, at least initially, in isolation. The newer organizations based in Yogyakarta, whose founders developed their skills during the political transition, tended to work more collaboratively with one another and with other sectors. These two parts of the movement worked in different ways, but the collective outcome of their efforts resulted in greater awareness among the broader population and decision makers of the importance of disability related issues and the translation of this new awareness into changes in policy.

The fact that so many different individuals and organizations from the disability movement had input into these laws demonstrates the extent to which democratization has created opportunities for participation. At the same time, there have been limits to the kinds of changes brought about by this increase in participation. Implementation of both the Yogyakarta law and the national law has been glacial, despite urgings from disability activists. As this suggests, while government officials were open to the idea of improving treatment of people with disability, they are less committed to making the necessary changes to ensure these ideas are put into practice. The challenges of implementing these two laws highlight a serious limitation of Indonesia's democratic system, namely that while the government has created mechanisms for participation, it has not developed appropriate mechanisms to hold itself to account for what it has committed to. Issues like disability, which are not necessarily considered a priority for the majority of the population, are particularly vulnerable to being overlooked. Fortunately, though, the disability movement does not have to deal with open hostility from opposing forces, as is the case with more politically controversial progressive social movements, which suggests that democracy may yet lead to positive changes for people with disability in Indonesia.

NOTES

1. Among disability activists, there is a distinction made between the medical and social models of disability (Kayess and French 2008). The medical model refers to the idea of people with disabilities as having a medical problem or impairment which needs addressing—the focus being on what the individual lacks and how to use welfare to provide support. The social model, on the other hand, frames disability as a consequence of social structures that obstruct the equal participation of people with disabilities (Kayess and French 2008; Oliver 1986). The welfare approach is based on a medical understanding of disability.
2. Before Indonesia ratified the United Nations Convention on the Rights of People with Disabilities, the official term for disability was *cacat* (crippled). Prior to this time, the names of these organizations were Persatuan Penyandang Cacat Indonesia (PPCI) and Himpunan Wanita Penyandang Cacat Indonesia (HWPCI).
3. "Difabel" is a term coined by disability activists from Yogyakarta meaning "differently abled." It was developed as an alternative to the term *penyandang cacat*, which means crippled or handicapped. The term is used primarily by activists from Yogyakarta and increasingly by their partners and collaborators in other parts of the country (Irwanto and Thohari 2017). Activists in Yogyakarta reported that there was some tension about the establishment of this group, as PPDI activists felt it threatened PPDI's role as the umbrella organization representing people with disabilities in Indonesia. Members of Komnas Difabel claimed that it was a different kind of organization type because it had no hierarchical structure and was more of a network than a centrally important body.
4. According to the Asia Foundation, they were approached by Komnas HAM to fund this process (Interview with Laurel MacLaren, December 2014).
5. Not all activists were in support of the National Disability Commission. Fuad (2015) argued that rather than establishing a separate commission, integrating a disability division into the existing commissions would ensure better engagement with disability across sectors.

REFERENCES

Afandi, Sugandi. 2014. "PPDI Pesimis RUU Disabilitas Bakal Disahkan Dalam Waktu Dekat." *Radio Republik Indonesia.* September 25. http://www.rri.co.id/post/berita/106252/nasional/ppdi_pesimis_ruu_disabilitas_bakal_disahkan_dalam_waktu_dekat.html.

Antlöv, Hans, and Anna Wetterberg. 2011. *Citizen Engagement, Deliberative Spaces and the Consolidation of a Post-Authoritarian Democracy: The Case of Indonesia.* Stockholm: Swedish International Centre for Local Democracy.

Anwar, Laraswati Ariadne. 2015a. "500 Pendemo Tuntut Penetapan RUU Disabilitas." *Kompas*. August 18. http://print.kompas.com/baca/2015/08/18/500-Pendemo-Tuntut-Penetapan-RUU-Disabilitas.

———. 2015b. "Masyarakat Tanda Tangani Petisi RUU Disabilitas." *Kompas* August 13. http://nasional.kompas.com/read/2015/08/13/21252931/Masyarakat.Tanda.Tangani.Petisi.RUU.Disabilitas?utm_source=RD&utm_medium=box&utm_campaign=Kaitrd.

Arief, Ajiwan. 2015. "Diskusi RUU Disabilitas SAPDA: Penuhi Hak Atas Kesehatan." Last Modified August 29, 2015. Accessed May 1, 2016. http://solider.or.id/2015/08/29/diskusi-ruu-disabilitas-sapda-penuhi-hak-atas-kesehatan.

Aspinall, Edward, and Greg Fealy. 2003. "Introduction: Decentralisation, Democratisation, and the Rise of the Local." In *Local Power and Politics in Indonesia: Decentralisation and Democratisation*, edited by Edward Aspinall and Greg Fealy, 1–12. Singapore: ISEAS–Yusof Ishak Institute.

Asrianti, Tifa. 2011. "RI Ratifies UN Convention on Rights of Persons with Disabilities." *Jakarta Post*. October 19.

Buehler, Michael. 2010. "Decentralisation and Local Democracy in Indonesia: The Marginalisation of the Public Sphere." In *Problems of Democratisation in Indonesia: Elections, Institutions, and Society*, edited by Edward Aspinall and Marcus Mietzner, 267–85. Singapore: ISEAS–Yusof Ishak Institute.

Butt, Simon. 2013. "Freedom of Information Law and Its Application in Indonesia: A Preliminary Assessment." *Asian Journal of Comparative Law* 8: 1–42.

CBM. 2015. *2015 Annual Report*.

Colbran, Nicola. 2010. "Access to Justice Persons with Disabilities Indonesia: Background Assessment Report." Geneva: International Labour Organization.

Commission VII DPR. 2016. "Komisi VIII Perjuangkan Knd Dalam RUU Penyandang Disabilitas." Accessed April 12, 2016. http://www.dpr.go.id/berita/detail/id/12526.

Crouch, Harold. 2000. "Indonesia: Democratization and the Threat of Disintegration." *Southeast Asian Affairs* 27: 115–33.

Dewi, Sita W. 2013. "No Barrier-Free Tourism in the City." *Jakarta Post*, February 25. http://www.thejakartapost.com/news/2013/02/25/no-barrier-free-tourism-city.html.

DFAT. 2015. *Development for All: 2015–2020: Strategy for Strengthening Disability-Inclusive Development in Australia's Aid Program*. Canberra: DFAT.

Edwards, Nicola J. 2014. "Disability Rights in Indonesia? Problems with Ratification of the United Nations Convention on the Rights of Persons with Disabilities." *Australian Journal of Asian Law* 15 (1): 1–15.

Febiyanto, Irwandi. 2015. "Draf RUU Disabilitas Masih Harus Disempurnakan." *Viva News*. June 1. http://politik.news.viva.co.id/news/read/632947-draf-ruu-disabilitas-masih-harus-disempurnakan.

Fuad, Bahrul. 2015. "Legalisasi Stigma." *Kompas*. September 22.

Gerkatin. 2008. "Gerkatin." Last Modified July 24, 2008. Accessed May 26, 2016. http://tunarungu.net76.net/node/6.

Global Disability Watch. 2016. "Indonesia to Set up National Disability Commission." *Global Disability*. March 10. http://globaldisability.org/2016/03/10/indonesia-set-national-disability-commission.

Grech, Shaun. 2009. "Disability, Poverty and Development: Critical Reflections on the Majority World Debate." *Disability and Society* 24 (6): 771–84.

HWDI. n.d. "Sejarah HWDI." Accessed May 19, 2016. http://www.hwdi.or.id/sejarah-hwdi.

Indo, Benni. 2014. "Diskusi Pleno RUU Penyandang Disabilitas Desak Kesetaraan Hak Difabel." Last Modified April 21, 2014. Accessed May 1, 2016. http://solider.or.id/2014/04/21/diskusi-pleno-ruu-penyandang-disabilitas-desak-kesetaraan-hak-difabel.

Irwanto, and Slamet Thohari. 2017. "Understanding National Implementation of the CRPD in Indonesia." In *Making Disability Rights Real in Southeast Asia: Implementing the UN Convention on the Rights of Persons with Disabilities in ASEAN*, edited by Derrick L. Cogburn and Tina Kempin Reuter, 91–118. Lanham, MD: Lexington Books.

Kanter, Arlene S. 2003. "The Globalization of Disability Rights Law." *Syracuse Journal of International Law and Commerce* 30 (2): 241–69.

Kayess, Rosemary, and Phillip French. 2008. "Out of Darkness into Light? Introducing the Convention on the Rights of Persons with Disabilities." *Human Rights Law Review* 8 (1): 1–34.

Komisi Nasional Hak Asasi Manusia. 2015. *Laporan Kinerja LKIP*. Jakarta: Komisi Nasional Hak Asasi Manusai.

Kurniawan, Bagus. 2004. "Ribuan Penyandang Cacat Tuntut Hak Ikut Coblosan Pilpres." *Detik News*. April 21. http://news.detik.com/read/2004/04/21/202503/128511/10/ribuan-penyandang-cacat-tuntut-hak-ikut-coblosan-pilpres?nd771104bcj.

Lutfia, Ismira. 2012. "1 Person, 1 Vote? Not for Many of Indonesia's Disabled." *Jakarta Globe*. February 2. http://www.thejakartaglobe.com/archive/1-person-1-vote-not-for-many-of-indonesias-disabled/.

Nurcaya, Ipak Ayu H. 2015. "Kaum Difabel Desak DPR Sahkan RUU Disabilitas." *Kabar24*. August 15. http://kabar24.bisnis.com/read/20150815/79/462801/kaum-difabel-desak-dpr-sahkan-ruu-disabilitas.

Nursyamsi, Fajri. 2017a. "Masyarakat Penyandang Disabilitas Menolak Pp 'Sapu Jagat.'" July 28, 2017. http://www.pshk.or.id/id/berita/aktivitas/masyarakat-penyandang-disabilitas-menolak-pp-sapu-jagat/.

———. 2017b. "Meninjau Kembali Pp 'Sapu Jagat' Implementasi Uu Penyandang Disabilitas." *Hukum Online*, August 3, 2017. http://www.hukumonline.com/berita/baca/lt5982cf6388274/meninjau-kembali-pp-sapu-jagat-implementasi-uu-penyandang-disabilitas-oleh--fajri-nursyamsi.

Oliver, Mike. 1986. "Social Policy and Disability: Some Theoretical Issues." *Disability, Handicap and Society* 1 (1): 5–17.

Osman, Nurfika. 2011. "Disabled Look to Ensure Equal Access in Elections." *Jakarta Globe*. April 1. http://www.thejakartaglobe.com/archive/disabled-look-to-ensure-equal-access-in-elections/.

Parawansa, Khofifah Indar, Tjahjo Kumolo, Ignatius Jonan, Basoeki Hadimoeljono, Yuddy Chrisnandi, Yasonna H. Laoly, Anies Baswedan, Mohamad Nasir, and Yohana Yambise. 2016. "Pandangan Dan Pendapat Presiden Terhadap Rancangan Undang-Undang Tentang Penyandang Disabilitas." Last Modified February 18, 2016. http://www.pshk.or.id/wp-content/uploads/2016/02/Pandangan-Pendapat-Presiden-thd-RUU-Penyandang-Disabilitas.pdf.

Pasandaran, Camelia. 2008. "People with Disabilities Call for Voting Rights." *Jakarta Globe*. December 19, 2008. http://www.thejakartaglobe.com/archive/people-with-disabilities-call-for-voting-rights/.

PNPM Special Program on Disability. 2015. "Scoping and Qualitative Needs Assessment of Disabled Persons Organizations in Eastern Indonesia." Unpublished.

Pusat Studi Hukum dan Kebijakan Indonesia. 2015. "Fajri Nursyamsi, Peneliti Pshk, Bersama Pokja RUU Penyandang Disabilitas Bertemu Menteri Sosial Perihal Koordinasi Antar Kementerian Terkait RUU Penyandang Disabilitas." Accessed March 26, 2015. http://www.pshk.or.id/id/berita/aktivitas/fajri-nursyamsi-peneliti-pshk-bersama-pokja-ruu-penyandang-disabilitas-bertemu-menteri-sosial-perihal-koordinasi-antar-kementerian-terkait-ruu-penyandang-disabilitas/.

Ridarineni, Neni. 2015. "Perda Perlindungan Penyandang Disabilitas Masih Diam Di Atas Kertas." *Republika*. March 14. http://nasional.republika.co.id/berita/nasional/daerah/15/03/13/nl5tq2-perda-perlindungan-penyandang-disabilitas-masih-diam-di-atas-kertas.

SAPDA. 2016. "Profil SAPDA." Last Modified January 25, 2016. Accessed May 24, 2016. http://sapdajogja.org/?cat=13.

Sherlock, Stephen. 2010. "The Parliament in Indonesia's Decade of Democracy: People's Forum or Chamber of Cronies?" In *Problems of Democratisation in Indonesia: Elections, Institutions, and Society*, edited by Edward Aspinall and Marcus Mietzner, 160–78. ISEAS–Yusof Ishak Institute.

Siagian, Sandra. 2013. "Garuda Apologizes to Passenger Who Filed Petition over Poor Treatment." *Jakarta Globe*, March 14. http://jakartaglobe.id/business/garuda-apologizes-to-passenger-who-filed-petition-over-poor-treatment/.

SIGAB. 2013. "Profil Lembaga SIGAB." Last Modified April 14, 2013. Accessed May 23, 2016. http://www.sigab.or.id/id/article/profil-lembaga-sigab.

Soekanwo, Ariani, Aria Indrawati, Yeni Rosa Damayanti, Maulani Rotinsulu, Mahmud Fasa, Tigor Hutapea, and Fajri Nursyamsi. 2016. "Masyarakat Penyandang Disabilitas Merespon Perkembangan Pembahasan RUU Penyandang Disabilitas." Last Modified February 18, 2016. http://www.pshk.or.id/wp-content/uploads/2016/02/Siaran-Pers-Konpres-Tagih-Janji-Jokowi-RUU-Penyandang-Disabilitas-10Feb16.pdf.

Suprobo, Novina. 2011. "Lesson Learnt from the Project: Mainstreaming Disability into Disability Risk Management Initiatives in Indonesia and Philippines." Manila: Handicap International.

Thohari, Slamet. 2013. *Disability in Java: Contesting Conception of Disability in Javanese Society after Soeharto Regime*. Saarbrucken: Lambert Academic Publishing.

Utami, Brita Putri. 2014. "Pembahasan RUU Disabilitas Perlu Libatkan Banyak Pihak." *SIGAB*. June 9. http://www.sigab.or.id/id/article/pembahasan-ruu-disabilitas-perlu-libatkan-banyak-pihak.

Wicaksono, Yovinus Guntur. 2015. "Penyandang Disabilitas Desak Pengesahan RUU Disabilitas." *Jatim Times*. December 3. http://www.jatimtimes.com/baca/111346/20151203/190441/penyandang-disabilitas-desak-pengesahan-ruu-disabilitas/.

Wijaya, Harta Nining. 2014. "Diskusi Lanjutan Draft RUU Disabilitas Bidang Pendidikan." Last Modified May 2, 2014. Accessed May 1, 2016. http://solider.or.id/2014/05/02/diskusi-lanjutan-draft-ruu-disabilitas-bidang-pendidikan.

Wulandari, Indah. 2014. "Kaum Difabel Ingin RUU Penyandang Disabilitas Segera Disahkan." *Republika*. December 3. http://nasional.republika.co.id/berita/nasional/umum/14/12/03/nfzhl6-kaum-difabel-ingin-ruu-penyandang-disabilitas-segera-disahkan.

CONCLUSION: SOCIAL MOVEMENTS, PATRONAGE DEMOCRACY, AND POPULIST BACKLASH IN INDONESIA

Edward Aspinall

Progressive social movements aiming to represent marginalized and disempowered groups and to expand democratic rights have become an important part of Indonesia's political landscape since the transition to democracy began two decades ago. The New Order regime's ambition to curb and control autonomous societal expression and organization was never fully realized in practice, but it crumbled once Suharto resigned and Habibie loosened restrictions on expression and association. As we have seen throughout this volume, coinciding with the *reformasi* years from 1998 to 2004, Indonesia experienced a dramatic expansion of civil society of a sort typical of countries that experience a sudden democratic breakthrough. In the years since that breakthrough, Indonesia has arguably come close to becoming a "social movement society," in which organized social movements and the protest repertoires they draw on, such as mass demonstrations, have become normalized (Juliawan 2011; Meyer and Tarrow 1998).

Further, as the chapters in this book also demonstrate, the social movements unleashed or empowered by democratization have made many important gains for their members and constituents. Though, as Yatun Sastramidjaja demonstrates in her chapter, the student movement—representing a relatively narrow and privileged group of Indonesians—was at the leading edge of the reformasi movement, and these gains were subsequently distributed relatively widely throughout Indonesian society. Together, we have seen that they amount to an impressive compendium of social movement success. Some of these gains were felt most acutely among groups that had been most marginalized, and whose political actions had been most ardently repressed, during the New Order. For example, as Iqra Anugrah explained in his chapter, agrarian movements in the post-Suharto period have on numerous occasions attained greater compensation for disenfranchised landowners or occupiers, successfully reclaimed land that has been lost, or frustrated attempts at land expropriation. Teri Caraway and Michele Ford likewise demonstrated how labor unions won significant improvements in wages and conditions. We have also seen how the reformasi climate allowed groups that had previously been almost invisible in the public sphere, such as LGBT persons and Indonesians with disabilities, as Hendri Wijaya and Sharyn Graham Davies and Thushara Dibley respectively explained, to seek new forms of self-expression and empowerment.

At times, these and similar social movements have been able to wield considerable influence when it comes to legislative and policy changes—whether achieving a national framework for agrarian reform in 2001 or lobbying for the introduction of a universal health insurance scheme in 2012 (e.g., Cole 2012). Social movement activists often enjoy considerable access to the national media, and human rights, women's, and other NGOs are routinely consulted during the drafting of national policy or legislation: witness, for example, the innovative forms of policy advocacy used by disability activists to gain access and achieve policy goals, as Thushara Dibley described in her chapter. There are also institutional pockets within the state bureaucracy—such as the National Human Rights Commission and the National Commission on Violence Against Women—that have been all but colonized by activists from these movements. As Elisabeth Kramer explained earlier in this book, anti-corruption activists have focused much of their energy on defending the Corruption Eradication Commission (Komisi Pemberantasan Korupsi, KPK), itself one of the signature achievements of the reformasi period. Finally, many former activists have joined political parties and been able to effect political change by working within the formal system (Mietzner 2013).

Despite such measures of progress, the accounts in this book present a picture that is somber. The part played by progressive social movements in post-Suharto Indonesia often recalls the labors of Sisyphus, with most of the gains such movements have made being fragile and insecure, under recurrent threat of rollback and constant pressure of erosion. Progress in one sector or region is frequently matched by regression in another. Such movements mostly lack strongly institutionalized, deeply rooted, and resilient organizations, with the national picture instead resembling an ever-changing kaleidoscope of small NGOs, action committees, and informal networks. A few of the larger labor unions are the main exception to this rule, but union density is low, at an estimated 3.6 percent of the total workforce and 11 percent in the formal sector in 2010 (Ford 2010, 5). No progressive social movement has been able to wield an institutionalized influence in electoral politics equivalent to, say, labor movements in countries with strong social democratic traditions, or Islamist movements in many other Muslim-majority countries. Some of the movements discussed in this book, such as those promoting women's equality, religious freedom, and LBGT rights, are challenged by other groups, who often appeal to conservative religious identities that oppose progressive goals. Other threats come from powerful economic actors—factory owners, property developers, plantation companies, and the like—whose interests and agendas conflict with those of social movements representing lower-class groups and promoting redistributive goals, and who have far more access to levers of formal and informal political power with which to defend their privileges. All in all, although progressive social movements have established a firm foothold in post-Suharto democratic life, they are far from being dominant political actors.

The reasons for the progress achieved by Indonesian social movements in the post-Suharto period are relatively clear. The opening of political space after the collapse of the Suharto regime, and widespread popular support for promoting democratic rights, empowering disenfranchised groups, and addressing social inequalities, allowed most of the movements discussed in this book to rapidly organize and advance their agendas. These movements were also able to draw on traditions of social activism and movement politics derived from Indonesia's nationalist struggle that, although badly crippled and distorted by the destruction of the communist Left in the 1960s, continue to legitimate and valorize the "little people" (*rakyat kecil*) as an important political actor and source of political legitimacy. The centrality of popular mobilization in the events leading to the resignation of Suharto and subsequent dismantling of his New Order further demonstrated the efficacy of social movement politics and established protest as a legitimate form of political expression in the successor democratic regime. Such dynamics need not detain us here, given that they have been addressed at length in other chapters in this book, as well as in many other works on Indonesian civil society and politics (for example, Aspinall 2005; Ford 2009; Nyman 2006; Uhlin 1997).

Instead, this concluding chapter drills down into the structural obstacles such movements have confronted when trying to achieve greater influence in post-Suharto Indonesia. It does so by contextualizing Indonesian social movements in terms of three deep features of Indonesia's post-Suharto social and political order. The first of these is the ubiquity of clientelistic patterns of political organization. Social movements seek to establish themselves on the basis of horizontal organization and identity, and can therefore splinter when they encounter the vertically arranged networks of personalized loyalty through which political influence and material resources flow in a patronage democracy such as Indonesia. The ubiquity of steeply hierarchical linkages connecting wealthy and powerful political actors to the grassroots makes social movements vulnerable to co-optation and can impede cooperation between them. A second related obstacle for social movements is the predominance of informal networks and extralegal methods as means of achieving political outcomes. Social movements of the sort discussed in this book are fundamentally about claiming *rights*: whether for equal treatment before the law, for access to resources, or for protection from abuse. But the rule of law in post-Suharto Indonesia is weak, making social movements vulnerable and throwing their potential supporters back onto reliance on informal and personalized connections with powerful actors. Finally, progressive social movements are challenged by rival forms of political organization, which contest their claims to represent and mobilize constituencies such as the urban poor, women, farmers, and industrial workers. As well as clientelist politicians distributing largesse to build personalized support networks, such rival political movements include populists and Islamists, which contest social movements' claims to represent the poor and seek to mobilize them for very different goals. Notably, such rivals and countermovements often have little commitment to the wider system of democratic representation and liberal rights in which the movements discussed in this book have prospered, and which they generally support.

SOCIAL MOVEMENTS AMID CLIENTELISM

There is a disjuncture between the structure and logic of social movements and the clientelistic relationships that infuse Indonesia's social and political order. As one author, writing on the Middle East, has put it, social movements "most often [follow] specific horizontal lines of social categorization, for example, race, gender, or class," whereas "patron-client relationships reflect an alternative structure, one based along vertical lines" (Clark 2004, 946). Social movements seek to mobilize individuals as members of broad-based collective identities and as citizens, claiming their collective rights by virtue of their membership in the nation and as part of the group advancing the claim. In contrast, when individuals seek to advance their interests through clientelistic ties, they do so on the basis of personalized relationships characterized by inequality in material resources, political power, and social status in which a lower-status person (the client) is dependent on someone of higher status (the patron).[1] In contrast to the social movement world of collective mobilization and rights claiming, the basic stuff of clientelistic relationships is *personalized* exchange of *favors*.

Indonesia's post-Suharto polity has been described as a patronage democracy (e.g., Blunt, Turner, and Lindroth 2012), in which the personalized distribution of material resources and other benefits in exchange for political support motivate social and political organization. In Indonesia, such dynamics are, most obviously, visible in the domain of political society. Most of Indonesia's political parties are highly clientelistic, with members seeking advancement by attaching themselves to powerful leaders, who in turn build clienteles by raising funds from their access to political office, and distributing them, and political authority, downward through the party structure. In the electoral arena itself, votes are routinely exchanged for patronage in the form of cash payments, material gifts, collective donations, and pork barrel projects, with such exchanges typically distributed via highly personalized and complex brokerage pyramids (Aspinall et al. 2017). Advancement within the civilian bureaucracy, as well as in state security agencies such as the police and army, is also to a large extent determined by personal relationships and informal payments, including the purchase of office, despite the complex formal hierarchies and rules that ostensibly govern these institutions (Kristiansen and Ramli 2006).

Importantly, these clientelistic patterns are found both at the base of society and at its apex. In both rural and urban neighborhoods, poor Indonesians often seek the assistance of their immediate social betters—local health workers or teachers, landlords, employers, civil servants, and the like—when they need to get a child into a school or hospital, or access a job, loan, or emergency help when times are hard. Community-level elected officials, such as village, neighborhood (*rukun warga*, RW), or subneighborhood (*rukun tetangga*, RT) heads are especially important local patrons because they exercise significant control over who gets access to government welfare programs and to the various government projects that circulate in both rural and urban areas. Poor citizens repay the help and favors imparted by local notables in part simply through expressing social deference and respect, but also by following the "advice" of such local elites about whom they should support at election time. Few poor Indonesians are entirely dependent on patrons, as in classical forms of clientelism such as those found between tenants and landlords. But in a context where many poor people derive their incomes from the informal economy rather than steady formal employment, most are constantly on the lookout for whatever minor payments, jobs, grants, and other benefits they can attain by attaching themselves, even temporarily, to community-level notables, as Ian Wilson's chapter in this volume makes clear. Meanwhile, such local notables themselves often depend for material and social advancement on their own connections with higher-level government officials, party activists, and businesspeople, as well as various fixers and brokers, who are in turn connected to yet higher-level patrons. Through such chains of personal connection, no matter how tenuous and attenuated, even the lowliest Indonesians are connected to the very peak of the social hierarchy, where Indonesia's wealthiest and most powerful actors themselves depend on personal relationships and the informal trading of favors to cement their authority and privilege, and where political and material wealth rise from the fusion of formal institutional and informal personal power (Robison and Hadiz 2004).

How does the ubiquity of clientelism affect social movements? We lack space to exhaustively cover the potential effects, but let us mention three. First, clientelism makes social movement organizations vulnerable to co-optation. In Indonesia, clientelistic politicians are constantly on the lookout for community leaders who can burnish their populist credentials and broker their attempts to mobilize voters in their constituencies (Aspinall 2014). Often, such politicians turn to local-level notables (such as village or neighborhood heads, *adat* chiefs, or preachers and religious teachers) for assistance in recruiting voters, but they also try to draw in the support of social movements of various types (for example, local NGOs, women's organizations, environmental groups). When community or social movement leaders attach themselves to politicians in this way they often become conduits for distribution of patronage—cash or in-kind donations, small-scale development projects, and the like—to their followers, but they can themselves often also gain personal benefits. Accordingly, virtually every social-movement sector is replete with stories of movement leaders who have been co-opted by their engagements with politics: the environmental activist who ends up owning a plot in an oil palm plantation, the student activist who becomes a mid-level party official and political fixer, the teacher union leader who becomes a project broker for the local district head. Of course, relationships between social movement leaders and politicians are often complex, with movement leaders often trying also to gain access to benefits for their constituents and not just for themselves. Even so, such relationships can lead to demobilization in cases in which a social movement organization finds itself channeling projects, jobs, or other forms of material assistance from the government to its members. In such circumstances, social movements can be caught by a "dual pressure" (Lapegna 2013), with constituents placing pressure on their leaders to assist them, and government officials requiring demobilization as a condition of continuing such assistance.

This points to a second effect: it can be hard for collectively oriented social movements to compete with clientelistic networks in conditions in which their constituents are constantly being drawn into personalized relationships based on material exchange. This dynamic is most obvious when social movement organizations engage in electoral politics. Indonesia's modern electoral history is full of failed attempts by leftist, labor, peasant, and other activists to form political parties or compete for elected office. Their attempts to promote programmatic politics often founder in the face of the clientelistic logic of the electoral arena: for example, in Savirani's (2016) study of labor union candidates in the 2014 legislative election in Bekasi, West Java, the union candidates found it difficult to compete with more conventional politicians who were distributing patronage to voters; these candidates often also confronted direct requests from voters for cash payments and other handouts. But a similar logic also operates outside the electoral arena: for instance, movements mobilizing in favor of agrarian reform, but unable to provide immediate benefits to their members, find it difficult to establish bases in rural communities. Yet rural areas are densely populated by farmers', livestock, and fishers' cooperatives, as well as by a variety of microenterprises and groups, whose primary function is to act as recipients of projects and aid packages from local government and development agencies.

Third, and finally, clientelistic patterns of organization also penetrate social movements themselves, blunting their effectiveness. One of the distinctive features of Indonesia's social movement terrain is its great fragmentation: in virtually every sector, an often dizzyingly complex array of organizations compete, duplicating geographic coverage and thematic concerns. As I have argued elsewhere (Aspinall 2013, 42–45), one source of this fragmentation is competition for funding, which is often doled out in the form of project support by foreign donor organizations or government agencies.

This pattern promotes a fragmentation of social movement organization, with competitive bidding for funding encouraging competition between groups that might otherwise cooperate on common goals, and encouraging relationships of dependency between major organizations in Jakarta and the regional branches and groups that are reliant on them. Moreover, given that success in the NGO world is often dependent on access to funding, leaders who possess connections to funding sources can wield disproportionate influence, with social movement organizations often coming to resemble clienteles of influential leaders-cum-patrons, in which personal enmities and competition can produce splintering.

Of course, it would be an error to overstate the influence of clientelism in Indonesia's political system, including among its social movements. Though clientelistic relationships are widespread, they do not represent the sum-total of Indonesian social and political organization. The explosion of social movement activism since the fall of Suharto has been thoroughgoing and has involved autonomous action by many ordinary Indonesians, independent of or in challenge to the hierarchical relationships that otherwise structure their lives. In fact, Indonesia's entire modern history can be read as a series of back-and-forth struggles between clientelistic and solidarity-based patterns of social and political organization. The era of mass politics in the 1950s and 1960s involved a complex mixture of clientelistic and horizontal modes, though popular mobilization—especially though not exclusively through the Indonesian Communist Party (Partai Komunis Indonesia, PKI) and other organizations on the Left—was an important feature that allowed many ordinary Indonesians to transform their own lives and personal circumstances in contravention of prevailing social mores and bonds (McVey 1990), though, as Mortimer (1974) notes, even the PKI grew partly by relying on clientelistic ties. The transition to the New Order saw active suppression of horizontal organization and deliberate corralling of social organizations into hierarchical and corporatist relationships with state authority. Since reformasi the obvious revival of social movements based on horizontal solidarities has, as we have seen, been far reaching, but has also involved hybridization with clientelist patterns.

Whatever the ultimate outcome of these processes, Indonesia's experience confirms that the transition to democracy involves not simply the establishment of formal representative institutions and civil liberties. For the promise of democracy to be realized for ordinary citizens, it also requires them to challenge an entire pattern of social organization in order to make, what has been called in other contexts, the transition from clientelism to citizenship (Fox 1994).

Rights Claiming amid Informality

A closely related obstacle for social movements—and one that helps explain the attraction of clientelistic and other forms of personalized connections to them—is what might be called the rule-of-law problem. Rights claiming is central to social movements in Indonesia and beyond. This book provides repeated evidence of that centrality. LGBT and women's movements claim rights of equal protection before the law, agrarian movements claim land rights and rights to other resources, labor movements claim rights to livelihoods and protection from arbitrary treatment by employers, and so on. Yet for such rights to be predictably and consistently enforced, and not merely invoked, a society requires a system in which the rule of law is respected, and the regulations produced as a result of social struggles are implemented in fact as well as merely rhetorically. Such a system is not yet present in Indonesia: after almost two decades of democratization what counts in Indonesian politics are typically not the regulations that formally govern the polity, but the informal relationships and networks through which power is organized (Aspinall and van Klinken 2011). The predominance of informality means that when social movements achieve gains, those gains are often ephemeral. At the same time, the totality of social movement demands can be read—at least in part—as an appeal for a rules- and rights-based order.

A fundamental problem here concerns the nature and effectiveness of the legal system. As with many countries, laws and regulations in Indonesia are frequently not implemented consistently, especially when they impose limitations or sanctions on powerful actors and empower or protect weak ones. For example, as we have seen, companies frequently do not feel bound by protections governing their workers, and plantation owners often do not respect the rights of landowners on whose land their crops are planted. Islamist or conservative vigilantes and militias often violate the rights of minority groups to assemble by breaking up their meetings or attacking their places of worship. The agencies of the state responsible for enforcing such legal regulations frequently collude with those who violate them. For example, the police and military often function as providers of informal security services for companies, enforcing rather than punishing their abrogation of employees' or landowners' rights. Wealthy businesspeople often provide financial sponsorship for the career paths of police officers, who later repay such favors with special treatment when required; in contrast, police officers often use great brutality to extract informal payments from poor or marginalized offenders—such as alleged drug users (Baker 2012, 2013). Meanwhile, the police collude with gangsters and vigilante organizations in order to extract fees from their protection rackets and to outsource some of their security functions (Nooteboom 2011; Wilson 2011). The state is penetrated with such informal networks and connections of mutual benefit, blurring the boundary between state and society, and impeding its ability to act as neutral arbiter in social and political disputes.

More perniciously still, Indonesian courts are penetrated by a "judicial mafia" (*mafia peradilan*) in which "case brokers" (*makelaar kasus*) facilitate payments from litigants to ensure favorable rulings—with bribes divided between police, prosecutors, lawyers, and especially, judges. Poor legal drafting facilitates such collusion: the country's thicket of laws and subordinate regulations frequently contains conflicting provisions, giving law enforcement agencies great leeway for picking and choosing those that will advantage the parties most willing to pay for protection. The bias and unpredictability of the judicial system poses a major obstacle for rights enforcement, and hence for social movements, given that "much of the power to define and shape the relationship between state and citizens is formally in the hands of the courts" (Butt and Lindsey 2011, 190). The upshot is that "for ordinary, unconnected citizens the formal legal system is something to be avoided rather than an avenue to realize one's rights" (Berenschot et al. 2017, 12).

For social movements, the result is that the political gains they achieve can be less substantive than they seem: a movement may succeed in pressuring the government to enact a new regulation granting certain rights that are not put into practice, or are put into practice unevenly. This gap between formal and substantive rights is part of the everyday political vernacular in Indonesia, wherein politicians, political activists, and ordinary citizens alike frequently state that the country's laws are strong, but implementation is weak, with this observation being the subject of countless seminars and news articles (e.g., *Antaranews* 2012). Of course, the degree of weakness in implementation varies widely across the archipelago: regulations that are upheld in the cities or in places with relatively diverse economies and strong civil societies are more readily ignored in remote districts dominated by local political dynasties or political mafias. Local political alignments greatly affect law enforcement generally, as those studying patterns of prosecutions of public officials for corruption have observed (Clark 2013; Davidson 2007).

For ordinary citizens, the weakness of law enforcement and the elusiveness of citizens' rights and entitlements mean that "in practice many everyday state–citizen interactions are shaped less by rules and laws, but rather by personal relations and norms of reciprocity that provide similar reassurances that state agents will award certain claims" (Berenschot et al. 2017, 9). Ordinary citizens cultivate close relationships with community-level officials, such as village heads, in order to turn to them for help when they need to access government services or assistance. Much the same logic applies to social movements: when legal enforcement is weak, the cultivation of informal relations with powerholders can assist them achieve their goals, helping to explain the ubiquity of the pattern of clientelistic relationships mentioned above.

All of this does not mean that laws or rights claims are insignificant for social movements in post-Suharto Indonesia. On the contrary, most social movements of the sort encountered in this book continue to view legal reform and rule of law as important goals, and they continue to place rights claiming at the center of their activities: look for example at Iqra Anugrah's analysis of agrarian movements, which he describes as movements for land rights. Numerous street demonstrations in Indonesia feature protestors holding posters or banners with phrases such as "give back our rights" (*kembalikan hak kami*). In every sector there are groups—those promoting religious pluralism are an obvious example—that expend much effort on documenting legal violations by state and social actors and drawing attention to the need for better enforcement of legal protections. Moreover, despite the power of the judicial mafia, the courts themselves remain an important arena of social-movement struggle, continuing the tradition of the Legal Aid Institute (Lembaga Bantuan Hukum, LBH) and allied organizations which during the New Order period provided legal representation to defendants in courtrooms not only to defend their individual human rights but also to promote the notion that Indonesia was a state ruled by law (Lev 1987; Aspinall 2005, 100–112). Such legal campaigning has greatly expanded in the post–New Order period, assisted by the establishment of new legal institutions, including new human rights protections in the Constitution and a Constitutional Court which has the power to rule legislation unconstitutional (Mietzner 2010). Human rights groups and other social organizations have won several cases extending citizen rights in the Constitutional Court, and have even used the court to claim socioeconomic rights (Rosser and van Diermen 2016).

The prominence of these strategies, again, points to the magnitude of the challenge confronting progressive social movements, which in order to secure advancement for their constituents, ultimately need not simply to achieve particular policy or legislative changes, but to remake the very framework of state-society relations. This would be an enormous task even if such movements had the political field to themselves. In fact, they face significant competition in post-Suharto Indonesia.

COMPETING CLAIMS AND COUNTERMOVEMENTS

Since the mid-2000s, Indonesia's new democracy has been challenged by a growing pushback against electoralism, liberalism, and pluralism. Indonesia is far from unique in this respect: for much of the last twenty years, the "third wave" of democratization that began in Southern Europe in the mid-1970s, before spreading through Latin America, Eastern Europe, Africa, and parts of Asia and even the Middle East through the 1980s and 1990s, has been arrested by democratic stagnation and even regression (Diamond 2015). Support for democracy has waned in both new and consolidated democracies, and an array of nativist, populist, and authoritarian forces has come together to challenge democratic rights and procedures in many countries. Critically, and largely differentiating the current trend from earlier tides of authoritarianism, democracy has largely been undermined by political leaders and movements relying on electoral support, rather than being overthrown by narrow coteries of elites using military coups or other nonelectoral means to seize power. In many parts of the world, often in the context of social dislocation associated with neoliberal economic policies and globalization, antiliberalism has become a popular force, mobilized at election times but also rooted in both offline and online social movements.

In Indonesia, democratic regression has not occurred to the extent witnessed in comparable regional powers such as Russia or Turkey, where authoritarian leaders have harnessed nationalist and authoritarian sentiment to centralize power, bridle opposition, and close space for public criticism. Popular support for democracy, as measured in public opinion surveys, has remained strong in Indonesia. However, as Mietzner (2012) has observed, deep skepticism about democracy is apparent in broad segments of Indonesia's political elite, including among national parliamentarians, party leaders, elected officials, bureaucrats, and military officers. Such views are dispersed, however, and often mix incoherently with support for aspects of the new democratic order. For example, some political parties whose leaders occasionally criticize such foundational democratic practices as voting—Megawati Sukarnoputri of the PDI-P is one prominent example—also contain former prodemocracy activists and in practice defend and even extend democratic reforms in parliament. Even so, that Indonesia's ruling elite contains deep reservoirs of skepticism regarding liberal democracy was demonstrated by the readiness with which a large share of the country's parties and leading political figures cohered around the authoritarian-populist challenge mounted by former general Prabowo Subianto during the 2014 presidential election and by subsequent erosions of democratic rights by President Joko Widodo.

As well as having elite sources, antiliberalism is also rooted in sections of the broader population and civil society. Since the transition to democracy began, progressive social movements have had to contend with a range of countermovements and organizations that seek to appeal to the very constituencies they seek as their own preserve, but in the service of antidemocratic and antipluralist goals. Such groups have been able to take advantage of Indonesia's democratic opening in much the same way as have progressive groups, giving rise to much discussion—especially early in the transition to democracy—about the presence of "uncivil society" in Indonesia (Beittinger-Lee 2009). The result is that there are competing claims to represent Indonesia's citizenry, including most of the constituencies targeted by progressive social movements.

One particularly prominent source of such contestation is Indonesia's range of Islamist organizations and networks: groups which seek thoroughgoing Islamization of Indonesia's social order and political system. The world of Indonesian Islamism is at least as fractured as that of progressive social movement activism, with groups divided on doctrine, strategy, and social constituency. Some groups are rooted in sections of the urban middle classes, pursue gradualist strategies of political change, and formally support democratic institutions. The most prominent example is the Prosperous Justice Party (Partai Keadilan Sejahtera, PKS), an organization that grew out of campus-based Islamic study groups inspired by the Muslim Brotherhood in the Middle East (Buehler 2013). Hizbut Tahrir Indonesia is a globally connected group that campaigns for the reestablishment of a universal caliphate and is mostly supported by university students and educated youth. Others, such as the Defenders of Islam Front (Front Pembela Islam, FPI), appeal to members of the urban poor and lower-middle classes. There are also salafi-jihadi groups that have engaged in terrorist attacks that operate on the fringes of more mainstream organization. But beyond such highly organized groups there is an enormous ecosystem of Islamist preachers, neighborhood-level Quranic study groups, and Islamic businesses and educational institutions found in virtually every sector of Indonesian society. As Greg Fealy explains in his chapter, this sprawling Islamist ecosystem has generated a conservative turn in Indonesian Islamic life over the last decade or so, restricting the space for many of the liberal groups that had flourished in the late New Order and initially hoped to take advantage of the reformasi space to promote even more progressive interpretations of Islamic doctrine.

Alongside Islamist groups, a second noteworthy category of organizations that challenge the claims of progressive social movements to represent the rakyat consists of organizations of thugs, gangsters, or vigilantes (*preman*). These are organizations of men, especially in urban and peri-urban settings, which run protection rackets, organize street parking, provide security at building sites, factories, marketplaces, nightclubs, brothels, gambling dens, and other venues, and often engage in out-and-out criminal activities such as the drug trade. Preman groups typically act in close coordination with members of the police, army, and other security agencies, and cultivate links in the worlds of politics and business. They are motivated by material concerns, providing income both to their leaders and members—many of whom are recruited from the ranks of the urban poor—though they often organize around some sort of ethnic, religious, or territorial identity (Wilson 2006). Preman groups lack the social goals and cohesion of the Islamist organizations, but they nevertheless draw on a discourse of popular representation, youthfulness, and struggle derived from Indonesia's revolutionary traditions (Ryter 1998) and frequently become involved in political affairs, though typically as guns for hire.

Though Islamist and preman organizations have distinctive raison d'être, it is useful to think of them in part as countermovements that advance claims to challenge those of their more progressive social-movement adversaries and which evolve in tandem with them (Mottl 1980; Andrews 2002). Though both sets of organizations have roots deep in Indonesian history—including, in part, in early contests with the political Left—they have also evolved *in response* to the claims for greater democratic space and pluralism expressed in Indonesian society during the post-Suharto era. Thus, in extreme cases, and as we have seen throughout this book, both Islamist and preman groups have mobilized violently against progressive social movements, seeking to roll back perceived gains or to restrict opportunities for them to organize and express themselves. For the Islamist groups, the main targets have been groups promoting greater pluralism and unsettling traditional gender roles—as the chapters on liberal Islam, women's rights, and LGBT rights especially demonstrate. One of the more notorious examples was a June 2008 attack by FPI and allied groups on a gathering called by liberal Islamic groups and NGOs to celebrate pluralism in Central Jakarta, in which more than seventy liberal activists were injured

(Wahid Institute 2008). This has to a large extent been a contest within the world of Indonesian Islam, with the primary targets being liberal Islamic groups, as Fealy's chapter explains. Since the early 2000s, however, FPI and similar Islamist vigilante groups have made numerous attacks on meetings or cultural events organized by LGBT organizations, discussions or film showings on the 1965–66 massacres, or meetings by leftist groups; they have also frequently attacked members of religious minorities. Preman groups, meanwhile, are frequently mobilized by local businesses or other powerful actors in order to break up protests by striking workers, land occupations by dispossessed farmers, or to enforce slum clearings, though in such cases their role tends to be that of hired muscle rather than seekers of wider social or political goals. At the same time, both the Islamist organizations and preman organizations, as Wilson demonstrates in his chapter, compete with progressive groups for the loyalties of the urban poor, making use of their political connections, brokerage skills, and street muscle, and offering a language of militancy and resolution that, for some at least, must feel like an attractive antidote to the precarity and uncertainty of life in the informal sector.

More broadly, the claims advanced by Islamist and, to a lesser degree, preman and other conservative groups in part respond to claim making by progressive social movements. For example, the new prominence of political homophobia in the discourse of contemporary Islamist groups is itself in part a reaction to the perceived gains that LGBT activists and communities have been making domestically, and their greater visibility as a result of media developments: for example, it is noteworthy that the major 2016 homophobic public backlash described by Hendri Wijaya and Sharyn Graham Davies in their chapter, was initially prompted by a response by the technology, research and higher education minister to activities by a progay group on campus (*Jakarta Post* 2016). More generally, the broad "conservative turn" (van Bruinessen 2013) that has been widely observed in Indonesian Islam since the mid-2000s—and is discussed by Fealy in this volume—has been a direct response to perceived advances that liberal Islamic groups, as well as wider forces of secularism, pluralism, and gender equality, were making in Indonesian society.

These countermovements often compete with progressive social movements for the exact same social constituencies and respond to the same discontent generated by social inequality and institutional defects. Such competition is visible in the *kampung* inhabited by members of Indonesia's urban poor. Particularly noteworthy in this regard is the FPI, an organization that has "articulated a populist notion of Islamic militancy that has struck a chord with many disenfranchised youth" (Wilson 2008, 209) and demonstrated solidarity with victims of urban resettlement programs in Jakarta, channeling their anger in 2016 into huge Islamic mobilizations against the ethnically Chinese and Christian Jakarta governor, Basuki Tjahaja Purnama (Wilson 2016). But Islamist groups have also made inroads into sectors such as labor organizing, while on campuses competition between leftists and Islamists has been a leitmotif of interstudent rivalry since even before the fall of the New Order.

Finally, it is worth setting these organizational challenges in a broader context of political contestation. As well as being fought over by rival social movements, the loyalties of Indonesia's poor and marginalized are also targeted by the populist campaigning of elite politicians with antipluralist and antidemocratic goals. Diffuse populist appeals to the sovereignty and dignity of the little people are a longstanding feature of Indonesian politics, but such traditions came into sharp relief in the 2014 presidential campaign of former general Prabowo Subianto. In common with authoritarian-populist leaders the world over, Prabowo depicted himself as representing the interests of the neglected poor, blamed Indonesia's ills on its elite and on foreigners, and offered strong leadership as the cure for those ills (Aspinall 2015). While, again in common with many populist politicians, Prabowo tried to appeal directly to the people, over the heads of established political parties, it is also noteworthy that he endeavored to establish organizational networks among farmers and built links with labor unions, and that numerous Islamist and preman groups flocked to his banner during the election. He succeeded, in other words, in building a grand antiliberal electoral coalition. By contrast, pluralist and prodemocratic groups have generally failed to coordinate themselves electorally, let alone to present themselves as a powerful electoral bloc, with some analyses presenting this failure as the chief weakness of democratic movements—and of democratic consolidation—in post-Suharto Indonesia (Savirani and Törnquist 2015).

CONCLUSION

The purpose of this discussion has not been to downplay the major advances and achievements that progressive social movements have recorded in the post-Suharto period. The role of popular and even leftist forces in Indonesia's democratic transition and its post-Suharto period of democratic maturation and contestation has been far from trivial. This book has rightly placed this remarkable record of achievement at the center of our understanding of post-Suharto politics. However, as we have seen in preceding chapters, such movements face significant structural challenges, and they are not alone in trying to reshape the social and political order, but also face challenges from determinedly illiberal forces. Meanwhile, the ubiquity of clientelism and other informal relationships as means of achieving material and political goals in post-Suharto Indonesia poses major challenges to social movements, whose organizing logic is to build horizontal solidarity and whose strategy is to mobilize through the public sphere rather to manipulate private relationships. The weakness of the rule of law likewise poses fundamental problems for movements that seek to attain legally enforceable rights for their constituents.

Both these factors draw attention to the enormity of the challenge facing progressive social movements in post-Suharto Indonesia, whose structural position thus necessitates that they do more than simply achieve discrete social and political goals, or even uphold Indonesia's new democratic system of government, if they wish to achieve secure improvements for their supporters. The logic of their position ultimately also requires social movements to strive for root-and-branch transformation of the social order, and to push forward Indonesia's transition from rule by a *particularistic* social order, in which social advancement depends on "widespread use of connections of any kind, exchange of favors, and, in their absence, monetary inducements" (Mungiu-Pippidi 2015, 22) to one based on *ethical universalism*, "where equal treatment applies to everyone regardless to the group to which one belongs" (Mungiu-Pippidi 2015, 14). Indonesia is far from being alone in undergoing such a transition, but the experience of other countries suggest that this transition can take multiple generations.

NOTE

1. For a classic description of clientelism in Southeast Asia, see Scott 1972.

REFERENCES

Andrews, Kenneth T. 2002. "Movement-Countermovement Dynamics and the Emergence of New Institutions: The Case of "White Flight" Schools in Mississippi." *Social Forces* 80 (3): 911–936.

Antaranews. 2012. "KY: Tujuh Faktor Sebabkan Penegakan Hukum Lemah" [Judicial Commission: Seven Factors Cause Weak Law Enforcement]. February 14. http://www.antaranews.com/berita/297354/ky--tujuh-faktor-sebabkan-penegakan-hukum-lemah Accessed May 11, 2017.

Aspinall, Edward. 2005. *Opposing Suharto: Compromise, Resistance, and Regime Change in Indonesia*. Stanford: Stanford University Press.

——. 2013. "A Nation in Fragments: Patronage and Neoliberalism in Contemporary Indonesia." *Critical Asian Studies* 45 (1): 27–54.

——. 2014. "When Brokers Betray: Social Networks and Electoral Politics in Indonesia." *Critical Asian Studies* 46 (4): 545–70.

——. 2015. Aspinall, Edward. "Oligarchic Populism: Prabowo Subianto's Challenge to Indonesian Democracy." *Indonesia* 99: 1–28.

Aspinall, Edward, Noor Rohman, Ahmad Zainul Hamdi, Rubaidi, and Zusiana Elly Triantini. 2017. "Vote Buying in Indonesia: Candidate Strategies, Market Logic, and Effectiveness." *Journal of East Asian Studies* 17 (1): 1–27.

Aspinall, Edward, and Gerry van Klinken, eds. 2011. *The State and Illegality in Indonesia*. Leiden: KITLV Press.

Baker, Jacqueline. 2012. *The Rise of Polri: Democratisation and the Political Economy of Security in Indonesia*. Ph.D. diss., London School of Economics and Political Science.

——. 2013. "The 'Parman' Economy: Post-Authoritarian Shifts in Indonesia's Illicit Security Economy." *Indonesia* 96: 123–50.

Beittinger-Lee, Verena. 2009. *(Un)civil Society and Political Change in Indonesia: A Contested Arena*. London: Routledge.

Berenschot, Ward, Henk Schulte Nordholt, and Laurens Bakker. 2017. "Introduction: Citizenship and Democratization in Postcolonial Southeast Asia." In *Citizenship and Democratization in Southeast Asia*, edited by Ward Berenschot, Henk Schulte Nordholt, and Laurens Bakker, 1–29. Leiden: Brill.

Blunt, Peter, Mark Turner, and Henrik Linroth. 2012. "Patronage's Progress in Post-Soeharto Indonesia." *Public Administration and Development*. 32 (1): 64–81.

Buehler, Michael. 2013. "Revisiting the Inclusion-Moderation Thesis in the Context of Decentralized Institutions: The Behavior of Indonesia's Prosperous Justice Party in National and Local Politics." *Party Politics* 19 (2): 210–29.

Butt, Simon, and Tim Lindsey. 2011. "Judicial Mafia: The Courts and State Illegality in Indonesia." In *The State and Illegality in Indonesia*, edited by Edward Aspinall and Gerry van Klinken, 189–215. Leiden: KITLV Press.

Clark, Janine. 2004. "Social Movement Theory and Patron-Clientelism: Islamic Social Institutions and the Middle Class in Egypt, Jordan, and Yemen." *Comparative Political Studies* 37 (8): 941–68.

Clark, Samuel. 2013. "Enforcing Corruption Laws: The Political Economy of Subnational Prosecutions in Indonesia." Ph.D. diss., University of Oxford.

Cole, Rachelle. 2012. "A New Tactical Toolkit." *Inside Indonesia* 11 (Oct–Dec). http://www.insideindonesia.org/current-edition/a-new-tactical-toolkit. Accessed May 12, 2007.

Davidson, Jamie S. 2007. "Politics-as-Usual on Trial: Regional Anticorruption Campaigns in Indonesia." *Pacific Review* 20 (1): 75–99.

Diamond, Larry. 2015. "Facing up to the Democratic Recession." *Journal of Democracy* 26 (1): 141–55.

Ford, Michele. 2009. *Workers and Intellectuals: NGOs, Trade Unions, and the Indonesian Labour Movement*. Singapore: National University of Singapore Press.

——. 2010. "Tusso/Guf Briefing Paper on Trade Unions in Indonesia." http://laborsta.ilo.org/applv8/data/TUM/TUD%20and%20CBC%20Technical%20Brief.pdf. Accessed May 3, 2017.

Ford, Michele, and George Martin Sirait. 2016. "The State, Democratic Transition, and Employment Relations in Indonesia." *Journal of Industrial Relations* 58 (2): 229–42.

Fox, Jonathan. 1994. "The Difficult Transition from Clientelism to Citizenship: Lessons from Mexico." *World Politics* 46 (2): 151–84.

Jakarta Post. 2016. "LGBT not Welcome at University: Minister." January 25. http://www.thejakartapost.com/news/2016/01/25/lgbt-not-welcome-university-minister.html. Accessed May 5, 2017.

Juliawan, Benny Hari. 2011. "Street-level Politics: Labour Protests in Post-Authoritarian Indonesia." *Journal of Contemporary Asia* 41 (3): 349–70.

Kristiansen, Stein, and Muhid Ramli. 2006. "Buying an Income: The Market for Civil Service Positions in Indonesia." *Contemporary Southeast Asia* 28 (2): 207–33.

Lapegna, Pablo. 2013. "Social Movements and Patronage Politics: Processes of Demobilization and Dual Pressure." *Sociological Forum* 28 (4): 842–63.

Lev, Daniel S. 1987. "Legal Aid in Indonesia." Centre of Southeast Asian Studies, Monash University. Working Paper No. 44. Clayton, Victoria.

McVey, Ruth T. 1990. "Teaching Modernity: The PKI as an Educational Institution." *Indonesia* 50: 5–28.

Meyer, David S., and Sidney Tarrow, eds. 1998. *The Social Movement Society: Contentious Politics for a New Century*. Lanham, MD: Rowman and Littlefield.

Mietzner, Marcus. 2010. "Political Conflict Resolution and Democratic Consolidation in Indonesia: The Role of the Constitutional Court." *Journal of East Asian Studies* 10: 397–424.

——. 2012. "Indonesia's Democratic Stagnation: Antireformist Elites and Resilient Civil Society." *Democratization* 19 (2): 209–29.

——. 2013. "Fighting the Hellhounds: Pro-Democracy Activists and Party Politics in Post-Suharto Indonesia." *Journal of Contemporary Asia* 43 (1): 28–50.

Mortimer, Rex. 1974. *Indonesian Communism under Sukarno: Ideology and Politics, 1959–1965*. Ithaca: Cornell University Press.

Mottl, Tahi L. 1980. "Analysis of Countermovements." *Social Problems* 27 (5): 620–35.

Mungiu-Pippidi, Alina. 2015. *The Quest for Good Governance: How Societies Develop Control of Corruption*. Cambridge: Cambridge University Press.

Nooteboom, Gerben. 2011. "Out of Wedlock: Migrant-Police Partnerships in East Kalimantan." In *The State and Illegality in Indonesia*, edited by Edward Aspinall and Gerry van Klinken, 215–37. Leiden: KITLV Press.

Nyman, Mikaela. 2006. *Democratising Indonesia: The Challenges of Civil Society in the Era of Reformasi*. Copenhagen: Nordic Institute of Asian Studies.

Robison, Richard, and Vedi R. Hadiz. 2004. *Reorganising Power in Indonesia: The Politics of Oligarchy in an Age of Markets*. London: Routledge.

Rosser, Andrew, and Maryke van Diermen. 2016. "Law, Democracy, and the Fulfilment of Socioeconomic Rights: Insights from Indonesia." *Third World Quarterly* 37 (2): 336–53.

Ryter, Loren. 1998. "Pemuda Pancasila: The Last Loyalist Free Men of Suharto's Order." *Indonesia* 66: 45–73.

Savirani, Amalinda. 2016. "Bekasi, West Java: From Patronage to Interest Groups Politics?" In *Electoral Dynamics in Indonesia: Money Politics, Patronage, and Clientelism at the Grassroots*, edited by Edward Aspinall and Mada Sukmajati, 184–202. Singapore: National University of Singapore Press.

Savirani, Amalinda, and Olle Törnquist, eds. 2015. *Reclaiming the State: Overcoming Problems of Democracy in Post-Soeharto Indonesia*. Yogyakarta: Penerbit Polgov.

Scott, James C. 1972. "Patron-Client Politics and Political Change in Southeast Asia." *American Political Science Review* 66 (1): 91–113.

Uhlin, Anders. 1997. *Indonesia and the "Third Wave of Democratization": The Indonesian Pro-Democracy Movement in a Changing World*. New York: St. Martin's Press.

van Bruinessen, Martin, ed. 2013. *Contemporary Developments in Indonesian Islam: Explaining the "Conservative Turn."* Singapore: Institute of Southeast Asian Studies.

Wahid Institute. 2008. *Monthly Report on Religious Issues*. June. http://www.wahidinsti tute.org/files/_docs/10.MonthlyRepost-X-english.pdf. Accessed May 3, 2017.

Wilson, Ian. 2006. "Continuity and Change: The Changing Contours of Organized Violence in Post–New Order Indonesia." *Critical Asian Studies* 38 (2): 265–97.

———. 2008. "'As Long as It's *Halal*: Islamic *Preman* in Jakarta." In *Expressing Islam: Religious Life and Politics in Indonesia*, edited by Greg Fealy and Sally White, 192–210. Singapore: Institute of Southeast Asian Studies.

———. 2011. "Reconfiguring Rackets: Racket Regimes, Protection, and the State in Post-New Order Jakarta." In *The State and Illegality in Indonesia*, edited by Edward Aspinall and Gerry van Klinken, 239–60. Leiden: KITLV Press.

———. 2016. "Making Enemies Out of Friends." *New Mandala*. November 3. http://www.newmandala.org/making-enemies-friends. Accessed May 5, 2017.

CONTRIBUTORS

Iqra Anugrah is a JSPS postdoctoral fellow at the Center for Southeast Asian Studies, Kyoto University. His main research interests are democracy, development, social movements, and critical theory. He has held fellowships with the Transparency for Development Project, the University of Sydney's Southeast Asia Centre, and New Mandala. He is also a contributing editor for *IndoProgress*, an online platform connecting progressive scholars and activists in Indonesia. His works have been published in venues such as *Indonesia* and *Journal of Current Southeast Asian Affairs*.

Edward Aspinall is a professor in the Department of Political and Social Change at the Australian National University. He researches politics in Indonesia, with interests in democratization, ethnicity, and clientelism. He is the author of *Opposing Suharto: Compromise, Resistance, and Regime Change in Indonesia* (Stanford University Press 2005), and *Islam and Nation: Separatist Rebellion in Aceh, Indonesia* (Stanford University Press 2009), and coauthor of *Democracy for Sale: Elections, Clientelism, and the State in Indonesia* (Cornell University Press 2019).

Teri Caraway is a professor of political science, University of Minnesota, Twin Cities. Her research focuses on comparative labor politics, comparative and international political economy, and the Indonesian labor movement. She is the author of *Assembling Women: The Feminization of Global Manufacturing* (ILR Press 2007), coauthor of *Labor and Politics in Indonesia* (Cambridge in press), and coeditor of *Working through the Past: Labor and Authoritarian Legacies in Comparative Perspective* (ILR Press 2015).

Sharyn Graham Davies is an associate professor in the School of Social Sciences and Public Policy at Auckland University of Technology in New Zealand. She is an anthropologist focusing on gender and sexuality in Indonesia and the author of two monographs and coeditor of *Sex and Sexualities in Contemporary Indonesia* (Routledge 2014), winner of the 2015 Ruth Benedict Prize for best edited collection. She has previously been Leverhulme Visiting Professor at Cambridge University and received a Fulbright award to present her work at Yale in the United States.

Thushara Dibley is the deputy director of the Sydney Southeast Asia Centre at the University of Sydney, Australia. Her research focuses on the system of international aid and development, its interface with grassroots and transnational activism and their influence on human rights–based policy and practice in Southeast Asia. She is the author of *Partnerships, Power, and Peacebuilding: NGOs as Agents of Peace in Aceh and Timor-Leste* (Palgrave MacMillan 2014). She has published in journals including *Antipode*.

Greg Fealy is an associate professor of Southeast Asian Politics in the Department of Political and Social Change at the Australian National University. He specializes in

Islamic politics and culture in Indonesia and is the coauthor of *Joining the Caravan? The Middle East, Islamism, and Indonesia; Radical Islam and Terrorism in Indonesia;* and *Zealous Democrats: Islamism and Democracy in Egypt, Indonesia, and Turkey.* He has published in journals including *Indonesia, Southeast Asian Affairs,* and *Bulletin of Indonesian Economic Studies.*

Michele Ford is the director of the Sydney Southeast Asia Centre and a professor of Southeast Asian studies at the University of Sydney, Australia. Her research focuses on labor internationalism and Southeast Asian labor movements. She is the author of *From Migrant to Worker: The Global Unions and Temporary Labor Migration in Asia* (ILR Press 2019); and *Workers and Intellectuals: NGOs, Unions, and the Indonesian Labour Movement* (NUS/Hawai'i/KITLV 2009); and coauthor of *Labor and Politics in Indonesia* (Cambridge in press).

Elisabeth Kramer is the deputy director at the Sydney Southeast Asia Centre at the University of Sydney, Australia. Her research interests include political communication, issues-based campaigning, and persuasion and symbolic politics in contemporary Indonesia. She completed a major study of anticorruption symbolism in Indonesia's 2014 national legislative elections focused on emerging political parties. She has published on this and other topics in journals such as *Critical Asian Studies, Asian Politics and Policy,* and *Media Asia.*

Rachel Rinaldo is an associate professor of sociology at the University of Colorado Boulder. She has been conducting research on gender, globalization, culture, and social change in Indonesia since 2002. She is the author of *Mobilizing Piety: Islam and Feminism in Indonesia* (Oxford 2013), an ethnographic study of Muslim and secular women activists. Her articles on Indonesian women's activism have been published in journals such as *Social Forces, Qualitative Sociology,* and *Gender & Society.*

Yatun Sastramidjaja is a lecturer in cultural anthropology and interdisciplinary social sciences at the University of Amsterdam. Her research focuses on student movements, youth cultures, citizenship, and memory cultures in Indonesia and more broadly Southeast Asia. Her publications include *Playing Politics: Power, Narrative, and Agency in the Making of the Indonesian Student Movement* (Brill forthcoming) and *Performance of the Past: Contested Heritage Politics in Globalizing Indonesia* (Brill forthcoming).

Ian Wilson is a senior lecturer in politics and international studies and security studies, and a research fellow at the Asia Research Centre, Murdoch University. His research focuses on the political economy of gangs, organized crime, and violence. He also has an interest in the political agency of the poor. He is the author of *The Politics of Protection Rackets in Post-New Order Indonesia: Coercive Capital, Authority, and Street Politics* (Routledge 2015) and has published in journals such as *Critical Asian Studies* and *Nationalism and Ethnic Politics.*

Hendri Wijaya obtained a masters degree in public policy from the National University of Singapore and a masters in research in gender and cultural studies from the University of Sydney. He is interested in queer studies, feminism, literary studies, the Indonesian LGBT movements, and sexual politics in Indonesia. Prior to continuing his studies, he worked in the development sector as a consultant, researcher, and officer in the UNDP's Indonesia office and the Asia Foundation.

INDEX

AGRA (Alliance of Agrarian Reform Movement), 85, 91n12, 92n14
agrarian reform: democratic transition and hopes for, 83; parliamentary decree on, 6, 83, 87; under Sukarno, 80, 87. *See also* land rights movement
Ahmadiyah, attacks on, 128–29, 130
Ahok (Basuki Tjahaja Purnama), 109; Islamic mobilization against, 35, 197; prosecution and jailing of, 35, 36, 143; urban poor and, 111, 112
Aisyiyah (organization), 141, 143, 146–47
AKAK (Advocacy for a Corruption Eradication Commission), 47, 49
AMAN (Alliance of Indigenous People of the Archipelago), 84, 88
anticommunist massacres, 7, 33, 63, 80, 136
Anticorruption Commission. *See* KPK
anticorruption courts (Tipikor), 42, 49
Anticorruption Law of 1999, 46, 51
anticorruption movement: achievements of, 49, 53; challenges facing, 14, 54; consolidation of, 46–47; and decentralization, support for, 52; democratic transition and, 11–12, 14, 41–42, 46–52, 53; elites' response to, 14, 47–48; and fall of Suharto's regime, 45–46; foreign funding for, 12, 46; idealized concepts of democracy and, 41, 54; Islamic groups and, 47, 53; and KPK, defense of, 50–51, 188; at local level, 52–53; during New Order regime, 41, 43; origins of, 42–43; students and, 43–44
Anti-Domestic Violence Law, 142, 144
Anti-Pornography Law, 142–43, 144, 147, 148, 161
API (Indonesian Peasant Alliance), 85
ARC (Agrarian Resource Center), 85
Ardhanary Institute, 159, 162
Argentina, same-sex marriage law in, 153
Arus Pelangi (organization), 156, 159
Asia: labor unions in, 62; student movements in, 33. *See also specific countries*

Asia Foundation, 123, 129, 130, 182n4
Asian financial crisis: and collapse of New Order regime, 8, 10, 23, 28, 45–46, 62, 66, 102; impact on jobs and wages, 66, 70; impact on urban poor, 102

Bank Century bailout, 50
Basic Agrarian Law, 80; Parliamentary Decree No. IX/2001 on, 6, 83, 87, 92n14
Beijing Declaration of Rights of People with Disability in the New Century, 175
Bina Desa (organization), 81
BPN (National Land Agency), 83
Brazil: peasant movement in, 79; same-sex marriage law in, 153
BTI (Indonesian Peasants' Front), 80

CEDAW (Convention on the Elimination of All Forms of Discrimination against Women), 137
censorship: in postauthoritarian era, 46, 148, 155; under Suharto, 44–45
Chandra Kirana (organization), 155
child protection legislation, 142, 144
China: LGBT activists in, 164; peasant protests in, 79
Chinese Indonesians, attacks on, 11, 46, 65, 140–41
Chosiyah, Ratu Atut, 52
CIQAL (Center for Improving Qualified Activity in Life of People with Disabilities), 177, 181
City Forum (Forum Kota, Forkot), 28, 29
CLD-KHI (Counter-Legal Draft on the Islamic Law Compilation), 130, 131, 143
clientelism, 3, 189; social movements and, 189–92, 194, 198; vs. solidarity-based organization, 192; urban poor and, 103–4, 190
coalition, of social movements, 4; and regime change, 4–5, 30–31
communists: persecution of, 7, 33, 63, 80, 136. *See also* PKI

CPSIA information can be obtained
at www.ICGtesting.com
Printed in the USA
LVHW101807221220
674912LV00014B/231